TEACHER'S EDITION

SENDEROS 1B

Spanish for a Connected World

VISTA
HIGHER LEARNING

Boston, Massachusetts

On the cover: El Morro Fortress, Puerto Rico.

Publisher: José A. Blanco
Editorial Development: Armando Brito, Jhonny Alexander Calle, Deborah Coffey, María Victoria Echeverri, Jo Hanna Kurth, Megan Moran, Jaime Patiño, Raquel Rodríguez, Verónica Tejeda, Sharla Zwirek
Project Management: Sally Giangrande, Tiffany Kayes
Rights Management: Ashley Poreda, Annie Pickert Fuller
Technology Production: Egle Gutiérrez, Jamie Kostecki, Reginald Millington, Fabián Montoya, Paola Ríos Schaaf
Design: Radoslav Mateev, Gabriel Noreña, Andrés Vanegas
Production: Oscar Díez, Adriana Jaramillo

© 2018 by Vista Higher Learning, Inc. All rights reserved.

No part of this work may be reproduced or distributed in any form or by any means, electronic or mechanical, including photocopying and recording, or by any information storage or retrieval system without prior written permission from Vista Higher Learning, 500 Boylston Street, Suite 620, Boston, MA 02116-3736.

Student Text (Casebound-SIMRA) ISBN: 978-1-68005-629-7

Teacher's Edition ISBN: 978-1-68005-631-0

Library of Congress Control Number: 2017949634

1 2 3 4 5 6 7 8 9 TC 22 21 20 19 18 17

Printed in Canada.

Teacher's Edition Table of Contents

Introduction T5

Scope & Sequence T6

Flexibility with **Senderos** T12

ACTFL Standards T19

Lesson Walkthrough T22

Assessment T47

The Vista Higher Learning Difference

As a specialized publisher, we focus on what we love and do best—developing world language materials that get teachers and students as excited about language and culture as we are.

What does that mean for you?

- Unparalleled service from day one, including personalized training by nationally-renowned world language educators.
- Superior technology support to ensure that your classes run smoothly throughout the year.
- Seamless integration of technology, content, and resources to ensure success for you and your students.

"My **Vista Higher Learning rep** is absolutely fantastic. He is **responsive to the needs** of my department and colleagues."

Sally Sefami, Sage High School
Newport Coast, CA

SENDEROS

Spanish for a Connected World

At Vista Higher Learning, we recognize that proficiency is best achieved through an articulated and extended sequence of study. **Senderos** was designed with this in mind, resulting in a fully integrated and scaffolded Spanish program with a variety of print offerings and superior technology.

With powerful and easy-to-use course management tools, you can shape **Senderos** to fit your instructional goals and teaching style—all while delivering an engaging, personalized learning experience to each and every student.

What sets Senderos apart?

- Vocabulary Tutorials
- Grammar Tutorials
- News and Cultural Updates
- Multi-part Video Collection
- Video Virtual Chat activities
- Partner Chat activities
- Heritage Speaker activities

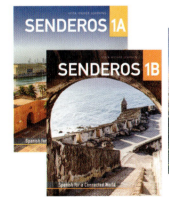
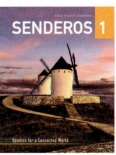

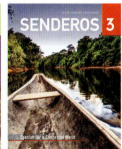
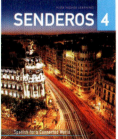

Scope & Sequence: Senderos 1A & 1B

1A

contextos	cultura	estructura	adelante

Lección preliminar A preview of the contexts and grammar of *Senderos 1A*, including an introduction to *Fotonovela* and *Cultura*.

avance/preview	avance/preview		avance/preview
Greetings	**En detalle:** Aquí se habla español		The classroom and school life
The alphabet	**Perfil:** Los salvadoreños de Washington, D.C.		School subjects
Identifying yourself			Days of the week

Lección 1 Hola, ¿qué tal?

Greetings and goodbyes	**En detalle:** Saludos y besos en los países hispanos	1.1 Nouns and articles	**En pantalla:** Anuncio de MasterCard (Estados Unidos)
Identifying yourself and others	**Perfil:** La plaza principal	1.2 Numbers 0–30	**Lectura:** Tira cómica de Quino
Courtesy expressions		1.3 Present tense of **ser**	**Panorama:** Estados Unidos y Canadá
		1.4 Telling time	

Lección 2 En la clase

The classroom and school life	**En detalle:** La escuela secundaria	2.1 Present tense of **–ar** verbs	**En pantalla:** Anuncio de Jumbo (Chile)
Fields of study and school subjects	**Perfil:** El INFRAMEN	2.2 Forming questions in Spanish	**Lectura:** ¡Español en Madrid!
Days of the week		2.3 Present tense of **estar**	**Panorama:** España
Class schedules		2.4 Numbers 31 and higher	

Lección 3 La familia

The family	**En detalle:** ¿Cómo te llamas?	3.1 Descriptive adjectives	**En pantalla:** Anuncio de banco Galicia (Argentina)
Identifying people	**Perfil:** La familia real española	3.2 Possessive adjectives	**Lectura:** Gente... Las familias
Professions and occupations		3.3 Present tense of **–er** and **–ir** verbs	**Panorama:** Ecuador
		3.4 Present tense of **tener** and **venir**	

1B

contextos	cultura	estructura	adelante

Lección preliminar A review of *Senderos 1A*, and a preview of the contexts and grammar of *Senderos 1B*, including a video recap of *Fotonovela* and *Cultura*.

repaso/review	avance/preview		avance/preview
School life	**En detalle:** El español en Latinoamérica		Sports
Family	**Perfil:** Día de la Independencia		Places in the city
Occupations			

Lección 4 Los pasatiempos

Pastimes	**En detalle:** Real Madrid y Barça: rivalidad total	4.1 Present tense of **ir**	**En pantalla:** *Ejes* (España)
Sports	**Perfil:** Miguel Cabrera and Paola Espinosa	4.2 Stem-changing verbs: e→ie, o→ue	**Lectura:** No sólo el fútbol
Places in the city		4.3 Stem-changing verbs: e→i	**Panorama:** México
		4.4 Verbs with irregular **yo** forms	

Lección 5 Las vacaciones

Travel and vacation	**En detalle:** Las cataratas del Iguazú	5.1 **Estar** with conditions and emotions	**En pantalla:** Anuncio de Santander LANPASS (Chile)
Months of the year	**Perfil:** Punta del Este	5.2 The present progressive	**Lectura:** Turismo ecológico en Puerto Rico
Seasons and weather		5.3 **Ser** and **estar**	**Panorama:** Puerto Rico
Ordinal numbers		5.4 Direct object nouns and pronouns	

Lección 6 ¡De compras!

Clothing and shopping	**En detalle:** Los mercados al aire libre	6.1 **Saber** and **conocer**	**En pantalla:** Anuncio de Juguettos (España)
Negotiating a price and buying	**Perfil:** Carolina Herrera	6.2 Indirect object pronouns	**Lectura:** ¡Real Liquidación en Corona!
Colors		6.3 Preterite tense of regular verbs	**Panorama:** Cuba
More adjectives		6.4 Demonstrative adjectives and pronouns	

Scope & Sequence: Senderos 1

contextos	cultura	estructura	adelante
Lección 1 Hola, ¿qué tal?			
Greetings and goodbyes Identifying yourself and others Courtesy expressions	**En detalle:** Saludos y besos en los países hispanos **Perfil:** La plaza principal	1.1 Nouns and articles 1.2 Numbers 0–30 1.3 Present tense of **ser** 1.4 Telling time	**En pantalla:** Anuncio de MasterCard (Estados Unidos) **Lectura:** Tira cómica de Quino **Panorama:** Estados Unidos y Canadá
Lección 2 En la clase			
The classroom and school life Fields of study and school subjects Days of the week Class schedules	**En detalle:** La escuela secundaria **Perfil:** El INFRAMEN	2.1 Present tense of **–ar** verbs 2.2 Forming questions in Spanish 2.3 Present tense of **estar** 2.4 Numbers 31 and higher	**En pantalla:** Anuncio de Jumbo (Chile) **Lectura:** ¡Español en Madrid! **Panorama:** España
Lección 3 La familia			
The family Identifying people Professions and occupations	**En detalle:** ¿Cómo te llamas? **Perfil:** La familia real española	3.1 Descriptive adjectives 3.2 Possessive adjectives 3.3 Present tense of **–er** and **–ir** verbs 3.4 Present tense of **tener** and **venir**	**En pantalla:** Anuncio de banco Galicia (Argentina) **Lectura:** Gente... Las familias **Panorama:** Ecuador
Lección 4 Los pasatiempos			
Pastimes Sports Places in the city	**En detalle:** Real Madrid y Barça: rivalidad total **Perfil:** Miguel Cabrera and Paola Espinosa	4.1 Present tense of **ir** 4.2 Stem-changing verbs: e→ie, o→ue 4.3 Stem-changing verbs: e→i 4.4 Verbs with irregular **yo** forms	**En pantalla:** Ejes (España) **Lectura:** No sólo el fútbol **Panorama:** México
Lección 5 Las vacaciones			
Travel and vacation Months of the year Seasons and weather Ordinal numbers	**En detalle:** Las cataratas del Iguazú **Perfil:** Punta del Este	5.1 **Estar** with conditions and emotions 5.2 The present progressive 5.3 **Ser** and **estar** 5.4 Direct object nouns and pronouns	**En pantalla:** Anuncio de Santander LANPASS (Chile) **Lectura:** Turismo ecológico en Puerto Rico **Panorama:** Puerto Rico
Lección 6 ¡De compras!			
Clothing and shopping Negotiating a price and buying Colors More adjectives	**En detalle:** Los mercados al aire libre **Perfil:** Carolina Herrera	6.1 **Saber** and **conocer** 6.2 Indirect object pronouns 6.3 Preterite tense of regular verbs 6.4 Demonstrative adjectives and pronouns	**En pantalla:** Anuncio de Juguettos (España) **Lectura:** ¡Real Liquidación en Corona! **Panorama:** Cuba

Scope & Sequence: Senderos 2

2 | contextos | cultura | estructura | adelante

Lección preliminar
A brief overview of the contexts and grammar from Level 1

Lección 1 La rutina diaria

contextos	cultura	estructura	adelante
Daily routine Personal hygiene Time expressions	**En detalle:** La siesta **Perfil:** El mate	1.1 Reflexive verbs 1.2 Indefinite and negative words 1.3 Preterite of **ser** and **ir** 1.4 Verbs like **gustar**	**En pantalla:** Anuncio de Asepxia (Argentina) **Lectura:** ¡Qué día! **Panorama:** Perú

Lección 2 La comida

contextos	cultura	estructura	adelante
Food Food descriptions Meals	**En detalle:** Frutas y verduras de América **Perfil:** Ferran Adrià: arte en la cocina	2.1 Preterite of stem-changing verbs 2.2 Double object pronouns 2.3 Comparisons 2.4 Superlatives	**En pantalla:** Anuncio de Sopas Roa (Colombia) **Lectura:** Menú y crítica: La feria del maíz **Panorama:** Guatemala

Lección 3 Las fiestas

contextos	cultura	estructura	adelante
Parties and celebrations Personal relationships Stages of life	**En detalle:** Semana Santa: vacaciones y tradición **Perfil:** Festival de Viña del Mar	3.1 Irregular preterites 3.2 Verbs that change meaning in the preterite 3.3 ¿Qué? and ¿cuál? 3.4 Pronouns after prepositions	**En pantalla:** Fiestas patrias: Chilevisión (Chile) **Lectura:** Vida social **Panorama:** Chile

Lección 4 En el consultorio

contextos	cultura	estructura	adelante
Health and medical terms Parts of the body Symptoms and medical conditions Health professions	**En detalle:** Servicios de salud **Perfil:** Curanderos y chamanes	4.1 The imperfect tense 4.2 The preterite and the imperfect 4.3 Constructions with **se** 4.4 Adverbs	**En pantalla:** Asociación Parkinson Alicante (España) **Lectura:** Libro de la semana **Panorama:** Costa Rica

Lección 5 La tecnología

contextos	cultura	estructura	adelante
Home electronics Computers and the Internet The car and its accessories	**En detalle:** Las redes sociales **Perfil:** Los mensajes de texto	5.1 Familiar commands 5.2 **Por** and **para** 5.3 Reciprocal reflexives 5.4 Stressed possessive adjectives and pronouns	**En pantalla:** BOOK (España) **Lectura:** Una tira cómica **Panorama:** Argentina

Lección 6 La vivienda

contextos	cultura	estructura	adelante
Parts of a house Household chores Table settings	**En detalle:** El patio central **Perfil:** Las islas flotantes del lago Titicaca	6.1 Relative pronouns 6.2 Formal (**usted/ustedes**) commands 6.3 The present subjunctive 6.4 Subjunctive with verbs of will and influence	**En pantalla:** Anuncio de Carrefour (España) **Lectura:** Bienvenidos al Palacio de las Garzas **Panorama:** Panamá

Scope & Sequence: Senderos 3

contextos	cultura	estructura	adelante
Lección preliminar			
A brief overview of the contexts and grammar from Levels 1 and 2			
Lección 1 La naturaleza			
Nature The environment Recycling and conservation	**En detalle:** ¡Los Andes se mueven! **Perfil:** La Sierra Nevada de Santa Marta	1.1 The subjunctive with verbs of emotion 1.2 The subjunctive with doubt, disbelief, and denial 1.3 The subjunctive with conjunctions	**En pantalla:** Anuncio de Ecovidrio (España) **Lectura:** Dos fábulas de Félix María Samaniego y Tomás de Iriarte **Panorama:** Colombia
Lección 2 En la ciudad			
City life Daily chores Money and banking At a post office	**En detalle:** Paseando en metro **Perfil:** Luis Barragán: arquitectura y emoción	2.1 The subjunctive in adjective clauses 2.2 **Nosotros/as** commands 2.3 Past participles used as adjectives	**En pantalla:** Anuncio de Banco Ficensa (Honduras) **Lectura:** *Inventario secreto de La Habana* (fragmento) de Abilio Estévez **Panorama:** Venezuela
Lección 3 El bienestar			
Health and well-being Exercise and physical activity Nutrition	**En detalle:** Spas naturales **Perfil:** La quinua	3.1 The present perfect 3.2 The past perfect 3.3 The present perfect subjunctive	**En pantalla:** *Iker pelos tiesos* (México) **Lectura:** *Un día de éstos* de Gabriel García Márquez **Panorama:** Bolivia
Lección 4 El mundo del trabajo			
Professions and occupations The workplace Job interviews	**En detalle:** Beneficios en los empleos **Perfil:** César Chávez	4.1 The future 4.2 The future perfect 4.3 The past subjunctive	**En pantalla:** *Sinceridad* (España) **Lectura:** *A Julia de Burgos* de Julia de Burgos **Panorama:** Nicaragua y La República Dominicana
Lección 5 Un festival de arte			
The arts Movies Television	**En detalle:** Museo de Arte Contemporáneo de Caracas **Perfil:** Fernando Botero: un estilo único	5.1 The conditional 5.2 The conditional perfect 5.3 The past perfect subjunctive	**En pantalla:** Anuncio de TV Azteca (México) **Lectura:** Tres poemas de Federico García Lorca **Panorama:** El Salvador y Honduras
Lección 6 Las actualidades			
Current events and politics The media Natural disasters	**En detalle:** Protestas sociales **Perfil:** Dos líderes en Latinoamérica	6.1 **Si** clauses 6.2 Summary of the uses of the subjunctive	**En pantalla:** Anuncio sobre elecciones chilenas (Chile) **Lectura:** *Don Quijote de la Mancha* de Miguel de Cervantes **Panorama:** Paraguay y Uruguay

Scope & Sequence: Senderos 4

contextos	el mundo hispano	estructura	videos y lecturas
Lección preliminar			
A brief overview of the contexts and grammar from Levels 1, 2, and 3			
Lección 1 Las relaciones personales			
La personalidad Los estados emocionales Los sentimientos Las relaciones personales	**En detalle:** Parejas sin fronteras **Perfil:** Isabel Allende y Willie Gordon	1.1 The present tense 1.2 **Ser** and **estar** 1.3 Progressive forms	**En pantalla:** *Di algo* **Literatura:** *Poema 20* de Pablo Neruda **Cultura:** *Sonia Sotomayor: la niña que soñaba*
Lección 2 Las diversiones			
La música y el teatro Los lugares de recreo Los deportes Las diversiones	**En detalle:** El nuevo cine mexicano **Perfil:** Gael García Bernal	2.1 Object pronouns 2.2 **Gustar** and similar verbs 2.3 Reflexive verbs	**En pantalla:** *El tiple* **Literatura:** *Idilio* de Mario Benedetti **Cultura:** *El toreo: ¿cultura o tortura?*
Lección 3 La vida diaria			
En casa De compras Expresiones La vida diaria	**En detalle:** La Familia Real **Perfil:** Letizia Ortiz	3.1 The preterite 3.2 The imperfect 3.3 The preterite vs. the imperfect	**En pantalla:** *Adiós mamá* **Literatura:** *Último brindis* de Nicanor Parra **Cultura:** *El arte de la vida diaria*
Lección 4 La salud y el bienestar			
Los síntomas y las enfermedades La salud y el bienestar Los médicos y el hospital Las medicinas y los tratamientos	**En detalle:** De abuelos y chamanes **Perfil:** La ciclovía de Bogotá	4.1 The subjunctive in noun clauses 4.2 Commands 4.3 **Por** and **para**	**En pantalla:** *Ayúdame a recordar* **Literatura:** *Mujeres de ojos grandes* de Ángeles Mastretta **Cultura:** *Colombia gana la guerra a una vieja enfermedad*
Lección 5 Los viajes			
De viaje El alojamiento La seguridad y los accidentes Las excursiones	**En detalle:** La ruta del café **Perfil:** El canal de Panamá	5.1 Comparatives and superlatives 5.2 Negative, affirmative, and indefinite expressions 5.3 The subjunctive in adjective clauses	**En pantalla:** *La autoridad* **Literatura:** *La luz es como el agua* de Gabriel García Márquez **Cultura:** *La ruta maya*
Lección 6 La naturaleza			
La naturaleza Los animales Los fenómenos naturales El medio ambiente	**En detalle:** Los bosques del mar **Perfil:** Parque Nacional Submarino La Caleta	6.1 The future 6.2 The subjunctive in adverbial clauses 6.3 Prepositions: **a**, **hacia**, and **con**	**En pantalla:** *Playa del Carmen: Tiburón Toro* **Literatura:** *El eclipse* de Augusto Monterroso **Cultura:** *La conservación de Vieques*

Scope & Sequence: Senderos 5

contextos	el mundo hispano	estructura	videos y lecturas

Lección preliminar

A brief overview of the contexts and grammar from Levels 1, 2, 3, and 4

Lección 1 La tecnología y la ciencia

La tecnología La astronomía y el universo Los científicos La ciencia y los inventos	**En detalle:** Argentina: tierra de animadores **Perfil:** Innovar	1.1 The present perfect 1.2 The past perfect 1.3 Diminutives and augmentatives	**En pantalla:** *Generación web: Smartcities* **Literatura:** *Ese bobo del móvil* de Arturo Pérez-Reverte **Cultura:** *Hernán Casciari: arte en la blogosfera*

Lección 2 La economía y el trabajo

El trabajo Las finanzas La economía La gente en el trabajo	**En detalle:** Las telenovelas **Perfil:** Carolina Herrera	2.1 The conditional 2.2 The past subjunctive 2.3 *Si* clauses with simple tenses	**En pantalla:** *Hispanos en la economía de los Estados Unidos* **Literatura:** *La abeja haragana* de Horacio Quiroga **Cultura:** *Gustavo Dudamel: la estrella de "El Sistema"*

Lección 3 La cultura popular y los medios de comunicación

La televisión, la radio, y el cine La cultura popular Los medios de comunicación La prensa	**En detalle:** El mate **Perfil:** Las murgas y el candombe	3.1 The present perfect subjunctive 3.2 Relative pronouns 3.3 The neuter *lo*	**En pantalla:** *Sintonía* **Literatura:** *Dos Palabras* de Isabel Allende **Cultura:** *Guaraní: la lengua vencedora*

Lección 4 La literatura y el arte

La literatura Los géneros literarios Los artistas El arte Las corrientes artísticas	**En detalle:** Las casas de Neruda **Perfil:** Neruda en el cine	4.1 The future perfect 4.2 The conditional perfect 4.3 The past perfect subjunctive	**En pantalla:** *Jóvenes valientes* **Literatura:** *Continuidad de los parques* de Julio Cortázar **Cultura:** *De Macondo a McOndo*

Lección 5 La política y la religión

La religión Las creencias religiosas Los cargos públicos La política	**En detalle:** El Carnaval de Oruro **Perfil:** Evo Morales	5.1 The passive voice 5.2 Uses of *se* 5.3 Prepositions: *de, desde, en, entre, hasta, sin*	**En pantalla:** *Hiyab* **Literatura:** *La noche de Tlatelolco* (fragmento) de Elena Poniatowska **Cultura:** *Cómo Bolivia perdió su mar*

Lección 6 La historia y la civilización

La historia y la civilización Los conceptos Las características Los gobernantes La conquista y la independencia	**En detalle:** La herencia de los incas **Perfil:** Machu Picchu	6.1 Uses of the infinitive 6.2 Summary of the indicative 6.3 Summary of the subjunctive	**En pantalla:** *Ramona* **Literatura:** *El milagro secreto* de Jorge Luis Borges **Cultura:** *El Inca Garcilaso: un puente entre dos imperios*

Flexibility with Senderos

SENDEROS PRIME vs. SENDEROS supersite

At Vista Higher Learning, we recognize that classrooms and districts across the country are at different stages in the implementation of technology. That's why we offer two levels of technology with **Senderos: Prime** or **Supersite**. Regardless of a school's resources and readiness, **Senderos** is the perfect fit with any curriculum and infrastructure. It meets customers where they are, and will take them where they want to be.

For the Teacher

COMPONENT	WHAT IS IT?	PRIME	supersite
Teacher's Edition	Teacher support for core instruction	•	•
Activity Pack (with Answer Key)	Supplementary activities, including: Additional structured language practice, additional activities using authentic sources, communication activities for practicing interpersonal speaking, lesson review activities, and the ¡Atrévete! Board Game.	•	•
Assessment Program (with Answer Key)	Quizzes, tests, and exams; includes IPAs	•	•
Assessment Program Audio	Audio to accompany all tests and exams	•	•
Audio files	Audio files for all textbook and Practice Workbook activities	•	•
Audio and Video Scripts	Scripts for all audio and video selections: • Textbook audio • Testing Program audio • Video Virtual Chat scripts • *Fotonovela, Flash cultura,* and *Panorama cultural* • Grammar Tutorials	•	•
Digital Image Bank	Images and maps from the text to use for presentation in class, plus a bank of illustrations to use with the Instructor-Created Content tool	•	•
Grammar Presentation Slides	Grammar presentation reformatted in PowerPoint	•	•
I Can Worksheets	Lesson Objectives broken down by section and written in student-friendly "I Can" statement format	•	•
Implementation Guides	In-depth support for every stage of instruction—from planning and implementation, to assessment and remediation	•	•
Index to AP® Themes and Contexts	Overview chart on where you can explore the various themes and contexts with students	•	•
Learning Templates	Pre-built course templates that provide flexible options to suit On-level, Above-level, and Heritage Speaker classes	•	
Lesson Plans	Editable block and standard schedules	•	•
Middle School Activity Pack	Hands-on vocabulary and grammar practice design for younger learners, but effective for kinesthetic instruction for all level 1 students	•	•
Pacing Guides	Guidelines for how to cover the level's instructional material for a variety of scenarios (standard, block, etc.)	•	•
Teacher's DVD Set	*Flash cultura/Fotonovela/Panorama cultural* DVD, Teacher Resources DVD	•	

For the Student

COMPONENT	WHAT IS IT?	PRIME	supersite
Student Edition	Core instruction for students	•	•
Audio-synced Readings	Audio to accompany all *Lecturas*	•	•
Dictionary	Easy digital access to dictionary	•	•
eBook	Downloadable Student Edition	•	•
eCompanion	Online version of the Student Edition	•	
En pantalla Video	Authentic TV clips from across the Spanish-speaking world	•	•
Enhanced Diagnostics	Embedded assessment activities provide immediate feedback to students	•	
Flash cultura Video	Young broadcasters from the Spanish-speaking world share cultural aspects of life	•	•
Fotonovela Video	Engaging storyline video	•	•
Grammar Tutorials	Animated tutorials feature embedded quick checks to engage students and ensure comprehension		•
Grammar Tutorials with Diagnostics	Animated tutorials feature embedded quick checks and a diagnostic activity at the end with real-time feedback and remediation	•	
Learning Progression	Unique learning progression logically contextualizes lesson content	•	
My Vocabulary	A variety of tools to practice vocabulary	•	
News and Cultural Updates	Monthly posting of authentic resource links with scaffolded activities	•	•
Online Information Gap Activities	Student pairs work synchronously to record a conversation as they negotiate for meaning to complete a task	•	
Panorama cultural Video	Short video showcases the nations of the Spanish-speaking world	•	•
Partner Chat Activities	Pairs of students work synchronously to record a conversation	•	•
Personalized Study Plan	Personalized prescriptive pathway highlights areas where students need more practice	•	
Practice Tests with Diagnostics	Students get feedback on what they need to study before a test or exam	•	•
Pronunciation Tutorials	Interactive presentation of Spanish pronunciation and spelling with Speech Recognition	•	
Speech Recognition	Innovative technology analyzes students' speech and provides real-time feedback	•	
vText	Virtual interactive textbook for browser-based exploration		•
Video Virtual Chat Activities	Students create simulated conversations by responding to questions delivered by video recordings of native speakers	•	•
Vocabulary Hotpots	Vocabulary presentation with embedded audio	•	
Vocabulary Spotlights	Automated spotlighting on images with audio	•	
Vocabulary Tutorials (Animated)	Animated tutorials allow students to practice vocabulary at their own pace		•
Vocabulary Tutorials (Interactive)	Lesson vocabulary taught in a cyclical learning sequence—Listen & repeat, Match, Say it—with Speech Recognition and diagnostics	•	
Web-enhanced Readings	Dynamic presentation with audio	•	

Senderos Prime

Teacher-Driven Technology

Senderos Prime allows your unique teaching style to shine through. With convenient, ready-made Learning Templates, you'll have the time and flexibility to create and incorporate your own activities, videos, assignments, and assessments. Adding your own voice is easy—and your students will hear your unique accent loud and clear.

So what are Learning Templates?

Learning Templates are pre-built lesson plans that provide flexible options to suit your On-level, Above-level, or Heritage Speaker Spanish classes.

Once you've selected a Learning Template as a base for your course, **Senderos Prime** will automatically set all of the assignments for the entire year, as well as create your gradebook. You can then add or delete activities, change due dates, and customize assessments. You can even add your own personal touches, including activities, videos, and notes to students.

Student-Directed Learning

To effectively learn a new language, students need opportunities for meaningful practice—both inside and outside of the classroom. **Senderos Prime** provides students with the interactive tools and engaging content they need to stay motivated and on track throughout the school year.

Senderos Prime is unique in its organization and delivery of lesson content. Each color-coded strand features a progression that contextualizes the learning experience for students by breaking lesson content into comprehensible language chunks.

Explore and Learn

Explore and Learn activities engage students, so they can actively learn and build confidence in a safe online environment. With these low-stakes activities, students receive credit for participation, not performance.

Explore

Explore activities activate students' prior knowledge and connect them with the material they are about to learn.

Contextos Explore features a multimodal presentation with audio, text, illustrations, and contemporary photos that immerses students in an engaging learning environment.

Contextos Spotlights capture and focus students' attention on key vocabulary from the lesson.

Fotonovela Explore mini video clips in an easy-to-follow storyboard format set the context for the entire episode.

Estructura Explore features carefully designed charts and diagrams that call out key grammatical structures as well as additional active vocabulary. Audio and point-of-use photos from the Vocabulary Tutorials and *Fotonovela* episode provide additional context.

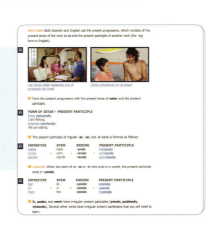

Senderos Prime

Learn

Learn activities shift from purely receptive to interactive learning, inviting students to be active participants and take ownership of their learning. Embedded quick checks give students immediate feedback, without grading or demotivating them.

Vocabulary Tutorials feature a cyclical learning sequence that optimizes comprehension and retention:

- **Listen & repeat:** How does the word look and sound?
- **Match:** Which picture represents the word?
- **Say it:** Do you recognize the picture? Do you know how to say the word?

Audio hints and cognate/false cognate icons help students understand and remember new vocabulary.

Speech Recognition, embedded in the Vocabulary Tutorials, Pronunciation Tutorials, and *Fotonovela*, identifies student utterances in real time and objectively determines whether a student knows the word.

This innovative technology increases student awareness of pronunciation through low-stakes production practice.

Learn

Pronunciation Tutorials require students to engage with the material via interactive quick checks throughout each tutorial.

Real-time feedback via embedded Speech Recognition gives students an opportunity to reflect on their language patterns and increases their awareness of pronunciation for more effective speaking and listening skills.

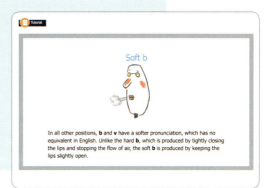

En detalle features a dynamic web-enhanced presentation of the reading with audio to engage 21st century learners.

Practice

Practice activities are carefully scaffolded—moving from discrete to open-ended—to support students as they acquire new language. This purposeful progression develops students' confidence and skills as they master new vocabulary and structures.

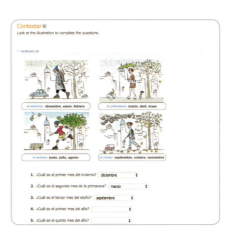

Senderos Prime

Communicate

Communicate activities provide opportunities for students to develop their oral skills and build confidence, reducing the affective filter. Scaffolded activities build on the three modes of communication: interpretive, interpersonal, and presentational.

Online Information Gap activities engage student partners in interpersonal communication as they negotiate meaning to solve a real-world task. They also provide opportunities for students to learn how to ask for clarification, request information, and use circumlocution or paraphrasing when faced with misunderstandings.

Self-check

Self-check activities support the self-directed nature of learning by enabling students to gauge their performance every step of the way. These low-stakes activities feature real-time feedback and personalized remediation that highlights areas where students may need more practice.

Autoevaluación is a Self-check activity that provides students with low-stakes diagnostic opportunities for vocabulary and each grammar point. Depending on their performance, students are provided with opportunities to review the vocabulary or each grammar point.

Assessment

A variety of formative and summative assessments allow for varied and ongoing evaluation of student learning and progress. Tailor these assessments to meet the needs of your students.

Prueba de práctica is a multi-question practice test that provides students with a low-stakes opportunity for assessing their knowledge of the vocabulary and grammar points covered in each lesson.

A **Personalized Study Plan** highlights areas where students need additional support and recommends remediation activities for completion prior to the lesson test.

ACTFL Standards

World-Readiness Standards for Learning Languages

Senderos blends the underlying principles of the World-Readiness Standards with features and strategies tailored specifically to build students' language and cultural competencies.

 This icon provides information on the specific standard(s) addressed in each section.

THE FIVE C'S OF FOREIGN LANGUAGE LEARNING

Communication

Students:
1. Interact and negotiate meaning in spoken, signed, or written conversations to share information, reactions, feelings, and opinions. (Interpersonal mode)
2. Understand, interpret, and analyze what is heard, read, or viewed on a variety of topics. (Interpretive mode)
3. Present information, concepts, and ideas to inform, explain, persuade, and narrate on a variety of topics using appropriate media and adapting to various audiences of listeners, readers, or viewers. (Presentational mode)

Cultures

Students use Spanish to investigate, explain, and reflect on:
1. The relationship of the practices and perspectives of the culture studied.
2. The relationship of the products and perspectives of the culture studied.

Connections

Students:
1. Build, reinforce, and expand their knowledge of other disciplines while using Spanish to develop critical thinking and to solve problems creatively.
2. Access and evaluate information and diverse perspectives that are available through Spanish and its cultures.

Comparisons

Students use Spanish to investigate, explain, and reflect on:
1. The nature of language through comparisons of the Spanish language and their own.
2. The concept of culture through comparisons of the cultures studied and their own.

Communities

Students:
1. Use Spanish both within and beyond the school to interact and collaborate in their community and the globalized world.
2. Set goals and reflect on their progress in using languages for enjoyment, enrichment, and advancement.

Adapted from ACTFL's *Standards for Foreign Language Learning in the 21st Century*

Preliminary Lesson

Designed with Middle School in Mind

The *Lección preliminar* provides a review of the contexts that were presented in **Senderos 1A**. In addition, it features a preview of Lessons 4–6. Highly visual presentations introduce vocabulary in small manageable chunks, while extensive practice sets students up for success in **Senderos 1B**.

Unique Lesson Structure

The *Lección preliminar* covers four core contexts, reviews the *Fotonovela* storyline, and explores the history of Spanish in the Americas.

Focus on Vocabulary

The *Lección preliminar* focuses on a lexical introduction and review of Spanish. Language models allow students to produce correct structures, while leaving detailed study of the rules to later lessons. This allows students to focus on simple communication without getting bogged down by grammar.

An appealing design and layout draw students to each presentation. Students encounter new terms in bilingual lists and dialogues that are illustrated with photos or drawings.

Multiple and multisensory input of new terms will aid comprehension and support vocabulary acquisition.

Senderos 1B *Lección preliminar* includes structures that support student language production.

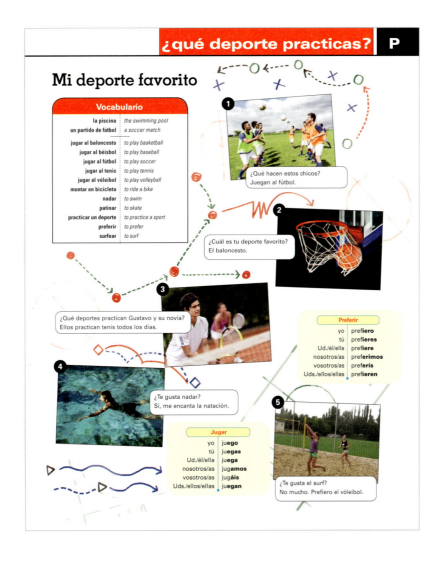

Enhance your Vocabulary Presentations
You can use digital versions of the vocabulary presentations in the Digital Image Bank online as an alternative to using a textbook in class.

Lesson Walkthrough: Senderos 1B

Senderos is built around Vista Higher Learning's proven six-step instructional design. Each lesson is organized into color-coded strands that present new material in clear, comprehensible, and communicative ways. With a focus on personalization, authenticity, cultural immersion, and the seamless integration of text and technology, Spanish-language learning comes to life in ways that are meaningful to each and every student.

Contextos ensures students' understanding and application of new vocabulary by presenting new words and phrases in real-life contexts.

Fotonovela storyline videos bridge language and culture, providing a glimpse into everyday life in the Spanish-speaking world.

Pronunciación provides students with training opportunities to be accurate and effective communicators.

Cultura exposes students to different aspects of contemporary Hispanic cultures tied to the lesson theme.

Estructura provides a clear and concise presentation of relevant grammar and scaffolded activities for building confidence, fluency, and accuracy. Grammar is presented as a tool, not a topic.

Adelante synthesizes students' listening, speaking, reading, and writing skills within a culturally rich context.

Icons

Familiarize yourself with these icons that appear throughout **Senderos**.

 Listening activity/section

 Pair activity

 Group activity

 Interpretive activity

 Interpersonal activity

 Presentational activity

Walkthrough Legend

Point-of-Use Suggestions support the presentation of new material and in-class implementation of activities and group work.

Online Features describe digital material integral to the instruction of each strand.

General Suggestions describe the purpose of each instructional section and how it supports learning.

Las vacaciones 5

Communicative Goals

You will learn how to:
- Discuss and plan a vacation
- Describe a hotel
- Talk about how you feel
- Talk about the seasons and the weather

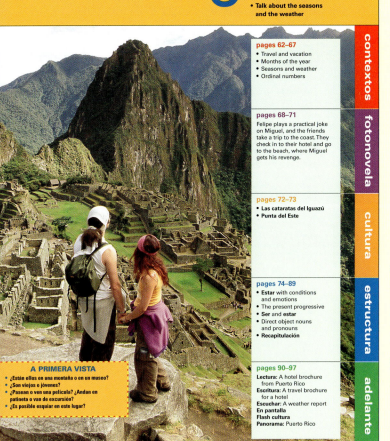

A PRIMERA VISTA
- ¿Están ellos en una montaña o en un museo?
- ¿Son viejos o jóvenes?
- ¿Pasean o ven una película? ¿Andan en patineta o van de excursión?
- ¿Es posible esquiar en este lugar?

contextos
pages 62–67
- Travel and vacation
- Months of the year
- Seasons and weather
- Ordinal numbers

fotonovela
pages 68–71
Felipe plays a practical joke on Miguel, and the friends take a trip to the coast. They check in to their hotel and go to the beach, where Miguel gets his revenge.

cultura
pages 72–73
- Las cataratas del Iguazú
- Punta del Este

estructura
pages 74–89
- **Estar** with conditions and emotions
- The present progressive
- **Ser** and **estar**
- Direct object nouns and pronouns
- Recapitulación

adelante
pages 90–97
- **Lectura:** A hotel brochure from Puerto Rico
- **Escritura:** A travel brochure for a hotel
- **Escuchar:** A weather report
- **En pantalla**
- **Flash cultura**
- **Panorama:** Puerto Rico

Lesson Goals
In **Lección 5**, students will be introduced to the following:
- terms for traveling and vacations
- seasons and months
- weather expressions
- ordinal numbers (1st–10th)
- **Las cataratas del Iguazú**
- **Punta del Este**, Uruguay
- **estar** with conditions and emotions
- adjectives for conditions and emotions
- present progressive of regular and irregular verbs
- comparison of the uses of **ser** and **estar**
- direct object nouns and pronouns
- personal **a**
- scanning to find specific information
- making an outline
- writing a brochure for a hotel
- listening for key words
- an ad for **LANPASS**, a Chilean airline loyalty program
- a video about **Machu Picchu**
- cultural, geographic, and historical information about Puerto Rico

A primera vista Here are some additional questions you can ask to personalize the photo: ¿Dónde te gusta pasar tus ratos libres? ¿Qué haces en tus ratos libres? ¿Te gusta explorar otras culturas? ¿Te gusta viajar a otros países? ¿Adónde quieres ir en las próximas vacaciones?

Teaching Tip Look for these icons for additional communicative practice:

→	Interpretive communication
↔	Presentational communication
⇄	Interpersonal communication

SUPPORT FOR BACKWARD DESIGN

Lección 5 Essential Questions
1. How do people discuss and plan a vacation?
2. How do people talk about how they feel?
3. What are some popular vacation destinations in the Spanish-speaking world and why?

Lección 5 Integrated Performance Assessment
Before teaching this chapter, review the Integrated Performance Assessment (IPA) and its accompanying scoring rubric. Use the IPA to assess students' progress toward proficiency targets at the end of the chapter. **IPA Context:** Six students from your Spanish class will be chosen to spend a week in Puerto Rico, at the **Hotel Vistahermosa** in Lajas. Students will be chosen in pairs based on their presentation to the selection committee.

Voice boards online allow you and your students to record and share up to five minutes of audio. Use voice boards for presentations, oral assessments, discussions, directions, etc.

Teacher's Edition • Lesson Five **61**

Lesson Openers outline the content of each lesson.

Lesson Goals provide an at-a-glance view of the vocabulary, grammar, and cultural topics covered in each lesson. Lesson strands are color-coded for easy use and navigation.

Communicative Goals introduce the lesson's learning objectives.

A primera vista questions jump-start the lesson, allowing students to use the Spanish they already know to talk about the photo.

Integrated Performance Assessments (IPAs) begin with a real-life task that engages students' interest. To complete the task, students progress through the three modes of communication: they read, view, and listen for information (interpretive mode); they talk and write with classmates about what they have experienced (interpersonal mode); and they share formally what they have learned (presentational mode).

A critical step in administering the IPA is to define and share rubrics with students before beginning the task. They need to be aware of what successful performance should look like.

Contextos

Contextos presents theme-related vocabulary through expansive, full-color illustrations and easy-to-use references.

Teacher Resources
Project digital images of the vocabulary illustrations to enhance in-class presentations.

For additional practice and variety, use the *Más práctica* worksheets from the Activity Pack.

Use the Illustration Bank to build your own image-rich activities.

Administer the Vocabulary Quiz to check comprehension.

Más vocabulario
Más vocabulario calls out active, theme-related vocabulary in easy-to-reference Spanish-English lists. For expansion, use the Additional Vocabulary handout online.

Variación léxica
Variación léxica highlights linguistic diversity in the Spanish-speaking world by presenting alternate words and expressions.

Middle School Activity Pack
The **Middle School Activity Pack** provides younger students with fun and engaging ways to practice new vocabulary and grammar. Each *Contextos* and *Estructura* strand has targeted practice in hands-on and game formats. Students who learn kinesthetically will particularly benefit from these additional activities, though they will be an entertaining addition to any middle school classroom.

---

5 contextos

Section Goals
In **Contextos**, students will learn and practice:
- travel- and vacation-related vocabulary
- seasons and months of the year
- weather expressions
- ordinal numbers

Communication 1.2
Comparisons 4.1

Teacher Resources
Read the front matter for suggestions on how to incorporate all the program's components. See pages 61A–61B for a detailed listing of Teacher Resources online.

In-Class Tips
- Ask: **¿A quién le gusta mucho viajar? ¿Cómo prefieres viajar?** Introduce cognates as suggestions: **¿Te gusta viajar en auto?** Write each term on the board as you say it. Ask: **¿Adónde te gusta viajar? ¿A México?** Ask students about their classmates' statements: **¿Adónde le gusta viajar a ____ ? ¿Cómo puede viajar?**
- Ask questions about transportation in your community. Ex: **Si quiero ir de la escuela al aeropuerto, ¿cómo puedo ir?** Ask what type of transportation students use to go home on school break.
- Use the **Lección 5 Contextos** vocabulary presentation online or the digital images in the Resources online to assist with this presentation.
- Give students two minutes to review the four scenes and then ask questions. Ex: **¿Quién trabaja en una agencia de viajes? (el/la agente de viajes)**

Note: At this point you may want to present *Vocabulario adicional: Más vocabulario para las vacaciones* from the online Resources.

Las vacaciones

Más vocabulario

la cama	bed
la habitación individual, doble	single, double room
el piso	floor (of a building)
la planta baja	ground floor
el campo	countryside
el paisaje	landscape
el equipaje	luggage
la estación de autobuses, del metro, de tren	bus, subway, train station
la llegada	arrival
el pasaje (de ida y vuelta)	(round-trip) ticket
la salida	departure; exit
la tabla de (wind)surf	surfboard/sailboard
acampar	to camp
estar de vacaciones	to be on vacation
hacer las maletas	to pack (one's suitcases)
hacer un viaje	to take a trip
hacer (wind)surf	to (wind)surf
ir de compras	to go shopping
ir de vacaciones	to go on vacation
ir en autobús (m.), auto(móvil) (m.), motocicleta (f.), taxi (m.)	to go by bus, car, motorcycle, taxi

Variación léxica
automóvil ↔ coche (*Esp.*), carro (*Amér. L.*)
autobús ↔ camión (*Méx.*), guagua (*Caribe*)
motocicleta ↔ moto (*coloquial*)

En la agencia de viajes

En el hotel

TEACHING OPTIONS

Extra Practice Ask questions about the people, places, and activities in **Contextos**. Ex: **¿Qué actividades pueden hacer los turistas en una playa? ¿Pueden nadar? ¿Tomar el sol? ¿Sacar fotos?** Then expand questions to ask students what they specifically do at these places. ____, **¿qué haces tú cuando vas a la playa?** Students should respond in complete sentences.

Variación léxica Point out that these are just some of the different Spanish names for vehicles. Ask heritage speakers if they are familiar with other terms. While some of these terms are mutually understood in different regions (**el coche, el carro, el auto, el automóvil**), others are specific to a region and may not be understood by others (**la guagua, el camión**). Stress that the feminine article **la** is used with the abbreviation **moto**.

sesenta y tres **63**

Práctica

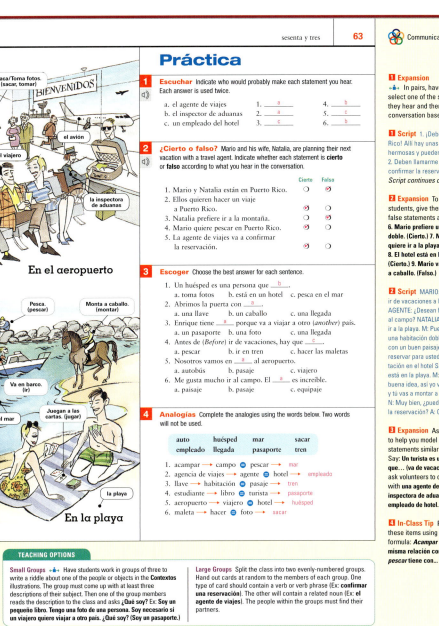

En el aeropuerto

En la playa

1 **Escuchar** Indicate who would probably make each statement you hear. Each answer is used twice.

a. el agente de viajes   1. _a_   4. _b_
b. el inspector de aduanas   2. _a_   5. _c_
c. un empleado del hotel   3. _c_   6. _b_

2 **¿Cierto o falso?** Mario and his wife, Natalia, are planning their next vacation with a travel agent. Indicate whether each statement is **cierto** or **falso** according to what you hear in the conversation.

	Cierto	Falso
1. Mario y Natalia están en Puerto Rico.	○	●
2. Ellos quieren hacer un viaje a Puerto Rico.	●	○
3. Natalia prefiere ir a la montaña.	○	●
4. Mario quiere pescar en Puerto Rico.	●	○
5. La agente de viajes va a confirmar la reservación.	●	○

3 **Escoger** Choose the best answer for each sentence.

1. Un huésped es una persona que _b_.
 a. toma fotos   b. está en un hotel   c. pesca en el mar
2. Abrimos la puerta con _a_.
 a. una llave   b. un caballo   c. una llegada
3. Enrique tiene _a_ porque va a viajar a otro (*another*) país.
 a. un pasaporte   b. una foto   c. una llegada
4. Antes de (*Before*) ir de vacaciones, hay que _c_.
 a. pescar   b. ir en tren   c. hacer las maletas
5. Nosotros vamos en _a_ al aeropuerto.
 a. autobús   b. pasaje   c. viajero
6. Me gusta mucho ir al campo. El _a_ es increíble.
 a. paisaje   b. pasaje   c. equipaje

4 **Analogías** Complete the analogies using the words below. Two words will not be used.

auto	huésped	mar	sacar
empleado	llegada	pasaporte	tren

1. acampar → campo ⊖ pescar → _mar_
2. agencia de viajes → agente ⊖ hotel → _empleado_
3. llave → habitación ⊖ pasaje → _tren_
4. estudiante → libro ⊖ turista → _pasaporte_
5. aeropuerto → viajero ⊖ hotel → _huésped_
6. maleta → hacer ⊖ foto → _sacar_

TEACHING OPTIONS

Small Groups Have students work in groups of three to write a riddle about one of the people or objects in the **Contextos** illustrations. The group must come up with at least three descriptions of their subject. Then one of the group members reads the description to the class and asks **¿Qué soy?** Ex: **Soy un pequeño libro. Tengo una foto de una persona. Soy necesario si un viajero quiere viajar a otro país. ¿Qué soy?** (Soy un pasaporte.)

Large Groups Split the class into two evenly-numbered groups. Hand out cards at random to the members of each group. One type of card should contain a verb or verb phrase (Ex: **confirmar una reservación**). The other will contain a related noun (Ex: **el agente de viajes**). The people within the groups must find their partners.

Contextos **63**

Communication 1.1, 1.2

1 Expansion In pairs, have students select one of the statements they hear and then write a conversation based on it.

1 Script 1. ¡Deben ir a Puerto Rico! Allí hay unas playas muy hermosas y pueden acampar. 2. Deben llamarme el lunes para confirmar la reservación. *Script continues on page 64.*

2 Expansion To challenge students, give them these true/false statements as items 6–9: **6. Mario prefiere una habitación doble. (Cierto.) 7. Natalia no quiere ir a la playa. (Falso.) 8. El hotel está en la playa. (Cierto.) 9. Mario va a montar a caballo. (Falso.)**

2 Script MARIO: Queremos ir de vacaciones a Puerto Rico. AGENTE: ¿Desean hacer un viaje al campo? NATALIA: Yo quiero ir a la playa. M: Pues, yo prefiero una habitación doble en un hotel con un buen paisaje. A: Puedo reservar para ustedes una habitación en el hotel San Juan que está en la playa. M: Es una buena idea, así yo voy a pescar y tú vas a montar a caballo. N: Muy bien, ¿puede confirmar la reservación? A: Claro que sí.

3 Expansion Ask a volunteer to help you model making statements similar to item 1. Say: **Un turista es una persona que…** (va de vacaciones). Then ask volunteers to do the same with **una agente de viajes, una inspectora de aduanas, un empleado de hotel.**

4 In-Class Tip Present these items using the following formula: **Acampar** tiene la misma relación con **campo** que **pescar** tiene con… (**mar**).

Práctica begins with listening exercises and continues with activities to practice new vocabulary in meaningful contexts. The practice sections always move from closed-ended and directed practice to more open-ended activities that require students to produce language.

Scripts are available to help you with planning. As an alternative, read the script aloud for your students instead of using the MP3 audio.

My Vocabulary enables students to identify, practice, and retain vocabulary for each lesson.

Students can print bilingual word lists. They can also create personalized word lists.

Interactive Flashcards featuring the Spanish word or expression (with audio) and the English translation are available for fast and effective review and practice.

T25

Contextos

In-Class Tips provide suggestions for how to enhance the vocabulary presentation. Ideas include asking personalized questions and emphasizing cognates to build connections to language students already know.

Expansion activities offer suggestions for more complex communication. Pair and group activities engage students as they collaborate and build fluency, while individual activities extend application.

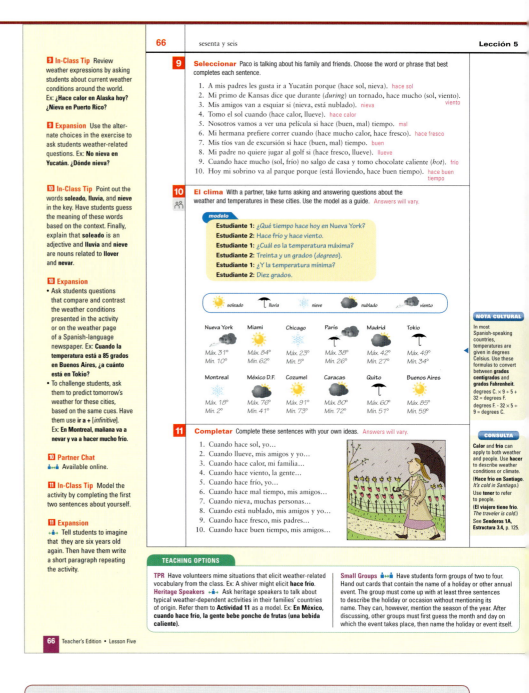

General Suggestions for Teaching Contextos

Encourage students to review vocabulary within the context of the lesson using the *Vocabulario* section. Color-coded vocabulary lists are categorized by topic for efficient study. This organization provides a handy way for students to find the right word as they complete activities.

References are made at the end of the list to the *Expresiones útiles* from *Fotonovela* and grammar charts. Students are also responsible for learning these terms for formative assessment.

See Implementation Guides for additional instructional support

Las vacaciones　　　　　　　sesenta y siete　　67

Comunicación

12 En la agencia de viajes Listen to the conversation between Mr. Vega and a travel agent. Then indicate whether the following conclusions are **lógico** or **ilógico**, based on what you heard.

	Lógico	Ilógico
1. El señor Vega quiere visitar la Antártida.	○	●
2. Hace calor en Puerto Rico.	●	○
3. El señor Vega va a ver el mar en Puerto Rico.	●	○
4. El señor Vega va a comprar un pasaje de ida y vuelta.	●	○
5. El señor Vega viaja con su familia.	○	●

13 Preguntas personales Answer your partner's questions.　Answers will vary.
1. ¿Cuál es la fecha de hoy? ¿Qué estación es?
2. ¿Te gusta esta estación? ¿Por qué?
3. ¿Qué estación prefieres? ¿Por qué?
4. ¿Prefieres el mar o las montañas? ¿La playa o el campo? ¿Por qué?
5. Cuando haces un viaje, ¿qué te gusta hacer y ver?
6. ¿Piensas ir de vacaciones este verano? ¿Adónde quieres ir? ¿Por qué?
7. ¿Qué deseas ver y qué lugares quieres visitar?
8. ¿Cómo te gusta viajar? ¿En avión? ¿En motocicleta...?

14 Itinerario Create a trip itinerary for a friend, a relative, or someone famous. First, choose a destination. Include information about transportation and accommodations, as well as a section for each day with activities.　Answers will vary.
- fechas
- lugar
- transporte
- hotel
- actividades

Síntesis

15 Un viaje With a partner, role-play a conversation between a travel agent and a client planning a trip. Discuss destinations, dates, transportation, hotel accommodations, and activities for the trip.　Answers will vary.

TEACHING OPTIONS

Pairs Tell students they are part of a scientific expedition to Antarctica (**la Antártida**). Have them write a letter back home about the weather conditions and their activities there. Begin the letter for them by writing **Queridos amigos** on the board.
Game Have each student create a *Bingo* card with 25 squares (five rows of five). Tell them to write **GRATIS** (*FREE*) in the center square and the name of a different city in each of the other squares. Have them exchange cards. Call out different weather expressions. Ex: **Hace viento.** Students who think this description fits a city or cities on their card should mark the square with the weather condition. In order to win, a student must have marked five squares in a row and be able to give the weather condition for each one. Ex: **Hace mucho viento en Chicago.**

Communication 1.1, 1.2, 1.3

12 In-Class Tip Ask students if they have ever been to a travel agency. Let them share their experiences before doing the activity.

12 Script *See the script for this activity on Interleaf page 61B.*

13 Expansion Have pairs imagine that one of them is a journalist and the other is a celebrity. Then have them conduct the interview using questions 3–8.

13 Virtual Chat Available online.

14 In-Class Tip Have students create a tourist brochure of the destination they selected for their trip.

15 In-Class Tip Encourage students to use the information they prepared in activity **14 Itinerario** as the basis of this conversation.

15 Expansion Divide the class in pairs and distribute the handouts for activity **Un viaje** from the online Resources (Lección 5/Activity Pack/ Information Gap Activities). Ask students to read the instructions and give them ten minutes to complete the activity.

Communication 1.1

15 In-Class Tip Set up the classroom chairs in two parallel rows so pairs of students face each other. The students in one row will be assigned the role of travel agents and the others will be the customers. Let them interact for two minutes and then ask one row to shift one seat to the right, and ask the new pairs to continue the role-play.

15 Partner Chat Available online.

Contextos 67

Comunicación provides scaffolded activities built around the three modes of communication:

- Interpretive communication activities target students' reading and listening comprehension skills.

- Interpersonal communication activities target the development of students' skills in real-time negotiation of meaning with one or more partners in both spoken and written communication settings.

- Presentational communication activities target students' skills in producing a variety of written and spoken language.

Teaching Options offer in-class activity ideas to reinforce new and previously taught vocabulary. Games, such as 20 questions or charades, enliven students' newly-acquired vocabulary.

Video Virtual Chat activities provide students with opportunities to develop their listening and speaking skills. They also help build students' confidence as they practice with video recordings of native speakers.

Students also benefit from nonverbal and articulatory cues that are essential for production and pronunciation.

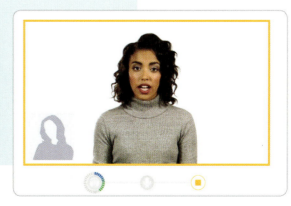

Fotonovela

Fotonovela is an episodic video series that follows the adventures of a group of students living and traveling in Mexico.

Video Recap helps students recall the events of the previous lesson's episode.

Teacher Resources
Videoscripts can be used to support comprehension or to work with listening.

Incorporate the Optional Testing Sections into a lesson test, or use them as additional practice.

Section Goals
In **Fotonovela**, students will:
- receive comprehensible input from free-flowing discourse
- learn functional phrases that preview lesson grammatical structures

Communication 1.2
Cultures 2.1, 2.2

Teacher Resources
Read the front matter for suggestions on how to incorporate all the program's components. See pages 61A–61B for a detailed listing of Teacher Resources online.

Video Recap: Lección 4
Review the previous episode with these questions:
1. ¿Qué prefiere hacer tía Ana María en sus ratos libres? (Ella nada, juega al tenis y al golf y va al cine y a los museos.)
2. ¿Adónde van Miguel, Maru, Marissa y Jimena? (Van a un cenote.)
3. ¿Qué van a hacer Felipe y Juan Carlos? (Van a jugar al fútbol con Eduardo y Pablo.)
4. ¿Qué quieren comer los chicos después de jugar al fútbol? (Quieren comer mole.)

Video Synopsis
The friends watch the weather report on TV and discuss weather and seasons in their hometowns. **Felipe** rouses **Miguel** so they don't miss the bus to the beach. The group checks in to their hotel. At the beach, **Maru** and **Miguel** windsurf. **Miguel** gets back at **Felipe**.

In-Class Tips
- Have the class glance over the **Fotonovela** captions and list words and phrases related to tourism.
- Ask individuals how they are today, using **cansado/a** and **aburrido/a**.
- Ask the class: ¿Cómo es el hotel ideal? ¿Cómo es la habitación de hotel perfecta?

5 fotonovela

¡Vamos a la playa!
Los seis amigos hacen un viaje a la playa.

PERSONAJES FELIPE JUAN CARLOS

TÍA ANA MARÍA ¿Están listos para su viaje a la playa?
TODOS Sí.
TÍA ANA MARÍA Excelente... ¡A la estación de autobuses!
MARU ¿Dónde está Miguel?
FELIPE Yo lo traigo.

(se escucha un grito de Miguel)
FELIPE Ya está listo. Y tal vez enojado. Ahorita vamos.

FELIPE No está nada mal el hotel, ¿verdad? Limpio, cómodo... ¡Oye, Miguel! ¿Todavía estás enojado conmigo? (a Juan Carlos) Miguel está de mal humor. No me habla.
JUAN CARLOS ¿Todavía?

EMPLEADO Bienvenidas. ¿En qué puedo servirles?
MARU Hola. Tenemos una reservación para seis personas para esta noche.
EMPLEADO ¿A nombre de quién?
JIMENA ¿Díaz? ¿López? No estoy segura.

EMPLEADO No encuentro su nombre. Ah, no, ahora sí lo veo, aquí está. Díaz. Dos habitaciones en el primer piso para seis huéspedes.

EMPLEADO Aquí están las llaves de sus habitaciones.
MARU Gracias. Una cosa más. Mi novio y yo queremos hacer windsurf, pero no tenemos tablas.
EMPLEADO El botones las puede conseguir para ustedes.

TEACHING OPTIONS
Video Tips General suggestions for using video clips in the classroom can be found in the front matter of this Teacher's Edition.
¡Vamos a la playa! Before viewing the **¡Vamos a la playa!** episode of the **Fotonovela**, ask students to brainstorm a list of things that might happen in an episode in which the characters check in to a hotel and go to the beach. Then play the **¡Vamos a la playa!** episode once without sound and have the class create a plot summary based on visual clues. Finally, show the video segment with sound and have the class correct any mistaken guesses and fill in any gaps. Ask comprehension questions as a follow-up.

68 Teacher's Edition • Lesson Five

Fotonovela storyline episodes combine new vocabulary and grammar with previously taught language, exposing students to a variety of authentic accents along the way.

T28 See Implementation Guides for additional instructional support

sesenta y nueve **69**

MARISSA JIMENA MARU MIGUEL MAITE FUENTES ANA MARÍA EMPLEADO

7

JUAN CARLOS ¿Qué hace este libro aquí? ¿Estás estudiando en la playa?
JIMENA Sí, es que tengo un examen la próxima semana.

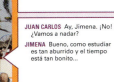

8

JUAN CARLOS Ay, Jimena. ¡No! ¿Vamos a nadar?
JIMENA Bueno, como estudiar es tan aburrido y el tiempo está tan bonito...

MARISSA Yo estoy un poco cansada. ¿Y tú? ¿Por qué no estás nadando?
FELIPE Es por causa de Miguel.

9

10

MARISSA Hmm, estoy confundida.
FELIPE Esta mañana. ¡Sigue enojado conmigo!
MARISSA No puede seguir enojado tanto tiempo.

Expresiones útiles

Talking with hotel personnel
¿En qué puedo servirles?
How can I help you?
Tenemos una reservación.
We have a reservation.
¿A nombre de quién?
In whose name?
¿Quizás López? ¿Tal vez Díaz?
Maybe López? Maybe Díaz?
Ahora lo veo, aquí está. Díaz.
Now I see it. Here it is. Díaz.
Dos habitaciones en el primer piso para seis huéspedes.
Two rooms on the first floor for six guests.
Aquí están las llaves.
Here are the keys.

Describing a hotel
No está nada mal el hotel.
The hotel isn't bad at all.
Todo está tan limpio y cómodo.
Everything is so clean and comfortable.
Es excelente/estupendo/fabuloso/ fenomenal/increíble/magnífico/ maravilloso/perfecto.
It's excellent/stupendous/fabulous/ phenomenal/incredible/magnificent/ marvelous/perfect.

Talking about how you feel
Yo estoy un poco cansado/a.
I am a little tired.
Estoy confundido/a. *I'm confused.*
Todavía estoy/Sigo enojado/a contigo.
I'm still angry with you.

Additional vocabulary
afuera *outside*
amable *nice; friendly*
el balde *bucket*
el/la botones *bellhop*
la crema de afeitar *shaving cream*
el frente (frío) *(cold) front*
el grito *scream*
la temporada *period of time*
entonces *so, then*
es igual *it's the same*

Expresiones útiles Remind students that **está**, **están**, and **estoy** are present-tense forms of the verb **estar**, which is often used with adjectives that describe conditions and emotions. Remind students that **Es** is a present-tense form of the verb **ser**, which is often used to describe characteristics of people and things and to make generalizations. Draw students' attention to video stills 7 and 9. Point out that **Estás estudiando** and **estás nadando** are examples of the present progressive, which is used to emphasize an action in progress. Finally, point out the captions for video stills 1, 4, and 6 and explain that **lo** and **las** are examples of direct object pronouns. Explain that these are words that replace direct object nouns in order to avoid repetition. Tell students that they will learn more about these concepts in **Estructura**.

In-Class Tip
Have students work in groups of six to read the **Fotonovela** captions aloud (have one student read the role of both **tía Ana María** and the **empleado**). Then have one group come to the front of the class and role-play the scenes. Encourage them to use props and gestures.

Nota cultural The **Yucatán** peninsula is warm year-round, but there are rainy and dry seasons. Generally, the dry season lasts from November to April and the wet season runs from May through October. Hurricanes occur in the late summer and fall. The **Yucatán's** average temperature is 25°C to 27°C (77°F to 81°F), rarely dropping below 16°C (61°F) or rising above 49°C (120°F).

TEACHING OPTIONS

Pairs Ask pairs to write five true/false statements based on the **¡Vamos a la playa!** captions. Then have them exchange papers with another pair, who will complete the activity and correct the false statements. Ask volunteers to read a few statements for the class, who will answer and point out the caption that contains the information.

Interpersonal Speaking Ask students to work in groups to rewrite the **¡Vamos a la playa!** episode using a different ending or location. Suggest new locations such as a ski resort, a big city, or a campground. Allow groups time to prepare, and ask them to ad-lib their new versions for the class. You may want to assign this activity as homework and have students present it in the next class period for review.

Personajes show the main characters who appear in the episode.

Expresiones útiles highlight active vocabulary from the episode. Lists are organized by language function, demonstrating their real, practical use.

Pre-AP® offers ideas on how students can build the skills needed for long-term success in Spanish-language learning.

AP and Advanced Placement Program are registered trademarks of the College Board, which was not involved in the production of, and does not endorse, this product.

Fotonovela

¿Qué pasó? practice activities are carefully scaffolded to support students as they acquire new language, thus building their confidence, skills, and fluency.

In-Class Tips help you engage students with the *Fotonovela* episode and its corresponding textbook section to enhance their comprehension.

Notas culturales provide a wide range of cultural information relevant to the topic of an activity or section. Background information helps you expand students' knowledge about cultural products and practices.

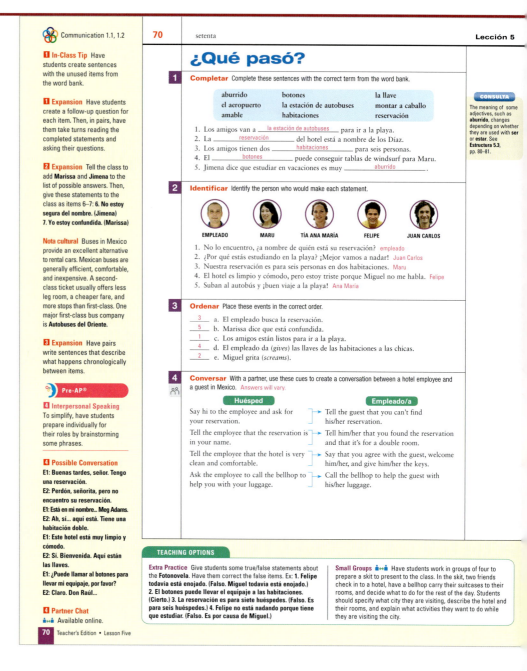

Using Fotonovela for grammar instruction

- Play parts of the episode that demonstrate the grammar point you are teaching.

- Show selected scenes that review known grammar topics and ask students to identify them.

- After completing the *Estructura* section, have students watch the corresponding *Resumen* section of the *Fotonovela* in its entirety for additional review.

Pronunciación

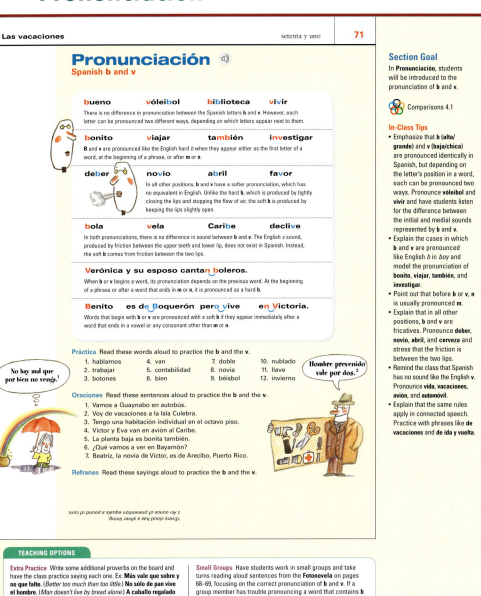

Section Goal
In **Pronunciación**, students will be introduced to the pronunciation of **b** and **v**.

Comparisons 4.1

In-Class Tips
- Emphasize that **b (alta/grande)** and **v (baja/chica)** are pronounced identically in Spanish, but depending on the letter's position in a word, each can be pronounced two ways. Pronounce **vóleibol** and **vivir** and have students listen for the difference between the initial and medial sounds represented by **b** and **v**.
- Explain the cases in which **b** and **v** are pronounced like English *b* in *boy* and model the pronunciation of **bonito, viajar, también,** and **investigar**.
- Point out that before **b** or **v**, **n** is usually pronounced **m**.
- Explain that in all other positions, **b** and **v** are fricatives. Pronounce **deber, novio, abril,** and **cerveza** and stress that the friction is between the two lips.
- Remind the class that Spanish has no sound like the English *v*. Pronounce **vida, vacaciones, avión,** and **automóvil**.
- Explain that the same rules apply in connected speech. Practice with phrases like **de vacaciones** and **de ida y vuelta**.

Pronunciación helps students demonstrate the accuracy necessary for effective communication.

Refranes feature illustrated sayings and proverbs, so students can practice the pronunciation point in an entertaining cultural context.

Teaching Options provide you with in-class activity ideas for extra practice and small group work.

TEACHING OPTIONS

Extra Practice Write some additional proverbs on the board and have the class practice saying each one. Ex: **Más vale que sobre y no que falte.** (*Better too much than too little.*) **No sólo de pan vive el hombre.** (*Man doesn't live by bread alone.*) **A caballo regalado no se le ve el colmillo.** (*Don't look a gift horse in the mouth.*) **Más vale dar que recibir.** (*It's better to give than to receive.*)

Small Groups Have students work in small groups and take turns reading aloud sentences from the **Fotonovela** on pages 68–69, focusing on the correct pronunciation of **b** and **v**. If a group member has trouble pronouncing a word that contains **b** or **v**, the rest of the group should supply the rule that explains how it should be pronounced.

General Suggestions for Teaching Pronunciación

Have the class work in pairs to practice the pronunciation of the *Fotonovela* captions. Encourage students to help their partners if they are having trouble pronouncing a particular word or phrase.

This collaborative communication activity provides students with an opportunity to try out new rules and modify their output accordingly. Circulate around the class and model correct pronunciation as needed.

Cultura

Cultura offers theme-driven coverage of cultural products, practices, and perspectives from throughout the Spanish-speaking world.

En detalle explores the lesson's cultural topic in-depth.

Actividades comprehension activities check understanding and solidify learning.

Teaching Options include cultural notes and suggestions for homework and projects that address the needs of various learning styles, age groups, and heritage speakers.

News and Cultural Updates provide real-world connections to language and culture via authentic articles and videos. From online newspaper articles to TV news segments, each source is chosen for its age-appropriate content, currency, and high interest to students. Each selection includes scaffolded pre-, during, and post-reading and viewing activities for a wide range of learning abilities.

Section Goals

In **Cultura**, students will:
- read about **Las cataratas del Iguazú**
- learn travel-related terms
- read about **Punta del Este**, Uruguay
- read about popular vacation destinations in the Spanish-speaking world

 Communication 1.1, 1.2
Cultures 2.1, 2.2
Connections 3.1, 3.2
Comparisons 4.2

En detalle

Antes de leer Ask students what kind of travel interests them. Ex: ¿Te gusta acampar o dormir en un hotel? ¿Adónde prefieres ir: a la ciudad, a las montañas…? Then ask students to predict what a tourist would see and do near a waterfall.

Lectura
- Explain that the **Guaraní** are an indigenous group who traditionally inhabit areas of Paraguay, northern Argentina, southern Brazil, and parts of Uruguay and Bolivia. The **Guaraní** language is one of the two official languages of Paraguay.
- The **Iguazú** Falls have been featured in many movies, most notably in *The Mission* (1986).

Después de leer Ask students through which country they would prefer to visit **Iguazú** and why.

1 Expansion Give students these true/false statements as items 11–12: 11. The **Tren Ecológico de la Selva** takes tourists to San Martín Island. (Falso. It takes them to the walkways.) 12. **Piedra Volada** is the tallest waterfall in Mexico. (Cierto.)

---

5 cultura

EN DETALLE

Las cataratas del Iguazú

Imagine the impressive and majestic Niagara Falls, the most powerful waterfall in North America. Now, if you can, imagine a waterfall four times as wide and almost twice as tall that caused Eleanor Roosevelt to exclaim "Poor Niagara!" upon seeing it for the first time. Welcome to **las cataratas del Iguazú**!

Iguazú is located in Iguazú National Park, an area of subtropical jungle where Argentina meets Brazil. Its name comes from the indigenous Guaraní word for "great water." A UNESCO World Heritage Site, **las cataratas del Iguazú** span three kilometers and comprise 275 cascades split into two main sections by San Martín Island. Most of the falls are about 82 meters (270 feet) high. The horseshoe-shaped cataract **Garganta del Diablo** (Devil's Throat) has the greatest water flow and is considered to be the most impressive; it also marks the border between Argentina and Brazil.

Each country offers different views and tourist options. Most visitors opt to use the numerous catwalks that are available on both sides; however, from the Argentinean side, tourists can get very close to the falls, whereas Brazil provides more panoramic views. If you don't mind getting wet, a jet boat tour is a good choice; those looking for wildlife—such as toucans, ocelots, butterflies, and jaguars—should head for San Martín Island. Brazil boasts less conventional ways to view the falls, such as helicopter rides and rappelling, while Argentina focuses on sustainability with its **Tren Ecológico de la Selva** (*Ecological Jungle Train*), an environmentally friendly way to reach the walkways.

No matter which way you choose to enjoy the falls, you are certain to be captivated.

Más cascadas° en Latinoamérica

Nombre	País	Altura°	Datos
Salto Ángel	Venezuela	979 metros	la más alta° del mundo°
Catarata del Gocta	Perú	771 metros	descubierta° en 2006
Piedra Volada	México	453 metros	la más alta de México

cascadas waterfalls Altura Height más alta tallest mundo world descubierta discovered

ACTIVIDADES

1 ¿Cierto o falso? Indicate whether these statements are cierto or falso. Correct the false statements.

1. Iguazú Falls is located on the border of Argentina and Brazil. Cierto.
2. Niagara Falls is four times as wide as Iguazú Falls. Falso. *Iguazú is four times as wide as Niagara Falls.*
3. Iguazú Falls has a few cascades, each about 82 meters. Falso. *Iguazú is composed of 275 cascades about 82 meters tall.*
4. Tourists visiting Iguazú can see exotic wildlife. Cierto.
5. *Iguazú* is the Guarani word for "blue water." Falso. *Iguazú is the Guaraní word for "great water."*
6. You can access the walkways by taking the **Garganta del Diablo**. Falso. *One way of accessing the walkways is taking the Tren Ecológico de la Selva.*
7. It is possible for tourists to visit Iguazú Falls by air. Cierto.
8. **Salto Ángel** is the tallest waterfall in the world. Cierto.
9. There are no waterfalls in Mexico. Falso. *The Piedra Volada is in Mexico.*
10. For the best views of Iguazú Falls, tourists should visit the Brazilian side. Cierto.

TEACHING OPTIONS

La leyenda Share this legend of the **Iguazú** Falls with students: Many ages ago, in the **Iguazú** River there lived a god-serpent, **Mboi**, to whom the **Guaraní** tribes sacrificed a young woman during their annual gathering. At one such gathering, a young man named **Tarobá** instantly fell in love with **Naipí**, who was to be sacrificed. After pleading in vain to have her spared, one night **Tarobá** took **Naipí** and tried to flee with her in his canoe.

The furious **Mboi** awoke and split the river in two, forming the waterfall and trapping the pair. He transformed **Naipí** into a rock at the base of the falls and **Tarobá** into a tree perched at the edge of the abyss. Lest the lovers try to reunite, the watchful **Mboi** keeps an eternal vigil from deep under the waters of the **Garganta del Diablo**. Now ask them to think of other creation legends they know (Ex: Paul Bunyan and the Great Lakes).

72 Teacher's Edition • Lesson Five

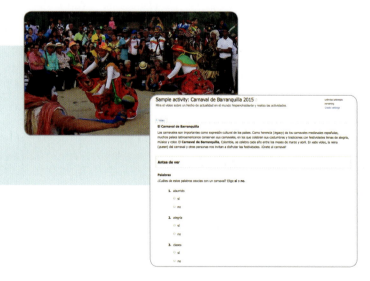

T32 See Implementation Guides for additional instructional support

setenta y tres **73**

ASÍ SE DICE
Viajes y turismo

el asiento del medio, del pasillo, de la ventanilla	center, aisle, window seat
el itinerario	itinerary
media pensión	breakfast and one meal included
el ómnibus (Perú)	el autobús
pensión completa	all meals included
el puente	long weekend (lit., bridge)

EL MUNDO HISPANO
Destinos populares

- **Las playas del Parque Nacional Manuel Antonio** (Costa Rica) ofrecen° la oportunidad de nadar y luego caminar por el bosque tropical°.
- **Teotihuacán** (México) Desde antes de la época° de los aztecas, aquí se celebra el equinoccio de primavera en la Pirámide del Sol.
- **Puerto Chicama** (Perú), con sus olas° de cuatro kilómetros de largo°, es un destino para surfistas expertos.
- **Tikal** (Guatemala) Aquí puedes ver las maravillas de la selva° y ruinas de la civilización maya.
- **Las playas de Rincón** (Puerto Rico) Son ideales para descansar y observar ballenas°.

ofrecen *offer* bosque tropical *rainforest*
Desde antes de la época *Since before the time* olas *waves*
de largo *in length* selva *jungle* ballenas *whales*

PERFIL
Punta del Este

One of South America's largest and most fashionable beach resort towns is Uruguay's **Punta del Este**, a narrow strip of land containing twenty miles of pristine beaches. Its peninsular shape gives it two very different seascapes. **La Playa Mansa**, facing the bay and therefore the more protected side, has calm waters. Here, people practice water sports like swimming, water skiing, windsurfing, and diving. **La Playa Brava**, facing the east, receives the Atlantic Ocean's powerful, wave-producing winds, making it popular for surfing, body boarding, and kite surfing. Besides the beaches, posh shopping, and world-famous nightlife, **Punta** offers its 600,000 yearly visitors yacht and fishing clubs, golf courses, and excursions to observe sea lions at the **Isla de Lobos** nature reserve.

Conexión Internet

¿Cuáles son los sitios más populares para el turismo en Puerto Rico?

Use the Web to find more cultural information related to this Cultura section.

ACTIVIDADES

2 Comprensión Complete the sentences.
1. En las playas de Rincón puedes ver __ballenas__.
2. Cerca de 600.000 turistas visitan __Punta del Este__ cada año.
3. En el avión pides un __asiento de la ventanilla__ si te gusta ver el paisaje.
4. En Punta del Este, la gente prefiere nadar en la Playa __Mansa__.
5. El __ómnibus__ es un medio de transporte en Perú.

3 De vacaciones Spring break is coming up, and you want to go on a short vacation with your family. Decide which of the locations featured on these pages best suits your likes and interests. Come to an agreement about how you will get there, where you prefer to stay and for how long, and what each of you will do during your free time. Answers will vary.

Estructura

Estructura provides a formal presentation of relevant grammar and scaffolded activities for building confidence, fluency, and accuracy.

Ante todo helps students ease into grammar with definitions of grammatical terms, comparisons to English grammar and syntax, and reminders of previously learned Spanish grammar.

In-Class Tips provide extensive suggestions on how to clarify the grammar point for enhanced student comprehension and to engage students with the material in class.

Teaching Options offer in-class activity ideas to reinforce new and previously taught grammar, such as working with the *Fotonovela* in order to demonstrate a grammar topic in action.

The **Middle School Activity Pack** can be especially helpful for grammar practice. A combination of the engaging Animated Grammar Tutorials, in addition to the hands-on and game formats in the Middle School Activity pack, will provide younger students with exposure to and practice with the new structures in formats more suited to their abilities and natural learning preferences.

T34   See Implementation Guides for additional instructional support

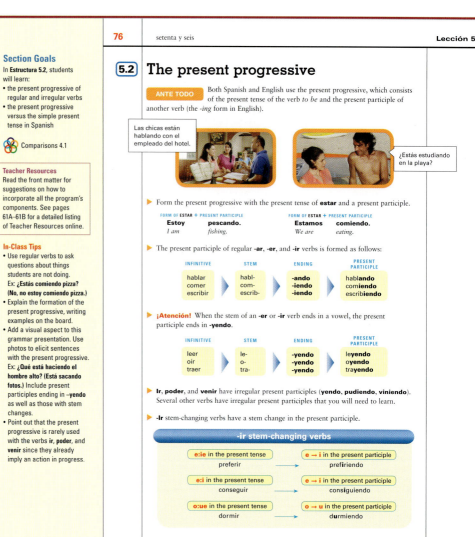

Section Goals
In **Estructura 5.2**, students will learn:
- the present progressive of regular and irregular verbs
- the present progressive versus the simple present tense in Spanish

Comparisons 4.1

Teacher Resources
Read the front matter for suggestions on how to incorporate all the program's components. See pages 61A–61B for a detailed listing of Teacher Resources online.

In-Class Tips
- Use regular verbs to ask questions about things students are not doing. Ex: **¿Estás comiendo pizza? (No, no estoy comiendo pizza.)**
- Explain the formation of the present progressive, writing examples on the board.
- Add a visual aspect to this grammar presentation. Use photos to elicit sentences with the present progressive. Ex: **¿Qué está haciendo el hombre alto? (Está sacando fotos.)** Include present participles ending in **–yendo** as well as those with stem changes.
- Point out that the present progressive is rarely used with the verbs **ir, poder,** and **venir** since they already imply an action in progress.

Las vacaciones   setenta y siete   **77**

COMPARE & CONTRAST

The use of the present progressive is much more restricted in Spanish than in English. In Spanish, the present progressive is mainly used to emphasize that an action is in progress at the time of speaking.

Maru **está escuchando** música latina **ahora mismo**.
Maru *is listening* to Latin music *right now*.

Felipe y su amigo **todavía están jugando** al fútbol.
Felipe and his friend *are still playing* soccer.

In English, the present progressive is often used to talk about situations and actions that occur over an extended period of time or in the future. In Spanish, the simple present tense is often used instead.

Xavier **estudia** computación este semestre.
Xavier *is studying* computer science this semester.

Marissa **sale** mañana para los Estados Unidos.
Marissa *is leaving* tomorrow for the United States.

¿Está pensando en su futuro?
Nosotros, sí.
BANCO CONGRESO
Preparándolo para el mañana

¡INTÉNTALO!   Create complete sentences by putting the verbs in the present progressive.

1. mis amigos / descansar en la playa   Mis amigos están descansando en la playa.
2. nosotros / practicar deportes   Estamos practicando deportes.
3. Carmen / comer en casa   Carmen está comiendo en casa.
4. nuestro equipo / ganar el partido   Nuestro equipo está ganando el partido.
5. yo / leer el periódico   Estoy leyendo el periódico.
6. él / pensar comprar una bicicleta   Está pensando comprar una bicicleta.
7. ustedes / jugar a las cartas   Ustedes están jugando a las cartas.
8. José y Francisco / dormir   José y Francisco están durmiendo.
9. Marisa / leer correo electrónico   Marisa está leyendo correo electrónico.
10. yo / preparar sándwiches   Estoy preparando sándwiches.
11. Carlos / tomar fotos   Carlos está tomando fotos.
12. ¿dormir / tú?   ¿Estás durmiendo?

TEACHING OPTIONS

Pairs Have students write eight sentences in Spanish modeled after the examples in the **Compare & Contrast** box. There should be two sentences modeled after each example. Ask students to replace the verbs with blanks. Then, have students exchange papers with a partner and complete the sentences.

Extra Practice For homework, ask students to find five photos from a magazine or create five simple drawings of people performing different activities. For each image, have them write one sentence telling where the people are, one explaining what they are doing, and one describing how they feel. Ex: **Juan está en la biblioteca. Está estudiando. Está cansado.**

Estructura **77**

In-Class Tips
- Discuss each point in the **Compare & Contrast** box.
- Write these statements on the board and ask students if they would use the present or the present progressive in Spanish for each item. 1. I'm going on vacation tomorrow. 2. She's packing her suitcase right now. 3. They are fishing in Puerto Rico this week. 4. Roberto is still working. Then ask students to translate the items. (1. **Voy de vacaciones mañana.** 2. **Está haciendo la maleta ahora mismo.** 3. **Pescan en Puerto Rico esta semana.** 4. **Roberto todavía está trabajando.**)
- In this lesson, students learn **todavía** to mean *still* in the present progressive tense. You may want to point out that **todavía** also means *yet*. They will be able to use that meaning in later lessons as they learn the past tenses.
- Have students rewrite the sentences in the **¡Inténtalo!** activity using the simple present. Ask volunteers to explain how the sentences change depending on whether the verb is in the present progressive or the simple present.

Middle School Activity Pack
Give students extra practice with **¡A la pizarra!** in Resources online (Lección 5/Middle School Activity Pack/Grammar 5.2 Activity 1).

¡Inténtalo! is a brief activity that practices the grammar forms that have just been presented. It is a quick way to check student accuracy.

Teacher Resources
Grammar Slides can be used as an additional in-class presentation tool.

For extra directed practice, use the *Más práctica* activities from the Activity Pack. An answer key is provided in PDF format.

Scripts for the interactive Grammar Tutorials are available to help you plan.

The *¡Atrévete!* Board Game in the Activity Pack is a fun and interactive way for students to practice and apply the grammar and vocabulary they've learned.

Quizzes for each grammar point may be assigned online or printed for in-class use. Either way, you can edit the assessments to address your exact needs.

Grammar Tutorials feature guided instruction to keep students on track and ensure comprehension. *El profesor* provides a humorous, engaging, and relatable approach to grammar instruction.

Estructura

Práctica guided exercises weave current and previously learned vocabulary together with the current grammar point.

In-Class Tips give you detailed ideas of how to make each activity work in your classroom, including ideas for simplifying an activity, challenging your students, and creating variations to provide more practice.

1 Expansion Ask students comprehension questions that elicit the present progressive. Ex: ¿Quién está buscando información? (Marta y José Luis están buscando información.) ¿Qué información están buscando? (Están buscando información sobre San Juan.)

2 In-Class Tips
- Use the Lección 5 Estructura online Resources to assist with the presentation of this activity.
- Before starting the activity, ask students questions about each drawing to elicit a description of what they see. Ex: ¿Quién está en el dibujo número 5? (Samuel está en el dibujo.) ¿Dónde está Samuel? (Está en la playa.) ¿Qué más ven en el dibujo? (Vemos una silla y el mar.)

3 In-Class Tip To simplify, first read through the names in column A as a class. Point out the profession clues in the **Ayuda** box, then guide students in matching each name with an infinitive. Finally, have students form sentences.

3 Expansion Have students choose five more celebrities and write descriptions of what they are doing at this moment.

Comparisons 4.1

Práctica

1 Completar Alfredo's Spanish class is preparing to travel to Puerto Rico. Use the present progressive of the verb in parentheses to complete Alfredo's description of what everyone is doing.

1. Yo _estoy investigando_ (investigar) la situación política de la isla (*island*).
2. La esposa del profesor _está haciendo_ (hacer) las maletas.
3. Marta y José Luis _están buscando_ (buscar) información sobre San Juan en Internet.
4. Enrique y yo _estamos leyendo_ (leer) un correo electrónico de nuestro amigo puertorriqueño.
5. Javier _está aprendiendo_ (aprender) mucho sobre la cultura puertorriqueña.
6. Y tú _estás practicando_ (practicar) el español, ¿verdad?

2 ¿Qué están haciendo? María and her friends are vacationing at a resort in San Juan, Puerto Rico. Complete her description of what everyone is doing right now.

1. Yo _estoy escribiendo una carta._
2. Javier _está buceando en el mar._
3. Alejandro y Rebeca _están jugando a las cartas._
4. Celia y yo _estamos tomando el sol._
5. Samuel _está escuchando música._
6. Lorenzo _está durmiendo._

CONSULTA
For more information about Puerto Rico, see **Panorama**, pp. 96–97.

3 Personajes famosos Say what these celebrities are doing right now, using the cues provided. *Answers will vary.*

modelo
Shakira
Shakira está cantando una canción ahora mismo.

A		B	
Isabel Allende	Nelly Furtado	bailar	hacer
Rachael Ray	Dwight Howard	cantar	jugar
James Cameron	Las Rockettes de	correr	preparar
Venus y Serena	Nueva York	escribir	¿?
Williams	¿?	hablar	¿?
Joey Votto	¿?		

AYUDA
Isabel Allende: **novelas**
Rachael Ray: **televisión, negocios** (*business*)
James Cameron: **cine**
Venus y Serena Williams: **tenis**
Joey Votto: **béisbol**
Nelly Furtado: **canciones**
Dwight Howard: **baloncesto**
Las Rockettes de Nueva York: **baile**

TEACHING OPTIONS

Pairs Have students bring in photos from a vacation. Ask them to describe the photos to a partner. Students should explain what the weather is like, who is in the photo, and what they are doing. The partner should try to guess the location the student is describing. Students can ask additional questions until they guess correctly.

Game Have the class form a circle. Appoint one student to be the starter, who will mime an action (Ex: eating) and say what he or she is doing (Ex: **Estoy comiendo.**). The next student mimes the same action, says what that person is doing (_____ **está comiendo.**), and then mimes and states a different action (Ex: sleeping/**Estoy durmiendo.**). Have students continue until the chain breaks. Have students see how long the chain can get in three minutes.

Comunicación

4 **Las vacaciones** Read Elena's description of her family vacation. Then indicate whether these conclusions are **lógico** or **ilógico**, based on what you read.

> Está lloviendo. Mis tres hermanos están jugando a las cartas. Mi hermana está leyendo una revista. Mi madre está buscando la llave de la habitación. Mi padre está durmiendo. ¿Y yo? Estoy escribiendo este mensaje electrónico...

	Lógico	Ilógico
1. Hace mal tiempo.	●	○
2. La familia es pequeña.	○	●
3. La madre está contenta.	○	●
4. El padre está en la cama.	●	○
5. La familia está en un hotel.	●	○

5 **Preguntar** Answer your partner's questions about what you are doing at these times. Answers will vary.

modelo
8:00 a.m.
Estudiante 1: Son las ocho de la mañana. ¿Qué estás haciendo?
Estudiante 2: Estoy desayunando.

1. 5:00 a.m.   3. 11:00 a.m.   5. 2:00 p.m.   7. 9:00 p.m.
2. 9:30 a.m.   4. 12:00 p.m.   6. 5:00 p.m.   8. 11:30 p.m.

6 **Describir** Use the present progressive to write a description of what is happening in this Spanish beach scene. Answers will vary.

NOTA CULTURAL
Nearly 60 million tourists travel to Spain every year, many of them drawn by the warm climate and beautiful coasts. Tourists wanting a beach vacation go mostly to the **Costa del Sol** or the **Balearic Islands**, in the Mediterranean.

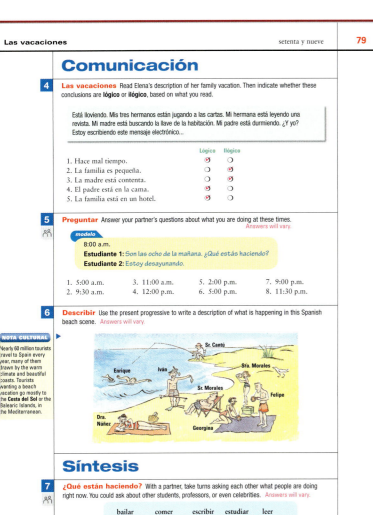

Síntesis

7 **¿Qué están haciendo?** With a partner, take turns asking each other what people are doing right now. You could ask about other students, professors, or even celebrities. Answers will vary.

| bailar | comer | escribir | estudiar | leer |
| cantar | enseñar | escuchar | jugar | mirar |

TEACHING OPTIONS

Video Show the **Fotonovela** episode again, pausing after each exchange. Ask students to describe what each person in the shot is doing at that moment.
TPR Write sentences with the present progressive on strips of paper. Call on volunteers to draw papers out of a hat to act out. The class should guess what the sentences are. Ex: **Yo estoy durmiendo en la cama.**

Pairs Add an auditory aspect to this grammar practice. Ask students to write a short paragraph using the present progressive. Students should try to make their sentences as complex as possible. Have students dictate their sentences to a partner. After pairs have finished dictating their sentences, have them exchange papers to check for accuracy. Circulate around the room and look over students' work.

Communication 1.1, 1.2, 1.3
Comparisons 4.1

4 Expansion After checking students' answers, ask volunteers to change the activities so they would be true for their family on a rainy day on vacation. Ex: **Está lloviendo. Mis hermanos están jugando a los videojuegos. Mi hermana está escuchando música en su habitación...**

5 Expansion Reverse the activity by having students state what they are doing. Their partner should guess the time of day. Alternatively, students could say that they are doing season-specific activities (Ex: **Estoy tomando el sol.**) and their partner will guess the month.

5 Virtual Chat Available online.

6 In-Class Tip Use the online Resources (Lección 5/Digital Image Bank/Estructura 5.2 Present Progessive) to assist with the presentation of this activity.

6 Expansion In pairs, have students write a conversation between two or more of the people in the drawing. Conversations should consist of at least three exchanges.

Communication 1.1

7 Expansion Divide the class in pairs and distribute the handouts for the activity **¿Qué están haciendo?** from the online Resources (Lección 5/Activity Pack/ Information Gap Activities). Ask students to read the instructions and give them ten minutes to complete the activity. Have volunteers report their findings to the class.

7 Partner Chat Available online.

Comunicación provides scaffolded activities built around the three modes of communication:

- Interpretive communication activities target students' reading and listening comprehension skills.

- Interpersonal communication activities target the development of students' skills in real-time negotiation of meaning with one or more partners in both spoken and written communication settings.

- Presentational communication activities target students' skills in producing a variety of written and spoken language.

Notas culturales and **¡Lengua viva!** boxes appear when there's an interesting cultural or linguistic note to give students even more real-world context as they communicate.

Partner Chat activities allow students to work in pairs to synchronously record a conversation in the target language. This collaborative activity allows for spontaneous and creative communication in a safe environment.

Adelante: Lectura

Lectura develops reading skills in the context of the lesson theme.

Context-based readings pull all of the lesson elements together, recycling vocabulary and grammar that students have learned.

Charts, graphic organizers, photos, and other visual elements support reading comprehension.

Estrategia features reading strategies and pre-reading activities that strengthen students' reading abilities in Spanish.

Examinar el texto prompts students to take an initial bird's-eye view of the reading and draw assumptions based on its format, photos, title, and other readily apparent elements.

---

5 adelante

Lectura
Antes de leer

Section Goals
In **Lectura**, students will:
- learn the strategy of scanning to find specific information in reading matter
- read a brochure about ecotourism in Puerto Rico

Communication 1.1, 1.2
Cultures 2.1, 2.2, 2.3
Connections 3.1, 3.2
Comparisons 4.2

Pre-AP®

Interpretive Reading: Estrategia
Explain to students that a good way to improve reading comprehension and to get an idea of what an article or other text is about is to scan it before reading. Scanning means running one's eyes over a text in search of specific information that can be used to infer the content of the text.

The Affective Dimension
Point out to students that becoming familiar with cognates will help them feel less overwhelmed when they encounter new Spanish texts.

Examinar el texto Do the activity orally as a class. Some cognates that give a clue to the content of the text are: **turismo ecológico, teléfono, TV por cable, Internet, hotel, aire acondicionado, perfecto, Parque Nacional Foresta, Museo de Arte Nativo, Reserva, Biosfera, Santuario**. These clues should tell a reader scanning the text that it is about a hotel promoting ecotourism.

Preguntas Ask the questions orally of the class. Possible responses: 1. travel brochure 2. Puerto Rico 3. photos of beautiful tropical beaches, bays, and forests; The document is trying to attract the reader. 4. **Hotel Vistahermosa** in Lajas, Puerto Rico; attract guests

Estrategia
Scanning

Scanning involves glancing over a document in search of specific information. For example, you can scan a document to identify its format, to find cognates, to locate visual clues about the document's content, or to find specific facts. Scanning allows you to learn a great deal about a text without having to read it word for word.

Examinar el texto
Scan the reading selection for cognates and write down a few of them. *Answers will vary.*

1. _____   4. _____
2. _____   5. _____
3. _____   6. _____

Based on the cognates you found, what do you think this document is about?
_____

Preguntas
Read these questions. Then scan the document again to look for answers. *Answers will vary.*

1. What is the format of the reading selection?

2. Which place is the document about?

3. What are some of the visual cues this document provides? What do they tell you about the content of the document?

4. Who produced the document, and what do you think it is for?

TEACHING OPTIONS

Heritage Speakers Ask heritage speakers of Puerto Rican descent who have lived on or visited the island to talk briefly about any experiences they have had with the beaches, nature preserves, or wildlife of Puerto Rico.
Small Groups Have students work in small groups to research and prepare a short presentation about the climate, geography, or people of Puerto Rico. If possible, ask them to illustrate their presentations with photos or illustrations.
Small Groups Lead a discussion about vacations. Have students work in groups to brainstorm what are important aspects of an "ideal" vacation. Each student should contribute at least one idea. When each group has its list, ask for volunteers to share the information with the rest of the class. How do the groups differ? How are they similar?

90 Teacher's Edition • Lesson Five

Lectura readings provide students with an opportunity to listen to native speakers as auto-sync highlighting of sentences guides their eyes.

T38 See Implementation Guides for additional instructional support

atracciones cercanas

aya Grande ¿Busca la playa perfecta? Playa ande es la playa que está buscando. Usted puede scar, sacar fotos, nadar y pasear en bicicleta. Playa ande es un paraíso para el turista que quiere acticar deportes acuáticos. El lugar es bonito e teresante y usted va a tener muchas oportunidades para descansar y disfrutar en familia.

Valle Niebla Ir de excursión, tomar café, montar a caballo, caminar, hacer picnics. Más de cien lugares para acampar.

Bahía Fosforescente Sacar fotos, salidas de noche, excursión en barco. Una maravillosa experiencia llena de luz°.

rrecifes de Coral Sacar fotos, bucear, explorar. un lugar único en el Caribe.

aya Vieja Tomar el sol, pasear en bicicleta, jugar a s cartas, escuchar música. eal para la familia.

arque Nacional oresta Sacar fotos, visitar Museo de Arte Nativo. eserva Mundial de la osfera.

ntuario de las Aves car fotos, observar aves°, guir rutas de excursión.

na de luz *full of light*   aves *birds*

Después de leer

Listas
Which amenities of Hotel Vistahermosa would most interest these potential guests? Explain your choices. *Answers will vary.*

1. dos padres con un hijo de seis años y una hija de ocho años

2. un hombre y una mujer en su luna de miel (*honeymoon*)

3. una persona en un viaje de negocios (*business trip*)

Conversaciones
Answer your partner's questions. *Answers will vary.*

1. ¿Quieres visitar el Hotel Vistahermosa? ¿Por qué?
2. Tienes tiempo de visitar sólo tres de las atracciones turísticas que están cerca del hotel. ¿Cuáles vas a visitar? ¿Por qué?
3. ¿Qué prefieres hacer en Valle Niebla? ¿En Playa Vieja? ¿En el Parque Nacional Foresta?

Situaciones
You have just arrived at Hotel Vistahermosa. Your partner is the concierge. Use the phrases below to express your interests and ask for suggestions about where to go. *Answers will vary.*

1. montar a caballo
2. bucear
3. pasear en bicicleta
4. pescar
5. observar aves

Contestar
Answer these questions. *Answers will vary.*

1. ¿Quieres visitar Puerto Rico? Explica tu respuesta.
2. ¿Adónde quieres ir de vacaciones el verano que viene? Explica tu respuesta.

TEACHING OPTIONS

Pairs Have pairs of students work together to read the brochure aloud and write three questions about it. After they have finished, ask pairs to exchange papers with another pair, who will work together to answer them. Alternatively, you might pick pairs to read their questions to the class. Ask volunteers to answer them.

Small Groups To practice scanning written material to infer its content, bring in short, simple Spanish-language magazine or newspaper articles you have read. Have small groups scan the articles to determine what they are about. Have them write down all the clues that help them. When each group has come to a decision, ask it to present its findings to the class. Confirm the accuracy of the inferences.

Listas
- Ask these comprehension questions. **1.** ¿El Hotel Vistahermosa está situado cerca de qué mar? (el mar Caribe) **2.** ¿Qué playa es un paraíso para el turista? (la Playa Grande) **3.** ¿Dónde puedes montar a caballo? (en el Valle Niebla)
- Encourage discussion of each of the items by asking questions such as: En tu opinión, ¿qué tipo de atracciones buscan los padres con hijos de seis y ocho años? ¿Qué esperan de un hotel? Y una pareja en su luna de miel, ¿qué tipo de atracciones espera encontrar en un hotel? En tu opinión, ¿qué busca una persona en un viaje de negocios?

Conversaciones Ask individuals about what their partners said. Ex: ¿Por qué (no) quiere ____ visitar el Hotel Vistahermosa? ¿Qué atracciones quiere ver? Ask other students: Y tú, ¿quieres visitar el Parque Nacional Foresta o prefieres visitar otro lugar?

Conversaciones
Available online as **Virtual Chat**

Situaciones
- Give students a couple of minutes to review **Más vocabulario** on page 62 and **Expresiones útiles** on page 69.
- To challenge students, add to the list activities such as **sacar fotos, correr, nadar,** and **ir de excursión**.

Situaciones
Available online as **Partner Chat**

Contestar Have volunteers explain how the reading selection might influence their choice of a vacation destination for next summer.

Después de leer includes scaffolded post-reading activities that check students' comprehension.

Teaching Options provide information about lexical variations that are touched upon in the reading.

General Suggestions: Reading

- Remind students to look over pre-reading activities or strategies and post-reading activities to anticipate the context.
- Ask students to read the selection once, focusing on the gist, *not* looking up words, but taking notes as needed.
- Ask students to read the selection a second time, consulting glosses for unfamiliar terms. Have students revisit post-reading activities to answer as many items as possible.
- Students will benefit from reading the selection a third time before you lead the class in a discussion of the topic, details, and real-world application.

Adelante: Escritura

Escritura helps students develop writing skills in the context of the lesson theme.

Estrategia offers strategies for preparing and executing the writing task related to the lesson theme. This writing task allows students to present information, concepts, and ideas to inform, explain, or persuade on a variety of topics.

Tema provides a writing topic and includes suggestions for approaching it.

Evaluation provides a sample rubric for the writing task. Consider sharing this criteria with your students as a tool for self-assessment.

Section Goals
In **Escritura**, students will:
- write a brochure for a hotel or resort
- integrate travel-related vocabulary and structures taught in **Lección 5**

Communication 1.3

Pre-AP®

Interpersonal Writing: Estrategia
Explain that outlines are a great way for a writer to think about what a piece of writing will be like before actually expending much time and effort on writing. An outline is also a great way of keeping a writer on track while composing the piece and helps the person keep the whole project in mind as he or she focuses on a specific part.

Tema Discuss the hotel or resort brochure students are to write. Go over the list of information that they might include. You might indicate a specific number of the points that should be included in the brochure. Tell students that the brochure for **Hotel Vistahermosa** in **Lectura**, pages 90–91, can serve as a model for their writing. Remind them that they are writing with the purpose of attracting guests to the hotel or resort. Suggest that, as they begin to think about writing, students should brainstorm as many details as they can remember about the hotel they are going to describe. Tell them to do this in Spanish.

In-Class Tip Have students write each of the individual items of their brainstorm lists on index cards so that they can arrange and rearrange them into different idea maps as they plan their brochures.

Escritura

Estrategia
Making an outline

When we write to share information, an outline can serve to separate topics and subtopics, providing a framework for the presentation of data. Consider the following excerpt from an outline of the tourist brochure on pages 90–91.

IV. Descripción del sitio (con foto)
  A. Playa Grande
   1. Playas seguras y limpias
   2. Ideal para tomar el sol, descansar, tomar fotografías, nadar
  B. El hotel
   1. Abierto los 365 días del año
   2. Rebaja para estudiantes universitarios

Mapa de ideas
Idea maps can be used to create outlines. The major sections of an idea map correspond to the Roman numerals in an outline. The minor idea map sections correspond to the outline's capital letters, and so on. Examine the idea map that led to the outline above.

Tema
Escribir un folleto

Write a tourist brochure for a hotel or resort you have visited. If you wish, you may write about an imaginary location. You may want to include some of this information in your brochure:

▸ the name of the hotel or resort
▸ phone and fax numbers that tourists can use to make contact
▸ the hotel website that tourists can consult
▸ an e-mail address that tourists can use to request information
▸ a description of the exterior of the hotel or resort
▸ a description of the interior of the hotel or resort, including facilities and amenities
▸ a description of the surrounding area, including its climate
▸ a listing of nearby scenic natural attractions
▸ a listing of nearby cultural attractions
▸ a listing of recreational activities that tourists can pursue in the vicinity of the hotel or resort

EVALUATION: Folleto

Criteria	Scale
Appropriate details	1 2 3 4 5
Organization	1 2 3 4 5
Use of vocabulary	1 2 3 4 5
Grammatical accuracy	1 2 3 4 5

Scoring	
Excellent	18–20 points
Good	14–17 points
Satisfactory	10–13 points
Unsatisfactory	< 10 points

General Suggestions: Writing

Presentational writing serves to communicate meaning, and students must ensure that their audience can understand their message. Remind students to take into account spelling, mechanics, and the logical sequencing of their work.

Remember that activities in other strands such as *Cultura* and *Estructura* provide writing practice with shorter tasks.

Adelante: Escuchar

Las vacaciones noventa y tres **93**

Escuchar

Estrategia
Listening for key words

By listening for key words or phrases, you can identify the subject and main ideas of what you hear, as well as some of the details.

> To practice this strategy, you will now listen to a short paragraph. As you listen, jot down the key words that help you identify the subject of the paragraph and its main ideas.

Preparación
Based on the illustration, who do you think Hernán Jiménez is, and what is he doing? What key words might you listen for to help you understand what he is saying?

Ahora escucha
Now you are going to listen to a weather report by Hernán Jiménez. Note which phrases are correct according to the key words and phrases you hear.

Santo Domingo
1. hace sol ✓
2. va a hacer frío
3. una mañana de mal tiempo
4. va a estar nublado ✓
5. buena tarde para tomar el sol
6. buena mañana para la playa ✓

San Francisco de Macorís
1. hace frío ✓
2. hace sol
3. va a nevar
4. va a llover ✓
5. hace calor
6. mal día para excursiones ✓

Comprensión

¿Cierto o falso?
Indicate whether each statement is **cierto** or **falso**, based on the weather report. Correct the false statements.

1. Según el meteorólogo, la temperatura en Santo Domingo es de 26 grados.
   Cierto.
2. La temperatura máxima en Santo Domingo hoy va a ser de 30 grados.
   Cierto.
3. Está lloviendo ahora en Santo Domingo.
   Falso. Hace sol.
4. En San Francisco de Macorís la temperatura mínima de hoy va a ser de 20 grados.
   Falso. La temperatura mínima va a ser de 18 grados.
5. Va a llover mucho hoy en San Francisco de Macorís.
   Cierto.

Preguntas
Answer these questions about the weather report.
1. ¿Hace viento en Santo Domingo ahora?
   Sí, hace viento en Santo Domingo.
2. ¿Está nublado en Santo Domingo ahora?
   No, no está nublado ahora en Santo Domingo.
3. ¿Está nevando ahora en San Francisco de Macorís?
   No, no está nevando ahora en San Francisco de Macorís.
4. ¿Qué tiempo hace en San Francisco de Macorís?
   Hace frío.

Section Goals
In **Escuchar**, students will:
- learn the strategy of listening for key words
- listen to a short paragraph and note the key words
- answer questions based on the content of a recorded conversation

Communication 1.2

Estrategia
Script Aquí está la foto de mis vacaciones en la playa. Ya lo sé; no debo pasar el tiempo tomando el sol. Es que vivo en una ciudad donde llueve casi todo el año y mis actividades favoritas son bucear, pescar en el mar y nadar.

In-Class Tip Have students look at the drawing and describe what they see. Guide them in saying what **Hernán Jiménez** is like and what he is doing.

Preguntas
Available online as **Virtual Chat**

Ahora escucha
Script Buenos días, queridos televidentes, les saluda el meteorólogo Hernán Jiménez, con el pronóstico del tiempo para nuestra bella isla.

Hoy, 17 de octubre, a las diez de la mañana, la temperatura en Santo Domingo es de 26 grados. Hace sol con viento del este a 10 kilómetros por hora.

En la tarde, va a estar un poco nublado con la posibilidad de lluvia. La temperatura máxima del día va a ser de 30 grados. Es una buena mañana para ir a la playa.

En las montañas hace bastante frío ahora, especialmente en el área de San Francisco de Macorís. La temperatura mínima de estas 24 horas va a ser de

(Script continues at far left in the bottom panels.)

Adelante **93**

---

18 grados. Va a llover casi todo el día. ¡No es buen día para excursiones a las montañas!

Hasta el noticiero del mediodía, me despido de ustedes. ¡Que les vaya bien!

Escuchar builds students' listening skills with a recorded conversation and narration.

Ahora escucha offers a variety of scaffolded activities to support listening comprehension. These activities provide students with an opportunity to understand, interpret, and analyze what they hear on a variety of engaging topics.

Scripts for listening activities are available to help you with planning. As an alternative, read the script aloud for your students instead of using the MP3 audio.

Adelante: En pantalla

En pantalla presents TV clips from around the Spanish-speaking world connected to the language, vocabulary, and theme of the lesson. These clips include commercials, newscasts, and TV shows.

A complete instructional sequence engages students through personal reflection, discussion, and real-world application of what they have seen and heard.

Conversación discussion questions invite student partners to expand on the themes explored in the TV clip and to make connections with their own experiences and opinions.

Aplicación activities engage students with interesting and personal applications of the topics covered in the TV clip.

Teacher Resources include Videoscripts, English Translations, and Optional Testing Sections.

Section Goals
In **En pantalla**, students will:
- read about airline travel in Latin America
- watch an ad for **LANPASS**, a Chilean airline loyalty program

 Communication 1.1, 1.2, 1.3
Cultures 2.2
Connections 3.2
Comparisons 4.2
Communities 5.2

Teacher Resources Read the front matter for suggestions on how to incorporate all the program's components. See pages 61A–61B for a detailed listing of Teacher Resources online.

El arte de viajar Check comprehension: 1. How will airline travel evolve in Latin America by the year 2034? 2. What is LAN? 3. What is LANPASS and what is its goal?

 Pre-AP®
Audiovisual Interpretive Communication
Antes de ver Strategy
Remind students to focus first on familiar words to identify the purpose of the video.

Comprensión Once students have marked the items they hear in the ad, ask them to make a list of other ways everyday life is different when we travel.

Aplicación Encourage students to use photos or videos of their own family trips when presenting their ad to the class.

---

en pantalla

Anuncio de **Santander LANPASS**

Con lo que realmente nos importa°.

Preparación
Answer these questions in Spanish. *Answers will vary.*
1. ¿Te gusta viajar? ¿Por qué? ¿Adónde te gusta viajar?
2. ¿Qué te gusta hacer cuando estás de vacaciones?
3. ¿Qué modo de transporte prefieres usar? ¿Por qué?

El arte de viajar
Millions of people travel on airlines every year for business and pleasure. The number of airline passengers is expected to double between 2014 and 2034 worldwide. This is true for Latin America, too, as airlines are looking at how to attract all those customers to their planes. The airline of Chile, LAN, has partnered with the international bank Santander to create the loyalty program LANPASS to encourage frequent travel on LAN. What does an airline say to travelers that captures their attention and makes their business seem like your pleasure?

importa *matters*

Vocabulario útil

arena	sand
cambiar	to change
destino	destination
medir	to measure
mismo/a	itself
piel	skin
puestas de sol	sunsets
recuerdos	memories
sentirse	to feel
sino	but

Comprensión
Mark an X next to the phrases you hear in the ad.
Irse es volver a....
- x cambiar de piel
- _ trabajar
- _ la oficina
- x desconectarnos
- x castillos de arena
- x sentirse vivo
- _ estudiar mucho
- _ destinos exóticos
- x las siestas
- x un mundo sin Internet
- x la esencia de todo
- _ tiempo en familia

Conversación *Answers will vary.*
Answer these questions with a classmate.
1. Según el anuncio, ¿cuáles son algunas cosas positivas de viajar?
2. ¿Cuáles de estas cosas positivas son importantes para ti? ¿Por qué?
3. Para tener experiencias positivas, ¿a dónde viajas tú? ¿A dónde viaja tu familia? ¿Y tus amigos?

Aplicación
With a classmate, prepare an ad inviting other peop[le] to travel to a special place. Explain why it is a perfe[ct] or ideal place. What evocative words and images wi[ll] you use? Present your ad to the class. *Answers will va[ry.]*

EXPANSION

Culture Note Although airline travel is becoming more popular throughout Latin America, in some countries people still use other means of transportation for their trips, especially intercity buses. This is in part a custom and in part due to the high costs of airline tickets. However, low-cost airlines have recently started operations in some countries.

Small Groups Have small groups of students research and create an oral presentation about other big airline companies in the Spanish-speaking world. Encourage them to include information on the alliances they have with other companies and the way they attract customers.

En pantalla clips are a great tool for exposing students to target language discourse. This authentic input provides evidence of the correct formulations of the language so that students can form hypotheses about how it works.

Adelante: Flash cultura

Las vacaciones noventa y cinco **95**

Between 1438 and 1533, when the vast and powerful Incan Empire was at its height, the Incas built an elaborate network of **caminos** (*trails*) that traversed the Andes Mountains and converged on the empire's capital, Cuzco. Today, hundreds of thousands of tourists come to Peru annually to walk the surviving trails and enjoy the spectacular scenery. The most popular trail, **el Camino Inca**, leads from Cuzco to **Intipunku** (*Sun Gate*), the entrance to the ancient mountain city of Machu Picchu.

Vocabulario útil

ciudadela	citadel
de cultivo	farming
el/la guía	guide
maravilla	wonder
quechua	Quechua (indigenous Peruvian)
sector (urbano)	(urban) sector

Preparación
Have you ever visited an archeological or historic site? Where? Why did you go there? *Answers will vary.*

Completar
Complete these sentences. Make the necessary changes.
1. Las ruinas de Machu Picchu son una antigua ___ciudadela___ inca.
2. La ciudadela estaba (*was*) dividida en tres sectores: ___urbano___, religioso y de cultivo.
3. Cada año los ___guías___ reciben a cientos (*hundreds*) de turistas de diferentes países.
4. Hoy en día, la cultura ___quechua___ está presente en las comunidades andinas (*Andean*) de Perú.

¡Vacaciones en Perú!

Machu Picchu [...] se encuentra aislada sobre° esta montaña...

... siempre he querido° venir [...] Me encantan° las civilizaciones antiguas°.

Somos una familia francesa [...] Perú es un país muy, muy bonito de verdad.

se encuentra aislada sobre it is isolated on   siempre he querido I have always wanted   Me encantan I love   antiguas ancient

TEACHING OPTIONS

Pairs Tell students to imagine that they are archeologists that belong to a future civilization and they are examining the remains of your school. In pairs, have students write a list of what they found. Then, based on this list, tell them to write and act out a dialogue where they discuss the kind of people that inhabited the school. Encourage them to use props. (Ex: **Son teleadictos. Hay restos de televisores por todas partes.**) You may wish to introduce key vocabulary or cognates, such as **restos, habitantes,** and **intacto/a**.

Extra Practice For homework, have students research and write a report about the different ways tourists can reach **Machu Picchu**. Have them state which method they prefer and why, and create a trip itinerary.

Section Goals
In **Flash cultura**, students will:
- read about Incan trails
- watch a video about **Machu Picchu**

Cultures 2.1, 2.2
Comparisons 4.2

Teacher Resources
Read the front matter for suggestions on how to incorporate all the program's components. See pages 61A–61B for a detailed listing of Teacher Resources online.

Introduction To check comprehension, ask these questions. 1. During what years was the Incan empire at its most powerful? (between 1438 and 1533) 2. How many tourists walk the Incan trails each year? (hundreds of thousands) 3. What is the most famous Incan trail called and to where does it lead? (**el Camino Inca**; to **Machu Picchu**)

Antes de ver
- Have students look at the video stills, read the captions, and predict the content of the video.
- Read through **Vocabulario útil** with students. Model the pronunciation.
- Explain that students do not need to understand every word they hear. Tell them to rely on visual cues, cognates, and words from **Vocabulario útil**.

Preparación Ask students how they felt while visiting the site, and what they learned about the people who created it.

Completar Have students write three additional cloze sentences for a partner to complete based on the content of the video.

Adelante **95**

Flash cultura videos feature young broadcasters from across the Spanish-speaking world sharing aspects of life related to each lesson's theme.

Preparación activities activate students' knowledge by asking about their own experience with topics related to the *Flash cultura* segment.

Teaching Options Go deeper into the content with activities that expand on the themes explored in the *Flash cultura*. Build student excitement around contemporary culture in Spanish-speaking countries.

Flash cultura videos provide valuable cultural insights as well as linguistic input, while introducing students to a variety of accents and vocabulary.

The similarities and differences among Spanish-speaking countries that come up through their adventures will challenge students to think about their own cultural practices and values.

Panorama

Panorama showcases the nations of the Spanish-speaking world with short features about each country's culture—history, places, fine arts, literature, and aspects of everyday life.

El país en cifras presents almanac information that orients students to key facts for each country or region, offering opportunities for comparison to their own community. Comprehension questions (with answers) are provided to check students' understanding.

¡Increíble pero cierto! highlights an intriguing, and often little-known fact about the featured country or its people.

Section Goal
In **Panorama**, students will read about the geography, history, and culture of Puerto Rico.

Communication 1.3
Cultures 2.1, 2.2
Connections 3.1, 3.2
Comparisons 4.2

Teacher Resources
Read the front matter for suggestions on how to incorporate all the program's components. See pages 61A–61B for a detailed listing of Teacher Resources online.

In-Class Tips
- Use the **Lección 5 Panorama** online Resources to assist with this presentation.
- Discuss Puerto Rico's location in relation to the U.S. mainland and the other Caribbean islands. Encourage students to describe what they see in the photos on this page.

El país en cifras After reading **Puertorriqueños célebres**, ask volunteers who are familiar with these individuals to tell a little more about each one. For example, **José Rivera** is a playwright and screenwriter who was nominated for an Academy Award for his screenplay of *Diarios de motocicleta* (2004). You might also mention **Rita Moreno**, the only Hispanic female performer to have won an Oscar, a Tony, an Emmy, and a Grammy, and novelist **Rosario Ferré**, whose *House on the Lagoon* (*La casa de la laguna*) gives a fictional portrait of a large part of Puerto Rican history.

¡Increíble pero cierto! The **río Camuy** caves are actually a series of karstic sinkholes, formed by water sinking into and eroding limestone. Another significant cave in this system is **Cueva Clara**, located in the **Parque de las Cavernas del Río Camuy**.

---

5 panorama

Puerto Rico

El país en cifras

▸ **Área:** 8.959 km² (3.459 millas²) menor° que el área de Connecticut
▸ **Población:** 3.667.084
Puerto Rico es una de las islas más densamente pobladas° del mundo. Más de la mitad de la población vive en San Juan, la capital.
▸ **Capital:** San Juan—2.730.000
▸ **Ciudades principales:** Arecibo, Bayamón, Fajardo, Mayagüez, Ponce
▸ **Moneda:** dólar estadounidense
▸ **Idiomas:** español (oficial); inglés (oficial)
Aproximadamente la cuarta parte de la población puertorriqueña habla inglés, pero en las zonas turísticas este porcentaje es mucho más alto. El uso del inglés es obligatorio para documentos federales.

Bandera de Puerto Rico

Puertorriqueños célebres
▸ **Raúl Juliá**, actor (1940–1994)
▸ **Roberto Clemente**, beisbolista (1934–1972)
▸ **Julia de Burgos**, escritora (1914–1953)
▸ **Benicio del Toro**, actor y productor (1967–)
▸ **Rosie Pérez**, actriz y bailarina (1964–)
▸ **José Rivera**, dramaturgo y guionista (1955–)

menor *less* pobladas *populated* río subterráneo *underground river* más largo *longest* cuevas *caves* bóveda *vault* fortaleza *fort* caber *fit*

¡Increíble pero cierto!
El río Camuy es el tercer río subterráneo° más largo° del mundo y tiene el sistema de cuevas° más grande del hemisferio occidental. La Cueva de los Tres Pueblos es una gigantesca bóveda°, tan grande que toda la fortaleza° del Morro puede caber° en su interior.

Playa en San Juan

Faro en Arecibo

Pescadores en Mayagüez

Iglesia en Ponce

TEACHING OPTIONS

Heritage Speakers Encourage heritage speakers of Puerto Rican descent who have visited or lived on the island to share their impressions of it with the class. Ask them to describe people they knew or met, places they saw, and experiences they had. Have the class ask follow-up questions.
El béisbol Baseball is a popular sport in Puerto Rico, home of the Winter League. **Roberto Clemente**, a player with the Pittsburgh Pirates who died tragically in a plane crash, was the first Latino to be inducted into the Baseball Hall of Fame. He is venerated all over the island with buildings and monuments. There are numerous Major League Baseball players that were born in Puerto Rico, such as **Carlos Beltrán, Iván Rodríguez, Jorge Posada, Carlos Delgado,** and **Yadier Molina**.

noventa y siete 97

Lugares • El Morro

El Morro es una fortaleza que se construyó para proteger° la bahía° de San Juan desde principios del siglo° XVI hasta principios del siglo XX. Hoy día muchos turistas visitan este lugar, convertido en un museo. Es el sitio más fotografiado de Puerto Rico. La arquitectura de la fortaleza es impresionante. Tiene misteriosos túneles, oscuras mazmorras° y vistas fabulosas de la bahía.

Artes • Salsa
La salsa, un estilo musical de origen puertorriqueño y cubano, nació° en el barrio latino de la ciudad de Nueva York. Dos de los músicos de salsa más famosos son Tito Puente y Willie Colón, los dos de Nueva York. Las estrellas° de la salsa en Puerto Rico son Felipe Rodríguez y Héctor Lavoe. Hoy en día, Puerto Rico es el centro internacional de este estilo musical. El Gran Combo de Puerto Rico es una de las orquestas de salsa más famosas del mundo°.

Ciencias • El Observatorio de Arecibo
El Observatorio de Arecibo tiene uno de los radiotelescopios más grandes del mundo. Gracias a este telescopio, los científicos° pueden estudiar las propiedades de la Tierra°, la Luna° y otros cuerpos celestes. También pueden analizar fenómenos celestiales como los quasares y pulsares, y detectar emisiones de radio de otras galaxias, en busca de inteligencia extraterrestre.

Historia • Relación con los Estados Unidos
Puerto Rico pasó a ser° parte de los Estados Unidos después de° la guerra° de 1898 y se hizo° un estado libre asociado en 1952. Los puertorriqueños, ciudadanos° estadounidenses desde° 1917, tienen representación política en el Congreso, pero no votan en las elecciones presidenciales y no pagan impuestos° federales. Hay un debate entre los puertorriqueños: ¿debe la isla seguir como estado libre asociado, hacerse un estado como los otros° o volverse° independiente?

¿Qué aprendiste? Contesta las preguntas con una oración completa.
1. ¿Cuál es la moneda de Puerto Rico? La moneda de Puerto Rico es el dólar estadounidense.
2. ¿Qué idiomas se hablan (*are spoken*) en Puerto Rico? Se hablan español e inglés en Puerto Rico.
3. ¿Cuál es el sitio más fotografiado de Puerto Rico? El Morro es el sitio más fotografiado de Puerto Rico.
4. ¿Qué es el Gran Combo? Es una orquesta de Puerto Rico.
5. ¿Qué hacen los científicos en el Observatorio de Arecibo? Los científicos estudian las propiedades de la Tierra y la Luna y detectan emisiones de otras galaxias.

Conexión Internet Investiga estos temas en Internet.
1. Describe a dos puertorriqueños famosos. ¿Cómo son? ¿Qué hacen? ¿Dónde viven? ¿Por qué son célebres?
2. Busca información sobre lugares en los que se puede hacer ecoturismo en Puerto Rico.

proteger *protect* bahía *bay* siglo *century* mazmorras *dungeons* nació *was born* estrellas *stars* mundo *world* científicos *scientists* Tierra *Earth* Luna *Moon* pasó a ser *became* después de *after* guerra *war* se hizo *became* ciudadanos *citizens* desde *since* pagan impuestos *pay taxes* otros *others* volverse *to become*

TEACHING OPTIONS

Variación léxica When the first Spanish colonists arrived on the island they were to name Puerto Rico, they found it inhabited by the Taínos, who called the island **Boriquen**. Puerto Ricans still use **Borinquen** to refer to the island, and they frequently call themselves **boricuas**. The Puerto Rican national anthem is *La borinqueña*. Some other Taíno words that have entered Spanish (and English) are **huracán, hamaca, canoa,** and **iguana. Juracán** was the name of the Taíno god of the winds whose anger stirred up the great storms that periodically devastated the island. The hammock, of course, was the device the Taínos slept in, and canoes were the boats made of great hollowed-out logs with which they paddled between islands. The Taíno language also survives in many Puerto Rican place names: **Arecibo, Bayamón, Guayama, Sierra de Cayey, Yauco,** and **Coamo.**

Adelante 97

El Morro
- Remind students that at the time **El Morro** was built, piracy was a major concern for Spain and its Caribbean colonies. If possible, show other photos of **El Morro**, San Juan Bay, and **Viejo San Juan**.
- For additional information about **El Morro** and **Viejo San Juan**, you may want to play the *Panorama cultural* video footage for this lesson.

Salsa
With students, listen to **salsa** or **merengue** from the Dominican Republic, and **rumba** or **mambo** from Cuba. Encourage them to identify common elements in the music (strong percussion patterns rooted in African traditions, alternating structure of soloist and ensemble, incorporation of Western instruments and musical vocabulary). Then, have them point out contrasts.

El Observatorio de Arecibo
The Arecibo Ionospheric Observatory has the world's most sensitive radio telescope. It can detect objects up to 13 billion light years away. The telescope dish is 1,000 feet in diameter and covers 20 acres. The dish is made of about 40,000 aluminum mesh panels. The Arecibo Observatory celebrated its 50th anniversary in 2013.

Relación con los Estados Unidos
Point out that only Puerto Ricans living on the island vote in plebiscites (or referenda) on the question of the island's political relationship with the United States.

Teaching Options provide expansion activities and additional culture notes.

Teacher Resources include Videoscripts, English Translations, Digital Image Bank, and Optional Testing Sections.

Panorama cultural videos present authentic documentary and travelogue footage of the featured Spanish-speaking country, exposing students to the sights and sounds of an aspect of its culture.

Here are the countries represented in each lesson in Panorama:

Senderos 1A
- USA and Canada
- Spain
- Ecuador

Senderos 1B
- Mexico
- Puerto Rico
- Cuba

T45

Recapitulación

Recapitulación provides diagnostic, scaffolded activities for targeted review of the lesson's key grammar points.

Expansion activities offer suggestions for more complex communication. Pair and group activities engage students as they collaborate and build fluency, while individual activities extend application.

Resumen gramatical provides a handy summary of the grammatical points presented in the lesson.

Section Goal
In **Recapitulación**, students will review the grammar concepts from this lesson.

1 Expansion Create a list of present participles and have students supply the infinitive. Ex: **durmiendo** (**dormir**)

2 In-Class Tip Ask students to explain why they chose **ser** or **estar** for each item.

2 Expansion Have students use **ser** and **estar** to write a brief paragraph describing **Julia's** first few days in Paris.

3 In-Class Tip To simplify, have students begin by underlining the direct object nouns and identifying the corresponding direct object pronouns.

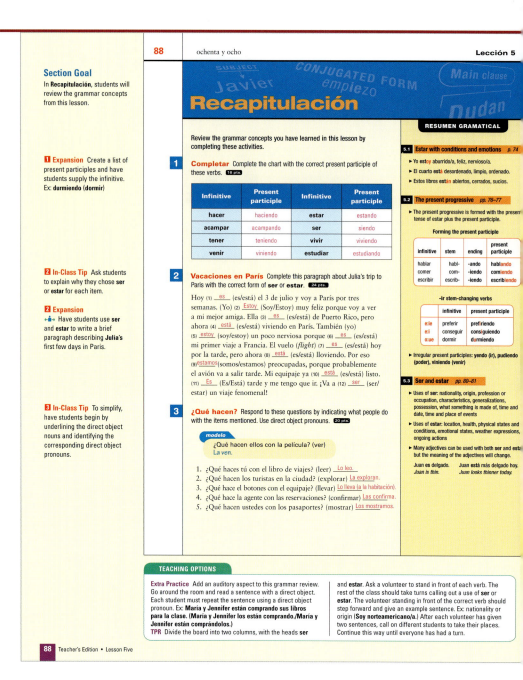

Recapitulación is an auto-gradable cumulative grammar section available for every lesson. The series of activities, moving from discrete to open-ended, systematically tests students' understanding of the lesson's grammar.

Students can choose to improve their score by watching the Grammar Tutorial again or by completing additional practice activities.

Assessment: Options

Tailor a variety of formative and summative assessments to meet the needs of your students. Assessments include downloadable and printable grammar and vocabulary quizzes, lesson tests, and multi-lesson exams.

Minipruebas assess students' knowledge of lesson vocabulary and each grammar point. These open-ended quizzes provide students with an opportunity to demonstrate their understanding and proficiency with the lesson content.

Pruebas focus on the grammar, vocabulary, and theme of a lesson. These formal assessments consist of three different sets of testing material per lesson, with two versions per set.

PRUEBAS A & B	PRUEBAS C & D	PRUEBAS E & F
• Open-ended question format requiring students to write sentences and paragraphs. • Discrete question format. • The listening activity consists of narrations (commercials, radio broadcasts, etc.) and focuses on global comprehension, as well as key details.	• Briefer versions of **Prueba A**. • Open-ended question format. • The listening activity consists of personalized questions, designed to incorporate the lesson's vocabulary and grammar.	• Test students' mastery of lesson vocabulary and grammar. • Discrete question format. • Completely auto-gradable. • Same listening activity type as **Pruebas A** and **B**.

Note: All versions are interchangeable.

Exámenes are cumulative assessments that encompass the vocabulary, grammar points, and language functions. Each *Examen* begins with a listening comprehension, continues with achievement and proficiency-oriented vocabulary and grammar checks, and ends with a reading activity and a personalized writing task.

General Suggestions for Assessment

Writing Assessment

In each lesson, the *Adelante* section includes an *Escritura* page that introduces a writing strategy, which students apply as they complete the writing activity. The Teacher's Edition contains suggested rubrics for evaluating students' written work.

These activities also include suggestions for peer- and self-editing that will focus students' attention on what is important for attaining clarity in written communication.

The tests are also available on the Teacher Resources DVD and in the Resources library so that you can customize them by adding, eliminating, or moving items according to your classroom and student needs.

Portfolio Assessment

Portfolios can provide further valuable evidence of your students' learning. They are useful tools for evaluating students' progress in Spanish and also suggest to students how they are likely to be assessed in the real world. Since portfolio activities often comprise classroom tasks that you would assign as part of a lesson or as homework, you should think of the planning, selecting, recording, and interpreting of information about individual performance as a way of blending assessment with instruction.

You may find it helpful to refer to portfolio contents, such as drafts, essays, and samples of presentations when writing student reports and conveying the status of a student's progress to his or her parents.

Ask students regularly to consider which pieces of their own work they would like to share with family and friends, and help them develop criteria for selecting representative samples of essays, stories, poems, recordings of plays or interviews, mock documentaries, and so on. Prompt students to choose a variety of media in their activities wherever possible to demonstrate development in all four language skills. Encourage them to seek peer and parental input as they generate and refine criteria to help them organize and reflect on their own work.

Strategies for Differentiating Assessment

Here are some strategies for modifying tests and other forms of assessment according to your students' needs and for your own purposes in administering the assessment.

Adjust Questions Direct complex or higher-level questions to students who are equipped to answer them adequately and modify questions for students with greater needs. Always ask questions that elicit thinking, but keep in mind students' abilities.

Provide Tiered Assignments Assign tasks of varying complexity depending on individual student needs. Appealing to learners of different abilities and learning styles will allow you to foster a positive teaching environment.

Promote Flexible Grouping Encourage movement among groups of students so that all learners are appropriately challenged. Group students according to interest, oral proficiency levels, or learning styles.

Adjust Pacing Pace the sequence and speed of assessments to suit your students' learning needs. Time advanced learners to challenge them and allow slower-paced learners more time to complete tasks or answer questions.

SENDEROS 1B

Spanish for a Connected World

Boston, Massachusetts

On the cover: El Morro Fortress, Puerto Rico.

Publisher: José A. Blanco
Editorial Development: Armando Brito, Jhonny Alexander Calle, Deborah Coffey, María Victoria Echeverri, Jo Hanna Kurth, Megan Moran, Jaime Patiño, Raquel Rodríguez, Verónica Tejeda, Sharla Zwirek
Project Management: Sally Giangrande, Tiffany Kayes
Rights Management: Ashley Poreda, Annie Pickert Fuller
Technology Production: Egle Gutiérrez, Jamie Kostecki, Reginald Millington, Fabián Montoya, Paola Ríos Schaaf
Design: Radoslav Mateev, Gabriel Noreña, Andrés Vanegas
Production: Oscar Díez, Adriana Jaramillo

© 2018 by Vista Higher Learning, Inc. All rights reserved.

No part of this work may be reproduced or distributed in any form or by any means, electronic or mechanical, including photocopying and recording, or by any information storage or retrieval system without prior written permission from Vista Higher Learning, 500 Boylston Street, Suite 620, Boston, MA 02116-3736.

Student Text (Casebound-SIMRA) ISBN: 978-1-68005-629-7

Teacher's Edition ISBN: 978-1-68005-631-0

Library of Congress Control Number: 2017949634

1 2 3 4 5 6 7 8 9 TC 22 21 20 19 18 17

Printed in Canada.

SENDEROS 1B

Spanish for a Connected World

Table of Contents

Lección Preliminar

Repaso/Review
De regreso a clases 2
Retrato familiar 8

Fotonovela
Review 12

Lección 4 Los pasatiempos

Contextos
Pastimes 26
Sports 26
Places in the city 28

Fotonovela
Fútbol, cenotes y mole 30
Pronunciación
  Word stress and
  accent marks 33

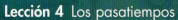

Lección 5 Las vacaciones

Travel and vacation 62
Months of the year 64
Seasons and weather 64
Ordinal numbers 65

¡Vamos a la playa! 68
Pronunciación
  Spanish **b** and **v** 71

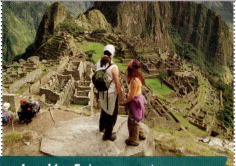

Lección 6 ¡De compras!

Clothing and shopping 100
Negotiating a price and buying ... 100
Colors 102
More adjectives 102

En el mercado 104
Pronunciación
  The consonants **d** and **t** 107

Consulta (*Reference*)

Vocabulario
  Spanish–English A-2
  English–Spanish A-18
Credits A-46
Índice A-47

iv

Cultura

En detalle: El español en Latinoamérica 14

Perfil: Día de la Independencia 15

Avance/Preview

Un paseo por la ciudad 16

¿Qué deporte practicas? 19

Síntesis

Recapitulación 22

Síntesis 24

Cultura

En detalle: Real Madrid y Barça: rivalidad total 34

Perfiles: Miguel Cabrera y Paola Espinosa 35

Estructura

4.1 Present tense of **ir** 36

4.2 Stem-changing verbs: **e→ie**, **o→ue** 39

4.3 Stem-changing verbs: **e→i** 43

4.4 Verbs with irregular **yo** forms 46

Recapitulación 50

Adelante

Lectura: *No sólo el fútbol* 52

Escritura 54

Escuchar 55

En pantalla: *Ejes* (España) 56

Flash cultura 57

Panorama: México 58

En detalle: Las cataratas del Iguazú 72

Perfil: Punta del Este 73

5.1 **Estar** with conditions and emotions 74

5.2 The present progressive 76

5.3 **Ser** and **estar** 80

5.4 Direct object nouns and pronouns 84

Recapitulación 88

Lectura: *Turismo ecológico en Puerto Rico* 90

Escritura 92

Escuchar 93

En pantalla: Anuncio de Santander LANPASS (Chile) 94

Flash cultura 95

Panorama: Puerto Rico 96

En detalle: Los mercados al aire libre 108

Perfil: Carolina Herrera 109

6.1 **Saber** and **conocer** 110

6.2 Indirect object pronouns 112

6.3 Preterite tense of regular verbs 116

6.4 Demonstrative adjectives and pronouns 120

Recapitulación 124

Lectura: *¡Real Liquidación en Corona!* 126

Escritura 128

Escuchar 129

En pantalla: Anuncio de Juguettos (España) 130

Flash cultura 131

Panorama: Cuba 132

Icons Familiarize yourself with these icons that appear throughout **Senderos**.

- 🔊 Listening activity/section
- 👥 Pair activity
- 👥👥 Group activity

The Spanish-Speaking World

Mexico

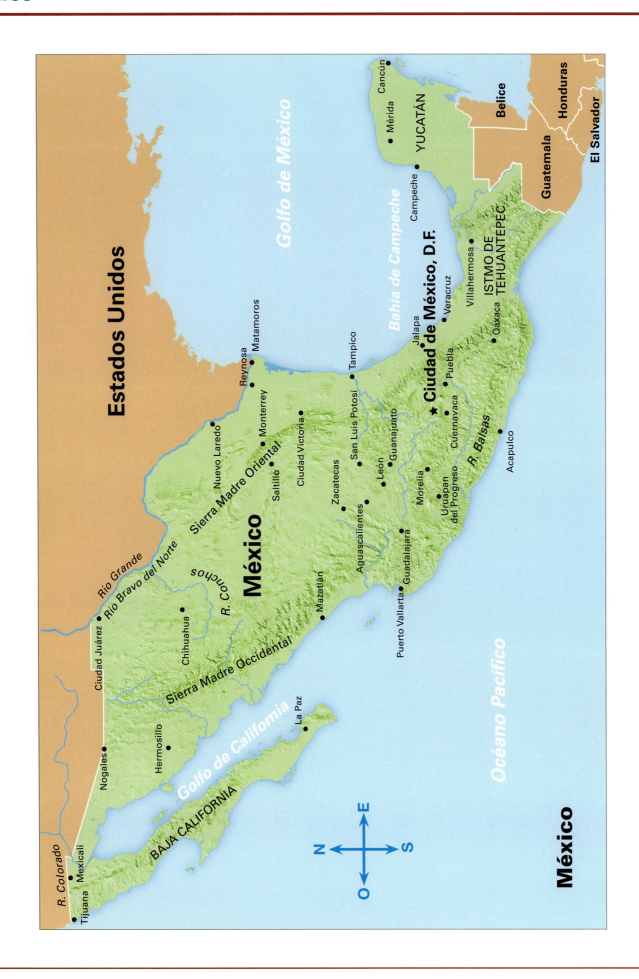

Central America and the Caribbean

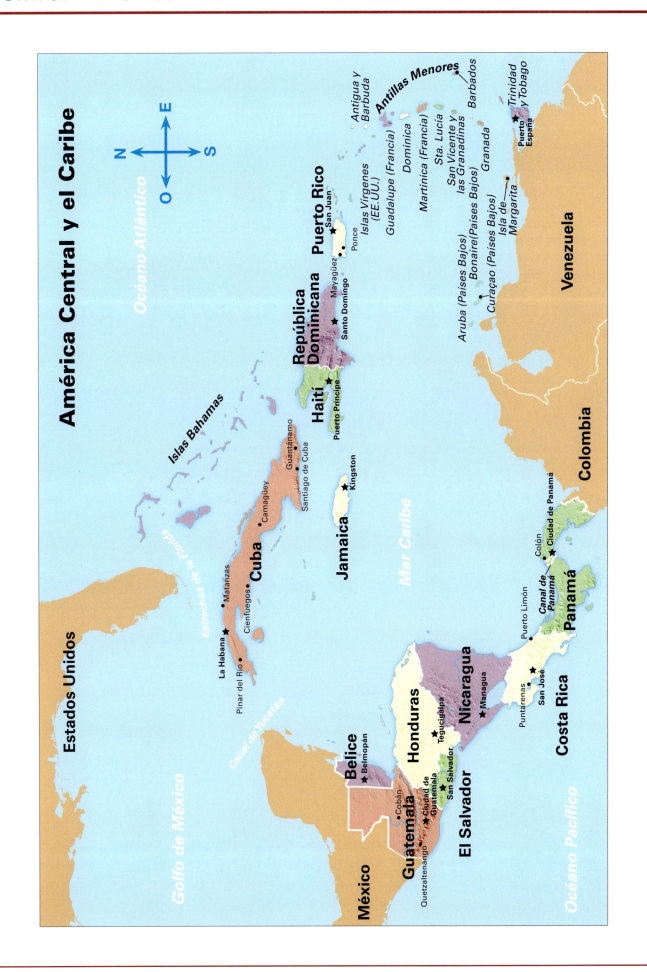

South America

Spain

Studying Spanish

The Spanish-Speaking World

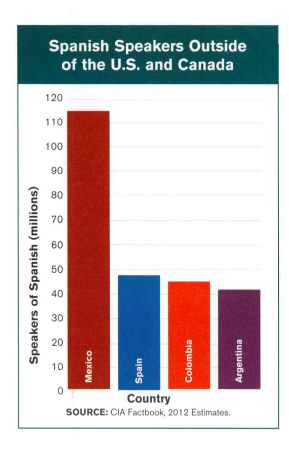

Spanish Speakers Outside of the U.S. and Canada

SOURCE: CIA Factbook, 2012 Estimates.

Do you know someone whose first language is Spanish? Chances are you do! More than approximately forty million people living in the U.S. speak Spanish; after English, it is the second most commonly spoken language in this country. It is the official language of twenty-two countries and an official language of the European Union and United Nations.

The Growth of Spanish

Have you ever heard of a language called Castilian? It's Spanish! The Spanish language as we know it today has its origins in a dialect called Castilian (castellano in Spanish). Castilian developed in the 9th century in north-central Spain, in a historic provincial region known as Old Castile. Castilian gradually spread towards the central region of New Castile, where it was adopted as the main language of commerce. By the 16th century, Spanish had become the official language of Spain and eventually, the country's role in exploration, colonization, and overseas trade led to its spread across Central and South America, North America, the Caribbean, parts of North Africa, the Canary Islands, and the Philippines.

Spanish in the United States

1500 — **1600** — **1700**

16th Century
Spanish is the official language of Spain.

1565
The Spanish arrive in Florida and found St. Augustine.

1610
The Spanish found Santa Fe, today's capital of New Mexico, the state with the most Spanish speakers in the U.S.

Spanish in the United States

Spanish came to North America in the 16th century with the Spanish who settled in St. Augustine, Florida. Spanish-speaking communities flourished in several parts of the continent over the next few centuries. Then, in 1848, in the aftermath of the Mexican-American War, Mexico lost almost half its land to the United States, including portions of modern-day Texas, New Mexico, Arizona, Colorado, California, Wyoming, Nevada, and Utah. Overnight, hundreds of thousands of Mexicans became citizens of the United States, bringing with them their rich history, language, and traditions.

This heritage, combined with that of the other Hispanic populations that have immigrated to the United States over the years, has led to the remarkable growth of Spanish around the country. After English, it is the most commonly spoken language in 43 states. More than 12 million people in California alone claim Spanish as their first or "home" language.

You've made a popular choice by choosing to take Spanish in school. Not only is Spanish found and heard almost everywhere in the United States, but it is the most commonly taught foreign language in classrooms throughout the country! Have you heard people speaking Spanish in your community? Chances are that you've come across an advertisement, menu, or magazine that is in Spanish. If you look around, you'll find that Spanish can be found in some pretty common places. For example, most ATMs respond to users in both English and Spanish. News agencies and television stations such as CNN and Telemundo provide Spanish-language broadcasts. When you listen to the radio or download music from the Internet, some of the most popular choices are Latino artists who perform in Spanish. Federal government agencies such as the Internal Revenue Service and the Department of State provide services in both languages. Even the White House has an official Spanish-language webpage! Learning Spanish can create opportunities within your everyday life.

1800

1848
Mexicans who choose to stay in the U.S. after the Mexican-American War become U.S. citizens.

1900

1959
After the Cuban Revolution, thousands of Cubans emigrate to the U.S.

2015

2015
Spanish is the 2nd most commonly spoken language in the U.S., with more than approximately 52.5 million speakers.

Studying Spanish

Why Study Spanish?

Learn an International Language
There are many reasons to learn Spanish, a language that has spread to many parts of the world and has along the way embraced words and sounds of languages as diverse as Latin, Arabic, and Nahuatl. Spanish has evolved from a medieval dialect of north-central Spain into the fourth most commonly spoken language in the world. It is the second language of choice among the majority of people in North America.

Understand the World Around You
Knowing Spanish can also open doors to communities within the United States, and it can broaden your understanding of the nation's history and geography. The very names Colorado, Montana, Nevada, and Florida are Spanish in origin. Just knowing their meanings can give you some insight into the landscapes for which the states are renowned. Colorado means "colored red;" Montana means "mountain;" Nevada is derived from "snow-capped mountain;" and Florida means "flowered." You've already been speaking Spanish whenever you talk about some of these states!

State Name	Meaning in Spanish
Colorado	"colored red"
Florida	"flowered"
Montana	"mountain"
Nevada	"snow-capped mountain"

Connect with the World
Learning Spanish can change how you view the world. While you learn Spanish, you will also explore and learn about the origins, customs, art, music, and literature of people in close to two dozen countries. When you travel to a Spanish-speaking country, you'll be able to converse freely with the people you meet. And whether in the U.S., Canada, or abroad, you'll find that speaking to people in their native language is the best way to bridge any culture gap.

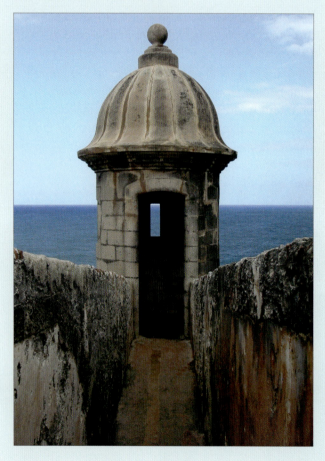

Why Study Spanish?

Expand Your Skills

Studying a foreign language can improve your ability to analyze and interpret information and help you succeed in many other subject areas. When you first begin learning Spanish, your studies will focus mainly on reading, writing, grammar, listening, and speaking skills. You'll be amazed at how the skills involved with learning how a language works can help you succeed in other areas of study. Many people who study a foreign language claim that they gained a better understanding of English. Spanish can even help you understand the origins of many English words and expand your own vocabulary in English. Knowing Spanish can also help you pick up other related languages, such as Italian, Portuguese, and French. Spanish can really open doors for learning many other skills in your school career.

Explore Your Future

How many of you are already planning your future careers? Employers in today's global economy look for workers who know different languages and understand other cultures. Your knowledge of Spanish will make you a valuable candidate for careers abroad as well as in the United States or Canada. Doctors, nurses, social workers, hotel managers, journalists, businessmen, pilots, flight attendants, and many other professionals need to know Spanish or another foreign language to do their jobs well.

Studying Spanish

How to Learn Spanish

Start with the Basics!
As with anything you want to learn, start with the basics and remember that learning takes time! The basics are vocabulary, grammar, and culture.

Vocabulary | Every new word you learn in Spanish will expand your vocabulary and ability to communicate. The more words you know, the better you can express yourself. Focus on sounds and think about ways to remember words. Use your knowledge of English and other languages to figure out the meaning of and memorize words like **conversación, teléfono, oficina, clase,** and **música**.

Grammar | Grammar helps you put your new vocabulary together. By learning the rules of grammar, you can use new words correctly and speak in complete sentences. As you learn verbs and tenses, you will be able to speak about the past, present, or future, express yourself with clarity, and be able to persuade others with your opinions. Pay attention to structures and use your knowledge of English grammar to make connections with Spanish grammar.

Culture | Culture provides you with a framework for what you may say or do. As you learn about the culture of Spanish-speaking communities, you'll improve your knowledge of Spanish. Think about a word like **salsa**, and how it connects to both food and music. Think about and explore customs observed on **Nochevieja** (New Year's Eve) or at a **fiesta de quince años** (a girl's fifteenth birthday party). Watch people greet each other or say goodbye. Listen for idioms and sayings that capture the spirit of what you want to communicate!

Teenagers celebrating at a **fiesta de quince años**.

Listen, Speak, Read, and Write

Listening | Listen for sounds and for words you can recognize. Listen for inflections and watch for key words that signal a question such as **cómo** (*how*), **dónde** (*where*), or **qué** (*what*). Get used to the sound of Spanish. Play Spanish pop songs or watch Spanish movies. Borrow audiobooks from your local library, or try to visit places in your community where Spanish is spoken. Don't worry if you don't understand every single word. If you focus on key words and phrases, you'll get the main idea. The more you listen, the more you'll understand!

Speaking | Practice speaking Spanish as often as you can. As you talk, work on your pronunciation, and read aloud texts so that words and sentences flow more easily. Don't worry if you don't sound like a native speaker, or if you make some mistakes. Time and practice will help you get there. Participate actively in Spanish class. Try to speak Spanish with classmates, especially native speakers (if you know any), as often as you can.

Reading | Pick up a Spanish-language newspaper or a pamphlet on your way to school, read the lyrics of a song as you listen to it, or read books you've already read in English translated into Spanish. Use reading strategies that you know to understand the meaning of a text that looks unfamiliar. Look for cognates, or words that are related in English and Spanish, to guess the meaning of some words. Read as often as you can, and remember to read for fun!

Writing | It's easy to write in Spanish if you put your mind to it. And remember that Spanish spelling is phonetic, which means that once you learn the basic rules of how letters and sounds are related, you can probably become an expert speller in Spanish! Write for fun—make up poems or songs, write e-mails or instant messages to friends, or start a journal or blog in Spanish.

Studying Spanish

Tips for Learning Spanish

- Listen to Spanish radio shows and podcasts. Write down words that you can't recognize or don't know and look up the meaning.
- Watch Spanish TV shows, movies, or YouTube clips. Read subtitles to help you grasp the content.
- Read Spanish-language newspapers, magazines, or blogs.
- Listen to Spanish songs that you like —anything from Shakira to a traditional mariachi melody. Sing along and concentrate on your pronunciation.

Practice, practice, practice!

Seize every opportunity you find to listen, speak, read, or write Spanish. Think of it like a sport or learning a musical instrument—the more you practice, the more you will become comfortable with the language and how it works. You'll marvel at how quickly you can begin speaking Spanish and how the world that it transports you to can change your life forever!

- Seek out Spanish speakers. Look for neighborhoods, markets, or cultural centers where Spanish might be spoken in your community. Greet people, ask for directions, or order from a menu at a Mexican restaurant in Spanish.
- Pursue language exchange opportunities (**intercambio cultural**) in your school or community. Try to join language clubs or cultural societies, and explore opportunities for studying abroad or hosting a student from a Spanish-speaking country in your home or school.
- Connect your learning to everyday experiences. Think about naming the ingredients of your favorite dish in Spanish. Think about the origins of Spanish place names in the U.S., like Cape Canaveral and Sacramento, or of common English words like *adobe*, *chocolate*, *mustang*, *tornado*, and *patio*.
- Use mnemonics, or a memorizing device, to help you remember words. Make up a saying in English to remember the order of the days of the week in Spanish (L, M, M, J, V, S, D).
- Visualize words. Try to associate words with images to help you remember meanings. For example, think of a **paella** as you learn the names of different types of seafood or meat. Imagine a national park and create mental pictures of the landscape as you learn names of animals, plants, and habitats.
- Enjoy yourself! Try to have as much fun as you can learning Spanish. Take your knowledge beyond the classroom and make the learning experience your own.

Useful Spanish Expressions

The following expressions will be very useful in getting you started learning Spanish. You can use them in class to check your understanding or to ask and answer questions about the lessons. Read En las **instrucciones** ahead of time to help you understand direction lines in Spanish, as well as your teacher's instructions. Remember to practice your Spanish as often as you can!

Expresiones útiles *Useful expressions*

¿Cómo se dice _____ en español?	How do you say _____ in Spanish?
¿Cómo se escribe _____?	How do you spell _____?
¿Comprende(n)?	Do you understand?
Con permiso.	Excuse me.
De acuerdo.	Okay.
De nada.	You're welcome.
¿De veras?	Really?
¿En qué página estamos?	What page are we on?
Enseguida.	Right away.
Más despacio, por favor.	Slower, please.
Muchas gracias.	Thanks a lot.
No entiendo.	I don't understand.
No sé.	I don't know.
Perdone.	Excuse me.
Pista	Clue
Por favor.	Please.
Por supuesto.	Of course.
¿Qué significa _____?	What does _____ mean?
Repite, por favor.	Please repeat.
Tengo una pregunta.	I have a question.
¿Tiene(n) alguna pregunta?	Do you have questions?
Vaya(n) a la página dos.	Go to page 2.

En las instrucciones *In direction lines*

Cierto o falso	True or false
Completa las oraciones de una manera lógica.	Complete the sentences logically.
Con un(a) compañero/a...	With a classmate...
Contesta las preguntas.	Answer the questions.
Corrige la información falsa.	Correct the false information.
Di/Digan...	Say...
En grupos...	In groups...
En parejas...	In pairs...
Entrevista...	Interview...
Forma oraciones completas.	Create/Make complete sentences.
Háganse preguntas.	Ask each other questions.
Haz el papel de...	Play the role of...
Haz los cambios necesarios.	Make the necessary changes.
Indica/Indiquen si las oraciones...	Indicate if the sentences...
Lee/Lean en voz alta.	Read aloud.
...que mejor completa...	...that best completes...
Toma nota...	Take note...
Tomen apuntes.	Take notes.
Túrnense...	Take turns...

Common Names

Get started learning Spanish by using a Spanish name in class. You can choose from the lists on these pages, or you can find one yourself. How about learning the Spanish equivalent of your name? The most popular Spanish female names are Lucía, María, Paula, Sofía, and Valentina. The most popular male names in Spanish are Alejandro, Daniel, David, Mateo, and Santiago. Is your name, or that of someone you know, in the Spanish top five?

Más nombres masculinos	Más nombres femeninos
Alfonso	Alicia
Antonio (Toni)	Beatriz (Bea, Beti, Biata)
Carlos	Blanca
César	Carolina (Carol)
Diego	Claudia
Ernesto	Diana
Felipe	Emilia
Francisco (Paco)	Irene
Guillermo	Julia
Ignacio (Nacho)	Laura
Javier (Javi)	Leonor
Leonardo	Liliana
Luis	Lourdes
Manolo	Margarita (Marga)
Marcos	Marta
Oscar (Óscar)	Noelia
Rafael (Rafa)	Patricia
Sergio	Rocío
Vicente	Verónica

Los 5 nombres masculinos más populares	Los 5 nombres femeninos más populares
Alejandro	Lucía
Daniel	María
David	Paula
Mateo	Sofía
Santiago	Valentina

Lección preliminar: Teacher Resources

Teaching with the Preliminary Lesson

The *Lección preliminar* for **Senderos 1B** was created with the Middle School classroom in mind. Each section in the *Lección preliminar* either reviews topics from **Senderos 1A** or previews the topics students will be studying in depth throughout the year—all broken into manageable chunks of new vocabulary, highly visual presentations, and straightforward practice activities. By teaching some of the key vocabulary from later lessons, you are setting learning expectations and helping students build confidence.

The curriculum is paced in a way that gives you time to use the program technology and incorporate hands-on activities in class. Students are given time to internalize and practice the vocabulary before moving on from controlled practice to interpersonal and presentational tasks.

Teaching Suggestions:

- Set a comfortable classroom routine while establishing expectations for the year. If you are going to ask students to use Spanish names, take time for all students to learn the new names and work together to build rapport. Students will later be more willing to take risks in a supportive environment.

- Provide students with a place to start. Use this preliminary lesson as an opportunity to get to know your students, activate their prior knowledge, and identify what they can do with the language. The first two contexts review the vocabulary and grammar concepts explored in **Senderos 1A**, while the last two preview the content of **Senderos 1B**.

- Whet students' appetite for more information about the cultures of Spanish-speaking people using the *Cultura* section and review the episodes from *Fotonovela*.

- Use the *Síntesis* activities to pull it all together at the end of the lesson by means of in-class group activities. Consider this section an opportunity to gain an understanding of your students' abilities and to inform instruction and curriculum for future lessons.

- For assessment in the preliminary lesson, create a collaborative environment in which you favor oral feedback over quantitative evaluation. Use the vocabulary quizzes to check students' progress and identify where additional practice may be needed. Correcting the quizzes in class with the help of volunteers allows you to give additional immediate feedback on the lesson. Don't forget that you can edit any quiz so that the testing material meets the needs of your classroom.

¡Buena suerte!

Lección preliminar: Teacher Resources

There is a wealth of resources online to support instruction using **Senderos**. For details on how to integrate these Teacher Resources into your lessons, see the front matter of this Teacher's Edition on pages T14 to T48.

Presentation	Practice & Communicate	Assess	

• Digital Images:
  • Hola, ¿qué tal?
  • En la clase
  • Present tense of **estar**
  • Conversaciones en la clase
• Grammar Slides
	• Audio MP3s for Classroom Presentations:
	  • Conversaciones en la clase (p. 2)
	• Digital Image Bank:
	  • Personal Interactions
	  • School and University
		• Vocabulary Quiz (with Answer Key)
		• Grammar Quiz (with Answer Key)
			de regreso a clases

• Digital Images:
  • Retrato familiar
  • Una familia
• Grammar Slides
	• Audio MP3s for Classroom Presentations:
	  • Te presento a mi familia (p. 8)
	• **¡Atrévete!** game (Activity Pack)
	• Digital Image Bank (Family)
		• Vocabulary Quiz (with Answer Key)
		• Grammar Quiz (with Answer Key)
			retrato familiar

• Digital Images:
  • Un paseo por la ciudad
  • En el centro
• Grammar Slides
	• Audio MP3s for Classroom Activities	• Vocabulary Quiz (with Answer Key)
		• Grammar Quiz (with Answer Key)
			un paseo por la ciudad

• Digital Images:
  • Mi deporte favorito
  • Los deportes
• Grammar Slides
	• Audio MP3s for Classroom Presentations:
	  • Mi deporte favorito (p. 19)
	• **¡Atrévete!** game (Activity Pack)
	• Digital Image Bank (Sports and outdoors activities)
		• Vocabulary Quiz (with Answer Key)
		• Grammar Quiz (with Answer Key)
			¿qué deporte practicas?

Additional Tools for Planning and Teaching

Go to the Teacher Resources online to find the following tools in PDF and DOCX formats:

- Essential Questions
- I Can Worksheets
- Lesson Plans
- Middle School Activity Pack
- Pacing Guides

Assessment

Lesson Test
- **Prueba A** with audio
- **Prueba B** with audio
- **Prueba C** with audio
- **Prueba D** with audio
- **Prueba F** with audio
- Tests Answer Key

Audio MP3s for Classroom Activities

- De regreso a clases. Activities 1 (p. 3) and 8 (p. 6)
- Retrato familiar. Activities 1 (p. 9) and 6 (p. 11)

Lección preliminar

Communicative Goals
I will be able to:
- Talk about myself and my classmates
- Talk about my family
- Identify different sports
- Identify places in the city

Lesson Goals
In **Lección preliminar**, students will be introduced to the following:
- identifying oneself
- classroom and school related terms
- terms for family relationships
- names of various occupations
- names of sports
- names of places in a city
- information about Spanish in Latin America
- numbers 31 and higher
- present tense of regular **-ar**, **-er**, and **-ir** verbs
- possessive adjectives
- the verb **gustar**
- the present tense of **estar**
- the present tense of **tener**, **venir**, and **ir**

de regreso a clases
pages 2–7
- basic greetings
- names for people and things at school
- names of academic courses
- the present tense of **estar**, **gustar** and other **-ar** verbs

retrato familiar
pages 8–11
- terms of family relationships
- possessive adjectives
- the present tense of **tener**, **venir** and other **-er** and **-ir** verbs

pages 12–13
- Review the first three episodes of the **Fotonovela** series featured in **Senderos 1A**.

pages 14–15
- The Spanish language in Latin America
- Independence Day in Mexico
- Pre-Columbian civilizations

un paseo por la ciudad
pages 16–18
- names of places in the city
- the present tense of **ir**

¿qué deporte practicas?
pages 19–21
- names of sports
- numbers 31 and higher

pages 22–24
- Recapitulación

repaso/review
fotonovela
cultura
avance/preview
síntesis

A primera vista This photo shows **La calleja de las Flores**, in Córdoba, Spain. Help students develop strategies for gleaning information from photos. They should ask themselves: **¿Dónde es este lugar? ¿Adónde va la mujer? ¿Te interesa viajar? ¿Quieres viajar a este lugar? ¿Por qué?** Tell them that gathering information from images is an important skill to apply to learning a new language.

Teaching Tip Look for these icons for additional communicative practice:

→👤←	Interpretive communication
←👤→	Presentational communication
👤↔👤	Interpersonal communication

SUPPORT FOR BACKWARD DESIGN

Lección preliminar **Essential Questions**
1. How do people describe themselves, their friends, and family members?
2. How do you talk about your favorite sports?
3. What do you know about pre-Columbian civilizations?

Lección preliminar **Síntesis**
Before teaching this preliminary lesson, review the **Síntesis** tasks at the end (p. 24). As you move through the lesson, make sure students are building the skills necessary to successfully complete the final tasks.

Section Goals

In **De regreso a clases**, students will review and practice:
- basic greetings
- names for people and things at school
- names of academic courses
- the present tense of **estar**, **gustar**, and other **-ar** verbs

 Communication 1.1, 1.2
Comparisons 4.1

Teacher Resources
Read the front matter for suggestions on how to incorporate all the program's components. See page 1B for a detailed listing of the Teacher Resources online.

In-Class Tips
- Circulate around the class, greeting students, making introductions, and encouraging responses.
- Have volunteers read the dialogues aloud, and clarify questions about pronunciation and vocabulary.
- Ask volunteers to point out the differences between **tú** and **usted** and formal and informal expressions. Then, ask students to convert these informal dialogues into formal ones and read them aloud for the class.

P | de regreso a clases

Conversaciones en la clase

Vocabulario

Hola.	Hi.
¿Cómo te llamas?	What's your name?
Encantado/a.	Pleased to meet you.
¿De dónde eres?	Where are you from?
la computación	computer science
el español	Spanish
la historia	history
el inglés	English
las matemáticas	mathematics
la música	music
enseñar	to teach
gustar	to like
estudiar	to study
preguntar	to ask
tomar (una clase)	to take (a class)

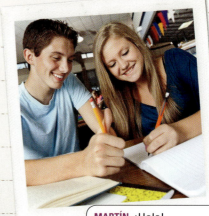

MARTÍN ¡Hola!
JESSICA ¡Hola! ¿Cómo te llamas?
MARTÍN Martín, ¿y tú?
JESSICA Jessica. Encantada.
MARTÍN Igualmente.
JESSICA ¿De dónde eres, Martín?
MARTÍN Soy de Argentina.

FELIPE ¡Hola, Andrés! ¿Cómo estás?
ANDRÉS Muy bien, ¿y tú?
FELIPE Bien, gracias. ¿Tienes clase de español a las ocho y cuarto?
ANDRÉS Sí, con la profesora Gómez.
FELIPE ¿Y te gusta la clase de español?
ANDRÉS Sí, me gusta mucho.

DIANA Ésa es la profesora Davis, y ésos son los profesores Pérez y Adams.
BEATRIZ ¿Qué enseña la profesora Pérez?
DIANA Ella enseña música, y el profesor Adams enseña computación.
BEATRIZ ¿Y te gustan esas clases?
DIANA La de computación sí, pero la de música no mucho.

TEACHING OPTIONS

Extra Practice Bring to class photos or magazine images of people talking or greeting each other. Working in pairs, have students write dialogues to accompany each photo. As a follow-up, have students act out one of their dialogues in front of the class. The class has to decide which image the dialogue is illustrating.

Heritage Speakers Have pairs create five or six more lines to the three dialogues. Encourage them to use vocabulary and expressions they know, and have them act out their dialogues in front of the class. Use these opportunities to diagnose your students' vocabulary and communicative skills.

Práctica

1 Lee y escucha Follow along while you listen to the dialogues on page 2. Listen for extra information at the end of each one. Then indicate whether the following conclusions are **falso** or **cierto**, based on what you heard.

1. Jessica es de los Estados Unidos, de California. cierto
2. A Felipe le gusta la clase de español. cierto
3. A Felipe no le gusta la clase de historia. falso
4. A Beatriz no le gusta la clase de música. falso
5. La profesora Davis enseña ciencias sociales. falso

Repaso: Present of *-ar* verbs

Juan Carlos estudia ciencias ambientales.

▶ Conjugate most regular **-ar** verbs in the present tense by dropping the **-ar** and adding the appropriate endings.

estudiar		preguntar	
yo	estudio	yo	pregunto
tú	estudias	tú	preguntas
Ud./él/ella	estudia	Ud./él/ella	pregunta
nosotros/as	estudiamos	nosotros/as	preguntamos
vosotros/as	estudiáis	vosotros/as	preguntáis
Uds./ellos/ellas	estudian	Uds./ellos/ellas	preguntan

▶ When two verbs are used together without a change in subject, the second verb is in the infinitive. To make the sentence negative, put **no** before the conjugated verbs.

Necesito comprar un libro.
I need to buy a book.

No necesito comprar un libro.
I don't need to buy a book.

Deseamos viajar hoy.
We want to travel today.

No deseamos viajar hoy.
We don't want to travel today.

The verb *gustar*

▶ To express your likes and dislikes, use:

(no) me gusta + [*singular nouns or infinitives*]
Me gust**a** el nuevo horario. No me gust**a** bailar.
I like the new schedule. I don't like to dance.

(no) me gustan + [*plural nouns*]
No me gust**an** las matemáticas.
I don't like mathematics.

▶ To ask a classmate about likes and dislikes, use **te**.
¿**Te** gusta la clase? ¿**Te** gustan las ciencias sociales?

TEACHING OPTIONS

TPR Bring images with foods and activities. Show one image at a time and have students say **me gusta** or **no me gusta** depending on their likes. If they like the food or activity, they should also raise their right hand. If not, they should wave their hand instead.

Game Have students sit in a circle. Say one of your students' names, an **-ar** infinitive, and a subject pronoun. The student has to say the correct verb form, and then call a classmate's name and continue the game by giving another **-ar** infinitive and pronoun. Help students by writing a list of **-ar** infinitives on the board.

---

1 Script

1. MARTÍN ¡Hola!
JESSICA ¡Hola! ¿Cómo te llamas?
MARTÍN Martín, ¿y tú?
JESSICA Jessica. Encantada.
MARTÍN Igualmente.
JESSICA ¿De dónde eres, Martín?
MARTÍN Soy de Argentina, ¿y tú?
JESSICA De los Estados Unidos, de California.

2. FELIPE ¡Hola, Andrés! ¿Cómo estás?
ANDRÉS Muy bien, ¿y tú?
FELIPE Bien, gracias. ¿Tienes clase de español a las ocho y cuarto?
ANDRÉS Sí, con la profesora Gómez.
FELIPE ¿Y te gusta la clase de español?
ANDRÉS Sí, me gusta mucho. ¿Y a ti?
FELIPE También. Y me gustan las clases de inglés e historia. La única clase que no me gusta es la de química.

3. DIANA Ésa es la profesora Davis, y ésos son los profesores Pérez y Adams.
BEATRIZ ¿Qué enseña la profesora Pérez?
DIANA Ella enseña música, y el profesor Adams enseña computación.
BEATRIZ ¿Y te gustan esas clases?
DIANA La de computación sí, pero la de música no mucho.
BEATRIZ A mí sí me gusta mucho la música. ¿Y qué enseña la profesora Davis?
DIANA Ella es la profesora de matemáticas.

In-Class Tips
- Remind students that **vosotros/as** forms will not be practiced actively in **Senderos**.
- Give students the following infinitives: **bailar, conversar, desayunar, practicar,** and **trabajar**, and have volunteers orally conjugate these verbs.

2 Completar
Complete the sentences with the correct forms of the verbs in parentheses.

1. Los profesores __explican__ (explicar) las lecciones.
2. Nosotras __cenamos__ (cenar) a las ocho.
3. Tú __desayunas__ (desayunar) en la cafetería.
4. ¿__Trabaja__ (Trabajar) usted los viernes?
5. Me __gusta__ (gustar) cantar y bailar.
6. Yo no __deseo__ (desear) tomar limonada ahora.
7. Los chicos __dibujan__ (dibujar) con tiza.
8. Julio y yo __escuchamos__ (escuchar) música rock.
9. ¿Te __gustan__ (gustar) las lenguas extranjeras?
10. Ustedes esperan __viajar__ (viajar) a Perú.

3 Gustar
Luisa studies science. For each item, write what Luisa would say about his preferences, according to the cue. Follow the model.

modelo
trabajar en el laboratorio 😞
No me gusta trabajar en el laboratorio.

1. las ciencias marinas 🙂 Me gustan las ciencias marinas.
2. los exámenes de física 😞 No me gustan los exámenes de física.
3. escuchar la radio cuando estudio 🙂 Me gusta escuchar la radio cuando estudio.
4. trabajar y conversar con los profesores 🙂 Me gusta trabajar y conversar con los profesores.
5. la tarea de química 😞 No me gusta la tarea de química.
6. la clase de biología 🙂 Me gusta la clase de biología.

4 Escribir
Use words from each column to create complete sentences. Pay attention to conjugations.

Answers will vary.

1	2	3
Daniela	desear	a las doce
Sebastián	enseñar	en la cafetería
La clase de español	estudiar	estudiantes de secundaria
La profesora Cruz	ser	hablar con el profesor
Mis hermanos	terminar	la clase de biología
Nosotros	tomar	la tarea de matemáticas
Yo	trabajar	siete clases

modelo
Daniela toma siete clases.

Comunicación

5 **Contestar** Answer these questions. *Answers will vary.*

1. ¿Cuántas clases tomas? ¿Cuál es tu clase favorita?
2. ¿Dónde estudias, en la biblioteca o en casa? ¿Escuchas música cuando estudias?
3. ¿A qué hora llegas a la escuela? ¿A qué hora regresas a casa?
4. ¿Con quién(es) cenas normalmente? ¿Quién prepara la comida (*food*)?
5. ¿Miras mucha televisión? ¿Qué programas te gustan?
6. ¿Te gusta viajar? ¿Qué países o culturas te gustan?
7. ¿Qué música escuchan tus amigos/as y tú? ¿Bailan ustedes? ¿Cantan?
8. ¿Qué te gusta hacer los fines de semana? ¿Descansas, preparas la tarea o pasas tiempo con tu familia?

6 **Actividades** With a partner, take turns asking each other if you do these activities. Also ask follow-up questions. Jot down your partner's answers and make note of which activities you both do. *Answers will vary.*

modelo
desayunar en casa
Estudiante 1: ¿Desayunas en casa?
Estudiante 2: Sí, desayuno en casa.
Estudiante 1: ¿A qué hora desayunas los días de semana?
Estudiante 2: Desayuno a las siete de la mañana.
Estudiante 1: ¿Con quién desayunas?
Estudiante 2: Desayuno con mis padres.

bailar bien
comprar música en iTunes
estudiar geografía
mirar la televisión
practicar deportes
tomar clases después de la escuela
trabajar como voluntario(a)
viajar por el país
visitar museos de arte

7 **Escribir** Write an e-mail to a new friend. Introduce yourself, describe what classes you take, your studying habits, and what you do on school days and weekends. Talk about your likes and dislikes, and ask about your friend's. *Answers will vary.*

modelo
Hola, Andrés:
Me llamo David y soy de Miami, Florida. Soy estudiante en una escuela secundaria. Tomo clases de historia, arte...

Repaso: Present of *estar*

Prepositions and adverbs often used with estar

al lado de	next to	delante de	in front of
a la derecha de	to the right of	detrás de	behind
a la izquierda de	to the left of	en	in; on
allá	over there	encima de	on top of
allí	there	entre	between
cerca de	near	lejos de	far from
con	with	sin	without
debajo de	below	sobre	on; over

COMPARE & CONTRAST

Compare the uses of the verb **estar** to those of the verb **ser**.

Uses of *estar*

Location
Estoy en casa.
I am at home.

Health
Juan Carlos **está** enfermo hoy.
Juan Carlos is sick today.

Well-being
—¿Cómo **estás**, Jimena?
How are you, Jimena?

—**Estoy** muy bien, gracias.
I'm very well, thank you.

Uses of *ser*

Identity
Hola, **soy** Maru.
Hello, I'm Maru.

Occupation
Soy estudiante.
I'm a student.

Origin
Ella **es** de México.
She is from Mexico.

Telling time
Son las cuatro.
It's four o'clock.

Práctica

8 Completar There is a substitute teacher in Clara's class today. Complete the conversation with the correct forms of **ser** or **estar**.

SRA. GARCÍA Buenos días. ¿Cómo (1) _estás_ ?

CLARA Bien, gracias. ¿Cómo (2) _está_ usted?

SRA. GARCÍA (3) _Estoy_ muy bien. (4) _Soy_ la señora García, la profesora de ciencias sociales. Y tú (5) _eres_ Clara Rivas, ¿verdad?

CLARA Sí. Perdón, señora García pero, ¿dónde (6) _está_ el profesor Duque?

SRA. GARCÍA (7) _Está_ en una conferencia, pero regresa mañana. Clara, ¿en qué parte del libro (8) _están_ ustedes?

CLARA (Nosotros) (9) _estamos_ en la lección 4.

SRA. GARCÍA Muchas gracias, Clara. Ya (11) _son_ las ocho, ¡es hora de comenzar la clase!

Lección preliminar   siete   **7**

9 Buscar You are in a school supply store and can't find various items. Ask the clerk (your partner) about the location of five items in the drawing. Then switch roles.   *Answers will vary.*

modelo
Estudiante 1: ¿Dónde están los diccionarios?
Estudiante 2: Los diccionarios están debajo de los libros de literatura.

10 Entrevista Take turns answering your classmate's questions.

1. ¿Cómo estás?
2. ¿Dónde estás ahora?
3. ¿Dónde está tu cuaderno de español?
4. ¿Dónde está tu diccionario de español?
5. ¿Dónde estás los sábados a las siete de la mañana?
6. ¿Dónde estás los miércoles a las ocho de la noche?
7. ¿Dónde están tus padres los lunes a las dos de la tarde?

11 Escribir A new student named Andrés just transferred into your Spanish class. With a partner, write a conversation where you greet each other, ask where you both are from, who the teacher is, and describe the location of items in the classroom. Use both **ser** and **estar**.

PRE-AP®

Interpersonal Writing Have pairs imagine they are already seniors in high school. Ask them to write each other a short e-mail in which they tell about themselves, where they live, their class schedule, and how they feel. Encourage students to finish their message with questions for their classmate.

TEACHING OPTIONS

Expansion Give students the following idiomatic expressions with **estar**, and ask them to guess their meaning: **estar en la luna** (to have one's head in the clouds); **estar en las nubes** (to daydream); **estar hecho polvo** (to be worn out); **estar loco de remate** (to be completely crazy); **estar de pie** (to be standing). Encourage the use of a dictionary to explore the meanings of these expressions.

---

9 Expansion
For visual learners, have pairs of students create another drawing of school supplies at a store. Have pairs exchange drawings with another pair. Students should take turns asking each other about the location of the items in the drawing.

10 Partner chat
Available online

10 Expansion
Have students switch partners every three or four minutes.

11 In-Class Tip Have students work in pairs. Suggest that they first outline their conversation by writing a question for each topic listed in the activity. Ask for volunteers to present their conversation to the class.

Section Goals

In **Retrato familiar**, students will review and practice:
- terms related to family relationships
- possessive adjectives
- the present tense of **tener**, **venir**, and other **-er** and **-ir** verbs

Communication 1.2
Comparisons 4.1, 4.2

Teacher Resources
Read the front matter for suggestions on how to incorporate all the program's components. See page 1B for a detailed listing of the Teacher Resources online.

In-Class Tips
- Have students cover the presentation text while they look at the photo and listen to the audio. Then ask them if they can tell you about any of the people in the photos.
- Ask volunteers to read the presentations aloud. As students listen, ask them to create lists of the terms they hear using the following categories: family, occupations, descriptive adjectives, and pets. After checking their answers, have students add as many items as they can to each category and share with the class.
- Point out the meanings of plural family terms and explain that the masculine plural forms can refer to mixed groups of males and females. Ex: **los padres, los hermanos, los primos, los sobrinos, los tíos**.

P retrato familiar

Te presento a mi familia

Vocabulario

los abuelos	grandparents
el/la hermano/a	brother/sister
los padres	parents
el/la primo/a	cousin
antipático/a	unpleasant
delgado/a	thin
gordo/a	fat
simpático/a	nice; likeable
el/la artista	artist
el/la doctor(a)	doctor
el/la periodista	journalist
el/la profesor(a)	professor, teacher

Me llamo Miguel, tengo 13 años y ésta es mi familia. Mi papá se llama Cristóbal, y es periodista y fotógrafo (*photographer*). Mi mamá se llama Anita y es artista. Tengo una hermana que se llama Valentina. Ella tiene 16 años y quiere ser artista como mi mamá y mi abuela. Mis abuelos se llaman Fernando y Sofía. Él tiene 61 años y ella 60. Ellos son los padres de mi mamá. ¿Y el perro? Se llama Rey y es un pastor alemán (*German Shepherd*). ¡Es el consentido (*spoiled one*) de la casa!

¡Hola! Mi nombre es Emily y vivo en Los Ángeles con mi familia. Mi mamá se llama Olivia y la quiero mucho. Ella tiene 50 años y es profesora de literatura latinoamericana en la universidad. El señor de lentes (*glasses*) es mi abuelo Michael. Él es muy inteligente y le gusta leer y escribir, y también le gusta correr en el parque y viajar por el mundo. La otra chica en la foto es mi prima Sara. Ella vive en Miami con su familia, pero le gusta visitarnos a menudo (*often*).

PRE-AP®
Cultural Comparison Have students point out the differences between the two families. Then, ask them to create a list of **similitudes** and **diferencias** between these families and other families they know (either real or fictional). Have pairs compare and discuss their lists, and then present the most interesting comparisons to the class.

TEACHING OPTIONS
Heritage Speakers Have volunteers describe their own families, and mention the terms they use to refer to their family members. These may include terms of endearment (**abue, ma, pa, mami, papi, mijo/a, mamita, papito, nana, tito/a**, etc.). As they are giving their descriptions, ask them questions that elicit more information.

Práctica

1 **La foto de mi familia** Listen to Felipe talk about his family and complete the chart with the missing information according to what you hear.

NOMBRE	EDAD	OCUPACIÓN	RELACIÓN
FELIPE	12 años	estudiante de secundaria	hijo
MARGARITA	60 años	artista	abuela
LAURA	36 años	profesora de idiomas	madre/mamá
ALBERTO	36 años	fotógrafo	padre/papá

Repaso: Descriptive adjectives

Felipe es gordo, antipático y muy feo.

▶ Adjectives are words that describe nouns. In Spanish, adjectives agree in both gender and number with the nouns they modify.

Forms and agreement of adjectives

Masculine		Feminine	
SINGULAR	PLURAL	SINGULAR	PLURAL
alt**o**	alt**os**	alt**a**	alt**as**
inteligent**e**	inteligent**es**	inteligent**e**	inteligent**es**
trabajad**or**	trabajad**ores**	trabajad**ora**	trabajad**oras**

▶ Descriptive adjectives, color words, and adjectives of nationality follow the noun:

el chico rubio, la mujer española, las sillas rojas

▶ Adjectives of quantity precede the noun:

muchos libros, dos turistas

▶ When placed before a singular masculine noun, the following adjectives are shortened:

bueno ⟶ buen; malo ⟶ mal
un buen día, un mal estudiante

▶ When placed before a singular noun, **grande** is shortened to **gran**, and the meaning changes to *great*.

una gran escuela

2 In-Class Tip To simplify, provide a word bank of the answers in masculine, singular form.

2 Expansion Have students use five of the adjectives in complete sentences.

3 In-Class Tip After checking answers as a class, ask a volunteer to explain why item 2 is in feminine form even though it refers to a group of males.

4 In-Class Tip Review the possessive adjectives with students before completing the activity. To simplify, provide a word bank.

4 Expansion Ask students to write questions that could have elicited these sentences as answers. For item 5, have them write a logical response to the question.

5 In-Class Tip Before beginning, ask students to list the family members they plan to describe.

5 Partner Chat Available online.

---

10   diez   **Lección preliminar**

2 Opuestos For each adjective, give an adjective that is opposite in meaning. Keep the gender and number the same.

1. tonto *inteligente*
2. baja *alta*
3. gordo *delgado*
4. viejos *jóvenes*
5. simpáticas *antipáticas*
6. bonito *feo*
7. difíciles *fáciles*
8. morena *rubia*
9. malas *buenas*
10. blanco *negro*

3 Completar Ernesto is talking about life at his new school. Complete the paragraph with the correct form of the adjectives from the list. Use each adjective only once. One adjective will not be used.

> bueno   mismo
> difícil   mucho
> feo   simpático
> inteligente   tonto
> interesante   tres

En la escuela donde estudio tengo (1) _tres_ amigos: Ignacio, Carlos y Tomás. Son personas muy (2) _simpáticas_; hablamos de todo. Ellos son (3) _inteligentes_; reciben A en todos los exámenes. Yo no soy (4) _tonto_, pero no tengo las (5) _mismas_ notas. Las materias son (6) _interesantes_ y los profesores son (7) _buenos_, pero en la clase de matemáticas hay (8) _mucha_ tarea y la clase de química es (9) _difícil_. Deseo tomar más clases de historia y de arte.

4 Posesivos Write the correct form of each possessive adjective.

1. _Tu_ (*Your*, fam.) sobrino es muy joven.
2. _Sus_ (*Her*) profesores son estrictos.
3. Olivia es _mi_ (*my*) hermana.
4. _Nuestra_ (*Our*) casa es azul.
5. ¿Juliana es _su_ (*your*, form.) esposa?
6. _Su_ (*His*) familia es pequeña.
7. Los libros viejos son de _nuestros_ (*our*) abuelos.
8. _Mis_ (*My*) tíos son argentinos.

Comunicación

5 Describe a tu familia With a classmate, take turns asking each other questions about your families.

> **modelo**
> **Estudiante 1:** ¿Cómo es tu mamá?
> **Estudiante 2:** Mi mamá es delgada, morena y muy simpática.

PRE-AP®

Presentational Speaking Have small groups prepare a description of a famous person, such as a politician, a movie star, or a sports figure, and his or her extended family. Tell them to feel free to invent details about this famous person's family members as necessary. Have groups present their descriptions to the class.

TEACHING OPTIONS

¡Atrévete! As an alternative to review, play the board game **¡Atrévete!** available in the Resources online (Lesson 4/ Activity Pack/Cards). Have students play the game and review vocabulary and grammar concepts by selecting the cards for **Lecciones 1–3**.

Lección preliminar

Repaso: Present of -er and -ir

▶ Create the present-tense forms of most regular verbs by dropping the -er or -ir and adding the appropriate endings.

comer		escribir	
com**o**	com**emos**	escrib**o**	escrib**imos**
com**es**	com**éis**	escrib**es**	escrib**ís**
com**e**	com**en**	escrib**e**	escrib**en**

Jimena lee.

Repaso: Present of *tener* and *venir*

Tengo una familia pequeña.

tener		venir	
ten**go**	tenemos	ven**go**	venimos
t**ie**nes	tenéis	v**ie**nes	venís
t**ie**ne	t**ie**nen	v**ie**ne	v**ie**nen

Práctica

6 **Conversación** Complete the conversation with the correct form of the appropriate verb. Then, act it out with a partner.

—Hola, Raquel. ¿Qué (1) __escribes__ (escribir/comprender) en el teléfono?
—Hola, Simón. (2) __Escribo__ (Comer/Escribir) un mensaje de texto (*text message*) para mi amiga Inés.
—¿Inés? Ella (3) __vive__ (abrir/vivir) cerca del parque, ¿verdad?
—Sí, exactamente. Por las tardes ella y yo (4) __corremos__ (correr/decidir) en el parque.
—¡Qué bien! A mí también me gusta (5) __correr__ (correr/leer).
—¿Ah, sí? ¿Por qué no (6) __vienes__ (tener/venir) con nosotras? Corremos y después (7) __bebemos__ (beber/creer) un batido.
—Em… no, gracias. (8) __Tengo__ (Recibir/Tener) que terminar la tarea y a las cinco (9) __asisto__ (describir/asistir) a una lección de piano.
—Ay, Simón. De verdad (10) __debes__ (deber/compartir) practicar más deportes.

Comunicación

7 **Un día común y corriente** Write a paragraph describing a typical day in your life. Include as many verbs ending in -er and -ir as possible.

TEACHING OPTIONS

Extra Practice Add an auditory aspect to this grammar review. Use these sentences as a dictation. Read each one twice, pausing to allow students to write. **1. Cuando tengo un mal día, hablo con mis padres. 2. Tenemos que escribir las listas de vocabulario. 3. Carlos lee muchos libros con sus hijos. 4. Elena tiene sed.**

Heritage Speakers Have heritage speakers make statements describing customs in their families or cultural communities, using -er/-ir verbs and **tener** expressions. Some statements should be false. The class will guess which are true and ask follow-up questions as needed.

In-Class Tip Review the present tense of **-ar** verbs. Write **canto** on the board and ask for the corresponding subject pronoun (**yo**). Continue until you have reviewed the entire paradigm. Underline the endings and contrast them with the conjugations of verbs ending in **-er** and **-ir**.

Tener Remind students that **tener** is used in many common phrases expressing feelings and age: **tener años, tener calor, tener frío, tener ganas de +** *inf.*, **tener hambre, tener prisa, tener razón, tener sed, tener sueño, tener que +** *inf.*

6 In-Class Tip Alternatively, have students listen to the dialogue to check their answers. Then, ask two volunteers to read the conversation aloud.

6 In-Class Tip Divide the class into pairs and give them a few minutes to role-play the conversations. Encourage students to ad-lib. Then, have them switch roles.

7 In-Class Tips
- To simplify the activity, first have students make a list of **-er** and **-ir** verbs using the Repaso and Activity 6.
- Provide these phrases so that students can organize their ideas by time of day: **por la mañana/por la tarde/por la noche**

Section Goals

In **Fotonovela**, students will:
- receive comprehensible input from free-flowing discourse
- review, practice, and preview lesson grammatical structures

 Communication 1.2
Comparisons 4.1, 4.2

Teacher Resources
Read the front matter for suggestions on how to incorporate all the program's components. See page 1B for a detailed listing of the Teacher Resources online.

Video Synopsis
Marissa, a student from Appleton, Wisconsin, arrives in Mexico City. There, she meets the Díaz family, with whom she will stay for a year to study and explore Mexico. The Díaz family includes husband and wife Carolina and Roberto, their son, Felipe, and their daughter, Jimena. Felipe takes Marissa around Mexico City, and along the way, they meet Felipe's friends, Juan Carlos and Miguel, and discuss the upcoming semester. Later, the Díaz family spends a Sunday afternoon in Xochimilco. Marissa meets their extended family and answers questions about her own family.

In-Class Tip
Have the class read through the entire **Fotonovela**, with volunteers playing the parts of **Felipe**, **Marissa**, and **Sra. Díaz**.

 Pre-AP®

Audiovisual Interpretive Communication
- Show the clips without sound and ask students what they remember from the **Fotonovela** episodes.
- Explain to students that they do not need to understand every word they hear, and that they should also rely on visual cues and cognates.

P fotonovela

Fotonovela Review

En los tres primeros episodios de la Fotonovela, Marissa viaja a México y conoce a la familia Díaz.

PERSONAJES

 MARISSA

 SRA. DÍAZ   SR. DÍAZ

 FELIPE   JIMENA

 MIGUEL   JUAN CARLOS

1
MARISSA ¿Quiénes son los dos chicos de las fotos? ¿Jimena y Felipe?
SRA. DÍAZ Sí. Ellos son estudiantes.

MARISSA ¡Qué bonitas son tus hijas! Y ¡qué simpáticas!

2
FELIPE Estás en México, ¿verdad? Nosotros somos tu diccionario.

FELIPE Oye, Marissa, ¿cuántas clases tomas?
MARISSA Tomo cuatro clases: … español, historia, literatura… y también geografía. Me gusta mucho la cultura mexicana.

3

SRA. DÍAZ Chicas, ¿compartimos una trajinera?
MARISSA ¡Claro que sí! ¡Qué bonitas son!

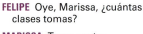

TEACHING OPTIONS

Video Tips General suggestions for using video clips in the classroom can be found in the front matter of this Teacher's Edition.

Expansion Have pairs choose video still 1, 3, or 5, and write three more exchanges to continue the characters' dialogue. Then ask them to share their conversations with the class.

En los próximos episodios, Marissa y sus nuevos amigos viajarán (*will travel*) a la Península de Yucatán para divertirse (*have fun*) y explorar lugares hermosos.

¿Qué pasó?

1 **Organizar** Organize the following events in chronological order.

- __3__ Marissa conoce a Felipe y a Jimena.
- __6__ Marissa pasea en una trajinera.
- __1__ Marissa llega a México.
- __4__ Marissa conoce a Juan Carlos y a Miguel.
- __5__ Marissa y la familia Díaz visitan a Xochimilco.
- __2__ Marissa conoce a la Sra. Díaz.

2 **¿Cierto o falso?** Indicate if each statement is **cierto** or **falso**. Then, correct the false statements.

1. El Sr. Díaz y la Sra. Díaz son de Cuba. **Falso.** El Sr. Díaz es de Mérida, México.
2. Marissa no necesita su diccionario en México, según Felipe. **Cierto.**
3. Marissa toma inglés, historia, arte y geografía. **Falso.** Marissa toma español, historia, arte y geografía.
4. Marissa tiene tres hermanos: Zack, Jennifer y Adam. **Cierto.**
5. La Sra. Díaz tiene dos hermanos: Roberto y Ramón. **Falso.** La Sra. Díaz es hija única.
6. Ana María es la tía de Felipe y Jimena. **Cierto.**

3 **Identificar** Indicate which person would make each statement. One name will be used twice, and one won't be used at all.

1. Ésta es la Ciudad de México.
   Felipe
2. Sí, de La Habana, y Roberto es de Mérida.
   Sra. Díaz
3. La verdad, mi familia es pequeña.
   Marissa
4. ¡Debes viajar a Mérida!
   Sra. Díaz
5. No, gracias. Tengo que leer.
   Jimena

 SRA. DÍAZ
 FELIPE
 MARISSA
 JIMENA
SR. DÍAZ

cultura

Lección preliminar

Section Goals

In **Cultura**, students will:
- read about the Spanish language in Latin America
- learn Spanish words that have indigenous origins
- read about Independence Day in Mexico and Central American nations
- read about pre-Columbian civilizations

Communication 1.1, 1.2
Cultures 2.1, 2.2
Connections 3.1, 3.2
Comparisons 4.2

En detalle

Antes de leer Tell students to look at the visual elements on the page.

Lectura

- Remind students that 1492 was a pivotal year in Spanish history: the Catholic monarchs Ferdinand and Isabel (**Fernando e Isabel**) completed the **Reconquista**, thus ending any Muslim rule on the Iberian Peninsula; it was decreed that Jews be forced to convert to Catholicism or face expulsion; Columbus sailed to America, a trip financed by the Spanish crown.
- **Guaraní** is the only indigenous language in the Americas that is spoken by a large proportion of nonindigenous people.

Después de leer Ask students to share any facts from the reading that were new or surprising to them.

1 Expansion Give this statement as item 11:
11. Ecuador has three official languages. (**Cierto**.)

EN DETALLE

El español en Latinoamérica

As a Spanish language learner, you are on your way to being able to communicate with a vast number of people from diverse regions, backgrounds, and cultures. There are about 500 million Spanish-speakers in the world, but less than 600 years ago, Spanish was used only in the northern and central regions of the Iberian Peninsula. In 1492, the **Reyes Católicos°** unified Spain under Christian rule and the Spanish language. In that same year, they commissioned **Cristóbal Colón°** to search for a new trade route to India, on which he carried the Spanish language to the Americas.

Although Columbus initially sought to explore and establish trade routes, a principal goal of the Spaniards in the Americas quickly became conquest and evangelism—spreading the Catholic faith. The Spanish encountered millions of indigenous people who spoke a vast number of languages and dialects. The Spanish **conquistadores** used various indigenous languages to communicate their religious message, and several were preserved this way throughout colonial times. For example, **quechua** was the main means of communication in the central Andean region between the Spaniards and the indigenous population. Over time, the geographic reach of quechua continued to expand, and words from many different indigenous languages were incorporated into Spanish. **Papa°** and **jaguar°** are just two examples.

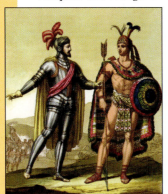

Over the following few centuries of colonial rule, descendants of the Spanish and majority **mestizo°** population perpetuated the use of Spanish. After the wars of independence, most nations opted to have Spanish as their official language. However, millions of Latin Americans continue to speak a multitude of indigenous languages, especially in rural areas. And in several Latin American countries, indigenous languages have co-official status: Bolivia (**quechua, aimará**), Ecuador (**quechua, aimará**), Paraguay (**guaraní**), and Peru (**quechua, aimará**).

Otras° lenguas indígenas

Lengua	Donde se habla	Más información
náhuatl	México	lengua de los aztecas
chibcha	(lengua extinta)	lengua dominante en Colombia y Panamá en tiempos precolombinos°
maya	Guatemala, México, Honduras	en tiempos precolombinos usan un sistema jeroglífico°
taíno	(lengua extinta)	lengua más dominante en la región del Caribe en tiempos precolombinos
mapuche	Chile	no tiene relación con otras lenguas indígenas

Reyes Católicos *the Catholic King Fernando of Aragón and Queen Isabel of Castilla* **Cristóbal Colón** *Christopher Columbus* **Papa** *Potato (from Quechua)* **jaguar** *jaguar (from Guaraní)* **mestizo** *mixed Spanish and indigenous ancestry* **Otras** *Other* **precolombinos** *pre-Columbian* **jeroglífico** *hieroglyphic*

ACTIVIDADES

1 Cierto o falso? Indicate whether each statement is **cierto** or **falso**. Correct the false statements.

1. About 500,000 people speak Spanish worldwide. **Falso.** About 500 million people speak Spanish worldwide.
2. The Spanish **conquistadores** often communicated Catholic teachings in indigenous languages. **Cierto.**
3. Indigenous languages did not survive the Spanish conquest. **Falso.** Many indigenous languages survived.
4. **Quechua** originated in the Caribbean. **Falso. Quechua** is an Andean language.
5. Many Spanish words have indigenous origins. **Cierto.**
6. Today, indigenous languages are not widely spoken in Latin America. **Falso.** Millions of Latin Americans speak indigenous languages.
7. **Aimará** is spoken in Paraguay. **Falso. Guaraní** is spoken in Paraguay.
8. **Taíno** and **chibcha** are extinct languages. **Cierto.**
9. The Aztecs spoke **maya**. **Falso.** The Aztecs spoke **náhuatl**.
10. **Mapuche** and **quechua** belong to the same linguistic family. **Falso. Mapuche** is not related to any other indigenous language.

PRE-AP®

Presentational Speaking with Cultural Comparison Have students research one indigenous group in Latin America and one in the present-day U.S. or Canada. Have students compare and contrast the two groups in terms of population size and territory, early contact with Europeans, and survival of language and culture. Have students present their findings to the class.

TEACHING OPTIONS

Heritage Speakers Ask heritage speakers to share with the class any words or expressions used in their cultural communities that are of indigenous origin. Also have them discuss the presence and influence of indigenous populations in their families' countries of origin.

ASÍ SE DICE

Palabras de origen indígena

el aguacate (náhuatl)	avocado
la barbacoa (taíno)	barbecue
la cancha (quechua)	field, court
el chile (náhuatl)	chili (pepper)
el coyote (náhuatl)	coyote
el huracán (taíno)	hurricane
la maraca (guaraní)	maraca
la palta (quechua)	avocado
el puma (quechua)	puma

EL MUNDO HISPANO

Civilizaciones precolombinas

La civilización maya This civilization is known for its art, architecture, mathematics, and astronomy. The Maya developed a counting system based on 20 and the concept of zero. Remains of Maya temples, such as **Tikal** in Guatemala and **Chichén Itzá** on the Yucatan Peninsula, are now popular tourist attractions.

El imperio azteca This civilization, based in Mexico's central valley, greatly expanded its domain through military conquest and alliances. The Aztecs founded their capital, **Tenochtitlán**, in 1325; by the time the Spanish arrived in 1519, it was one of the largest cities in the world.

El imperio incaico The Incas developed an innovative agricultural system of terraces and constructed a vast network of roads with the capital, Cusco, at its center. One of the most famous legacies of the Incan Empire is the mountaintop ruins of **Machu Picchu**.

PERFIL

Día de la Independencia

During the early morning hours of September 16, 1810, a Mexican priest rang his church bell in the town of Dolores and gave a rousing call for a free, independent Mexico: ¡Viva° la Independencia! ¡Muera el mal gobierno°! After 11 years of war, Mexico won its independence from Spain, which it commemorates on the 16th of September. Although Mexico's **Día de la Independencia** is officially September 16th, the celebrations begin the night before. Father Miguel Hidalgo's act, now known as **el Grito° de Dolores**, is reenacted every year in **zócalos°** across Mexico, accompanied by fireworks, music, and revelers dressed in the colors of the Mexican flag.

Beginning in 1811, similar movements for freedom ignited all over Central America. Finally, on September 15, 1821, Costa Rica, El Salvador, Guatemala, Honduras, and Nicaragua signed the **Acta de Independencia de Centroamérica**, thus proclaiming their autonomy from Spain. These five countries all celebrate their independence on September 15th.

Viva *Long live* Muera el mal gobierno *Down with bad government* Grito *Shout* zócalos *plazas*

Conexión Internet

When did Colombia, Ecuador, Perú, and Bolivia win their independence from Spain?

Use the web to find more cultural information related to this **Cultura** section.

ACTIVIDADES

2. Comprensión Complete these sentences.
1. Mexicans reenact _el Grito de Dolores_ as part of Independence Day.
2. The capital of the _Aztec_ Empire was one of the largest cities in the world.
3. **Palta** and _aguacate_ both mean avocado.
4. Honduras and Nicaragua celebrate their independence on _September 15th_.
5. _Coyote_ is a Nahuatl word referring to an animal.

3. Los indígenas With a classmate, research one of the indigenous groups mentioned on these pages, or another pre-Columbian civilization in Latin America. Prepare a brief oral presentation about the group's culture, language, customs, and place in history. Answers will vary.

P | un paseo por la ciudad

Section Goals
In **Un paseo por la ciudad,** students will preview and practice:
- places in the city
- the present tense of **ir**

 Communication 1.1, 1.2
Comparisons 4.1

Teacher Resources
Read the front matter for suggestions on how to incorporate all the program's components. See page 1B for a detailed listing of the Teacher Resources online.

In-Class Tips
- Ask volunteers to identify each location, using the vocabulary list. Answers:
  1. el almacén 2. el museo 3. el cine/teatro 4. el mercado 5. el parque 6. el gimnasio 7. el centro comercial 8. el estadio
- Alternatively, ask students to identify the places using questions. Ex: **¿En dónde hacemos ejercicio? En el gimnasio. ¿En dónde vemos una película? En el cine. ¿En dónde vemos obras de arte? En un museo.**

Expansion Introduce additional city places: **el banco, el restaurante, la librería.** In pairs, have students pick 3–4 places and write down three sentences of things they do there (ask them to look up new words). Have them read the sentences to a classmate, who should guess where they are. Ex: **Hago ejercicio, bebo mucha agua, tomo una clase de aeróbicos. / Estás en el gimnasio.**

¿Cuál es el nombre de los siguientes lugares?

Vocabulario

la agencia de viajes	travel agency
el almacén	department store
el centro comercial	shopping mall
el cine	cinema
la estación de autobuses	bus station
el estadio	stadium
el gimnasio	gym
el hotel	hotel
la librería	book store
el mercado	market
el museo	museum
el parque	park
el restaurante	restaurant
la tienda	store

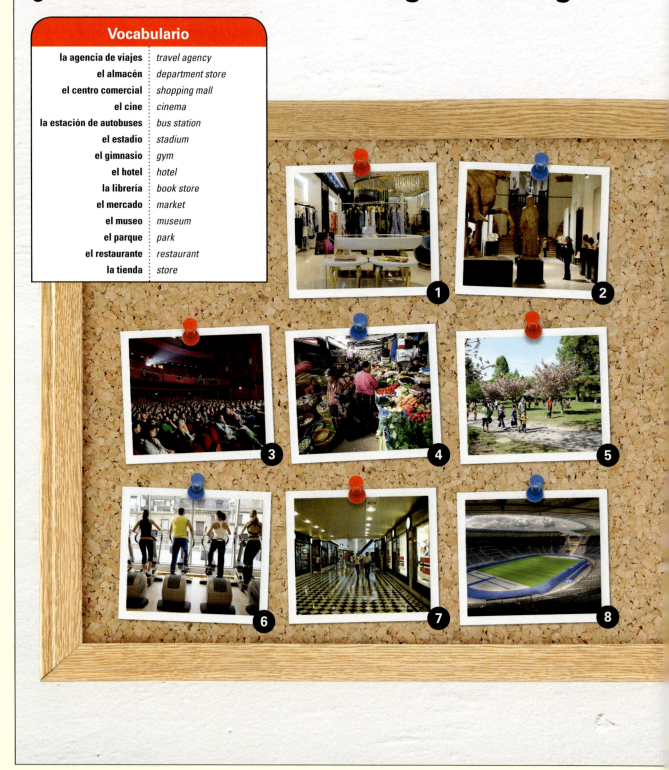

TEACHING OPTIONS

Heritage Speakers Have volunteers name local spots they regularly visit. Write their answers on the board, and then ask students **¿Qué hacemos en ____?** Ex:**¿Qué hacemos en la piscina? En la piscina nadamos/entrenamos. ¿Qué hacemos en el hospital? En el hospital visitamos al médico.**

Game Add a visual aspect to this vocabulary presentation by playing **Concentración**. On ten cards, write the words introduced on page 16. On another ten cards, paste a picture or have students make a drawing that matches each word. Place the cards facedown and in pairs, students select two cards. If the cards match, the pair keeps them. If the cards do not match, students replace them in their original position. The pair with the most cards at the end wins the game.

Preview: Present of *ir*

Él va a los museos.

Ellos van a parque.

ir	
yo	**voy**
tú	**vas**
Ud./él/ella	**va**
nosotros/as	**vamos**
vosotros/as	**vais**
Uds./ellos/ellas	**van**

▶ **Ir** is often used with the preposition **a**; if **a** is followed by the definite article **el**, they form a contraction: **a + el = al**.

Vamos al [a + el] parque.

▶ **Ir** has many everyday uses, including expressing future plans:

ir a + [*infinitive*] = *to be going to* + [*infinitive*]
ir a nadar, ir a correr

vamos a [*infinitive*] = *let's* [*infinitive*]
¡Vamos a nadar a la piscina! - *Let's swim in the pool.*
Vamos a correr al parque. - *Let's run in the park.*
Vamos a ver un partido de fútbol en el estadio. - *Let's watch a soccer game in the stadium.*

Práctica

1 **¡Vamos!** Complete the following sentences using the vocabulary on the previous page.

modelo
Para planear un viaje, vamos *a la agencia de viajes*.

1. Para tomar un autobús, vas _a la estación de autobuses_.
2. Para correr, vamos _al parque / al estadio_.
3. Para aprender sobre historia y arte, vas _al museo / a la biblioteca / a la escuela / a la clase_.
4. Para comprar ropa (*clothes*), vas _a la tienda / al almacén / al centro comercial_.
5. Para ver una película, vamos _al cine / al centro comercial_.
6. Para ver un partido de fútbol americano, vamos _al estadio_.
7. Para comprar comida (*food*), vas _al mercado / al restaurante_.

Lección preliminar

2 **El verbo** *ir* Complete the sentences with the correct form of the verb **ir** and **a**, **al**, or **a la**.

1. Los jóvenes __van__ __a la__ plaza.
2. ¿Ustedes __van__ __al__ estadio?
3. Mi abuela __va__ __a la__ iglesia.
4. Tú __vas__ __al__ restaurante.
5. Yo __voy__ __al__ gimnasio.
6. Fernanda y yo __vamos__ __al__ cine.

3 **¿Adónde?** With a partner, take turns asking and answering questions about where these people are going and what they are going to do there. *Some answers will vary.*

modelo
Estudiante 1: ¿Adónde va Estela?
Estudiante 2: Va a la Librería Sol.
          ¿Qué va a comprar allí?
Estudiante 1: Va a comprar un libro.

Estela

¿Adónde van Álex y Miguel? Van al parque. Van a…

¿Adónde va mi amigo? Va al gimnasio. Va a…

1. Álex y Miguel
2. mi amigo

¿Adónde vas? Voy al partido de tenis. Voy a…

¿Adónde van los estudiantes? Van al estadio. Van a…

3. tú
4. los estudiantes

¿Adónde va la profesora Torres? Va a la Biblioteca Nacional. Va a…

¿Adónde van ustedes? Vamos a la piscina. Vamos a…

5. la profesora Torres
6. ustedes

Comunicación

4 **El fin de semana** Write a short text about your schedule and the places you visit on Saturdays and Sundays. Don't forget to use **ir a**.

modelo
Todos los sábados a las nueve de la mañana voy a clases de piano. Luego, a las doce, voy a un restaurante con mi familia…

¿qué deporte practicas?

Mi deporte favorito

Vocabulario

la piscina	the swimming pool
un partido de fútbol	a soccer match
jugar al baloncesto	to play basketball
jugar al béisbol	to play baseball
jugar al fútbol	to play soccer
jugar al tenis	to play tennis
jugar al vóleibol	to play volleyball
montar en bicicleta	to ride a bike
nadar	to swim
patinar	to skate
practicar un deporte	to practice a sport
preferir	to prefer
surfear	to surf

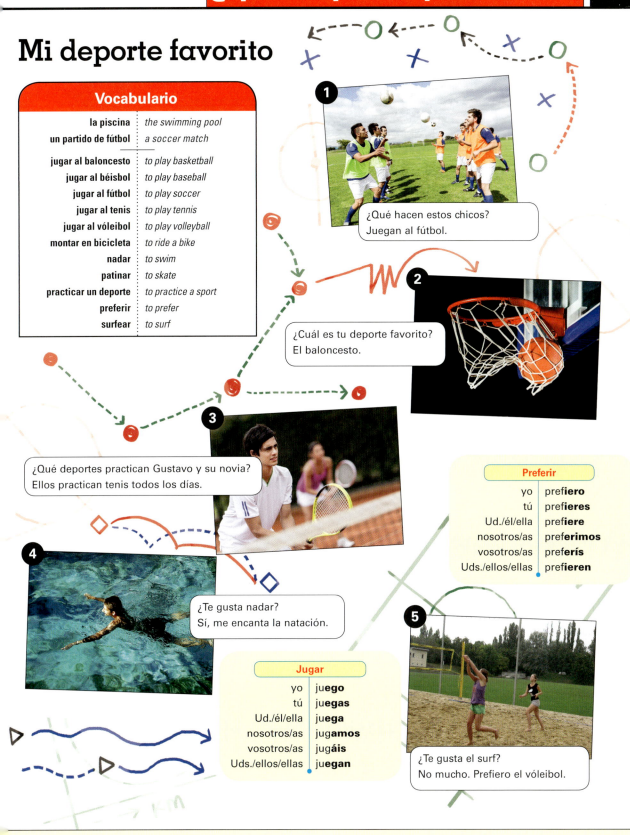

1. ¿Qué hacen estos chicos?
   Juegan al fútbol.

2. ¿Cuál es tu deporte favorito?
   El baloncesto.

3. ¿Qué deportes practican Gustavo y su novia?
   Ellos practican tenis todos los días.

4. ¿Te gusta nadar?
   Sí, me encanta la natación.

5. ¿Te gusta el surf?
   No mucho. Prefiero el vóleibol.

Preferir

yo	pref**iero**
tú	pref**ieres**
Ud./él/ella	pref**iere**
nosotros/as	pref**erimos**
vosotros/as	pref**erís**
Uds./ellos/ellas	pref**ieren**

Jugar

yo	ju**ego**
tú	ju**egas**
Ud./él/ella	ju**ega**
nosotros/as	jug**amos**
vosotros/as	jug**áis**
Uds./ellos/ellas	ju**egan**

Section Goals
In **¿Qué deporte practicas?**, students will preview and practice:
- names of sports
- numbers 31 and higher

Communication 1.1, 1.2
Comparisons 4.1

Teacher Resources
Read the front matter for suggestions on how to incorporate all the program's components. See page 1B for a detailed listing of the Teacher Resources online.

In-Class Tips
- Start this presentation by asking students what sports vocabulary they already know. Ask students what sports they play or that they would like to play. If they mention sports that are not included on the vocabulary list on this page, write them on the board and model their pronunciation.
- Preview the first ordinal numbers: Teach **primero/a, segundo/a, tercero/a, cuarto/a** and **quinto/a**. Then, ask questions about each photo to elicit a description using the new vocabulary. Ex: **¿Qué vemos en la primera foto? (Los chicos juegan al fútbol/practican fútbol). ¿En dónde está el chico de la cuarta foto? (Está en la piscina). ¿(A) qué juegan las chicas en la última foto? (Las chicas juegan al vóleibol).** You may need to preview the conjugation of **jugar** and **preferir**, which will be later presented in **Estructura 4.2**.

TEACHING OPTIONS

Extra Practice Bring photos or magazine images of people playing different sports. Ask students to write dialogue captions for each photo, similar to those presented on this page.

PRE-AP®

Cultural Activity For homework, have students research the most popular sports in different Spanish-speaking countries. Encourage them to bring photos and statistics, and present their findings to the class.

Práctica

1 **¡Fútbol!** Read the following paragraph. Then, work with a classmate to answer the questions based on the reading.

¿Cómo traduces la palabra *football* al español? Ten cuidado y no te confundas (*don't make a mistake*). El deporte que en los Estados Unidos llaman *soccer*, en el mundo hispano se llama fútbol. Y el deporte que los estadounidenses llaman *football*, los hispanohablantes lo llaman fútbol americano. Son deportes diferentes, pero tienen también muchas similitudes: los dos se juegan con once jugadores, utilizan balones o pelotas (*balls*) y son deportes de contacto. Además, millones de personas celebran y ven los partidos de ambos (*both*) deportes en la televisión y en los estadios. Pero, ¿sabes por qué a diferencia del resto del mundo el fútbol se llama *soccer* en los Estados Unidos?

1. ¿Cómo se dice *soccer* en los países hispanohablantes?
2. ¿Cuáles son las similitudes entre el fútbol y el fútbol americano?
3. ¿Practicas fútbol o fútbol americano? ¿Cuál de los dos prefieres?
4. ¿Qué otros deportes practicas?
5. ¿Prefieres practicar deportes, o verlos en la televisión? ¿Por qué?

Repaso: Numbers 31 and higher

Hay cuarenta y siete estudiantes en la clase de geografía.

31	treinta y uno	101	ciento uno
32	treinta y dos	200	doscientos/as
	(*and so on*)	500	quinientos/as
40	cuarenta	700	setecientos/as
50	cincuenta	900	novecientos/as
60	sesenta	1.000	mil
70	setenta	2.000	dos mil
80	ochenta	5.100	cinco mil cien
90	noventa	100.000	cien mil
100	cien, ciento	1.000.000	un millón (de)

▸ The numbers 200 through 999 agree in gender with the nouns they modify.

324 plum**as** ⟶ trescient**as** veinticuatro plum**as**

500 flor**es** ⟶ quinient**as** flor**es**

2 Resultados
Provide these basketball scores in Spanish.

1. sesenta y nueve, ochenta y cuatro
2. ochenta y nueve, ciento uno

3. ciento once, noventa y dos
4. setenta y siete, sesenta y nueve

5. ochenta, cincuenta
6. cincuenta y ocho, sesenta y tres

3 Matemáticas básicas
Solve the following math problems. Write out the numbers in Spanish.

modelo
150 + 20 = ciento setenta

1. 325 + 189 = quinientos catorce
2. 500 − 222 = doscientos setenta y ocho
3. 101 + 32 + 13 = ciento cuarenta y seis
4. 410 + 509 + 678 = mil quinientos noventa y siete
5. 800 + 500 + 1.050 = dos mil trescientos cincuenta
6. 1.900 + 2.019 = tres mil novecientos diecinueve
7. 5.421 + 7.693 = trece mil ciento catorce
8. 90.000 − 80.300 = nueve mil setecientos
9. 25.000 + 168.005 = ciento noventa y tres mil cinco
10. 205.000 − 178.040 = veintiséis mil novecientos sesenta

2 Expansion In pairs, have each student write six additional scores and dictate them to his or her classmate, who writes them down.

3 In-Class Tip Remind students that Spanish uses a period to indicate thousands and millions.

3 Expansion Do simple multiplication problems. Review the phrases **multiplicado por** and **dividido por**. Ex: **Veinte multiplicado por ocho son...** (ciento sesenta). **Cien dividido por cuatro son...** (veinticinco).

TEACHING OPTIONS

Extra Practice Remind students of the math terms **más** (*plus*), **menos** (*minus*), and **son/es igual a** (*equals*). Review numbers from 1 to 30, and the numbers reviewed here. Then have students write ten math problems for a classmate to solve.

Small Groups Provide students with a list of historical events relevant to Spanish and Latin American history and a scrambled list of the years in which they occurred. Have them match the events and the years. Remind them to read the years as complete numbers. Possible events: **los moros invaden España (711), los aztecas fundan Tenochtitlán (1345), México gana independencia de España (1821)**, etc.

Recapitulación

Lección preliminar

1 Emparejar
Match each question or expression in the first column with an answer in the second.

1. ¿Cómo se llama usted?
2. ¿De dónde es usted?
3. ¿Cuántos años tienes?
4. ¿Cuántos años tiene Jimena?
5. Muchas gracias.
6. ¿A qué hora es la clase de español?
7. ¿Tienes clase de historia a las diez y media?

__2__ Soy de Mérida.
__7__ No, tengo clase de biología.
__6__ A las ocho y cuarto.
__1__ Francisco, mucho gusto.
__3__ Tengo 14 años, ¿y tú?
__5__ No hay de qué.
__4__ Ella tiene 19 años.

2 Analogías
Complete the following analogies.

1. maleta → pasajero = mochila → **estudiante**
2. Cristina → chica = Felipe → **chico**
3. once → doce = jueves → **viernes**
4. abuela → abuelo = padre → **madre**
5. biología → materia = martes → **día**
6. Miguel → nombre = Díaz → **apellido**
7. papel → cuaderno = miércoles → **semana**
8. Argentina → Buenos Aires = Estados Unidos → **Washington, D.C.**
9. Picasso → arte = Cervantes → **literatura**

3 Adjetivos
Complete each phrase with the appropriate adjective from the list. Each adjective can only be used once.

alemán	gordo
altas	interesante
difícil	jóvenes
española	simpáticos

Adjetivos calificativos p. 9

1. El novio de mi prima es **alemán**. Vive en Berlín.
2. Mis abuelos no son **jóvenes**, pero tampoco son viejos.
3. Jimena y Francisco son jóvenes y muy **simpáticos**.
4. La tarea de biología es **difícil**. No la entiendo.
5. Esta novela es muy **interesante**. Me gusta mucho.
6. Mis primas Ana y Cecilia son dos chicas muy **altas**.
7. Mi papá come mucho y es muy **gordo**.
8. Mi nueva profesora de literatura es **española**.

Lección preliminar

veintitrés 23

Los números
p. 20

4 Números Write these numbers in Spanish.

1. 751 _setecientos cincuenta y uno_
2. 99 _noventa y nueve_
3. 4.010 _cuatro mil diez_
4. 844 _ochocientos cuarenta y cuatro_
5. 738.266 _setecientos treinta y ocho mil doscientos sesenta y seis_
6. 23.110.680 _veintitrés millones ciento diez mil seiscientos ochenta_
7. 1.033 _mil treinta y tres_
8. 1.500.307 _un millón quinientos mil trescientos siete_

5 Identificar Find the word that does not belong.

1. (profesor) – padre – nieto – sobrino
2. literatura – español – historia – (miércoles)
3. martes – sábado – (semana) – lunes
4. baloncesto – (natación) – fútbol – vóleibol
5. prima – (sobrino) – mamá – tía
6. (museo) – almacén – centro comercial – mercado
7. escuela – (matemáticas) – biblioteca - librería
8. piscina – gimnasio – (restaurante) - estadio

Tener and venir
p. 11

Ir
p. 17

Jugar
p. 19

6 Verbos Provide the appropriate present tense form of each verb.

1. Los gemelos Ana María y Carlos _tienen_ (tener) 13 años.
2. Todos los días a las seis (yo) _corro_ (correr) en el parque.
3. (Yo) _vivo_ (vivir) en un apartamento con mis padres y mi abuela.
4. Los chicos _abren_ (abrir) sus libros de historia.
5. Mi hermana _aprende_ (aprender) a nadar los sábados en la piscina de la escuela.
6. ¿Adónde _va_ (ir) tu hermano con tanta prisa (in such a hurry)?
7. ¿Ustedes _juegan_ (jugar) al fútbol y _montan_ (montar) en bicicleta todos los días?
8. ¿De dónde _vienes_ (venir) tú? (Yo) _vengo_ (venir) del museo.
9. Mañana (yo) _voy_ (ir) a leer un buen libro toda la tarde.

-er verbs comer	
yo	com**o**
tú	com**es**
Ud./él/ella	com**e**
nosotros/as	com**emos**
vosotros/as	com**éis**
Uds./ellos/ellas	com**en**

-ir verbs escribir	
yo	escrib**o**
tú	escrib**es**
Ud./él/ella	escrib**e**
nosotros/as	escrib**imos**
vosotros/as	escrib**ís**
Uds./ellos/ellas	escrib**en**

4 Expansion Have students use each number in a logical sentence. Encourage them to use the verb form **hay**. Ex: **Hay cuatro mil diez libros en la biblioteca de la escuela**. Remind them that numbers 200 through 999 agree in number and gender with the noun they modify.

5 Expansion Challenge small groups of students to create five original questions for this activity. Ex: **antipático - paciente - contento - pelirrojo** (the first three being personality traits and **pelirrojo** being a physical characteristic).

6 In-Class Tip Before starting the main activity, do a rapid-response drill. Write an infinitive reviewed in the lesson on the board. Call out subject pronouns and/or names, and have students respond with the correct verb from. Then, reverse the drill; write a verb from on the board and have students say the subject pronouns.

6 Expansion Ask students to create six additional cloze sentences. Then have them exchange papers with a classmate and complete the items.

TEACHING OPTIONS

Small Groups Have small groups role-play a conversation using the verbs and adjectives taught in this lesson. Remind students to use the present tense in the appropriate situations. Give them time to prepare, and then have a few groups present their conversations to the class.

¡Atrévete! As an alternative to review, play the board game **¡Atrévete!** available in the Resources online (Lesson 4/ Activity Pack/Cards). Have students play the game and review vocabulary and grammar concepts by selecting the cards for **Lecciones 1–3**.

Recapitulación 23

Section Goals

In **Síntesis** students will apply what they have reviewed and previewed in this lesson in communicative activities.

 Communication 1.1, 1.3

In-Class Tips
- Make sure students understand these are diagnostic activities that will help you adjust the course to their needs.
- Try to group quieter students with extroverts, heritage speakers and more advanced students with those needing more support, and so on.
- Have students review the **Fotonovela** synopsis on page 12 or watch together the first three episodes in **Senderos 1A**.
- In the first activity, these four characters are recommended because they are the ones with the most lines and screen time during the first three episodes of the **Fotonovela** series. However, if students prefer a different character (like Miguel or Juan Carlos), allow them that possibility.
- In the second activity, students can act out the scene in class, or you can assign it as homework by having them record the skit and present the videos during the next class. In any case, ask them to be as accurate with the pronunciation and fluency of the dialogues as possible.

Assessment Use **Síntesis** as a diagnostic activity, providing students with a comfortable environment where they can have fun and show their oral skills at the same time. When students are done presenting their skits, give oral feedback on their performance (pronunciation, accuracy, and fluency).

P | síntesis
Lección preliminar

1 **Mi personaje favorito** Pick two of the **Fotonovela** characters and write a paragraph describing them. Don't forget to mention their family members and their likes and dislikes.

2 **Mi escena favorita** In groups of three or four, choose one or two of the **Fotonovela** scenes you have liked the most, and recreate them. Plan a dialogue based on the scenes below, or choose another scene that you liked from the **Fotonovela**.

1. Marissa conoce a la familia Díaz.

2. Marissa conoce a nuevos amigos y habla sobre las clases.

3. Un picnic en un lugar muy especial.

TEACHING OPTIONS

Heritage Speakers Challenge heritage speakers or advanced students by asking them to create a scene of their own with the **Fotonovela** characters and add it to the one(s) they already picked from the first three episodes. Suggest they use their imagination to write a coherent conversation that is likely to have taken place in the **Fotonovela** storyline, and have them act it out. As a diagnostic activity to check students' writing skills, have them turn in the script of the conversation they created. Choose and assign the length of the new scene and conversation based on how advanced your students are.

Lección 4: Teacher Resources

There is a wealth of resources online to support instruction using **Senderos**. For details on how to integrate these Teacher Resources into your lessons, see the front matter of this Teacher's Edition on pages T14 to T48.

Presentation	Practice & Communicate	Assess*	Scripts and Translations	

• Digital Images:
  • **Los pasatiempos**
  • **En el centro**
	• Information Gap Activity
	• Activity Pack Practice Activities (with Answer Key): **Contextos**
	• Additional Vocabulary (**Más vocabulario para el fin de semana**)
	• Digital Image Bank:
	  • Leisure and Entertainment
	  • Sports and Outdoor Activities
		• Vocabulary Quiz (with Answer Key)		contextos

		• **Fotonovela** Optional Testing Sections (with Answer Key)	• **Fotonovela** Videoscript • **Fotonovela** English Translation	fotonovela
• **Estructura 4.1** Grammar Slides	• Information Gap Activity* • Activity Pack Practice Activities (with Answer Key): Present tense of **ir** • Surveys: Worksheet for classroom survey	• Grammar 4.1 Quiz (with Answer Key)	• Tutorial Script: Present tense of **ir**	estructura
• **Estructura 4.2** Grammar Slides	• Information Gap Activity* • Activity Pack Practice Activities (with Answer Key): Stem-changing verbs: e→ie, o→ue • Surveys: Worksheet for classroom survey	• Grammar 4.2 Quiz (with Answer Key)	• Tutorial Script: Stem-changing verbs: e→ie, o→ue	
• **Estructura 4.3** Grammar Slides	• Activity Pack Practice Activities (with Answer Key): Stem-changing verbs: e→i	• Grammar 4.3 Quiz (with Answer Key)	• Tutorial Script: Stem-changing verbs: e→i	
• **Estructura 4.4** Grammar Slides	• Activity Pack Practice Activities (with Answer Key): Verbs with irregular **yo** forms	• Grammar 4.4 Quiz (with Answer Key)	• Tutorial Script: Verbs with irregular **yo** forms	
			• **En pantalla** Videoscript • **En pantalla** English Translation	En pantalla / adelante
		• **Flash cultura** Optional Testing Sections (with Answer Key)	• **Flash cultura** Videoscript • **Flash cultura** English Translation	Flash cultura
• Digital Images: • **México**		• **Panorama** Optional Testing Sections (with Answer Key) • **Panorama cultural** (video)	• **Panorama cultural** Videoscript • **Panorama cultural** English Translation	Panorama

*Can also be assigned online.

Lección 4: Teacher Resources

Pulling It All Together

Practice and Communicate
- Role-plays
- Activity Pack Practice Activities (¡A repasar!) (with Answer Key)

Assessment

Tests and Exams*
- **Prueba A** with audio
- **Prueba B** with audio
- **Prueba C** with audio
- **Prueba D** with audio
- **Prueba E** with audio
- **Prueba F** with audio
- Tests Answer Key
- Oral Testing Suggestions
- **Examen A** with audio (lessons 4-6)
- **Examen B** with audio (lessons 4-6)
- Exams Answer Key

Audioscripts
- Tests and Exams Audioscripts
- Alternative Listening Sections Audioscript

Additional Tools for Planning and Teaching
- Essential Questions
- I Can Worksheets
- IPAs & Rubrics
- Lesson Plans
- Middle School Activity Pack
- Pacing Guides

Audio MP3s for Classroom Activities
- **Contextos**. Activities 1 and 2 (p. 27)
- **Estructura 4.1. Comunicación**: Activity 4 (p. 38)
- **Estructura 4.4. Comunicación**: Activity 4 (p. 49)
- **Escuchar** (p. 55)

Script for Comunicación: Actividad 4 (p. 38)

Enrique Hola, Rosa. ¿Adónde vas esta noche?
Rosa Voy al cine con Mercedes. ¿Quieres venir?
Enrique No, gracias. Pedro y yo vamos al partido de béisbol.
Rosa ¡Oh! Fenomenal. Va a ser un partido muy bueno.
Enrique ¡Sí! Y después vamos a ir a un restaurante. ¿Quieren venir después de la película?
Rosa Voy a hablar con Mercedes. ¿A qué restaurante van?
Enrique Vamos a Osaka, el restaurante japonés del centro.
Rosa ¡Oh! Es mi restaurante favorito.
Enrique ¡Tienen que venir! Vamos a estar en el restaurante a las nueve y media.

Script for Comunicación: Actividad 4 (p. 49)

Francisco Salgo de casa a las siete y media de la mañana después de desayunar. Comienzo el día con mi clase favorita, la de matemáticas, a las siete y cuarenta y cinco. Almuerzo a las once y cuarto, y salgo de mi clase de arte a las dos y cuarenta y cinco de la tarde. Después de clases, practico baloncesto con el equipo escolar. A las cinco, llego a casa y uso mi tableta. Veo mis programas favoritos y hago mi tarea. Por la noche oigo un poco de música y leo mi blog favorito antes de ir a dormir.

*Tests and Exams can also be assigned online.

Los pasatiempos 4

Communicative Goals
You will learn how to:
- Talk about pastimes, weekend activities, and sports
- Make plans and invitations

Lesson Goals
In **Lección 4**, students will be introduced to the following:
- names of sports and other pastimes
- names of places in a city
- soccer rivalries
- Mexican diver **Paola Espinosa** and Venezuelan baseball player **Miguel Cabrera**
- present tense of **ir**
- the contraction **al**
- **ir a** + [*infinitive*]
- present tense of common stem-changing verbs
- verbs with irregular **yo** forms
- predicting content from visual elements
- using a Spanish-English dictionary
- writing an events pamphlet
- listening for the gist
- an excerpt of a documentary about skateboarding and BMX
- a video about soccer in Spain
- cultural, historical, economic, and geographic information about Mexico

A primera vista Ask these additional questions to personalize the photo: ¿Te gusta practicar los deportes? ¿Crees que son importantes los pasatiempos? ¿Estudias mucho los sábados y domingos? ¿Bailas? ¿Lees? ¿Escuchas música?

Teaching Tip Look for these icons for additional communicative practice:

→👤←	Interpretive communication
←👤→	Presentational communication
👤↔👤	Interpersonal communication

contextos
pages 26–29
- Pastimes
- Sports
- Places in the city

fotonovela
pages 30–33
The friends spend the day exploring Mérida and the surrounding area. Maru, Jimena, and Miguel take Marissa to a **cenote**; Felipe and Juan Carlos join Felipe's cousins for soccer and lunch.

cultura
pages 34–35
- Soccer rivalries
- Miguel Cabrera and Paola Espinosa

estructura
pages 36–51
- Present tense of **ir**
- Stem–changing verbs: e→ie; o→ue
- Stem–changing verbs: e→i
- Verbs with irregular **yo** forms
- **Recapitulación**

adelante
pages 52–59
Lectura: Popular sports in Latin America
Escritura: A pamphlet about activities in your area
Escuchar: A conversation about pastimes
En pantalla
Flash cultura
Panorama: México

A PRIMERA VISTA
- ¿Es esta persona un atleta o un artista?
- ¿En qué tiene interés, en el ciclismo o en el tenis?
- ¿Es viejo? ¿Es delgado?
- ¿Tiene frío o calor?

SUPPORT FOR BACKWARD DESIGN

Lección 4 Essential Questions
1. How do people talk about pastimes, weekend activities, and sports?
2. How do people make plans and extend invitations?
3. What sports and sports figures are popular in the Spanish-speaking world?

Lección 4 Integrated Performance Assessment
Before teaching this chapter, review the Integrated Performance Assessment (IPA) and its accompanying scoring rubric. Use the IPA to assess students' progress toward proficiency targets at the end of the chapter. **IPA Context:** Your school is having an election for student council, and you need to decide what attributes are important in the person you elect. You are going to listen to two people describe themselves. Then, you and a partner will talk about the characteristics that would make each of them a better candidate. Finally, you will describe the characteristics of your ideal candidate to the class.

Voice boards online allow you and your students to record and share up to five minutes of audio. Use voice boards for presentations, oral assessments, discussions, directions, etc.

Section Goals

In **Contextos**, students will learn and practice:
- names of sports and other pastimes
- names of places in a city

 Communication 1.2
Comparisons 4.1

Teacher Resources
Read the front matter for suggestions on how to incorporate all the program's components. See pages 25A–25B for a detailed listing of Teacher Resources online.

In-Class Tips
- Write **practicar un deporte** on the board and explain what it means. Ask: **¿Qué deportes practicas?** Offer some cognates as suggestions: **¿Practicas el béisbol? ¿El vóleibol? ¿El tenis? ¿El golf?** After the student answers, ask another student: **¿Qué deporte practica ____?**
- Use the **Lección 4 Contextos** vocabulary presentation online or the digital images in the Resources online to assist with this presentation.
- Ask true/false questions about the illustration. Ex: **¿Cierto o falso? Una chica nada en la piscina. (Falso. Es un chico.)** Next, name famous athletes and have students give the sports they play. Ex: **¿Qué deporte practica Novak Djokovic?**
- Point out that, except for the **nosotros/as** and **vosotros/as** forms, all present tense forms of **esquiar** carry an accent over the **i**: **esquío, esquías, esquía, esquían**.

Note: At this point you may want to present **Vocabulario adicional: Más vocabulario para el fin de semana** from the online Resources.

4 contextos

Los pasatiempos

Más vocabulario

el béisbol	baseball
el ciclismo	cycling
el esquí (acuático)	(water) skiing
el fútbol americano	football
el golf	golf
el hockey	hockey
la natación	swimming
el tenis	tennis
el vóleibol	volleyball
el equipo	team
el parque	park
el partido	game; match
la plaza	city or town square
andar en patineta	to skateboard
bucear	to scuba dive
escalar montañas (*f., pl.*)	to climb mountains
esquiar	to ski
ganar	to win
ir de excursión	to go on a hike
practicar deportes (*m., pl.*)	to play sports
escribir una carta/ un mensaje electrónico	to write a letter/ an e-mail
leer el correo electrónico	to read e-mail
leer una revista	to read a magazine
deportivo/a	sports-related

Variación léxica

piscina ↔ pileta (*Arg.*); alberca (*Méx.*)
baloncesto ↔ básquetbol (*Amér. L.*)
béisbol ↔ pelota (*P. Rico, Rep. Dom.*)

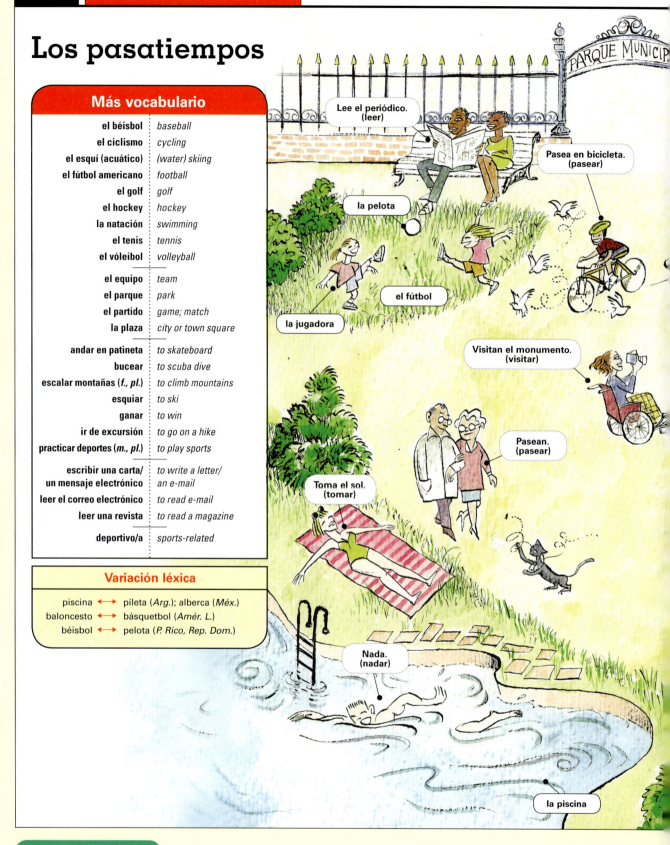

Lee el periódico. (leer)
Pasea en bicicleta. (pasear)
la pelota
el fútbol
la jugadora
Visitan el monumento. (visitar)
Pasean. (pasear)
Toma el sol. (tomar)
Nada. (nadar)
la piscina

TEACHING OPTIONS

Pairs Ask students to write down in Spanish their three favorite sports or leisure activities. Have students pair up and share the information using complete sentences. Ex: **Me gusta practicar la natación. Es un deporte divertido. Nado en mi piscina. ¿Qué deportes practicas?** As a class, call on individuals to report their partners' favorite pastimes. Partners will confirm or correct the information.

Variación léxica Point out that many sports in Spanish are referred to by names derived from English (**básquetbol, béisbol, fútbol**), including many in **Más vocabulario: el golf, el hockey, el vóleibol**. Ask students to guess the meaning of these activities (be sure to use Spanish pronunciation): **el footing** (*jogging*), **el camping, el surf(ing), el windsurf**.

Patina en línea. (patinar)
el baloncesto
el jugador

Práctica

1 **Escuchar** Indicate the letter of the activity in Column B that best corresponds to each statement you hear. Two items in Column B will not be used.

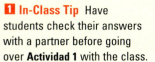

A	B
1. b	a. leer el correo electrónico
2. d	b. tomar el sol
3. f	c. pasear en bicicleta
4. c	d. ir a un partido de fútbol americano
5. g	e. escribir una carta
6. h	f. practicar muchos deportes
	g. nadar
	h. ir de excursión

2 **Ordenar** Order these activities according to what you hear in the narration.

- 5 a. pasear en bicicleta
- 1 b. nadar
- 4 c. leer una revista
- 3 d. tomar el sol
- 6 e. practicar deportes
- 2 f. patinar en línea

3 **¿Cierto o falso?** Indicate whether each statement is **cierto** or **falso** based on the illustration.

	Cierto	Falso
1. Un hombre nada en la piscina.	✓	
2. Un hombre lee una revista.		✓
3. Un chico pasea en bicicleta.	✓	
4. Dos muchachos esquían.		✓
5. Una mujer y dos niños visitan un monumento.	✓	
6. Un hombre bucea.		✓
7. Hay un equipo de hockey.		✓
8. Una mujer toma el sol.	✓	

4 **Clasificar** Fill in the chart below with as many terms from **Contextos** as you can. Answers will vary.

Actividades	Deportes	Personas

En el centro

Más vocabulario

la diversión	fun activity; entertainment; recreation
el fin de semana	weekend
el pasatiempo	pastime; hobby
los ratos libres	spare (free) time
el videojuego	video game
la iglesia	church
el lugar	place
ver películas (f., pl.)	to watch movies
favorito/a	favorite

5 Identificar Identify the place where these activities would take place.

modelo
Esquiamos. **Es una montaña.**

1. Tomamos una limonada. **Es un café./Es un restaurante.**
2. Vemos una película. **Es un cine.**
3. Nadamos y tomamos el sol. **Es una piscina./Es un parque.**
4. Hay muchos monumentos. **Es un parque./Es una plaza.**
5. Comemos tacos y fajitas. **Es un restaurante.**
6. Miramos pinturas (*paintings*) de Diego Rivera y Frida Kahlo. **Es un museo.**
7. Hay mucho tráfico. **Es el centro.**
8. Practicamos deportes. **Es un gimnasio./Es un parque.**

6 Lugares Indicate what you do in the places mentioned below. **Answers will vary.**

modelo
una plaza
Camino por la plaza y miro a las personas.

beber	escalar	mirar	practicar
caminar	escribir	nadar	tomar
correr	leer	patinar	visitar

1. una biblioteca
2. un estadio
3. una plaza
4. una piscina
5. las montañas
6. un parque
7. un café
8. un museo

TEACHING OPTIONS

Extra Practice Give students five minutes to write a short description of three to five sentences about a typical weekend: what they do and where, and with whom they spend time. Circulate through the class and help with unfamiliar vocabulary. Have volunteers share their paragraphs with the class. Then have the class discuss what a "typical weekend" consists of; compose a description on the board.

Game Have students tell a chain story. For example, one student begins with: **Es el sábado por la mañana y voy [al café]**. The next student continues with: **Estoy en el café y tomo una limonada.** You may need to provide some phrases on the board: **voy a/al/a la…, luego, después**. The story may change location; set a time limit for each response. The game ends after ten minutes or when all students have participated.

Comunicación

7 **Guadalajara** Read this description of Guadalajara. Then indicate whether the following conclusions are **lógico** or **ilógico**, based on what you read.

> Guadalajara es una gran ciudad del estado de Jalisco, México. ¿Te gustan los parques? El Parque Mirador Independencia es un buen lugar para pasear en bicicleta, andar en patineta o tomar el sol. ¿Te gusta el cine? Guadalajara es un importante centro cultural, famosa por el Festival de Cine de Guadalajara. ¿Tienes hambre? Hay fabulosos restaurantes por toda la ciudad. ¿Te gustan los deportes? Debes asistir a un partido del Club Deportivo Guadalajara, uno de los equipos de fútbol más populares de México. ¿Te gusta el arte? Guadalajara es también muy famosa por sus museos y sus monumentos.

	Lógico	Ilógico
1. En el Parque Mirador Independencia, hay lugar para la diversión.	✓	
2. Asistes al Festival de Cine de Guadalajara para ver películas.	✓	
3. En Guadalajara, la gente come bien.	✓	
4. No hay estadios de fútbol en Guadalajara.		✓
5. En Guadalajara, los turistas visitan monumentos.	✓	

8 **Entrevista** Answer your partner's questions. *Answers will vary.*

1. ¿Hay un café cerca de tu casa?
2. ¿Cuál es tu restaurante favorito?
3. ¿Te gusta viajar y visitar monumentos?
4. ¿Te gusta ir al cine los fines de semana?
5. ¿Cuáles son tus películas favoritas?
6. ¿Te gusta practicar deportes?
7. ¿Cuáles son tus deportes favoritos?
8. ¿Cuáles son tus pasatiempos favoritos?

CONSULTA
To review expressions with **gustar**, see **Senderos 1A, Estructura 2.1**, p. 76.

9 **Pasatiempos** Write a paragraph about the pastimes three of your friends and family members enjoy. *Answers will vary.*

> **modelo**
> Mi hermana pasea mucho en bicicleta, pero mis padres practican la natación.
> Mi hermano no nada, pero visita muchos museos.

10 **Conversación** Using the words and expressions provided, work with a partner to prepare a short conversation about pastimes. *Answers will vary.*

| ¿a qué hora? | ¿con quién(es)? | ¿dónde? |
| ¿cómo? | ¿cuándo? | ¿qué? |

> **modelo**
> **Estudiante 1:** ¿Cuándo patinas en línea?
> **Estudiante 2:** Patino en línea los domingos. Y tú, ¿patinas en línea?
> **Estudiante 1:** No, no me gusta patinar en línea. Me gusta practicar el béisbol.

TEACHING OPTIONS

Large Group Have students write down six activities they enjoy and then circulate around the room to collect signatures from others who enjoy the same activities (**¿Te gusta...? Firma aquí, por favor.**). Ask volunteers to report back to the class.

Game Ask students to take out a piece of paper and write anonymously a set of activities that best corresponds to their interests. Collect and shuffle the slips of paper. Divide the class into two teams. Pull out and read aloud each slip of paper, and have the teams take turns guessing the student's identity.

Communication 1.1, 1.2

7 In-Class Tip Before beginning the activity, review the verb **gustar**.

7 Expansion Have pairs or groups of students create a video ad promoting activities and interesting places to visit in their community. Then, ask students to present their ads to the class.

8 Expansion Have the same pairs ask each other additional questions. Then ask volunteers to share their mini-conversations with the class.

8 Virtual Chat Available online.

9 Expansion
- Ask volunteers to share any pastimes they and their partners, friends, and families have in common.
- In pairs, have students write sentences about the pastimes of a famous person without using their name. Encourage them to also recycle the descriptive adjectives and adjectives of nationality they learned in Lesson 3. Then have them work with another pair, asking questions as necessary, to guess the identity of the person being described.

10 In-Class Tip After students have asked and answered questions, ask volunteers to report their partners' activities back to the class. The partners should verify the information and provide at least one additional detail.

10 Partner Chat Available online.

Section Goals

In **Fotonovela**, students will:
- receive comprehensible input from free-flowing discourse
- learn functional phrases that preview lesson grammatical structures

Communication 1.2
Cultures 2.1, 2.2

Teacher Resources
Read the front matter for suggestions on how to incorporate all the program's components. See pages 25A–25B for a detailed listing of Teacher Resources online.

Video Recap: Lección 3
Before doing this **Fotonovela** section, review the previous episode with these fill-in-the-blank sentences:
1. Marta y Valentina son las _____ de Jimena y Felipe. (primas) **2.** Marissa tiene _____ hermanos y una hermana. (dos) **3.** _____ es hija única. (la Sra. Díaz) **4.** Las mujeres comparten una _____. (trajinera) **5.** Marissa tiene planes para visitar a _____. (tía Ana María)

Video Synopsis
The friends have arrived at **tía Ana María's** house in **Mérida**. **Juan Carlos** and **Felipe** head off to play soccer with **Felipe's** cousins, **Eduardo** and **Pablo**. Meanwhile, **Maru**, **Miguel**, and **Jimena** take **Marissa** to explore a **cenote**.

In-Class Tips
- Have students quickly glance over the **Fotonovela** captions and make a list of the cognates they find. Then, ask them to predict what this episode is about.
- Have students look for a few expressions used to talk about pastimes. Then ask a few questions. Ex: ¿Qué te gusta hacer en tus ratos libres? ¿Te gusta el fútbol?

4 fotonovela

Fútbol, cenotes y mole

Maru, Miguel, Jimena y Marissa visitan un cenote, mientras Felipe y Juan Carlos van a un partido de fútbol.

PERSONAJES MIGUEL PABLO

1
MIGUEL Buenos días a todos.
TÍA ANA MARÍA Hola, Miguel. Maru, ¿qué van a hacer hoy?
MARU Miguel y yo vamos a llevar a Marissa a un cenote.

2
MARISSA ¿No vamos a nadar? ¿Qué es un cenote?
MIGUEL Sí, sí vamos a nadar. Un cenote... difícil de explicar. Es una piscina natural en un hueco profundo.
MARU ¡Ya vas a ver! Seguro que te va a gustar.

(*unos minutos después*)
EDUARDO Hay un partido de fútbol en el parque. ¿Quieren ir conmigo?
PABLO Y conmigo. Si no consigo más jugadores, nuestro equipo va a perder.

3
ANA MARÍA Marissa, ¿qué te gusta hacer? ¿Escalar montañas? ¿Ir de excursión?
MARISSA Sí, me gusta ir de excursión y practicar el esquí acuático. Y usted, ¿qué prefiere hacer en sus ratos libres?

6
FELIPE ¿Recuerdas el restaurante del mole?
EDUARDO ¿Qué restaurante?
JIMENA El mole de mi tía Ana María es mi favorito.
MARU Chicos, ya es hora. ¡Vamos!

4
PABLO Mi mamá tiene muchos pasatiempos y actividades.
EDUARDO Sí. Ella nada y juega al tenis y al golf.
PABLO Va al cine y a los museos.
ANA MARÍA Sí, salgo mucho los fines de semana.

TEACHING OPTIONS

Video Tips General suggestions for using video clips in the classroom can be found in the front matter of this Teacher's Edition.
Fútbol, cenotes y mole Play the last half of the **Fútbol, cenotes y mole** episode and have the class give you a description of what they saw. Write their observations on the board, pointing out any incorrect information. Repeat this process to allow the class to pick up more details of the plot. Then ask students to use the information they have accumulated to guess what happened at the beginning of the episode. Write their guesses on the board. Then play the entire episode and, through discussion, help the class summarize the plot.

ANA MARÍA MARU MARISSA EDUARDO FELIPE JUAN CARLOS JIMENA DON GUILLERMO

7

(*más tarde, en el parque*)
PABLO No puede ser. ¡Cinco a uno!
FELIPE ¡Vamos a jugar! Si perdemos, compramos el almuerzo. Y si ganamos...
EDUARDO ¡Empezamos!

8

(*mientras tanto, en el cenote*)
MARISSA ¿Hay muchos cenotes en México?
MIGUEL Sólo en la península de Yucatán.
MARISSA ¡Vamos a nadar!

9

(*Los chicos visitan a don Guillermo, un vendedor de paletas heladas.*)
JUAN CARLOS Don Guillermo, ¿dónde podemos conseguir un buen mole?
FELIPE Eduardo y Pablo van a pagar el almuerzo. Y yo voy a pedir un montón de comida.

10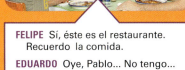

FELIPE Sí, éste es el restaurante. Recuerdo la comida.
EDUARDO Oye, Pablo... No tengo...
PABLO No te preocupes, hermanito.
FELIPE ¿Qué buscas? (*muestra la cartera de Pablo*) ¿Esto?

Expresiones útiles

Making invitations

Hay un partido de fútbol en el parque. ¿Quieren ir conmigo?
There's a soccer game in the park. Do you want to come with me?
¡Yo puedo jugar!
I can play!
Mmm... no quiero.
Hmm... I don't want to.
Lo siento, pero no puedo.
I'm sorry, but I can't.
¡Vamos a nadar!
Let's go swimming!
Sí, vamos.
Yes, let's go.

Making plans

¿Qué van a hacer hoy?
What are you going to do today?
Vamos a llevar a Marissa a un cenote.
We are taking Marissa to a cenote.
Vamos a comprar unas paletas heladas.
We're going to buy some popsicles.
Vamos a jugar. Si perdemos, compramos el almuerzo.
Let's play. If we lose, we'll buy lunch.

Talking about pastimes

¿Qué te gusta hacer? ¿Escalar montañas? ¿Ir de excursión?
What do you like to do? Mountain climbing? Hiking?
Sí, me gusta ir de excursión y practicar esquí acuático.
Yes, I like hiking and water skiing.
Y usted, ¿qué prefiere hacer en sus ratos libres?
And you, what do you like to do in your free time?
Salgo mucho los fines de semana.
I go out a lot on the weekends.
Voy al cine y a los museos.
I go to the movies and to museums.

Additional vocabulary

el/la aficionado/a fan
la cartera wallet   **el hueco** hole
un montón de a lot of

Expresiones útiles
- Point out the written accents in the words **fútbol, sí, ¿Qué?,** and **excursión**. Explain that accents indicate a stressed syllable in a word. Remind students that all question words have accent marks. Tell students that they will learn more about word stress and accent marks in **Pronunciación**.
- Mention that **Vamos, van,** and **Voy** are present-tense forms of the verb **ir**. Point out that **ir a** is used with an infinitive to tell what is going to happen. Ask: **¿Qué vas a hacer esta noche? ¿Por qué no vamos al parque?** Explain that **Quieren, quiero,** and **siento** are forms of **querer** and **sentir**, which undergo a stem change from **e** to **ie** in certain forms. Tell students that they will learn more about these concepts in **Estructura**.

In-Class Tip Have the class read through the entire **Fotonovela**, with volunteers playing various parts. Have students take turns playing the roles so that more students participate.

Nota cultural Traditionally, **mole** ingredients are ground on a flat slab of volcanic stone known as a **metate**, using a **mano**, or rounded grinding stone. The **metate** has been used for grinding grains (especially corn) and spices since pre-Columbian times, and although electric blenders and grinders have replaced many **metates** in Mexican homes, this utensil has experienced a resurgence. Many claim that using the **metate**, although time-consuming, gives dishes better flavor.

TEACHING OPTIONS

Extra Practice Ask students to write six true/false statements about the **Fotonovela** episode. Have them exchange papers with a classmate, who will complete the activity, correcting any false information.

Large Groups Go through the **Expresiones útiles** as a class. Then have students stand and form a circle. Call out a question or statement from **Expresiones útiles** and toss a ball to a student. He or she must respond appropriately and toss the ball back to you.

¿Qué pasó?

1 **Escoger** Choose the answer that best completes each sentence.

1. Marissa, Maru y Miguel desean ___a___.
   a. nadar   b. correr por el parque   c. leer el periódico
2. A Marissa le gusta ___c___.
   a. el tenis   b. el vóleibol   c. ir de excursión y practicar esquí acuático
3. A la tía Ana María le gusta ___b___.
   a. jugar al hockey   b. nadar y jugar al tenis y al golf   c. hacer ciclismo
4. Pablo y Eduardo pierden el partido de ___a___.
   a. fútbol   b. béisbol   c. baloncesto
5. Juan Carlos y Felipe desean ___c___.
   a. patinar   b. esquiar   c. comer mole

2 **Identificar** Identify the person who would make each statement.

1. A mí me gusta nadar, pero no sé qué es un cenote. ___Marissa___
2. Mamá va al cine y al museo en sus ratos libres. ___Pablo/Eduardo___
3. Yo voy a pedir mucha comida. ___Felipe___
4. ¿Quieren ir a jugar al fútbol con nosotros en el parque? ___Pablo/Eduardo___
5. Me gusta salir los fines de semana. ___tía Ana María___

MARISSA
FELIPE
EDUARDO
PABLO
TÍA ANA MARÍA

NOTA CULTURAL

Mole is a typical sauce in Mexican cuisine. It is made from pumpkin seeds, chile, and chocolate, and it is usually served with chicken, beef, or pork.

NOTA CULTURAL

Cenotes are deep, freshwater sinkholes found in caves throughout the Yucatán peninsula. They were formed in prehistoric times by the erosion and collapse of cave walls. The Mayan civilization considered the **cenotes** sacred, and performed rituals there. Today, they are popular destinations for swimming and diving.

3 **Preguntas** Answer the questions using the information from the **Fotonovela**.

1. ¿Qué van a hacer Miguel y Maru?
   Miguel y Maru van a llevar a Marissa a un cenote.
2. ¿Adónde van Felipe y Juan Carlos mientras sus amigos van al cenote?
   Felipe y Juan Carlos van a jugar al fútbol con Pablo y Eduardo.
3. ¿Quién gana el partido de fútbol?
   Felipe y Juan Carlos ganan el partido de fútbol.
4. ¿Quiénes van al cenote con Maru y Miguel?
   Marissa y Jimena van al cenote con Maru y Miguel.

4 **Conversación** With a partner, prepare a conversation in which you talk about pastimes and invite each other to do some activity together. Use these expressions and also look at **Expresiones útiles** on the previous page. Answers will vary.

¿A qué hora?	¿Dónde? *Where?*	Nos vemos a las siete.
(At) What time?	No puedo porque...	*See you at seven.*
contigo *with you*	*I can't because...*	

▶ ¿Eres aficionado/a a...?   ▶ ¿Por qué no...?   ▶ ¿Qué vas a hacer esta noche?
▶ ¿Te gusta...?   ▶ ¿Quieres... conmigo?

TEACHING OPTIONS

Small Groups Have the class quickly glance at frames 7, 8, and 10 of the **Fotonovela**. Then have students work in groups of three to ad-lib what transpires between the friends. Assure them that it is not necessary to follow the **Fotonovela** word for word. Students should be creative while getting the general meaning across with the vocabulary and expressions they know.

Extra Practice Have students close their books and complete these statements with words from the **Fotonovela**. 1. ¿Qué prefiere _____ usted en sus ratos libres? (hacer) 2. ¿Dónde _____ conseguir un buen mole? (podemos) 3. Nosotros _____ a nadar? (vamos) 4. Eduardo y Pablo _____ a pagar el almuerzo. (van) 5. ¿Ustedes _____ ir conmigo al partido de fútbol? (quieren)

Pronunciación
Word stress and accent marks

pe-lí-cu-la   e-di-fi-cio   ver   yo

Every Spanish syllable contains at least one vowel. When two vowels are joined in the same syllable they form a **diphthong***. A **monosyllable** is a word formed by a single syllable.

bi-blio-te-ca   vi-si-tar   par-que   fút-bol

The syllable of a Spanish word that is pronounced most emphatically is the "stressed" syllable.

pe-lo-ta   pis-ci-na   ra-tos   ha-blan

Words that end in **n**, **s**, or a **vowel** are usually stressed on the next-to-last syllable.

na-ta-ción   pa-pá   in-glés   Jo-sé

If words that end in **n**, **s**, or a **vowel** are stressed on the last syllable, they must carry an accent mark on the stressed syllable.

bai-lar   es-pa-ñol   u-ni-ver-si-dad   tra-ba-ja-dor

Words that do not end in **n**, **s**, or a **vowel** are usually stressed on the last syllable.

béis-bol   lá-piz   ár-bol   Gó-mez

If words that do not end in **n**, **s**, or a **vowel** are stressed on the next-to-last syllable, they must carry an accent mark on the stressed syllable.

*The two vowels that form a diphthong are either both weak or one is weak and the other is strong.

En la unión está la fuerza.²

Práctica Pronounce each word, stressing the correct syllable. Then give the word stress rule for each word.

1. profesor
2. Puebla
3. ¿Cuántos?
4. Mazatlán
5. examen
6. ¿Cómo?
7. niños
8. Guadalajara
9. programador
10. México
11. están
12. geografía

Oraciones Read the conversation aloud to practice word stress.

MARINA Hola, Carlos. ¿Qué tal?
CARLOS Bien. Oye, ¿a qué hora es el partido de fútbol?
MARINA Creo que es a las siete.
CARLOS ¿Quieres ir?
MARINA Lo siento, pero no puedo. Tengo que estudiar biología.

Quien ríe de último, ríe mejor.¹

Refranes Read these sayings aloud to practice word stress.

¹ He who laughs last, laughs best. ² United we stand.

Section Goals

In **Pronunciación**, students will be introduced to:
- the concept of word stress
- diphthongs and monosyllables
- accent marks

Comparisons 4.1

In-Class Tips

- You can use the Explore selection online to support your presentation of this pronunciation point.
- Write **película**, **edificio**, **ver**, and **yo** on the board. Model their pronunciation. Ask the class to identify the diphthongs and the monosyllables.
- Remind students of the strong and weak vowels that they learned about in **Lección 3**. Strong: **a, e, o**; Weak: **i, u**
- Write **biblioteca**, **visitar**, and **parque** on the board. Model their pronunciation, then ask which syllables are stressed.
- As you go through each point in the explanation, write the example words on the board, pronounce them, and have students repeat. Then, ask students to provide words they learned in **Lecciones 1–3** and **Contextos** and **Fotonovela** of this lesson that exemplify each point.

TEACHING OPTIONS

Extra Practice Write on the board a list of Mexican place names. Have the class pronounce each name, paying particular attention to word stress. Ex: **Campeche, Durango, Culiacán, Tepic, Chichén Itzá, Zacatecas, Colima, Nayarit, San Luis Potosí, Sonora, Puebla, Morelos, Veracruz, Toluca, Guanajuato, Pachuca, El Tajín, Chetumal.** Model pronunciation as necessary.

Small Groups On the board, write a list of words that students already know. Then have the class work in small groups to come up with the word stress rule that applies to each word. Ex: **lápiz, equipo, pluma, Felipe, chicas, comer, mujer, tenis, hombre, libros, papel, parque, béisbol, excursión, deportes, fútbol, pasear, esquí.**

4 cultura

Section Goals

In **Cultura**, students will:
- read about soccer rivalries
- learn sports-related terms
- read about **Miguel Cabrera** and **Paola Espinosa**
- read about renowned athletes

Communication 1.1, 1.2
Cultures 2.1, 2.2
Connections 3.1, 3.2
Comparisons 4.2

En detalle

Antes de leer Ask students to predict the content of this reading based on the title and photos. Have them share what they know about these teams or about other sports rivalries.

Lectura

- Use the map on page 98 of **Senderos 1A** to point out the locations of Barcelona and Madrid. Briefly explain that Spain's regional cultures (Basque, Catalan, Galician, etc.) were at odds with the authoritarian, centralized approach of **Franco's** regime, which banned the public use of regional languages. Point out that the nickname **Barça** is Catalan, which is why it has a cedilla to indicate a soft **c**.

- Describe the stadiums: **Camp Nou** (Catalan for *new field*) holds about 100,000 spectators and is the largest soccer stadium in Europe. Madrid's **Estadio Santiago Bernabéu**, named after an ex-player and club president, can seat about 80,000.

- Remind students that **el fútbol** is *soccer* and **el fútbol americano** is *football*.

1 Expansion To challenge students, ask them to write two additional items. Then have them exchange papers with a classmate and complete the activity.

EN DETALLE

Real Madrid y Barça: rivalidad total

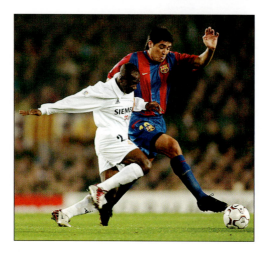

Soccer in Spain is a force to be reckoned with, and no two teams draw more attention than **Real Madrid** and the **Fútbol Club Barcelona**. Whether the venue is Madrid's **Santiago Bernabéu** or Barcelona's **Camp Nou**, the two cities shut down for the showdown, paralyzed by **fútbol** fever. A ticket to the actual game is always the hottest ticket in town.

The rivalry between **Real Madrid** and **Barça** is about more than soccer. As the two biggest, most powerful cities in Spain, Barcelona and Madrid are constantly compared to one another and have a natural rivalry. There is also a political component to the dynamic. Barcelona, with its distinct language and culture, has long struggled for increased autonomy from Madrid's centralized government. Under Francisco Franco's rule (1939–1975), when repression of the Catalan identity was at its height, a game between **Real Madrid** and **FC Barcelona** was wrapped up with all the symbolism of the regime versus the resistance, even though both teams suffered casualties in Spain's civil war and the subsequent Franco dictatorship.

Although the dictatorship is long over, the momentum of all those decades of competition still transforms both cities into a frenzied, tense panic leading up to the game. Once the final score is announced, one of those cities is transformed again, this time into the best party in the country.

Rivalidades del fútbol

Argentina:	Boca Juniors vs River Plate
México:	Águilas del América vs Chivas del Guadalajara
Chile:	Colo Colo vs Universidad de Chile
Guatemala:	Comunicaciones vs Municipal
Uruguay:	Peñarol vs Nacional
Colombia:	Millonarios vs Independiente Santa Fe

ACTIVIDADES

1 ¿Cierto o falso? Indicate whether each statement is **cierto** or **falso**. Correct the false statements.

1. People from Spain don't like soccer. **Falso.** People from Spain like soccer very much.
2. Madrid and Barcelona are the most important cities in Spain. **Cierto.**
3. Santiago Bernabéu is a stadium in Barcelona. **Falso.** It is a stadium in Madrid.
4. The rivalry between Real Madrid and FC Barcelona is not only in soccer. **Cierto.**
5. Barcelona has resisted Madrid's centralized government. **Cierto.**
6. Only the FC Barcelona team was affected by the civil war. **Falso.** Both teams were affected by the civil war.
7. During Franco's regime, the Catalan culture thrived. **Falso.** Catalan culture was repressed during Franco's regime.
8. There are many famous rivalries between soccer teams in the Spanish-speaking world. **Cierto.**
9. River Plate is a popular team from Argentina. **Cierto.**
10. Comunicaciones and Peñarol are famous rivals in Guatemala. **Falso.** Comunicaciones and Municipal are important rivals in Guatemala.

TEACHING OPTIONS

Project Have small groups choose famous soccer rivalries, then split up to research and create a web page for each of the rival teams. The pages should feature each team's colors, players, home stadium, official song, and other significant or interesting information. Have the groups present their rivals' web pages to the class.

¡Goooooooool! Explain that sportscasters in the Spanish-speaking world are famous for their theatrical commentaries. One example is **Andrés Cantor**, who provides commentary for soccer matches on Spanish-language stations in the U.S. Each time a goal is scored, fans know they can hear a drawn-out bellow of **¡Goooooooool!** Cantor's call, which can last for nearly thirty seconds, was made into a ringtone for cell phones in the U.S.

ASÍ SE DICE
Los deportes

el/la árbitro/a	referee
el/la atleta	athlete
la bola; el balón	la pelota
el campeón/la campeona	champion
la carrera	race
competir	to compete
empatar	to tie
la medalla	medal
el/la mejor	the best
mundial	worldwide
el torneo	tournament

EL MUNDO HISPANO
Atletas importantes

World-renowned Hispanic athletes:

- **Rafael Nadal** (España) has won 14 Grand Slam singles titles and the 2008 Olympic gold medal in singles tennis.
- **Lionel Andrés Messi** (Argentina) is one of the world's top soccer players. He plays for **FC Barcelona** and for the Argentine national team.
- **Mireia Belmonte García** (España) won two silver medals in swimming at the 2012 Olympics.
- **Lorena Ochoa** (México) was the top-ranked female golfer in the world when she retired in 2010 at the age of 28. She still hosts an LPGA golf tournament, the Lorena Ochoa Invitational, every year.

PERFILES
Miguel Cabrera y Paola Espinosa

Miguel Cabrera, considered one of the best hitters in baseball, now plays first base for the Detroit Tigers. Born in Venezuela in 1983, he made his Major League debut at the age of 20. Cabrera has been selected for both the National League and American League All-Star Teams. In 2012, he became the first player since 1967 to win the Triple Crown.

Mexican diver **Paola Milagros Espinosa Sánchez**, born in 1986, has competed in three Olympics (2004, 2008, and 2012). She and her partner Tatiana Ortiz took home a bronze medal in 2008. In 2012, she won a silver medal with partner Alejandra Orozco. She won three gold medals at the Pan American Games in 2007 and again in 2011.

Conexión Internet

¿Qué deportes son populares en los países hispanos?

Use the Web to find more cultural information related to this **Cultura** section.

ACTIVIDADES

2 Comprensión Write the name of the athlete described in each sentence.
1. Es un jugador de fútbol de Argentina. _Lionel Messi_
2. Es una mujer que practica el golf. _Lorena Ochoa_
3. Es un jugador de béisbol de Venezuela. _Miguel Cabrera_
4. Es una mujer mexicana que practica un deporte en la piscina. _Paola Milagros Espinosa Sánchez_

3 ¿Quién es? Write a short paragraph describing an athlete that you like. What does he/she look like? What sport does he/she play? Where does he/she live? _Answers will vary._

PRE-AP®
Presentational Speaking For homework, ask students to research one of the athletes from **El mundo hispano**. They should write five Spanish sentences about the athlete's life and career, and bring in a photo from the Internet. Have students who researched the same person work as a group to present that athlete to the class.

TEACHING OPTIONS
Heritage Speakers Ask heritage speakers to describe sports preferences in their families' countries of origin, especially ones that are not widely known in the United States, such as **jai-alai**. What well-known athletes in the U.S. are from their families' countries of origin?

4 estructura

4.1 Present tense of ir

ANTE TODO The verb **ir** (*to go*) is irregular in the present tense. Note that, except for the **yo** form (**voy**) and the lack of a written accent on the **vosotros** form (**vais**), the endings are the same as those for regular present tense **-ar** verbs.

The verb ir (to go)

Singular forms		Plural forms	
yo	voy	nosotros/as	vamos
tú	vas	vosotros/as	vais
Ud./él/ella	va	Uds./ellos/ellas	van

▶ **Ir** is often used with the preposition **a** (*to*). If **a** is followed by the definite article **el**, they combine to form the contraction **al**. If **a** is followed by the other definite articles (**la, las, los**), there is no contraction.

$$a + el = al$$

Voy **al** parque con Juan.
I'm going to the park with Juan.

Mis amigos van **a las** montañas.
My friends are going to the mountains.

▶ The construction **ir a** + [*infinitive*] is used to talk about actions that are going to happen in the future. It is equivalent to the English *to be going* + [*infinitive*].

Va a leer el periódico.
He is going to read the newspaper.

Van a pasear por el pueblo.
They are going to walk around town.

¡Voy a ir con ellos!

Ella va al cine y a los museos.

▶ **Vamos a** + [*infinitive*] can also express the idea of *let's (do something)*.

Vamos a pasear.
Let's take a walk.

¡Vamos a comer!
Let's eat!

AYUDA

When asking a question that contains a form of the verb **ir**, remember to use **adónde**:

¿Adónde vas?
(To) Where are you going?

¡INTÉNTALO!

Provide the present tense forms of **ir**.

1. Ellos ___van___.
2. Yo ___voy___.
3. Tu amigo ___va___.
4. Adela ___va___.
5. Mi prima y yo ___vamos___.
6. Tú ___vas___.
7. Ustedes ___van___.
8. Nosotros ___vamos___.
9. Usted ___va___.
10. Nosotras ___vamos___.
11. Miguel ___va___.
12. Ellas ___van___.

Práctica

1 **¿Adónde van?** Everyone in your neighborhood is dashing off to various places. Say where they are going.

1. la señora Castillo / el centro La señora Castillo va al centro.
2. las hermanas Gómez / la piscina Las hermanas Gómez van a la piscina.
3. tu tío y tu papá / el partido de fútbol Tu tío y tu papá van al partido de fútbol.
4. yo / el Museo de Arte Moderno (Yo) Voy al Museo de Arte Moderno.
5. nosotros / el restaurante Miramar (Nosotros) Vamos al restaurante Miramar.

2 **¿Qué van a hacer?** These sentences describe what several students in a college hiking club are doing today. Use **ir a** + [*infinitive*] to say that they are also going to do the same activities tomorrow.

> **modelo**
> Martín y Rodolfo nadan en la piscina.
> Van a nadar en la piscina mañana también.

1. Sara lee una revista. Va a leer una revista mañana también.
2. Yo practico deportes. Voy a practicar deportes mañana también.
3. Ustedes van de excursión. Van a ir de excursión mañana también.
4. El presidente del club patina. Va a patinar mañana también.
5. Tú tomas el sol. Vas a tomar el sol mañana también.
6. Paseamos con nuestros amigos. Vamos a pasear con nuestros amigos mañana también.

3 **Actividades** Indicate where the people are going and what they are going to do there. Some answers will vary.

> **modelo**
> Estela va a la Librería Sol.
> Va a comprar un libro.

Estela

1. Álex y Miguel
Álex y Miguel van al parque.
Van a…

2. mi amigo
Mi amigo va al gimnasio.
Va a…

3. tú
Voy al restaurante. Voy a…

4. los estudiantes
Los estudiantes van al estadio.
Van a…

5. la profesora Torres
La profesora Torres va a la Biblioteca Nacional. Va a…

6. ustedes
Vamos a la piscina.
Vamos a…

Comunicación

4 Esta noche Listen to the conversation between Enrique and Rosa. Then indicate whether the following conclusions are **lógico** or **ilógico**, based on what you heard.

	Lógico	Ilógico
1. Rosa y Mercedes van a ver una película esta noche.	●	○
2. A Enrique le gustan los deportes.	●	○
3. Enrique va a ir al estadio esta noche.	●	○
4. Enrique y Pedro van a cenar mientras (*while*) miran el partido.	○	●
5. A Rosa no le gustan los restaurantes japoneses.	○	●
6. Rosa y Enrique conversan en el cine.	○	●

5 Situaciones Work with a partner and say where you and your friends go in these situations. *Answers will vary.*

1. Cuando deseo descansar…
2. Cuando mi mejor amigo/a tiene que estudiar…
3. Si deseo hablar con mis amigos…
4. Cuando mis amigos y yo tenemos hambre…
5. En mis ratos libres…
6. Cuando mis amigos desean esquiar…
7. Si estoy de vacaciones…
8. Si tengo ganas de leer…

6 Entrevista With a partner, take turns asking each other where you are going and what you are going to do on your next vacation. *Answers will vary.*

modelo
Estudiante 1: ¿Adónde vas de vacaciones (*on vacation*)?
Estudiante 2: Voy a Guadalajara con mi familia.
Estudiante 1: ¿Y qué van a hacer (*to do*) ustedes en Guadalajara?
Estudiante 2: Vamos a visitar unos monumentos y museos. ¿Y tú?

Síntesis

7 Planes Make a schedule of your activities for the weekend. *Answers will vary.*

▶ For each day, list at least three things you have to do.
▶ For each day, list at least two things you will do for fun.

Los pasatiempos

4.2 Stem-changing verbs: e→ie, o→ue

ANTE TODO Stem-changing verbs deviate from the normal pattern of regular verbs. When stem-changing verbs are conjugated, they have a vowel change in the last syllable of the stem.

INFINITIVE	VERB STEM	STEM CHANGE	CONJUGATED FORM
empezar	empez-	emp**ie**z-	emp**ie**zo
volver	volv-	v**ue**lv-	v**ue**lvo

CONSULTA
To review the present tense of regular -ar verbs, see **Senderos 1A, Estructura 2.1**, p. 74.
...
To review the present tense of regular -er and -ir verbs, see **Senderos 1A, Estructura 3.3**, p. 120.

▶ In many verbs, such as **empezar** (*to begin*), the stem vowel changes from **e** to **ie**. Note that the **nosotros/as** and **vosotros/as** forms don't have a stem change.

The verb empezar (e:ie) (to begin)

Singular forms		Plural forms	
yo	emp**ie**zo	nosotros/as	empezamos
tú	emp**ie**zas	vosotros/as	empezáis
Ud./él/ella	emp**ie**za	Uds./ellos/ellas	emp**ie**zan

Los chicos empiezan a hablar de su visita al cenote.

Ellos vuelven a comer en el restaurante.

▶ In many other verbs, such as **volver** (*to return*), the stem vowel changes from **o** to **ue**. The **nosotros/as** and **vosotros/as** forms have no stem change.

The verb volver (o:ue) (to return)

Singular forms		Plural forms	
yo	v**ue**lvo	nosotros/as	volvemos
tú	v**ue**lves	vosotros/as	volvéis
Ud./él/ella	v**ue**lve	Uds./ellos/ellas	v**ue**lven

▶ To help you identify stem-changing verbs, they will appear as follows throughout the text:

empezar (e:ie), volver (o:ue)

Common stem-changing verbs

e:ie		o:ue	
cerrar	to close	almorzar	to have lunch
comenzar (a + *inf.*)	to begin	contar	to count; to tell
empezar (a + *inf.*)	to begin	dormir	to sleep
entender	to understand	encontrar	to find
pensar	to think	mostrar	to show
perder	to lose; to miss	poder (+ *inf.*)	to be able to; can
preferir (+ *inf.*)	to prefer	recordar	to remember
querer (+ *inf.*)	to want; to love	volver	to return

¡LENGUA VIVA!

The verb **perder** can mean *to lose* or *to miss*, in the sense of "to miss a train."
Siempre pierdo mis llaves.
I always lose my keys.
Es importante no perder el autobús.
It's important not to miss the bus.

▶ **Jugar** (*to play a sport or a game*) is the only Spanish verb that has a **u:ue** stem change. **Jugar** is followed by **a** + [*definite article*] when the name of a sport or game is mentioned.

Ella juega al tenis y al golf.

Los chicos juegan al fútbol.

▶ **Comenzar** and **empezar** require the preposition **a** when they are followed by an infinitive.

Comienzan a jugar a las siete.
They begin playing at seven.

Ana **empieza a** escribir una postal.
Ana is starting to write a postcard.

▶ **Pensar** + [*infinitive*] means *to plan* or *to intend to do something*. **Pensar en** means *to think about someone* or *something*.

¿**Piensan** ir al gimnasio?
Are you planning to go to the gym?

¿**En** qué **piensas**?
What are you thinking about?

¡INTÉNTALO!   Provide the present tense forms of these verbs.

cerrar (e:ie)
1. Ustedes _cierran_.
2. Tú _cierras_.
3. Nosotras _cerramos_.
4. Mi hermano _cierra_.
5. Yo _cierro_.
6. Usted _cierra_.
7. Los chicos _cierran_.
8. Ella _cierra_.

dormir (o:ue)
1. Mi abuela no _duerme_.
2. Yo no _duermo_.
3. Tú no _duermes_.
4. Mis hijos no _duermen_.
5. Usted no _duerme_.
6. Nosotros no _dormimos_.
7. Él no _duerme_.
8. Ustedes no _duermen_.

In-Class Tips

- Write **e:ie** and **o:ue** on the board and explain that some very common verbs have these types of stem changes. Point out that all the verbs listed are conjugated like **empezar** or **volver**. Model the pronunciation of the verbs and ask students a few questions using verbs of each type. Have them answer in complete sentences. Ex: **¿A qué hora cierra la biblioteca? ¿Duermen los estudiantes hasta tarde, por lo general? ¿Qué piensan hacer este fin de semana? ¿Quién quiere comer en un restaurante esta noche?**

- Point out the structure **jugar al** used with sports. Practice it by asking students about the sports they play. Have them answer in complete sentences. Ex: ____, ¿te gusta jugar al fútbol? Y tú, ____, ¿juegas al fútbol? ¿Prefieres jugar al fútbol o ver un partido en el estadio? ¿Cuántos juegan al tenis? ¿Qué prefieres, ____, jugar al tenis o jugar al fútbol?

- Prepare a few dehydrated sentences. Ex: **Raúl / empezar / la lección; ustedes / mostrar / los trabajos; nosotros / jugar / al fútbol** Write them on the board one at a time, and ask students to form complete sentences based on the cues.

Middle School Activity Pack

Have students play the game **La ruleta de la fortuna** in Resources online (Lección 4/ Middle School Activity Pack/ Grammar 4.2 Activity 3).

TEACHING OPTIONS

TPR Add an auditory aspect to this grammar presentation. At random, call out infinitives of regular and **e:ie** stem-changing verbs. Have students raise their hands if the verb has a stem change. Repeat for **o:ue** stem-changing verbs.

Extra Practice For additional drills of stem-changing verbs, do the **¡Inténtalo!** activity orally using infinitives other than **cerrar** and **dormir**. Keep a brisk pace.

TPR Have the class stand in a circle. As you toss a ball to a student, call out the infinitive of a stem-changing verb, followed by a pronoun. (Ex: **querer, tú**) The student should say the appropriate verb form (**quieres**), then name a different pronoun (Ex: **usted**) and throw the ball to another student. When all subject pronouns have been covered, start over with another infinitive.

Práctica

1 Completar Complete this conversation with the appropriate forms of the verbs.

PABLO Óscar, voy al centro ahora.
ÓSCAR ¿A qué hora (1) _piensas_ (pensar) volver? El partido de fútbol
(2) _empieza_ (empezar) a las dos.
PABLO (3) _Vuelvo_ (Volver) a la una. (4) _Quiero_ (Querer) ver el partido.
ÓSCAR (5) ¿_Recuerdas_ (Recordar) que (*that*) nuestro equipo es muy bueno?
(6) ¡_Puede_ (Poder) ganar!
PABLO No, (7) _pienso_ (pensar) que va a (8) _perder_ (perder). Los jugadores de Guadalajara son salvajes (*wild*) cuando (9) _juegan_ (jugar).

NOTA CULTURAL

Dominó (*Dominoes*) is a popular pastime throughout Colombia, Venezuela, Central America, and the Spanish-speaking countries of the Caribbean. It's played both socially and competitively by people of all ages.

2 Preferencias Indicate what these people want to do, using the cues provided.

modelo
Guillermo: estudiar / pasear en bicicleta
Guillermo no quiere estudiar. Prefiere pasear en bicicleta.

1. tú: trabajar / dormir
   Tú no quieres trabajar. Prefieres dormir.
2. ustedes: mirar la televisión / jugar al dominó
   Ustedes no quieren mirar la televisión. Prefieren jugar al dominó.
3. tus amigos: ir de excursión / descansar
   Tus amigos no quieren ir de excursión. Prefieren descansar.
4. tú: comer en la cafetería / ir a un restaurante
   Tú no quieres comer en la cafetería. Prefieres ir a un restaurante.
5. Elisa: ver una película / leer una revista
   Elisa no quiere ver una película. Prefiere leer una revista.
6. María y su hermana: tomar el sol / practicar el esquí acuático
   María y su hermana no quieren tomar el sol. Prefieren practicar el esquí acuático.

3 Describir Use a verb from the list to describe what these people are doing.

almorzar   cerrar   contar   dormir   encontrar   mostrar

1. las niñas Las niñas duermen.

2. yo (Yo) Cierro la ventana.

3. nosotros (Nosotros) Almorzamos.

4. tú (Tú) Encuentras una maleta.

5. Pedro Pedro muestra una foto.

6. Teresa Teresa cuenta.

Comunicación

4 Frecuencia Use the verbs from the list and other stem-changing verbs you know to explain which activities you do daily (**todos los días**), which you do once a month (**una vez al mes**), and which you do once a year (**una vez al año**). Answers will vary.

> **modelo**
> Yo recuerdo a mi familia todos los días. Yo pierdo uno de mis libros una vez al año...

cerrar	encontrar	poder	recordar
dormir	jugar	preferir	¿?
empezar	perder	querer	

5 En la televisión Read the television listings for Saturday. With a partner, role-play a conversation between two siblings arguing about what to watch. Answers will vary.

> **modelo**
> **Hermano:** Podemos ver la Copa Mundial.
> **Hermana:** ¡No, no quiero ver la Copa Mundial! Prefiero ver...

	13:00	14:00	15:00	16:00	17:00	18:00	19:00	20:00	21:00	22:00	23:00
7	Copa Mundial (*World Cup*) de fútbol				República Deportiva	Campeonato (*Championship*) Mundial de Vóleibol: México-Argentina				Torneo de Natación	
8	Abierto (*Open*) Mexicano de Tenis: Santiago González (México) vs. Nicolás Almagro (España). Semifinales			Campeonato de baloncesto: Los Correcaminos de Tampico vs. los Santos de San Luis				Aficionados al buceo		Cozumel: Aventuras	
12	Yo soy Betty, la fea		Héroes		Hermanos y hermanas			Película: Sin nombre		Película: El coronel no tiene quien le escriba	
13	El padrastro			60 Minutos				El esquí acuático		Patinaje artístico	
17	Biografías: La artista Frida Kahlo			Música de la semana			Entrevista del día: Iker Casillas y su pasión por el fútbol			Cine de la noche: Elsa y Fred	

> **NOTA CULTURAL**
> **Iker Casillas Fernández** is a famous goalkeeper for **Real Madrid**. A native of Madrid, he is among the best goalkeepers of his generation.

Síntesis

6 Deportes Write a paragraph about your favorite sport. Mention why you like it, and whether you practice it or watch it on TV. Include some facts you know about the sport. Use at least three stem-changing verbs. Answers will vary.

> **modelo**
> Mi deporte favorito es el béisbol porque es un deporte interesante. Esta noche pienso ver el partido de los Padres en la televisión. Empieza a las siete...

TEACHING OPTIONS

Small Groups Have students choose their favorite pastime and work in small groups with other students who have chosen that same activity. Have each group write six sentences about the activity, using a different stem-changing verb in each.

Pairs Ask students to write incomplete dehydrated sentences (only subjects and infinitives) about people and groups at the school. Ex: **el equipo de béisbol / perder / ¿?** Then have them exchange papers with a classmate, who will form a complete sentence by conjugating the verb and inventing an appropriate ending. Ask volunteers to write sentences on the board.

Los pasatiempos

4.3 Stem-changing verbs: e→i

ANTE TODO You've already seen that many verbs in Spanish change their stem vowel when conjugated. There is a third kind of stem-vowel change in some verbs, such as **pedir** (*to ask for; to request*). In these verbs, the stressed vowel in the stem changes from **e** to **i**, as shown in the diagram.

INFINITIVE	VERB STEM	STEM CHANGE	CONJUGATED FORM
pedir	p**e**d-	p**i**d-	p**i**do

▶ As with other stem-changing verbs you have learned, there is no stem change in the **nosotros/as** or **vosotros/as** forms in the present tense.

The verb pedir (e:i) (to ask for; to request)

Singular forms		Plural forms	
yo	p**i**do	nosotros/as	pedimos
tú	p**i**des	vosotros/as	pedís
Ud./él/ella	p**i**de	Uds./ellos/ellas	p**i**den

▶ To help you identify verbs with the **e:i** stem change, they will appear as follows throughout the text:

pedir (e:i)

▶ These are the most common **e:i** stem-changing verbs:

conseguir	**decir**	**repetir**	**seguir**
to get; to obtain	*to say; to tell*	*to repeat*	*to follow; to continue; to keep (doing something)*

Pido favores cuando es necesario.
I ask for favors when it's necessary.

Sigue con su tarea.
He continues with his homework.

Javier **dice** la verdad.
Javier is telling the truth.

Consiguen ver buenas películas.
They get to see good movies.

▶ **¡Atención!** The verb **decir** is irregular in its **yo** form: **yo digo**.

▶ The **yo** forms of **seguir** and **conseguir** have a spelling change in addition to the stem change **e:i**.

Sigo su plan.
I'm following their plan.

Consigo novelas en la librería.
I get novels at the bookstore.

¡LENGUA VIVA!

As you learned in **Lección 2**, **preguntar** means *to ask a question*. **Pedir**, however, means *to ask for something:*
Ella me pregunta cuántos años tengo. *She asks me how old I am.*
Él me pide ayuda. *He asks me for help.*

¡INTÉNTALO! Provide the correct forms of the verbs.

repetir (e:i)
1. Arturo y Eva **repiten**.
2. Yo **repito**.
3. Nosotros **repetimos**.
4. Julia **repite**.
5. Sofía y yo **repetimos**.

decir (e:i)
1. Yo **digo**.
2. Él **dice**.
3. Tú **dices**.
4. Usted **dice**.
5. Ellas **dicen**.

seguir (e:i)
1. Yo **sigo**.
2. Nosotros **seguimos**.
3. Tú **sigues**.
4. Los chicos **siguen**.
5. Usted **sigue**.

TEACHING OPTIONS

Game Divide the class into two teams. Name an infinitive and a subject pronoun (Ex: **decir / yo**). Have the first member of team A give the appropriate conjugated form of the verb. If the team member answers correctly, team A gets one point. If not, give the first member of team B the same example. If he or she does not know the answer, give the correct verb form and move on. The team with the most points at the end wins.

Extra Practice Add a visual aspect to this grammar presentation. Bring in magazine pictures or photos of parks and city centers where people are doing fun activities. In small groups, have students describe the photos using as many stem-changing verbs from **Estructura 4.2** and **4.3** as they can. Give points to the groups who use the most stem-changing verbs.

Section Goal
In **Estructura 4.3**, students will learn the present tense of stem-changing verbs: **e → i**.

Communication 1.1
Comparisons 4.1

Teacher Resources
Read the front matter for suggestions on how to incorporate all the program's components. See pages 25A–25B for a detailed listing of Teacher Resources online.

In-Class Tips
- Take a survey of students' habits. Ask questions like: **¿Quiénes piden limonada?** Make a chart on the board. Then form sentences based on the chart.
- Ask volunteers to answer questions using **conseguir**, **decir**, **pedir**, **repetir**, and **seguir**.
- Reiterate that the personal endings for the present tense of all the verbs listed are the same as those for the present tense of regular –**ir** verbs.
- Point out the spelling changes in the **yo** forms of **seguir** and **conseguir**.
- Prepare dehydrated sentences and write them on the board one at a time. Ex: 1. tú / pedir / café 2. usted / repetir / la pregunta 3. nosotros / decir / la verdad Have students form complete sentences based on the cues.
- For additional drills with stem-changing verbs, do the ¡Inténtalo! activity orally using other infinitives, such as **conseguir**, **impedir**, **pedir**, and **servir**. Keep a brisk pace.

Note: Students will learn more about **decir** with indirect object pronouns in **Estructura 6.2**.

Comparisons 4.1

1 Expansion
Have students use **conseguir, decir, pedir, repetir,** and **seguir** to write sentences about their own family members. Then have them exchange papers with a partner for peer editing.

Nota cultural
Have students read about **El Bosque de Chapultepec** in Spanish in either the library or on the Internet and bring a photo of the park to class. Ask them to share one new fact they learned about the park.

2 In-Class Tips
- Before beginning the activity, point out that not all verbs in column B have an **e:i** stem change. Have students identify those that do not (**poder, dormir, perder**).
- In pairs, have students decide which activities in column B are characteristic of a good student. Ex: **Un buen estudiante repite el vocabulario.**

2 Expansion In pairs, have students read their sentences aloud. Their partner must decide if they are true or false.

3 Expansion Have students create a survey using the list of activities provided or new ones. Let them walk around the class asking their classmates if they are going to do those activities that day. Tell them to be prepared to report their findings to the class.

Model the activity with volunteers:
—¿Vas a leer el periódico hoy?
—Sí, voy a leer el periódico hoy.
—No, no voy a leer el periódico hoy.

44 Teacher's Edition • Lesson Four

---

44 cuarenta y cuatro · Lección 4

Práctica

1 Completar Complete these sentences with the correct form of the verb provided.

1. Cuando mi familia pasea por la ciudad, mi madre siempre (*always*) va a un café y ___pide___ (pedir) una soda.
2. Pero mi padre ___dice___ (decir) que perdemos mucho tiempo. Tiene prisa por llegar al Bosque de Chapultepec.
3. Mi padre tiene suerte, porque él siempre ___consigue___ (conseguir) lo que (*that which*) desea.
4. Cuando llegamos al parque, mis hermanos y yo ___seguimos___ (seguir) conversando (*talking*) con nuestros padres.
5. Mis padres siempre ___repiten___ (repetir) la misma cosa: "Nosotros tomamos el sol aquí sin ustedes".
6. Yo siempre ___pido___ (pedir) permiso para volver a casa un poco más tarde porque me gusta mucho el parque.

2 Combinar Combine words from the two columns to create sentences about yourself and people you know. *Answers will vary.*

A	B
yo	(no) pedir muchos favores
mi madre	nunca (*never*) pedir perdón
mi mejor (*best*) amigo/a	nunca seguir las instrucciones
mi familia	siempre seguir las instrucciones
mis amigos/as	conseguir libros en Internet
mis amigos/as y yo	repetir el vocabulario
mis padres	poder hablar dos lenguas
mi hermano/a	dormir hasta el mediodía
mi profesor(a) de español	siempre perder sus libros

3 ¿Sí o no? Indicate whether you do the following. *Answers will vary.*

> **modelo**
> pedir consejos con frecuencia
> Pido consejos con frecuencia./No pido consejos con frecuencia.

1. conseguir libros en la librería
2. almorzar en casa
3. perder cosas con frecuencia
4. pedir favores
5. seguir las instrucciones de un manual
6. volver tarde a casa
7. dormir mucho
8. jugar al tenis

NOTA CULTURAL
A popular weekend destination for residents and tourists, **el Bosque de Chapultepec** is a beautiful park located in Mexico City. It occupies over 1.5 square miles and includes lakes, wooded areas, several museums, and a botanical garden. You may recognize this park from **Fotonovela, Lección 2**.

TEACHING OPTIONS

Pairs Ask students to write four simple statements using **e:i** verbs. Then have them read their sentences to a partner, who will guess where the situation takes place. Ex: **Consigo libros para las clases. (Estás en la biblioteca.)** Then reverse the activity, allowing them to answer with verbs from **Estructura 4.2**.

Small Groups Explain to students that movie titles for English-language films are frequently not directly translated into Spanish and that titles may vary from country to country. Bring in a list of movie titles in Spanish. Ex: **La guerra de las galaxias** (*Star Wars*); **Lo que el viento se llevó** (*Gone with the Wind*). In groups, have students guess the movies based on the Spanish titles. Then ask them to state which movies they'd prefer to watch.

Comunicación

4 **Una entrevista** Read this interview with actress Andrea de la Palma. Then indicate whether the following conclusions are **lógico** or **ilógico**, based on what you read.

MANUEL Andrea, ¿qué tipo de persona eres?
ANDREA Creo que soy una persona introvertida. No les pido demasiados favores a mis amigos. En general, pienso que soy una buena amiga; siempre digo la verdad.
MANUEL ¿Qué pides en un restaurante?
ANDREA Siempre (*Always*) pido comida (*food*) vegetariana. Hay un restaurante español muy bueno. Siempre pido tortilla española (*potato omelet*) y ¡siempre repito!
MANUEL ¿Qué deportes sigues?
ANDREA Sigo el béisbol, pero no consigo entender bien los partidos.
MANUEL Sí, ¡pueden ser muy complicados! Andrea, muchas gracias por la entrevista y por ser tan buena actriz. Siempre veo tus películas.
ANDREA El gusto es mío. ¡Muchas gracias!

	Lógico	Ilógico
1. Andrea es honesta.	☑	○
2. Andrea siempre come en casa.	○	☑
3. Andrea pide pollo (*chicken*) en los restaurantes.	○	☑
4. A Manuel le gustan las películas.	☑	○
5. Manuel sigue la carrera de Andrea.	☑	○

5 **Las películas** Answer your partner's questions. *Answers will vary.*

1. ¿Prefieres las películas románticas, las películas de acción o las películas de terror? ¿Por qué?
2. ¿Dónde consigues información sobre (*about*) cine y televisión?
3. ¿Dónde consigues las entradas (*tickets*) para el cine?
4. Para decidir qué películas vas a ver, ¿sigues las recomendaciones de los críticos de cine? ¿Qué dicen los críticos en general?
5. ¿Qué cines de tu comunidad muestran las mejores (*best*) películas?
6. ¿Vas a ver una película esta semana? ¿A qué hora empieza la película?

6 **El cine** With a partner, discuss good and bad movies you have seen. Use stem-changing verbs in your conversation. *Answers will vary.*

> **modelo**
> **Estudiante 1:** *Pienso que Gravedad es una película muy buena. Los efectos especiales son excelentes.*
> **Estudiante 2:** *Sí. Digo que Sandra Bullock es la mejor actriz...*

Síntesis

7 **Mi película favorita** Write a paragraph about your favorite movie. Use stem-changing verbs in your description. *Answers will vary.*

4.4 Verbs with irregular yo forms

ANTE TODO In Spanish, several verbs have irregular **yo** forms in the present tense. You have already seen three verbs with the **-go** ending in the **yo** form: **decir → digo**, **tener → tengo**, and **venir → vengo**.

▸ Here are some common expressions with **decir**.

decir la verdad	**decir mentiras**
to tell the truth	to tell lies
decir que	**decir la respuesta**
to say that	to say the answer

▸ The verb **hacer** is often used to ask questions about what someone does. Note that when answering, **hacer** is frequently replaced with another, more specific action verb.

Verbs with irregular yo forms

	hacer (to do; to make)	poner (to put; to place)	salir (to leave)	suponer (to suppose)	traer (to bring)
SINGULAR FORMS	hago	pongo	salgo	supongo	traigo
	haces	pones	sales	supones	traes
	hace	pone	sale	supone	trae
PLURAL FORMS	hacemos	ponemos	salimos	suponemos	traemos
	hacéis	ponéis	salís	suponéis	traéis
	hacen	ponen	salen	suponen	traen

Salgo mucho los fines de semana.

Yo no salgo, yo hago la tarea y veo películas en la televisión.

▸ **Poner** can also mean to *turn on* a household appliance.

Carlos **pone** la radio.
Carlos turns on the radio.

María **pone** la televisión.
María turns on the television.

▸ **Salir de** is used to indicate that someone is leaving a particular place.

Hoy **salgo del** hospital.
Today I leave the hospital.

Sale de la clase a las cuatro.
He leaves class at four.

Los pasatiempos

- **Salir para** is used to indicate someone's destination.

    Mañana **salgo para** México.
    Tomorrow I leave for Mexico.

    Hoy **salen para** España.
    Today they leave for Spain.

- **Salir con** means *to leave with someone* or *something*, or *to date someone*.

    Alberto **sale con** su mochila.
    Alberto is leaving with his backpack.

    Margarita **sale con** Guillermo.
    Margarita is going out with Guillermo.

The verbs ver and oír

- The verb **ver** (*to see*) has an irregular **yo** form. The other forms of **ver** are regular.

    ### The verb ver (to see)

Singular forms		Plural forms	
yo	**veo**	nosotros/as	vemos
tú	ves	vosotros/as	veis
Ud./él/ella	ve	Uds./ellos/ellas	ven

- The verb **oír** (*to hear*) has an irregular **yo** form and the spelling change **i:y** in the **tú**, **usted/él/ella**, and **ustedes/ellos/ellas** forms. The **nosotros/as** and **vosotros/as** forms have an accent mark.

    ### The verb oír (to hear)

Singular forms		Plural forms	
yo	**oigo**	nosotros/as	o**í**mos
tú	o**y**es	vosotros/as	o**í**s
Ud./él/ella	o**y**e	Uds./ellos/ellas	o**y**en

- While most commonly translated as *to hear*, **oír** is also used in contexts where the verb *to listen* would be used in English.

    Oigo a unas personas en la otra sala.
    I hear some people in the other room.

    ¿**Oyes** la radio por la mañana?
    Do you listen to the radio in the morning?

¡INTÉNTALO! Provide the appropriate forms of these verbs.

1. salir — Isabel *sale*. Nosotros *salimos*. Yo *salgo*.
2. ver — Yo *veo*. Uds. *ven*. Tú *ves*.
3. poner — Rita y yo *ponemos*. Yo *pongo*. Los niños *ponen*.
4. hacer — Yo *hago*. Tú *haces*. Ud. *hace*.
5. oír — Él *oye*. Nosotros *oímos*. Yo *oigo*.
6. traer — Ellas *traen*. Yo *traigo*. Tú *traes*.
7. suponer — Yo *supongo*. Mi amigo *supone*. Nosotras *suponemos*.

Práctica

1 **Completar** Complete this conversation with the appropriate forms of the verbs.

ERNESTO David, ¿qué (1) _haces_ (hacer) hoy?
DAVID Ahora estudio biología, pero esta noche (2) _salgo_ (salir) con Luisa. Vamos al cine. Los críticos (3) _dicen_ (decir) que la nueva (*new*) película de Almodóvar es buena.
ERNESTO ¿Y Diana? ¿Qué (4) _hace_ (hacer) ella?
DAVID (5) _Sale_ (Salir) a comer con sus padres.
ERNESTO ¿Qué (6) _hacen_ (hacer) Andrés y Javier?
DAVID Tienen que (7) _hacer_ (hacer) las maletas. (8) _Salen_ (Salir) para Monterrey mañana.
ERNESTO Pues, ¿qué (9) _hago_ (hacer) yo?
DAVID Yo (10) _supongo_ (suponer) que puedes estudiar o (11) _ver_ (ver) la televisión.
ERNESTO No quiero estudiar. Mejor (12) _pongo_ (poner) la televisión. Mi programa favorito empieza en unos minutos.

2 **Oraciones** Form sentences using the cues provided and verbs from **Estructura 4.4**.

modelo
tú / _____ / cosas / en / su lugar / antes de (*before*) / salir
Tú pones las cosas en su lugar antes de salir.

1. mis amigos / _____ / conmigo / centro Mis amigos salen conmigo al centro.
2. tú / _____ / mentiras / pero / yo _____ / verdad Tú dices mentiras, pero yo digo la verdad.
3. Alberto / _____ / música del café Pasatiempos Alberto oye la música del café Pasatiempos.
4. yo / no / _____ / muchas películas Yo no veo muchas películas.
5. domingo / nosotros / _____ / mucha / tarea El domingo nosotros hacemos mucha tarea.
6. si / yo / _____ / que / yo / querer / ir / cine / mis amigos / ir / también Si yo digo que quiero ir al cine, mis amigos van también.

3 **Describir** Use the verbs from **Estructura 4.4** to describe what these people are doing.

1. Fernán Fernán pone la mochila en el escritorio/trae una mochila.

2. los aficionados Los aficionados salen del estadio/para sus casas.

3. yo Yo traigo/salgo con una cámara.

4. nosotros Nosotros vemos el monumento.

5. la señora Vargas La señora Vargas no oye bien.

6. el estudiante El estudiante hace su tarea.

Comunicación

4 El día de Francisco Listen to Francisco's description of his day. Then indicate whether the following conclusions are **lógico** or **ilógico**, based on what you heard.

	Lógico	Ilógico
1. Francisco duerme hasta (*until*) el mediodía.	○	●
2. A Francisco no le gustan las matemáticas.	○	●
3. Francisco almuerza en casa.	○	●
4. A Francisco le gustan los deportes.	●	○
5. Francisco sale para la casa antes de las cinco.	●	○

5 Tu rutina Answer your partner's questions. *Answers will vary.*

1. ¿Siempre (*Always*) pones tus cosas en su lugar?
2. ¿Qué prefieres hacer, oír la radio o ver la televisión?
3. ¿Oyes música cuando estudias?
4. ¿Ves películas en casa o prefieres ir al cine?
5. ¿Haces mucha tarea los fines de semana?
6. ¿Sales con tus amigos los fines de semana? ¿A qué hora? ¿Qué hacen?

6 Un día típico Write a short paragraph about what you do on a typical day. Use at least six of the verbs you have learned in this lesson. *Answers will vary.*

modelo
Hola, me llamo Julia y vivo en Houston. Por la mañana, yo...

Síntesis

7 Situación Imagine that you are speaking with a member of your family. With a partner, prepare a conversation using these cues. *Answers will vary.*

Estudiante 1
- Ask your partner what he or she is doing.
- Say what you suppose he or she is watching.
- Say no, because you are going out with friends, and tell where you are going.
- Say what you are going to do, and ask your partner whether he or she wants to come along.

Estudiante 2
- Tell your partner that you are watching TV.
- Say that you like the show _____. Ask if he or she wants to watch.
- Say you think it's a good idea, and ask what your partner and his or her friends are doing there.
- Say no and tell your partner what you prefer to do.

TEACHING OPTIONS

Pairs Have pairs of students role-play an awful first date. Students should write their script first, then present it to the class. Encourage students to use descriptive adjectives as well as the new verbs learned in **Estructura 4.4**.

Heritage Speakers Ask heritage speakers to talk about a social custom in their cultural community. Remind them to use familiar vocabulary and simple sentences.

Charades Divide the class into small groups and have each group choose one student act out everyday actions. (You will need to provide cards or slips of paper with the actions.) The rest of the group will have a limited amount of time to guess the activities.

Communication 1.1, 1.2, 1.3

4 In-Class Tip Have students listen once and ask them to list the activities they hear. Let them compare their answers with a classmate and then check their lists by listening again.

4 Script *See the script for this activity on Interleaf page 25B.*

5 Virtual Chat Available online.

5 Expansion Ask volunteers to call out some of their answers. The class should speculate about the reason behind each answer and offer more information. Have the volunteer confirm or deny the speculation.
Ex: —Traigo mi tarea a clase.
—Eres un(a) buen(a) estudiante.
—Sí, soy un(a) buen(a) estudiante porque hago mi tarea.

6 In-Class Tip Before assigning the activity, provide an example of your own routine as a teacher, asking the students to help you write it.

6 Expansion Have students write reading comprehension questions about their paragraph. Have pairs of students read their routines to each other and then ask their questions.

Communication 1.1

7 Possible Conversation
E1: ¿Qué haces?
E2: Veo la tele.
E1: Supongo que ves *Los Simpson*.
E2: Sí. Me gusta el programa. ¿Quieres ver la tele conmigo?
E1: No puedo. Salgo con mis amigos a la plaza.
E2: Buena idea. ¿Qué hacen en la plaza?
E1: Vamos a escuchar música y a pasear. ¿Quieres venir?
E2: No. Prefiero descansar.

7 Partner Chat Available online.

Recapitulación

Review the grammar concepts you have learned in this lesson by completing these activities.

1 Completar
Complete the chart with the correct verb forms. **30 pts.**

Infinitive	yo	nosotros/as	ellos/as
volver	**vuelvo**	volvemos	vuelven
comenzar	comienzo	comenzamos	comienzan
hacer	hago	hacemos	hacen
ir	voy	vamos	van
jugar	juego	jugamos	juegan
repetir	repito	repetimos	**repiten**

2 Un día típico
Complete the paragraph with the appropriate forms of the verbs in the word list. Not all verbs will be used. Some may be used more than once. **30 pts.**

almorzar	ir	salir
cerrar	jugar	seguir
empezar	mostrar	ver
hacer	querer	volver

¡Hola! Me llamo Cecilia y vivo en Puerto Vallarta, México. ¿Cómo es un día típico en mi vida (*life*)? Por la mañana bebo café con mis padres y juntos (*together*) (1) **vemos** las noticias (*news*) en la televisión. A las siete y media, (yo) (2) **salgo** de mi casa y tomo el autobús. Me gusta llegar temprano (*early*) a la escuela porque siempre (*always*) (3) **veo** a mis amigos en la cafetería. Tomamos jugo y planeamos lo que (4) **queremos** hacer cada (*each*) día. A las ocho y cuarto, mi amiga Sandra y yo (5) **vamos** al laboratorio de lenguas. La clase de francés (6) **empieza** a las ocho y media. ¡Es mi clase favorita! A las doce y media (yo) (7) **almuerzo** en la cafetería con mis amigos. Después (*Afterwards*), yo (8) **sigo** con mis clases. Por las tardes, mis amigos (9) **vuelven** a sus casas, pero yo (10) **juego** al vóleibol con mi amigo Tomás.

RESUMEN GRAMATICAL

4.1 Present tense of *ir*   *p. 36*

yo	voy	nos.	vamos
tú	vas	vos.	vais
él	va	ellas	van

▶ ir a + [*infinitive*] = *to be going* + [*infinitive*]
▶ a + el = al
▶ vamos a + [*infinitive*] = *let's* (*do something*)

4.2 Stem-changing verbs e:ie, o:ue, u:ue   *pp. 39–40*

	empezar	volver	jugar
yo	emp**ie**zo	v**ue**lvo	j**ue**go
tú	emp**ie**zas	v**ue**lves	j**ue**gas
él	emp**ie**za	v**ue**lve	j**ue**ga
nos.	empezamos	volvemos	jugamos
vos.	empezáis	volvéis	jugáis
ellas	emp**ie**zan	v**ue**lven	j**ue**gan

▶ Other e:ie verbs: cerrar, comenzar, entender, pensar, perder, preferir, querer
▶ Other o:ue verbs: almorzar, contar, dormir, encontrar, mostrar, poder, recordar

4.3 Stem-changing verbs e:i   *p. 43*

pedir

yo	p**i**do	nos.	pedimos
tú	p**i**des	vos.	pedís
él	p**i**de	ellas	p**i**den

▶ Other e:i verbs: conseguir, decir, repetir, seguir

4.4 Verbs with irregular yo forms   *pp. 46–47*

hacer	poner	salir	suponer	traer
hago	pongo	salgo	supongo	traigo

▶ ver: veo, ves, ve, vemos, veis, ven
▶ oír: oigo, oyes, oye, oímos, oís, oyen

Los pasatiempos

3 **Oraciones** Arrange the cues provided in the correct order to form complete sentences. Make all necessary changes. **36 pts.**

1. tarea / los / hacer / sábados / nosotros / la
   Los sábados nosotros hacemos la tarea./Nosotros hacemos la tarea los sábados.
2. en / pizza / Andrés / una / restaurante / el / pedir
   Andrés pide una pizza en el restaurante.
3. a / ? / museo / ir / ¿ / el / (tú)
   ¿(Tú) Vas al museo?
4. de / oír / amigos / bien / los / no / Elena
   Los amigos de Elena no oyen bien./ No oímos bien a los amigos de Elena.
5. libros / traer / yo / clase / mis / a
   Yo traigo mis libros a clase.
6. película / ver / en / Jorge y Carlos / pensar / cine / una / el
   Jorge y Carlos piensan ver una película en el cine.
7. unos / escribir / Mariana / electrónicos / querer / mensajes
   Mariana quiere escribir unos mensajes electrónicos.
8. centro / conseguir / en / nosotros / el / videojuegos
   Nosotros conseguimos videojuegos en el centro.
9. tú / favores / el / pedir / tiempo / todo
   Tú pides favores todo el tiempo.

4 **Rima** Complete the rhyme with the appropriate forms of the correct verbs from the list. **4 pts.**

contar   poder
oír   suponer

"Si no ___puedes___ dormir
y el sueño deseas,
lo vas a conseguir
si ___cuentas___ ovejas°."

ovejas *sheep*

3 In-Class Tip To simplify, provide the first word for each sentence.

3 Expansion Give students these sentences as items 8–11: **8.** la / ? / ustedes / cerrar / ventana / ¿ / poder (¿Pueden ustedes cerrar la ventana?) **9.** cine / del / tú / las / salir / once / a (Tú sales del cine a las once.) **10.** el / conmigo / a / en / ellos / tenis / el / jugar / parque (Ellos juegan al tenis conmigo en el parque.) **11.** que / partido / mañana / un / decir / hay / Javier (Javier dice que hay un partido mañana.)

4 In-Class Tip Point out the inverted word order in line 2 of the rhyme and ask students what the phrase would be in everyday Spanish (**y deseas el sueño**).

4 Expansion Come up with similar rhymes and have students complete them. Ex: **Si no ____ descansar y diversión deseas, lo vas a encontrar si ____ con ellas.** (quieres, juegas)

TEACHING OPTIONS

Game Make a *Bingo* card of places at school or around town, such as libraries, cafeterias, movie theaters, and cafés. Give each student a card and model possible questions (Ex: for a cafeteria, ¿**Almuerzas en _____?/¿Dónde almuerzas?**). Encourage them to circulate around the room, asking only one question per person; if they get an affirmative answer, they should write that person's name in the square. The first student to complete a horizontal, vertical, or diagonal row and yell **¡Bingo!** is the winner.

Heritage Speakers Ask heritage speakers if counting sheep is common advice for sleeplessness in their families. Have them describe other insomnia remedies they have heard of or practiced.

4 adelante

Lectura

Antes de leer

> **Estrategia**
> **Predicting content from visuals**
>
> When you are reading in Spanish, be sure to look for visual clues that will orient you as to the content and purpose of what you are reading. Photos and illustrations, for example, will often give you a good idea of the main points that the reading covers. You may also encounter very helpful visuals that are used to summarize large amounts of data in a way that is easy to comprehend; these include bar graphs, pie charts, flow charts, lists of percentages, and other sorts of diagrams.

Examinar el texto
Take a quick look at the visual elements of the magazine article in order to generate a list of ideas about its content.

Contestar
Read the list of ideas you wrote in **Examinar el texto**, and look again at the visual elements of the magazine article. Then answer these questions:

1. Who is the woman in the photo, and what is her role? *María Úrsula Echevarría is the author of this article.*
2. What is the article about? *The article is about sports in the Hispanic world.*
3. What is the subject of the pie chart? *The most popular sports among college students.*
4. What is the subject of the bar graph? *Hispanic countries in world soccer championships.*

---

por María Úrsula Echevarría

El fútbol es el deporte más popular en el mundo° hispano, según° una encuesta° reciente realizada entre estudiantes de secundaria. Mucha gente practica este deporte y tiene un equipo de fútbol favorito. Cada cuatro años se realiza la Copa Mundial°. Argentina y Uruguay han ganado° este campeonato° más de una vez°. Los aficionados siguen los partidos de fútbol en casa por tele y en muchos otros lugares como bares, restaurantes, estadios y clubes deportivos. Los jóvenes juegan al fútbol con sus amigos en parques y gimnasios.

Países hispanos en campeonatos mundiales de fútbol (1930–2014)

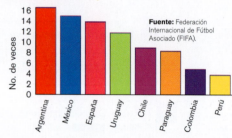

Fuente: Federación Internacional de Fútbol Asociado (FIFA).

Pero, por supuesto°, en los países de habla hispana también hay otros deportes populares. ¿Qué deporte sigue al fútbol en estos países? Bueno, ¡depende del país y de otros factores!

Después de leer

Evaluación y predicción
Which of the following sporting events would be most popular among the high school students surveyed? Rate them from one (most popular) to five (least popular). Which would be the most popular at your school?
Answers will vary.

_____ 1. la Copa Mundial de Fútbol

_____ 2. los Juegos Olímpicos

_____ 3. el Campeonato de Wimbledon

_____ 4. la Serie Mundial de Béisbol

_____ 5. el Tour de Francia

No sólo el fútbol

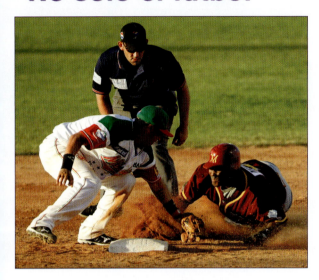

En Colombia, el béisbol también es muy popular después del fútbol, aunque° esto varía según la región del país. En la costa del norte de Colombia, el béisbol es una pasión. Y el ciclismo también es un deporte que los colombianos siguen con mucho interés.

Donde el béisbol es más popular
En los países del Caribe, el béisbol es el deporte predominante. Éste es el caso en Puerto Rico, Cuba y la República Dominicana. Los niños empiezan a jugar cuando son muy pequeños. En Puerto Rico y la República Dominicana, la gente también quiere participar en otros deportes, como el baloncesto, o ver los partidos en la tele. Y para los espectadores aficionados del Caribe, el boxeo es número dos.

Donde el fútbol es más popular
En México, el béisbol es el segundo° deporte más popular después° del fútbol. Pero en Argentina, después del fútbol, el rugby tiene mucha importancia. En Perú a la gente le gusta mucho ver partidos de vóleibol. ¿Y en España? Muchas personas prefieren el baloncesto, el tenis y el ciclismo.

Deportes más populares

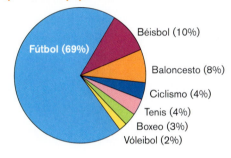

Fútbol (69%)
Béisbol (10%)
Baloncesto (8%)
Ciclismo (4%)
Tenis (4%)
Boxeo (3%)
Vóleibol (2%)

---

mundo *world* según *according to* encuesta *survey* se realiza la Copa Mundial *the World Cup is held* han ganado *have won* campeonato *championship* más de una vez *more than once* por supuesto *of course* segundo *second* después *after* aunque *although*

¿Cierto o falso?
Indicate whether each sentence is **cierto** or **falso**, then correct the false statements.

	Cierto	Falso
1. El vóleibol es el segundo deporte más popular en México. Es el béisbol.	○	●
2. En España a la gente le gustan varios deportes como el baloncesto y el ciclismo.	●	○
3. En la costa del norte de Colombia, el tenis es una pasión. El béisbol es una pasión.	○	●
4. En el Caribe, el deporte más popular es el béisbol.	●	○

Preguntas
Answer these questions in Spanish. Answers will vary.

1. ¿Dónde ven el fútbol los aficionados? Y tú, ¿cómo ves tus deportes favoritos?
2. ¿Te gusta el fútbol? ¿Por qué?
3. ¿Miras la Copa Mundial en la televisión?
4. ¿Qué deportes miras en la televisión?
5. En tu opinión, ¿cuáles son los tres deportes más populares en tu escuela? ¿En tu comunidad? ¿En tu país?
6. ¿Practicas deportes en tus ratos libres?

Section Goals

In **Escritura**, students will:
- write a pamphlet listing different events in their area
- integrate recreation-related vocabulary and structures taught in **Lección 4**

 Communication 1.3

Estrategia Explain that when students look up an English word in a Spanish-English dictionary, they will frequently find more than one definition. They must decide which one best fits the context. Discuss the meanings of *racket* that might be found in a Spanish-English dictionary and how the explanatory notes and abbreviations can be useful. Tell students that a good way to verify the meaning of a Spanish translation is to look it up and see the English translation.

Tema Discuss the three topics. You may want to introduce terms like **comité**, **guía de orientación**. Remind students of some common graphic features used in pamphlets: headings, times and places, brief events descriptions, and prices.

Successful Language Learning Tell students that they should resist the temptation to look up every unknown word. Advise them to guess the word's meaning based on context clues.

 Pre-AP®

Presentational Writing Remind students that they are writing with the purpose of attracting attendees to events and activities. Encourage them to brainstorm in Spanish as many details as possible about the activities that they are going to describe.

Teacher's Edition • Lesson Four

Escritura

Estrategia
Using a dictionary

A common mistake made by beginning language learners is to embrace the dictionary as the ultimate resource for reading, writing, and speaking. While it is true that the dictionary is a useful tool that can provide valuable information about vocabulary, using the dictionary correctly requires that you understand the elements of each entry.

If you glance at a Spanish-English dictionary, you will notice that its format is similar to that of an English dictionary. The word is listed first, usually followed by its pronunciation. Then come the definitions, organized by parts of speech. Sometimes the most frequently used definitions are listed first.

To find the best word for your needs, you should refer to the abbreviations and the explanatory notes that appear next to the entries. For example, imagine that you are writing about your pastimes. You want to write, "I want to buy a new racket for my match tomorrow," but you don't know the Spanish word for "racket." In the dictionary, you may find an entry like this:

> **racket** *s* **1**. alboroto; **2**. raqueta (*dep.*)

The abbreviation key at the front of the dictionary says that *s* corresponds to **sustantivo** (*noun*). Then, the first word you see is **alboroto**. The definition of **alboroto** is *noise* or *racket*, so **alboroto** is probably not the word you're looking for. The second word is **raqueta**, followed by the abbreviation *dep.*, which stands for **deportes**. This indicates that the word **raqueta** is the best choice for your needs.

Tema
Escribir un folleto

Choose one topic to write a brochure.   Answers will vary.

1. You are the head of the Homecoming Committee at your school this year. Create a pamphlet that lists events for Friday night, Saturday, and Sunday. Include a brief description of each event and its time and location. Include activities for different age groups, since some alumni will bring their families.

2. You are on the Freshman Student Orientation Committee and are in charge of creating a pamphlet for new students that describes the sports offered at your school. Write the flyer and include activities for both men and women.

3. You volunteer at your community's recreation center. It is your job to market your community to potential residents. Write a brief pamphlet that describes the recreational opportunities your community provides, the areas where the activities take place, and the costs, if any. Be sure to include activities that will appeal to singles as well as couples and families; you should include activities for all age groups and for both men and women.

EVALUATION: Folleto

Criteria	Scale
Appropriate details	1 2 3 4
Organization	1 2 3 4
Use of vocabulary	1 2 3 4
Grammatical accuracy	1 2 3 4
Mechanics	1 2 3 4

Scoring	
Excellent	18–20 points
Good	14–17 points
Satisfactory	10–13 points
Unsatisfactory	< 10 points

Escuchar

Estrategia
Listening for the gist

Listening for the general idea, or gist, can help you follow what someone is saying even if you can't hear or understand some of the words. When you listen for the gist, you simply try to capture the essence of what you hear without focusing on individual words.

🔊 To help you practice this strategy, you will listen to a paragraph made up of three sentences. Jot down a brief summary of what you hear.

Preparación

Based on the photo, what do you think Anabela is like? Do you and Anabela have similar interests?
Answers will vary.

Ahora escucha

You will hear first José talking, then Anabela. As you listen, check off each person's favorite activities.

Pasatiempos favoritos de José

1. ✔ leer el correo electrónico
2. ___ jugar al béisbol
3. ✔ ver películas de acción
4. ✔ ir al café
5. ✔ ir a partidos de béisbol
6. ___ ver películas románticas
7. ✔ dormir la siesta
8. ✔ escribir mensajes electrónicos

Pasatiempos favoritos de Anabela

9. ✔ esquiar
10. ✔ nadar
11. ✔ practicar el ciclismo
12. ✔ jugar al golf
13. ___ jugar al baloncesto
14. ___ ir a ver partidos de tenis
15. ✔ escalar montañas
16. ___ ver televisión

Comprensión

Preguntas
Answer these questions about José's and Anabela's pastimes.

1. ¿Quién practica más deportes? *Anabela*
2. ¿Quién piensa que es importante descansar? *José*
3. ¿A qué deporte es aficionado José? *Le gusta el béisbol.*
4. ¿Por qué Anabela no practica el baloncesto? *Ella no es alta.*
5. ¿Qué películas le gustan a la novia de José? *Le gustan las películas románticas.*
6. ¿Cuál es el deporte favorito de Anabela? *el ciclismo*

Seleccionar
Which person do these statements best describe?

1. Le gusta practicar deportes. *Anabela*
2. Prefiere las películas de acción. *José*
3. Le gustan las computadoras. *José*
4. Le gusta nadar. *Anabela*
5. Siempre (*Always*) duerme una siesta por la tarde. *José*
6. Quiere ir de vacaciones a las montañas. *Anabela*

---

pero también estudio mucho y necesito diversión. Aunque prefiero practicar el ciclismo, me gustan mucho la natación, el tenis, el golf… bueno, en realidad todos los deportes. No, eso no es cierto; no juego al baloncesto porque no soy alta. Para mis vacaciones, quiero esquiar o escalar la montaña, depende si nieva. Suena divertido, ¿no?

Section Goals
In **Escuchar**, students will:
- listen to and summarize a short paragraph
- learn the strategy of listening for the gist
- answer questions based on the content of a recorded conversation

Communication 1.2

Estrategia
Script Buenas tardes y bienvenidos a la clase de español. En esta clase van a escuchar, escribir y conversar en cada clase, y ustedes también deben estudiar y practicar todos los días. Ahora encuentran el español difícil, pero cuando termine el curso van a comprender y comunicarse bien en español.

In-Class Tip
Have students look at the photo and write a short paragraph describing what they see. Guide them in saying what **Anabela** is like and guessing what her favorite pastimes might be.

Preguntas Students can submit this activity online. Their paragraphs will appear in your gradebook.

Ahora escucha
Script JOSÉ: No me gusta practicar deportes, pero sí tengo muchos pasatiempos. Me gusta mucho escribir y recibir correo electrónico. Me gusta también ir con mis amigos a mi café favorito. Siempre duermo una siesta por la tarde. A veces voy a ver un partido de béisbol. Me gusta mucho ver películas de acción pero mi novia prefiere las de romance… y por lo tanto veo muchas películas de romance.
ANABELA: Todos mis parientes dicen que soy demasiado activa. Soy aficionada a los deportes,

(Script continues at far left in the bottom panels.)

Section Goals

In **En pantalla**, students will:
- read about extreme sports
- watch an excerpt from the documentary **Ejes** (*Axis*), about bikers and skaters in Spain.

Communication 1.1, 1.2, 1.3
Cultures 2.1
Connections 3.1
Comparisons 4.2
Communities 5.1

Teacher Resources
Read the front matter for suggestions on how to incorporate all the program's components. See pages 25A–25B for a detailed listing of Teacher Resources online.

 Pre-AP®

Audiovisual interpretive Communication
Antes de ver Strategy
Explain to students that they do not need to understand every word they hear, but rely on visual clues and cognates.

Comprensión
Have students correct the false statements. **(1. A Diego le gusta la patineta/patinar. 3. Pequesaurio prefiere la bicicleta.)**

Aplicación
Students can also prepare this presentation as an informational brochure or video that helps to promote the message of encouraging participation in sports at an early age.

en pantalla

Ejes

Preparación
Answer these questions in English. *Answers will vary.*
1. What role do sports play in your life? Which sports do you enjoy? Why?
2. Is there a sport you enjoy with other members of your family? With a group of friends? Is there a special season for that sport?

Más que un deporte
For many, extreme sports aren't just games but an art form and a lifestyle. BMX, skateboarding, surfing, and other sports are passions for many young men and women who, in search of speed and adrenaline, make their bikes and boards the center of their lives. Communities around the world are responding to the demand for extreme sports by constructing bike and skate parks, and Spanish-speaking countries are no exception. The UCI BMX World Championship was held in Medellín in 2016. Colombian Olympic Gold Medalist Mariana Pajón has won gold at the games three times (2011, 2014, 2016). Argentinian professional BMX cyclist Gabriela Díaz won the championship in 2001, 2002, and 2004.

Me quedo con la bici I stay with the bike

A mí me gusta la bici y me quedo con la bici°.

Vocabulario útil
andar	go
bici	bike
callejón	alley
campeonato	championship
conocer	to be acquainted with
molar	be cool
rampas	ramps

Comprensión
Indicate whether each statement is **cierto** or **falso**.

	Cierto	Falso
1. A Diego le gusta la bici.	○	●
2. Sarini cree que patinar es un arte.	●	○
3. Pequesaurio prefiere la patineta.	○	●
4. A Pequesaurio le gusta la rampa.	●	○

 ### Conversación
Answers will vary.
With a partner, discuss these questions in Spanish.
1. ¿Qué deportes se pueden practicar fácilmente en tu comunidad? ¿Qué deportes son fomentados (*encouraged*) en tu comunidad?
2. ¿Cuál es la diferencia entre un deporte y un juego? ¿Cuál es la diferencia entre un deporte y un deporte extremo?

 ### Aplicación
Participation in sports and other physical activities is important for one's well-being. With two classmates, prepare an oral presentation for your community. Your objective is to convince families and communities to encourage participation in sports among kids from an early age. Include illustrations in your presentation. *Answers will vary.*

TEACHING OPTIONS

Language Notes In its normal usage, **andar** means *to walk*. However, in many cases, **andar** can mean *to travel* or *to go*: **Ando en bicicleta para ir a la escuela**. In some cases, **andar** can be followed by a gerund to form a continuous tense: **Mi hermano anda estudiando mucho**. Sometimes it is a synonym of **estar**: **Mi madre siempre anda muy ocupada**. Note that **andar** is irregular in the indicative preterite and the past subjunctive tenses. The verb **molar** is used to express that something is cool: **La bici mola**. It can also be conjugated like the verb **gustar**: **¿Te mola el rap?** It is mainly used in Spain. **¡Cómo mola!**

Los pasatiempos

¡Fútbol en España!

The rivalry between the teams **Real Madrid** and **FC Barcelona** is perhaps the fiercest in all of soccer—just imagine if they occupied the same city! Well, each team also has competing clubs within its respective city: Spain's capital has the **Club Atlético de Madrid**, and Barcelona is home to **Espanyol**. In fact, across the Spanish-speaking world, it is common for a city to have more than one professional team, often with strikingly dissimilar origins, identity, and fan base. For example, in Bogotá, the **Millonarios** were so named for the large sums spent on players, while the **Santa Fe** team is one of the most traditional in Colombian soccer. **River Plate** and **Boca Juniors**, who enjoy a famous rivalry, are just two of twenty-four clubs in Buenos Aires—the city with the most professional soccer teams in the world.

Vocabulario útil

afición	fans
celebran	they celebrate
preferido/a	favorite
rivalidad	rivalry
se junta con	it's tied up with

Preparación

What is the most popular sport at your school? What teams are your rivals? How do students celebrate a win?

Answers will vary.

Escoger

Select the correct answer.

1. Un partido entre el Barça y el Real Madrid es un ___evento___ (deporte/evento) importante en toda España.
2. Los aficionados ___celebran___ (miran/celebran) las victorias de sus equipos en las calles (*streets*).
3. La rivalidad entre el Real Madrid y el Barça está relacionada con la ___política___ (religión/política).

(Hay mucha afición al fútbol en España.)

¿Y cuál es vuestro jugador favorito?

—¿Y quién va a ganar?
—El Real Madrid.

TEACHING OPTIONS

Small Groups In small groups, have students research one of the teams on this page. Have them focus on the team's key players, colors, team song (**himno**), any historical or political points of interest, and its fan base. Have groups present their findings to the class.

Heritage Speakers Ask heritage speakers to share their experiences with soccer as they were growing up. Ask them to discuss whether they played/watched formal or informal matches, whether girls were allowed or expected to play, and if they would watch soccer in their household and celebrate wins.

4 panorama

México

El país en cifras

▸ **Área:** 1.972.550 km^2 (761.603 millas^2), casi° tres veces° el área de Texas

La situación geográfica de México, al sur° de los Estados Unidos, ha influido en° la economía y la sociedad de los dos países. Una de las consecuencias es la emigración de la población mexicana al país vecino°. Hoy día, más de 33 millones de personas de ascendencia mexicana viven en los Estados Unidos.

▸ **Población:** 118.818.000
▸ **Capital:** México, D.F. (y su área metropolitana)—19.319.000
▸ **Ciudades principales:** Guadalajara —4.338.000, Monterrey—3.838.000, Puebla—2.278.000, Ciudad Juárez—1.321.000
▸ **Moneda:** peso mexicano
▸ **Idiomas:** español (oficial), náhuatl, otras lenguas indígenas

Bandera de México

Mexicanos célebres
▸ **Benito Juárez,** héroe nacional (1806–1872)
▸ **Octavio Paz,** poeta (1914–1998)
▸ **Elena Poniatowska,** periodista y escritora (1932–)
▸ **Mario Molina,** Premio Nobel de Química, 1995; químico (1943–)
▸ **Paulina Rubio,** cantante (1971–)

casi *almost* veces *times* sur *south* ha influido en *has influenced* vecino *neighboring* se llenan de luz *get filled with light* flores *flowers* Muertos *Dead* se ríen *laugh* muerte *death* lo cual se refleja *which is reflected* calaveras de azúcar *sugar skulls* pan *bread* huesos *bones*

¡Increíble pero cierto!

Cada dos de noviembre los cementerios de México se llenan de luz°, música y flores°. El Día de Muertos° no es un evento triste; es una fiesta en honor a las personas muertas. En ese día, los mexicanos se ríen° de la muerte°, lo cual se refleja° en detalles como las calaveras de azúcar° y el pan° de muerto —pan en forma de huesos°.

Cabo San Lucas

ESTADOS UNIDOS

Autorretrato con mono (Self-portrait with monkey), 1938, Frida Kahlo

Ciudad Juárez

Río Grande / Río Bravo del Norte

Golfo de California

Baja California

Sierra Madre Oriental

Sierra Madre Occidental

ESTADOS UNIDOS
MÉXICO
OCÉANO ATLÁNTICO
OCÉANO PACÍFICO
AMÉRICA DEL SUR

Monterrey

Océano Pacífico

Puerto Vallarta

Ciudad de México

Guadalajara

Puebla

Acapulco

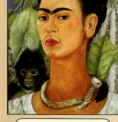
Artesanías en Taxco, Guerrero

Pirámide de Kukulcán en Chichén Itzá

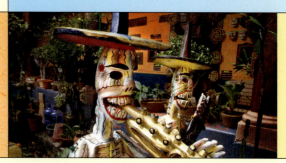

Section Goals

In **Panorama**, students will read about:
- the geography, history, economy, and culture of Mexico
- Mexico's relationship with the United States

Communication 1.3
Cultures 2.1, 2.2
Connections 3.1, 3.2
Comparisons 4.2

Teacher Resources
Read the front matter for suggestions on how to incorporate all the program's components. See pages 25A–25B for a detailed listing of Teacher Resources online.

In-Class Tips
- Use the **Lección 4 Panorama** online Resources to assist with this presentation.
- Have students look at the map of Mexico. Ask them questions about the locations of cities and natural features of Mexico. Ex: **¿Dónde está la capital? (en el centro del país)**

El país en cifras
Ask questions related to section content. Ex: After looking at the map, ask: **¿Qué ciudad mexicana está en la frontera con El Paso, Texas? (Ciudad Juárez)** Ask students if they can name other sister cities **(ciudades hermanas)** on the Mexico-U.S. border. (Tijuana/San Diego, Calexico/Mexicali, Laredo/Nuevo Laredo, etc.)

¡Increíble pero cierto!
Mexico's **Día de Muertos**, like many holidays in Latin America, blends indigenous and Catholic practices. The date coincides with the Catholic All Saints' Day; however, the holiday's indigenous origins are evident in the gravesite offerings, **el pan de muertos**, and the belief that on this day the deceased can communicate with the living.

TEACHING OPTIONS

Extra Practice Mexico is a large and diverse nation, with many regions and regional cultures. Have students select a region that interests them, research it, and present a short oral report to the class. Encourage them to include information about the cities, art, history, geography, customs, and cuisine of the region.

Small Groups Many of the dishes that distinguish Mexican cuisine have pre-Hispanic origins. To these native dishes have been added elements of Spanish and French cuisines, making Mexican food, like Mexican civilization, a dynamic mix of ingredients. Have groups of students research recipes that exemplify this fusion of cultures. Have each group describe one recipe's origins to the class.

58 Teacher's Edition • Lesson Four

Ciudades • México, D.F.

La Ciudad de México, fundada° en 1525, también se llama el D.F. o Distrito Federal. Muchos turistas e inmigrantes vienen a la ciudad porque es el centro cultural y económico del país. El crecimiento° de la población es de los más altos° del mundo. El D.F. tiene una población mayor que las de Nueva York, Madrid o París.

Artes • Diego Rivera y Frida Kahlo

Frida Kahlo y Diego Rivera eran° artistas mexicanos muy famosos. Se casaron° en 1929. Los dos se interesaron° en las condiciones sociales de la gente indígena de su país. Puedes ver algunas° de sus obras° en el Museo de Arte Moderno de la Ciudad de México.

Historia • Los aztecas

Los aztecas dominaron° en México del siglo° XIV al siglo XVI. Sus canales, puentes° y pirámides con templos religiosos eran muy importantes. El fin del imperio azteca comenzó° con la llegada° de los españoles en 1519, pero la presencia azteca sigue hoy. La Ciudad de México está situada en la capital azteca de Tenochtitlán, y muchos turistas van a visitar sus ruinas.

Economía • La plata

México es el mayor productor de plata° del mundo°. Estados como Zacatecas y Durango tienen ciudades fundadas cerca de los más grandes yacimientos° de plata del país. Estas ciudades fueron° en la época colonial unas de las más ricas e importantes. Hoy en día, aún° conservan mucho de su encanto° y esplendor.

¿Qué aprendiste? Responde a cada pregunta con una oración completa.

1. ¿Qué lenguas hablan los mexicanos?
   Los mexicanos hablan español y lenguas indígenas.
2. ¿Cómo es la población del D.F. en comparación con la de otras ciudades?
   La población del D.F. es mayor.
3. ¿En qué se interesaron Frida Kahlo y Diego Rivera? Se interesaron en las condiciones sociales de la gente indígena de su país.
4. Nombra algunas de las estructuras de la arquitectura azteca. Hay canales, puentes y pirámides con templos religiosos.
5. ¿Dónde está situada la capital de México?
   Está situada en la capital azteca de Tenochtitlán.
6. ¿Qué estados de México tienen los mayores yacimientos de plata? Zacatecas y Durango tienen los mayores yacimientos de plata.

Conexión Internet Investiga estos temas en Internet.

1. Busca información sobre dos lugares de México. ¿Te gustaría (*Would you like*) vivir allí? ¿Por qué?
2. Busca información sobre dos artistas mexicanos. ¿Cómo se llaman sus obras más famosas?

---

fundada *founded* crecimiento *growth* más altos *highest* eran *were* Se casaron *They got married* se interesaron *were interested* algunas *some* obras *works* dominaron *dominated* siglo *century* puentes *bridges* comenzó *started* llegada *arrival* plata *silver* mundo *world* yacimientos *deposits* fueron *were* aún *still* encanto *charm*

vocabulario

Comparisons 4.1

Teacher Resources
Read the front matter for suggestions on how to incorporate all the program's components. See pages 25A–25B for a detailed listing of Teacher Resources online.

In-Class Tip Ask students to prepare a list of the three products or perspectives they learned about in this lesson to share with the class. You may ask them to focus specifically on the **Cultura** and **Panorama** sections.

Pasatiempos

andar en patineta	to skateboard
bucear	to scuba dive
escalar montañas (*f., pl.*)	to climb mountains
escribir una carta	to write a letter
escribir un mensaje electrónico	to write an e-mail
esquiar	to ski
ganar	to win
ir de excursión	to go on a hike
leer el correo electrónico	to read e-mail
leer un periódico	to read a newspaper
leer una revista	to read a magazine
nadar	to swim
pasear	to take a walk
pasear en bicicleta	to ride a bicycle
patinar (en línea)	to (inline) skate
practicar deportes (*m., pl.*)	to play sports
tomar el sol	to sunbathe
ver películas (*f., pl.*)	to watch movies
visitar monumentos (*m., pl.*)	to visit monuments
la diversión	fun activity; entertainment; recreation
el fin de semana	weekend
el pasatiempo	pastime; hobby
los ratos libres	spare (free) time
el videojuego	video game

Deportes

el baloncesto	basketball
el béisbol	baseball
el ciclismo	cycling
el equipo	team
el esquí (acuático)	(water) skiing
el fútbol	soccer
el fútbol americano	football
el golf	golf
el hockey	hockey
el/la jugador(a)	player
la natación	swimming
el partido	game; match
la pelota	ball
el tenis	tennis
el vóleibol	volleyball

Adjetivos

deportivo/a	sports-related
favorito/a	favorite

Lugares

el café	café
el centro	downtown
el cine	movie theater
el gimnasio	gymnasium
la iglesia	church
el lugar	place
el museo	museum
el parque	park
la piscina	swimming pool
la plaza	city or town square
el restaurante	restaurant

Verbos

almorzar (o:ue)	to have lunch
cerrar (e:ie)	to close
comenzar (e:ie)	to begin
conseguir (e:i)	to get; to obtain
contar (o:ue)	to count; to tell
decir (e:i)	to say; to tell
dormir (o:ue)	to sleep
empezar (e:ie)	to begin
encontrar (o:ue)	to find
entender (e:ie)	to understand
hacer	to do; to make
ir	to go
jugar (u:ue)	to play (a sport or a game)
mostrar (o:ue)	to show
oír	to hear
pedir (e:i)	to ask for; to request
pensar (e:ie)	to think
pensar (+ *inf.*)	to intend
pensar en	to think about
perder (e:ie)	to lose; to miss
poder (o:ue)	to be able to; can
poner	to put; to place
preferir (e:ie)	to prefer
querer (e:ie)	to want; to love
recordar (o:ue)	to remember
repetir (e:i)	to repeat
salir	to leave
seguir (e:i)	to follow; to continue
suponer	to suppose
traer	to bring
ver	to see
volver (o:ue)	to return

Decir expressions	See page 46.
Expresiones útiles	See page 31.

Lección 5: Teacher Resources

There is a wealth of resources online to support instruction using **Senderos**. For details on how to integrate these Teacher Resources into your lessons, see the front matter of this Teacher's Edition on pages T14 to T48.

Presentation	Practice & Communicate	Assess*	Scripts and Translations	

• Digital Images:
  • **Las vacaciones**
  • **Las estaciones**
  • **El tiempo**
	• Information Gap Activities*
	• Activity Pack Practice Activities (with Answer Key): **Contextos**
	• Additional Vocabulary (**Más vocabulario para las vacaciones**)
	• Digital Image Bank (Travel)
	• Surveys: Worksheet for classroom survey
		• Vocabulary Quiz (with Answer Key)		**contextos**

		• **Fotonovela** Optional Testing Sections (with Answer Key)	• **Fotonovela** Videoscript • **Fotonovela** English Translation	**fotonovela**
• **Estructura 5.1** Grammar Slides	• Information Gap Activities* • Activity Pack Practice Activities (with Answer Key): **Estar** with conditions and emotions	• Grammar 5.1 Quiz (with Answer Key)	• Tutorial Script: **Estar** with conditions and emotions	**estructura**
• **Estructura 5.2** Grammar Slides	• Information Gap Activities* • Activity Pack Practice Activities (with Answer Key): The present progressive	• Grammar 5.2 Quiz (with Answer Key)	• Tutorial Script: The present progressive	
• **Estructura 5.3** Grammar Slides	• Activity Pack Practice Activities (with Answer Key): **Ser** and **estar**	• Grammar 5.3 Quiz (with Answer Key)	• Tutorial Script: **Ser** and **estar**	
• **Estructura 5.4** Grammar Slides	• Activity Pack Practice Activities (with Answer Key): Direct object nouns and pronouns	• Grammar 5.4 Quiz (with Answer Key)	• Tutorial Script: Direct object nouns and pronouns	
			• **En pantalla** Videoscript • **En pantalla** English Translation	**En pantalla** / **adelante**
		• **Flash cultura** Optional Testing Sections (with Answer Key)	• **Flash cultura** Videoscript • **Flash cultura** English Translation	**Flash cultura**
Digital Images: • **Puerto Rico**		• **Panorama** Optional Testing Sections (with Answer Key) • **Panorama cultural** (video)	• **Panorama cultural** Videoscript • **Panorama cultural** English Translation	**Panorama**

*Can also be assigned online.

Lección 5: Teacher Resources

Pulling It All Together

Practice and Communicate
- Role-plays
- Activity Pack Practice Activities (¡A repasar!) (with Answer Key)

Assessment

Tests and Exams*
- **Prueba A** with audio
- **Prueba B** with audio
- **Prueba C** with audio
- **Prueba D** with audio
- **Prueba E** with audio
- **Prueba F** with audio
- Tests Answer Key
- Oral Testing Suggestions
- **Examen A** with audio (lessons 4-6)
- **Examen B** with audio (lessons 4-6)
- Exams Answer Key

Audioscripts
- Tests and Exams Audioscripts
- Alternative Listening Sections Audioscript

Additional Tools for Planning and Teaching

- Essential Questions
- I Can Worksheets
- IPAs & Rubrics
- Lesson Plans
- Middle School Activity Pack
- Pacing Guides

Audio MP3s for Classroom Activities

- **Contextos. Práctica**: Activities 1 and 2 (p. 63)
- **Contextos. Comunicación**: Activity 12 (p. 67)
- **Estructura 5.3. Comunicación**: Activity 4 (p. 83)
- **Estructura 5.4. Comunicación**: Activity 4 (p. 87)
- **Escuchar** (p. 93)

Script for Comunicación: Actividad 12 (p. 67)

Agente de viajes	Buenas tardes. ¿Qué desea?
Sr. Vega	Quiero ir de vacaciones a un lugar interesante y bonito.
Agente de viajes	¿Qué le gusta hacer? ¿Acampar? ¿Esquiar? ¿Bucear?
Sr. Vega	Me gusta pescar y montar a caballo.
Agente de viajes	¿Por qué no va a las montañas?
Sr. Vega	No, gracias. Prefiero ir a un lugar donde hace calor.
Agente de viajes	¿Qué tal Puerto Rico? Puerto Rico tiene muchas playas bonitas. Puede pescar, montar a caballo, nadar, bucear e ir de compras.
Sr. Vega	¿Cuánto cuesta el hotel en Puerto Rico?
Agente de viajes	Voy a ver en la computadora. ¿Cuándo quiere ir?
Sr. Vega	La primera semana de marzo.
Agente de viajes	Pues, hay Las Tres Palmas. Es un hotel de segunda categoría. Tiene restaurante, piscina y jacuzzi. También está muy cerca a la playa. Una habitación individual cuesta ochenta y cinco dólares la noche. ¿Hago una reservación?
Sr. Vega	Sí, por favor, por cinco noches.

Script for Comunicación: Actividad 4 (p. 83)

¡Hola! Me llamo Carolina y ahora estoy de vacaciones en Ponce. Ponce es la segunda ciudad más grande de Puerto Rico. Está cerca del mar Caribe y es una ciudad muy bonita. Hoy no voy a la playa porque está lloviendo. Esperaba visitar el Parque de Bombas, que es ahora un museo, pero hoy es martes y está cerrado. Así que voy a visitar el Museo de Arte. Oigo que tiene una colección fenomenal de pinturas.

Script for Comunicación: Actividad 4 (p. 87)

Mercedes	Gabriel, ¿necesitas un pasaporte para tu viaje?
Gabriel	No, no lo necesito.
Mercedes	¿Tienes que comprar un pasaje de ida y vuelta?
Gabriel	Sí, tengo que comprarlo.
Mercedes	¿Vas a llevar tu tabla de surf?
Gabriel	Sí, la voy a llevar.
Mercedes	¿Qué más vas a hacer?
Gabriel	Voy a nadar en el mar y tomar el sol.
Mercedes	Ah, tienes suerte. Aquí va a nevar.

*Tests and Exams can also be assigned online.

Las vacaciones

5

Communicative Goals

You will learn how to:
- Discuss and plan a vacation
- Describe a hotel
- Talk about how you feel
- Talk about the seasons and the weather

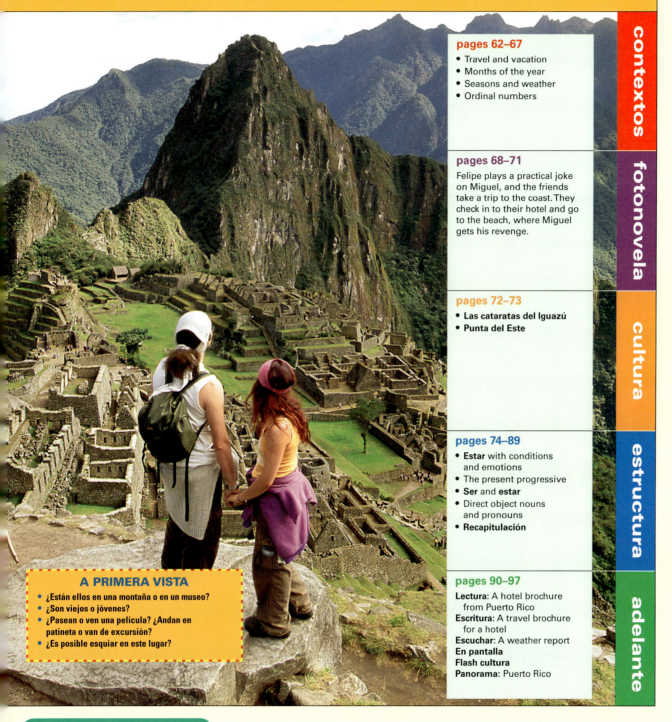

A PRIMERA VISTA
- ¿Están ellos en una montaña o en un museo?
- ¿Son viejos o jóvenes?
- ¿Pasean o ven una película? ¿Andan en patineta o van de excursión?
- ¿Es posible esquiar en este lugar?

contextos
pages 62–67
- Travel and vacation
- Months of the year
- Seasons and weather
- Ordinal numbers

fotonovela
pages 68–71
Felipe plays a practical joke on Miguel, and the friends take a trip to the coast. They check in to their hotel and go to the beach, where Miguel gets his revenge.

cultura
pages 72–73
- Las cataratas del Iguazú
- Punta del Este

estructura
pages 74–89
- Estar with conditions and emotions
- The present progressive
- Ser and estar
- Direct object nouns and pronouns
- Recapitulación

adelante
pages 90–97
Lectura: A hotel brochure from Puerto Rico
Escritura: A travel brochure for a hotel
Escuchar: A weather report
En pantalla
Flash cultura
Panorama: Puerto Rico

Lesson Goals
In **Lección 5**, students will be introduced to the following:
- terms for traveling and vacations
- seasons and months
- weather expressions
- ordinal numbers (1st–10th)
- **Las cataratas del Iguazú**
- **Punta del Este**, Uruguay
- **estar** with conditions and emotions
- adjectives for conditions and emotions
- present progressive of regular and irregular verbs
- comparison of the uses of **ser** and **estar**
- direct object nouns and pronouns
- personal **a**
- scanning to find specific information
- making an outline
- writing a brochure for a hotel
- listening for key words
- an ad for **LANPASS**, a Chilean airline loyalty program
- a video about **Machu Picchu**
- cultural, geographic, and historical information about Puerto Rico

A primera vista Here are some additional questions you can ask to personalize the photo: ¿Dónde te gusta pasar tus ratos libres? ¿Qué haces en tus ratos libres? ¿Te gusta explorar otras culturas? ¿Te gusta viajar a otros países? ¿Adónde quieres ir en las próximas vacaciones?

Teaching Tip Look for these icons for additional communicative practice:

→🏃←	Interpretive communication
←🏃→	Presentational communication
🏃↔🏃	Interpersonal communication

SUPPORT FOR BACKWARD DESIGN

Lección 5 Essential Questions
1. How do people discuss and plan a vacation?
2. How do people talk about how they feel?
3. What are some popular vacation destinations in the Spanish-speaking world and why?

Lección 5 Integrated Performance Assessment
Before teaching this chapter, review the Integrated Performance Assessment (IPA) and its accompanying scoring rubric. Use the IPA to assess students' progress toward proficiency targets at the end of the chapter. **IPA Context**: Six students from your Spanish class will be chosen to spend a week in Puerto Rico, at the **Hotel Vistahermosa** in Lajas. Students will be chosen in pairs based on their presentation to the selection committee.

 Voice boards online allow you and your students to record and share up to five minutes of audio. Use voice boards for presentations, oral assessments, discussions, directions, etc.

Section Goals

In **Contextos**, students will learn and practice:
- travel- and vacation-related vocabulary
- seasons and months of the year
- weather expressions
- ordinal numbers

 Communication 1.2
Comparisons 4.1

Teacher Resources
Read the front matter for suggestions on how to incorporate all the program's components. See pages 61A–61B for a detailed listing of Teacher Resources online.

In-Class Tips
- Ask: **¿A quién le gusta mucho viajar? ¿Cómo prefieres viajar?** Introduce cognates as suggestions: **¿Te gusta viajar en auto?** Write each term on the board as you say it. Ask: **¿Adónde te gusta viajar? ¿A México?** Ask students about their classmates' statements: **¿Adónde le gusta viajar a _____? ¿Cómo puede viajar?**
- Ask questions about transportation in your community. Ex: **Si quiero ir de la escuela al aeropuerto, ¿cómo puedo ir?** Ask what type of transportation students use to go home on school break.
- Use the **Lección 5 Contextos** vocabulary presentation online or the digital images in the Resources online to assist with this presentation.
- Give students two minutes to review the four scenes and then ask questions. Ex: **¿Quién trabaja en una agencia de viajes? (el/la agente de viajes)**

Note: At this point you may want to present *Vocabulario adicional: Más vocabulario para las vacaciones* from the online Resources.

5 contextos

Las vacaciones

Más vocabulario

la cama	bed
la habitación individual, doble	single, double room
el piso	floor (of a building)
la planta baja	ground floor
el campo	countryside
el paisaje	landscape
el equipaje	luggage
la estación de autobuses, del metro, de tren	bus, subway, train station
la llegada	arrival
el pasaje (de ida y vuelta)	(round-trip) ticket
la salida	departure; exit
la tabla de (wind)surf	surfboard/sailboard
acampar	to camp
estar de vacaciones	to be on vacation
hacer las maletas	to pack (one's suitcases)
hacer un viaje	to take a trip
hacer (wind)surf	to (wind)surf
ir de compras	to go shopping
ir de vacaciones	to go on vacation
ir en autobús (m.), auto(móvil) (m.), motocicleta (f.), taxi (m.)	to go by bus, car, motorcycle, taxi

Variación léxica

automóvil ↔ coche (*Esp.*), carro (*Amér. L.*)
autobús ↔ camión (*Méx.*), guagua (*Caribe*)
motocicleta ↔ moto (*coloquial*)

En la agencia de viajes

En el hotel

TEACHING OPTIONS

Extra Practice Ask questions about the people, places, and activities in **Contextos**. Ex: **¿Qué actividades pueden hacer los turistas en una playa? ¿Pueden nadar? ¿Tomar el sol? ¿Sacar fotos?** Then expand questions to ask students what they specifically do at these places. _____, **¿qué haces tú cuando vas a la playa?** Students should respond in complete sentences.

Variación léxica Point out that these are just some of the different Spanish names for vehicles. Ask heritage speakers if they are familiar with other terms. While some of these terms are mutually understood in different regions (**el coche, el carro, el auto, el automóvil**), others are specific to a region and may not be understood by others (**la guagua, el camión**). Stress that the feminine article **la** is used with the abbreviation **moto**.

En el aeropuerto

En la playa

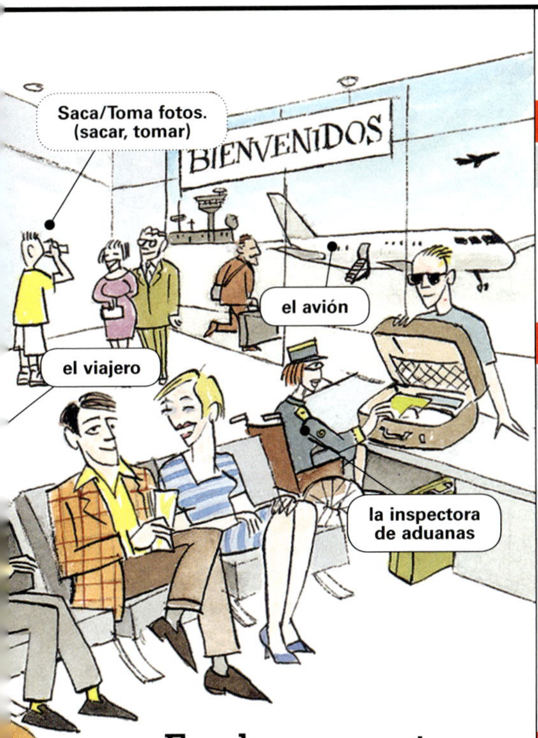

Práctica

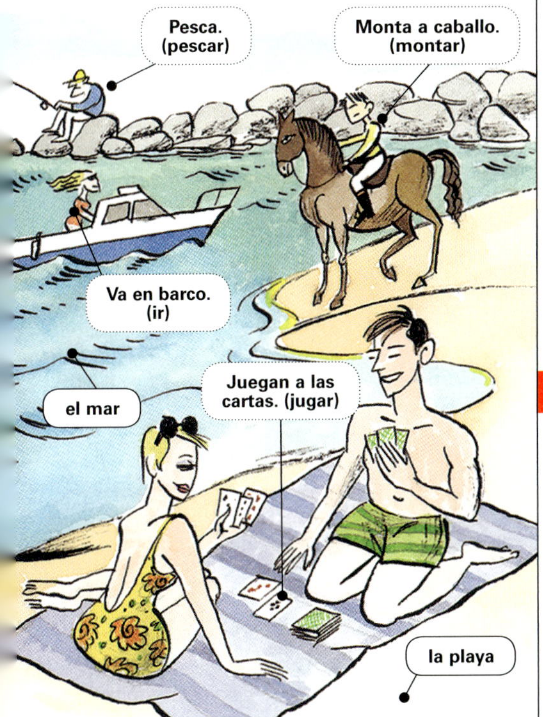

1 Escuchar Indicate who would probably make each statement you hear. Each answer is used twice.

a. el agente de viajes
b. el inspector de aduanas
c. un empleado del hotel

1. a
2. a
3. c
4. b
5. c
6. b

2 ¿Cierto o falso? Mario and his wife, Natalia, are planning their next vacation with a travel agent. Indicate whether each statement is **cierto** or **falso** according to what you hear in the conversation.

	Cierto	Falso
1. Mario y Natalia están en Puerto Rico.	○	✓
2. Ellos quieren hacer un viaje a Puerto Rico.	✓	○
3. Natalia prefiere ir a la montaña.	○	✓
4. Mario quiere pescar en Puerto Rico.	✓	○
5. La agente de viajes va a confirmar la reservación.	✓	○

3 Escoger Choose the best answer for each sentence.

1. Un huésped es una persona que __b__.
   a. toma fotos b. está en un hotel c. pesca en el mar
2. Abrimos la puerta con __a__.
   a. una llave b. un caballo c. una llegada
3. Enrique tiene __a__ porque va a viajar a otro (*another*) país.
   a. un pasaporte b. una foto c. una llegada
4. Antes de (*Before*) ir de vacaciones, hay que __c__.
   a. pescar b. ir en tren c. hacer las maletas
5. Nosotros vamos en __a__ al aeropuerto.
   a. autobús b. pasaje c. viajero
6. Me gusta mucho ir al campo. El __a__ es increíble.
   a. paisaje b. pasaje c. equipaje

4 Analogías Complete the analogies using the words below. Two words will not be used.

auto	huésped	mar	sacar
empleado	llegada	pasaporte	tren

1. acampar → campo = pescar → mar
2. agencia de viajes → agente = hotel → empleado
3. llave → habitación = pasaje → tren
4. estudiante → libro = turista → pasaporte
5. aeropuerto → viajero = hotel → huésped
6. maleta → hacer = foto → sacar

Communication 1.1, 1.2

1 Expansion In pairs, have students select one of the statements they hear and then write a conversation based on it.

1 Script 1. ¡Deben ir a Puerto Rico! Allí hay unas playas muy hermosas y pueden acampar. 2. Deben llamarme el lunes para confirmar la reservación. *Script continues on page 64.*

2 Expansion To challenge students, give them these true/false statements as items 6–9: **6. Mario prefiere una habitación doble. (Cierto.) 7. Natalia no quiere ir a la playa. (Falso.) 8. El hotel está en la playa. (Cierto.) 9. Mario va a montar a caballo. (Falso.)**

2 Script MARIO: Queremos ir de vacaciones a Puerto Rico. AGENTE: ¿Desean hacer un viaje al campo? NATALIA: Yo quiero ir a la playa. M: Pues, yo prefiero una habitación doble en un hotel con un buen paisaje. A: Puedo reservar para ustedes una habitación en el hotel San Juan que está en la playa. M: Es una buena idea, así yo voy a pescar y tú vas a montar a caballo. N: Muy bien, ¿puede confirmar la reservación? A: Claro que sí.

3 Expansion Ask a volunteer to help you model making statements similar to item 1. Say: **Un turista es una persona que… (va de vacaciones).** Then ask volunteers to do the same with **una agente de viajes, una inspectora de aduanas, un empleado de hotel.**

4 In-Class Tip Present these items using the following formula: ***Acampar* tiene la misma relación con *campo* que *pescar* tiene con… (*mar*).**

TEACHING OPTIONS

Small Groups Have students work in groups of three to write a riddle about one of the people or objects in the **Contextos** illustrations. The group must come up with at least three descriptions of their subject. Then one of the group members reads the description to the class and asks **¿Qué soy?** Ex: **Soy un pequeño libro. Tengo una foto de una persona. Soy necesario si un viajero quiere viajar a otro país. ¿Qué soy? (Soy un pasaporte.)**

Large Groups Split the class into two evenly-numbered groups. Hand out cards at random to the members of each group. One type of card should contain a verb or verb phrase (Ex: **confirmar una reservación**). The other will contain a related noun (Ex: **el agente de viajes**). The people within the groups must find their partners.

Las estaciones y los meses del año

el invierno: diciembre, enero, febrero

la primavera: marzo, abril, mayo

el verano: junio, julio, agosto

el otoño: septiembre, octubre, noviembre

—¿Cuál es la fecha de hoy? *What is today's date?*
—Es el primero de octubre. *It's the first of October.*
—Es el dos de marzo. *It's March 2nd.*
—Es el diez de noviembre. *It's November 10th.*

El tiempo

—¿Qué tiempo hace? *How's the weather?*
—Hace buen/mal tiempo. *The weather is good/bad.*

Hace (mucho) calor. *It's (very) hot.*   **Hace (mucho) frío.** *It's (very) cold.*

Llueve. (llover o:ue) *It's raining.*   **Nieva. (nevar e:ie)** *It's snowing.*

Está lloviendo. *It's raining.*   **Está nevando.** *It's snowing.*

Más vocabulario

Está (muy) nublado.	It's (very) cloudy.
Hace fresco.	It's cool.
Hace (mucho) sol.	It's (very) sunny.
Hace (mucho) viento.	It's (very) windy.

Las vacaciones

5 El Hotel Regis
Label the floors of the hotel.

Números ordinales

primer *(before a masculine singular noun)*, **primero/a**	first
segundo/a	second
tercer *(before a masculine singular noun)*, **tercero/a**	third
cuarto/a	fourth
quinto/a	fifth
sexto/a	sixth
séptimo/a	seventh
octavo/a	eighth
noveno/a	ninth
décimo/a	tenth

a. _séptimo_ piso
b. _sexto_ piso
c. _quinto_ piso
d. _cuarto_ piso
e. _tercer_ piso
f. _segundo_ piso
g. _primer_ piso
h. _planta_ baja

6 Contestar
Look at the illustrations of the months and seasons on the previous page. Then answer these questions.

modelo
Estudiante 1: ¿Cuál es el primer mes de la primavera?
Estudiante 2: marzo

1. ¿Cuál es el primer mes del invierno? diciembre
2. ¿Cuál es el segundo mes de la primavera? abril
3. ¿Cuál es el tercer mes del otoño? noviembre
4. ¿Cuál es el primer mes del año? enero
5. ¿Cuál es el quinto mes del año? mayo
6. ¿Cuál es el octavo mes del año? agosto
7. ¿Cuál es el décimo mes del año? octubre
8. ¿Cuál es el segundo mes del verano? julio
9. ¿Cuál es el tercer mes del invierno? febrero
10. ¿Cuál es el sexto mes del año? junio

7 Las estaciones
Name the season that applies to the description. *Some answers may vary.*

1. Las clases terminan. la primavera
2. Vamos a la playa. el verano
3. Acampamos. el verano
4. Nieva mucho. el invierno
5. Las clases empiezan. el otoño
6. Hace mucho calor. el verano
7. Llueve mucho. la primavera
8. Esquiamos. el invierno
9. el entrenamiento (*training*) de béisbol la primavera
10. el Día de Acción de Gracias (*Thanksgiving*) el otoño

8 ¿Cuál es la fecha?
Give the dates for these holidays.

modelo
el día de San Valentín 14 de febrero

1. el día de San Patricio 17 de marzo
2. el día de Halloween 31 de octubre
3. el primer día de verano 20–23 de junio
4. el Año Nuevo primero de enero
5. mi cumpleaños (*birthday*) Answers will vary.
6. mi día de fiesta favorito Answers will vary.

TEACHING OPTIONS

TPR Ask ten volunteers to line up facing the class. Make sure students know the starting point and what number in line they are. At random, call out ordinal numbers. The student to which each ordinal number corresponds has three seconds to step forward. If the student does not, he or she sits down and the order changes for the rest of the students further down the line. Who will be the last student(s) standing?

Game Ask four or five volunteers to come to the front of the room and hold races. (Make it difficult to reach the finish line; for example, have students hop on one foot or recite the ordinal numbers backwards.) Teach the words **llegó** and **fue** and, after each race, ask the class to summarize the results. Ex: ____ **llegó en quinto lugar.** ____ **fue la tercera persona (en llegar).**

---

5 In-Class Tips
- Point out that for numbers greater than ten, Spanish speakers tend to use cardinal numbers instead: **Está en el piso veintiuno.**
- Add a visual aspect to this vocabulary presentation. Write out each ordinal number on a separate sheet of paper and distribute them at random among ten students. Ask them to go to the front of the class, hold up their signs, and stand in the correct order.

5 Expansion Ask students questions about their lives, using ordinal numbers. Ex: **¿En qué piso vives? ¿En qué piso está tu clase de español?**

6 In-Class Tip Before beginning this activity, have students close their books. Review seasons and months of the year by asking questions. Ex: **¿Qué estación tiene los meses de junio, julio y agosto?**

6 Expansion Ask a student which month his or her birthday is in. Ask another student to give the season the first student's birthday falls in.

7 Expansion Ask volunteers to describe events, situations, or holidays that are important to them or their families. Have the class guess the event and name the season that applies.

8 In-Class Tip Bring in a Spanish-language calendar. Ask students to name the important events and their scheduled dates.

8 Expansion
- Give these holidays to students as items 7–10:
7. Independencia de los EE.UU. (4 de julio) 8. Navidad (25 de diciembre) 9. Día de Acción de Gracias (cuarto jueves de noviembre) 10. Día de los Inocentes (primero de abril)
- Ask heritage speakers to provide other important holidays, such as saints' days.

9 Seleccionar
Paco is talking about his family and friends. Choose the word or phrase that best completes each sentence.

1. A mis padres les gusta ir a Yucatán porque (hace sol, nieva). **hace sol**
2. Mi primo de Kansas dice que durante (*during*) un tornado, hace mucho (sol, viento). **viento**
3. Mis amigos van a esquiar si (nieva, está nublado). **nieva**
4. Tomo el sol cuando (hace calor, llueve). **hace calor**
5. Nosotros vamos a ver una película si hace (buen, mal) tiempo. **mal**
6. Mi hermana prefiere correr cuando (hace mucho calor, hace fresco). **hace fresco**
7. Mis tíos van de excursión si hace (buen, mal) tiempo. **buen**
8. Mi padre no quiere jugar al golf si (hace fresco, llueve). **llueve**
9. Cuando hace mucho (sol, frío) no salgo de casa y tomo chocolate caliente (*hot*). **frío**
10. Hoy mi sobrino va al parque porque (está lloviendo, hace buen tiempo). **hace buen tiempo**

10 El clima
With a partner, take turns asking and answering questions about the weather and temperatures in these cities. Use the model as a guide. **Answers will vary.**

> **modelo**
> **Estudiante 1:** ¿Qué tiempo hace hoy en Nueva York?
> **Estudiante 2:** Hace frío y hace viento.
> **Estudiante 1:** ¿Cuál es la temperatura máxima?
> **Estudiante 2:** Treinta y un grados (*degrees*).
> **Estudiante 1:** ¿Y la temperatura mínima?
> **Estudiante 2:** Diez grados.

soleado | lluvia | nieve | nublado | viento

Nueva York	Miami	Chicago	París	Madrid	Tokio
Máx. 31°	Máx. 84°	Máx. 23°	Máx. 38°	Máx. 42°	Máx. 49°
Mín. 10°	Mín. 62°	Mín. 5°	Mín. 26°	Mín. 27°	Mín. 34°

Montreal	México D.F.	Cozumel	Caracas	Quito	Buenos Aires
Máx. 18°	Máx. 76°	Máx. 91°	Máx. 80°	Máx. 60°	Máx. 85°
Mín. 2°	Mín. 41°	Mín. 73°	Mín. 72°	Mín. 51°	Mín. 59°

11 Completar
Complete these sentences with your own ideas. **Answers will vary.**

1. Cuando hace sol, yo…
2. Cuando llueve, mis amigos y yo…
3. Cuando hace calor, mi familia…
4. Cuando hace viento, la gente…
5. Cuando hace frío, yo…
6. Cuando hace mal tiempo, mis amigos…
7. Cuando nieva, muchas personas…
8. Cuando está nublado, mis amigos y yo…
9. Cuando hace fresco, mis padres…
10. Cuando hace buen tiempo, mis amigos…

NOTA CULTURAL
In most Spanish-speaking countries, temperatures are given in degrees Celsius. Use these formulas to convert between **grados centígrados** and **grados Fahrenheit**.
degrees C. × 9 ÷ 5 + 32 = degrees F.
degrees F. − 32 × 5 ÷ 9 = degrees C.

CONSULTA
Calor and **frío** can apply to both weather and people. Use **hacer** to describe weather conditions or climate.
(**Hace frío en Santiago**. *It's cold in Santiago.*)
Use **tener** to refer to people.
(**El viajero tiene frío**. *The traveler is cold.*)
See **Senderos 1A**, **Estructura 3.4**, p. 125.

TEACHING OPTIONS
TPR Have volunteers mime situations that elicit weather-related vocabulary from the class. Ex: A shiver might elicit **hace frío**.
Heritage Speakers Ask heritage speakers to talk about typical weather-dependent activities in their families' countries of origin. Refer them to **Actividad 11** as a model. Ex: **En México, cuando hace frío, la gente bebe ponche de frutas (una bebida caliente).**

Small Groups Have students form groups of two to four. Hand out cards that contain the name of a holiday or other annual event. The group must come up with at least three sentences to describe the holiday or occasion without mentioning its name. They can, however, mention the season of the year. After discussing, other groups must first guess the month and day on which the event takes place, then name the holiday or event itself.

Las vacaciones — sesenta y siete

Comunicación

12 En la agencia de viajes Listen to the conversation between Mr. Vega and a travel agent. Then indicate whether the following conclusions are **lógico** or **ilógico**, based on what you heard.

	Lógico	Ilógico
1. El señor Vega quiere visitar la Antártida.	○	●
2. Hace calor en Puerto Rico.	●	○
3. El señor Vega va a ver el mar en Puerto Rico.	●	○
4. El señor Vega va a comprar un pasaje de ida y vuelta.	●	○
5. El señor Vega viaja con su familia.	○	●

13 Preguntas personales Answer your partner's questions. Answers will vary.

1. ¿Cuál es la fecha de hoy? ¿Qué estación es?
2. ¿Te gusta esta estación? ¿Por qué?
3. ¿Qué estación prefieres? ¿Por qué?
4. ¿Prefieres el mar o las montañas? ¿La playa o el campo? ¿Por qué?
5. Cuando haces un viaje, ¿qué te gusta hacer y ver?
6. ¿Piensas ir de vacaciones este verano? ¿Adónde quieres ir? ¿Por qué?
7. ¿Qué deseas ver y qué lugares quieres visitar?
8. ¿Cómo te gusta viajar? ¿En avión? ¿En motocicleta...?

14 Itinerario Create a trip itinerary for a friend, a relative, or someone famous. First, choose a destination. Include information about transportation and accommodations, as well as a section for each day with activities. Answers will vary.

- fechas
- lugar
- transporte
- hotel
- actividades

Síntesis

15 Un viaje With a partner, role-play a conversation between a travel agent and a client planning a trip. Discuss destinations, dates, transportation, hotel accommodations, and activities for the trip. Answers will vary.

TEACHING OPTIONS

Pairs Tell students they are part of a scientific expedition to Antarctica (**la Antártida**). Have them write a letter back home about the weather conditions and their activities there. Begin the letter for them by writing **Queridos amigos** on the board.
Game Have each student create a *Bingo* card with 25 squares (five rows of five). Tell them to write **GRATIS** (*FREE*) in the center square and the name of a different city in each of the other squares. Have them exchange cards. Call out different weather expressions. Ex: **Hace viento.** Students who think this description fits a city or cities on their card should mark the square with the weather condition. In order to win, a student must have marked five squares in a row and be able to give the weather condition for each one. Ex: **Hace mucho viento en Chicago.**

Communication 1.1, 1.2, 1.3

12 In-Class Tip Ask students if they have ever been to a travel agency. Let them share their experiences before doing the activity.

12 Script *See the script for this activity on Interleaf page 61B.*

13 Expansion Have pairs imagine that one of them is a journalist and the other is a celebrity. Then have them conduct the interview using questions 3–8.

13 Virtual Chat Available online.

14 In-Class Tip Have students create a tourist brochure of the destination they selected for their trip.

15 In-Class Tip Encourage students to use the information they prepared in activity **14 Itinerario** as the basis of this conversation.

15 Expansion Divide the class in pairs and distribute the handouts for activity **Un viaje** from the online Resources (Lección 5/Activity Pack/Information Gap Activities). Ask students to read the instructions and give them ten minutes to complete the activity.

Communication 1.1

15 In-Class Tip Set up the classroom chairs in two parallel rows so pairs of students face each other. The students in one row will be assigned the role of travel agents and the others will be the customers. Let them interact for two minutes and then ask one row to shift one seat to the right, and ask the new pairs to continue the role-play.

15 Partner Chat Available online.

Contextos

Section Goals

In **Fotonovela**, students will:
- receive comprehensible input from free-flowing discourse
- learn functional phrases that preview lesson grammatical structures

 Communication 1.2
Cultures 2.1, 2.2

Teacher Resources
Read the front matter for suggestions on how to incorporate all the program's components. See pages 61A–61B for a detailed listing of Teacher Resources online.

Video Recap: Lección 4
Review the previous episode with these questions:
1. ¿Qué prefiere hacer tía Ana María en sus ratos libres? (Ella nada, juega al tenis y al golf y va al cine y a los museos.)
2. ¿Adónde van Miguel, Maru, Marissa y Jimena? (Van a un cenote.) 3. ¿Qué van a hacer Felipe y Juan Carlos? (Van a jugar al fútbol con Eduardo y Pablo.) 4. ¿Qué quieren comer los chicos después de jugar al fútbol? (Quieren comer mole.)

Video Synopsis
The friends watch the weather report on TV and discuss weather and seasons in their hometowns. **Felipe** rouses **Miguel** so they don't miss the bus to the beach. The group checks in to their hotel. At the beach, **Maru** and **Miguel** windsurf. **Miguel** gets back at **Felipe**.

In-Class Tips
- Have the class glance over the **Fotonovela** captions and list words and phrases related to tourism.
- Ask individuals how they are today, using **cansado/a** and **aburrido/a**.
- Ask the class: **¿Cómo es el hotel ideal? ¿Cómo es la habitación de hotel perfecta?**

---

5 fotonovela

¡Vamos a la playa!

Los seis amigos hacen un viaje a la playa.

PERSONAJES FELIPE JUAN CARLOS

1
TÍA ANA MARÍA ¿Están listos para su viaje a la playa?
TODOS Sí.
TÍA ANA MARÍA Excelente... ¡A la estación de autobuses!
MARU ¿Dónde está Miguel?
FELIPE Yo lo traigo.

2
(se escucha un grito de Miguel)
FELIPE Ya está listo. Y tal vez enojado. Ahorita vamos.

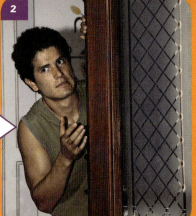

FELIPE No está nada mal el hotel, ¿verdad? Limpio, cómodo... ¡Oye, Miguel! ¿Todavía estás enojado conmigo? (a Juan Carlos) Miguel está de mal humor. No me habla.
JUAN CARLOS ¿Todavía?

3
EMPLEADO Bienvenidas. ¿En qué puedo servirles?
MARU Hola. Tenemos una reservación para seis personas para esta noche.
EMPLEADO ¿A nombre de quién?
JIMENA ¿Díaz? ¿López? No estoy segura.

4
EMPLEADO No encuentro su nombre. Ah, no, ahora sí lo veo, aquí está. Díaz. Dos habitaciones en el primer piso para seis huéspedes.

6
EMPLEADO Aquí están las llaves de sus habitaciones.
MARU Gracias. Una cosa más. Mi novio y yo queremos hacer windsurf, pero no tenemos tablas.
EMPLEADO El botones las puede conseguir para ustedes.

TEACHING OPTIONS

Video Tips General suggestions for using video clips in the classroom can be found in the front matter of this Teacher's Edition.
¡Vamos a la playa! Before viewing the **¡Vamos a la playa!** episode of the **Fotonovela**, ask students to brainstorm a list of things that might happen in an episode in which the characters check in to a hotel and go to the beach. Then play the **¡Vamos a la playa!** episode once without sound and have the class create a plot summary based on visual clues. Finally, show the video segment with sound and have the class correct any mistaken guesses and fill in any gaps. Ask comprehension questions as a follow-up.

68 Teacher's Edition • Lesson Five

MARISSA   JIMENA   MARU   MIGUEL   MAITE FUENTES   ANA MARÍA   EMPLEADO

7

JUAN CARLOS ¿Qué hace este libro aquí? ¿Estás estudiando en la playa?
JIMENA Sí, es que tengo un examen la próxima semana.

8

JUAN CARLOS Ay, Jimena. ¡No! ¿Vamos a nadar?
JIMENA Bueno, como estudiar es tan aburrido y el tiempo está tan bonito...

9

MARISSA Yo estoy un poco cansada. ¿Y tú? ¿Por qué no estás nadando?
FELIPE Es por causa de Miguel.

10

MARISSA Hmm, estoy confundida.
FELIPE Esta mañana. ¡Sigue enojado conmigo!
MARISSA No puede seguir enojado tanto tiempo.

Expresiones útiles

Talking with hotel personnel

¿En qué puedo servirles?
How can I help you?
Tenemos una reservación.
We have a reservation.
¿A nombre de quién?
In whose name?
¿Quizás López? ¿Tal vez Díaz?
Maybe López? Maybe Díaz?
Ahora lo veo, aquí está. Díaz.
Now I see it. Here it is. Díaz.
Dos habitaciones en el primer piso para seis huéspedes.
Two rooms on the first floor for six guests.
Aquí están las llaves.
Here are the keys.

Describing a hotel

No está nada mal el hotel.
The hotel isn't bad at all.
Todo está tan limpio y cómodo.
Everything is so clean and comfortable.
Es excelente/estupendo/fabuloso/ fenomenal/increíble/magnífico/ maravilloso/perfecto.
It's excellent/stupendous/fabulous/ phenomenal/incredible/magnificent/ marvelous/perfect.

Talking about how you feel

Yo estoy un poco cansado/a.
I am a little tired.
Estoy confundido/a. *I'm confused.*
Todavía estoy/Sigo enojado/a contigo.
I'm still angry with you.

Additional vocabulary

afuera *outside*
amable *nice; friendly*
el balde *bucket*
el/la botones *bellhop*
la crema de afeitar *shaving cream*
el frente (frío) *(cold) front*
el grito *scream*
la temporada *period of time*
entonces *so, then*
es igual *it's the same*

¿Qué pasó?

1 Completar Complete these sentences with the correct term from the word bank.

aburrido	botones	la llave
el aeropuerto	la estación de autobuses	montar a caballo
amable	habitaciones	reservación

1. Los amigos van a __la estación de autobuses__ para ir a la playa.
2. La __reservación__ del hotel está a nombre de los Díaz.
3. Los amigos tienen dos __habitaciones__ para seis personas.
4. El __botones__ puede conseguir tablas de windsurf para Maru.
5. Jimena dice que estudiar en vacaciones es muy __aburrido__.

2 Identificar Identify the person who would make each statement.

EMPLEADO   MARU   TÍA ANA MARÍA   FELIPE   JUAN CARLOS

1. No lo encuentro, ¿a nombre de quién está su reservación? empleado
2. ¿Por qué estás estudiando en la playa? ¡Mejor vamos a nadar! Juan Carlos
3. Nuestra reservación es para seis personas en dos habitaciones. Maru
4. El hotel es limpio y cómodo, pero estoy triste porque Miguel no me habla. Felipe
5. Suban al autobús y ¡buen viaje a la playa! Ana María

3 Ordenar Place these events in the correct order.

_3_ a. El empleado busca la reservación.
_5_ b. Marissa dice que está confundida.
_1_ c. Los amigos están listos para ir a la playa.
_4_ d. El empleado da (*gives*) las llaves de las habitaciones a las chicas.
_2_ e. Miguel grita (*screams*).

4 Conversar With a partner, use these cues to create a conversation between a hotel employee and a guest in Mexico. Answers will vary.

Huésped

Say hi to the employee and ask for your reservation.

Tell the employee that the reservation is in your name.

Tell the employee that the hotel is very clean and comfortable.

Ask the employee to call the bellhop to help you with your luggage.

Empleado/a

Tell the guest that you can't find his/her reservation.

Tell him/her that you found the reservation and that it's for a double room.

Say that you agree with the guest, welcome him/her, and give him/her the keys.

Call the bellhop to help the guest with his/her luggage.

CONSULTA

The meaning of some adjectives, such as **aburrido**, changes depending on whether they are used with **ser** or **estar**. See **Estructura 5.3**, pp. 80–81.

Pronunciación
Spanish b and v

| bueno | vóleibol | biblioteca | vivir |

There is no difference in pronunciation between the Spanish letters **b** and **v**. However, each letter can be pronounced two different ways, depending on which letters appear next to them.

| bonito | viajar | también | investigar |

B and **v** are pronounced like the English hard *b* when they appear either as the first letter of a word, at the beginning of a phrase, or after **m** or **n**.

| deber | novio | abril | favor |

In all other positions, **b** and **v** have a softer pronunciation, which has no equivalent in English. Unlike the hard **b**, which is produced by tightly closing the lips and stopping the flow of air, the soft **b** is produced by keeping the lips slightly open.

| bola | vela | Caribe | declive |

In both pronunciations, there is no difference in sound between **b** and **v**. The English *v* sound, produced by friction between the upper teeth and lower lip, does not exist in Spanish. Instead, the soft **b** comes from friction between the two lips.

Verónica y su esposo cantan boleros.

When **b** or **v** begins a word, its pronunciation depends on the previous word. At the beginning of a phrase or after a word that ends in **m** or **n**, it is pronounced as a hard **b**.

Benito es de Boquerón pero vive en Victoria.

Words that begin with **b** or **v** are pronounced with a soft **b** if they appear immediately after a word that ends in a vowel or any consonant other than **m** or **n**.

Práctica Read these words aloud to practice the **b** and the **v**.

1. hablamos
2. trabajar
3. botones
4. van
5. contabilidad
6. bien
7. doble
8. novia
9. béisbol
10. nublado
11. llave
12. invierno

Oraciones Read these sentences aloud to practice the **b** and the **v**.

1. Vamos a Guaynabo en autobús.
2. Voy de vacaciones a la Isla Culebra.
3. Tengo una habitación individual en el octavo piso.
4. Víctor y Eva van en avión al Caribe.
5. La planta baja es bonita también.
6. ¿Qué vamos a ver en Bayamón?
7. Beatriz, la novia de Víctor, es de Arecibo, Puerto Rico.

Refranes Read these sayings aloud to practice the **b** and the **v**.

No hay mal que por bien no venga.[1]

Hombre prevenido vale por dos.[2]

[1] Every cloud has a silver lining.
[2] An ounce of prevention equals a pound of cure.

cultura

EN DETALLE

Las cataratas del Iguazú

Garganta del Diablo
Isla San Martín

Imagine the impressive and majestic Niagara Falls, the most powerful waterfall in North America. Now, if you can, imagine a waterfall four times as wide and almost twice as tall that caused Eleanor Roosevelt to exclaim "Poor Niagara!" upon seeing it for the first time. Welcome to **las cataratas del Iguazú!**

Iguazú is located in Iguazú National Park, an area of subtropical jungle where Argentina meets Brazil. Its name comes from the indigenous Guaraní word for "great water." A UNESCO World Heritage Site, **las cataratas del Iguazú** span three kilometers and comprise 275 cascades split into two main sections by San Martín Island. Most of the falls are about 82 meters (270 feet) high. The horseshoe-shaped cataract **Garganta del Diablo** (Devil's Throat) has the greatest water flow and is considered to be the most impressive; it also marks the border between Argentina and Brazil.

Each country offers different views and tourist options. Most visitors opt to use the numerous catwalks that are available on both sides; however, from the Argentinean side, tourists can get very close to the falls, whereas Brazil provides more panoramic views. If you don't mind getting wet, a jet boat tour is a good choice; those looking for wildlife—such as toucans, ocelots, butterflies, and jaguars—should head for San Martín Island. Brazil boasts less conventional ways to view the falls, such as helicopter rides and rappelling, while Argentina focuses on sustainability with its **Tren Ecológico de la Selva** (*Ecological Jungle Train*), an environmentally friendly way to reach the walkways.

No matter which way you choose to enjoy the falls, you are certain to be captivated.

Más cascadas° en Latinoamérica

Nombre	País	Altura°	Datos
Salto Ángel	Venezuela	979 metros	la más alta° del mundo°
Catarata del Gocta	Perú	771 metros	descubierta° en 2006
Piedra Volada	México	453 metros	la más alta de México

cascadas *waterfalls* Altura *Height* más alta *tallest* mundo *world* descubierta *discovered*

ACTIVIDADES

1 **¿Cierto o falso?** Indicate whether these statements are cierto or falso. Correct the false statements.

1. Iguazú Falls is located on the border of Argentina and Brazil. **Cierto.**
2. Niagara Falls is four times as wide as Iguazú Falls. **Falso.** Iguazú is four times as wide as Niagara Falls.
3. Iguazú Falls has a few cascades, each about 82 meters. **Falso.** Iguazú is composed of 275 cascades about 82 meters tall.
4. Tourists visiting Iguazú can see exotic wildlife. **Cierto.**
5. *Iguazú* is the Guaraní word for "blue water." **Falso.** *Iguazú* is the Guaraní word for "great water."
6. You can access the walkways by taking the **Garganta del Diablo**. **Falso.** One way of accessing the walkways is taking the **Tren Ecológico de la Selva**.
7. It is possible for tourists to visit Iguazú Falls by air. **Cierto.**
8. **Salto Ángel** is the tallest waterfall in the world. **Cierto.**
9. There are no waterfalls in Mexico. **Falso.** The **Piedra Volada** is in Mexico.
10. For the best views of Iguazú Falls, tourists should visit the Brazilian side. **Cierto.**

ASÍ SE DICE
Viajes y turismo

el asiento del medio, del pasillo, de la ventanilla	center, aisle, window seat
el itinerario	itinerary
media pensión	breakfast and one meal included
el ómnibus (Perú)	el autobús
pensión completa	all meals included
el puente	long weekend (lit., bridge)

EL MUNDO HISPANO
Destinos populares

- **Las playas del Parque Nacional Manuel Antonio** (Costa Rica) ofrecen° la oportunidad de nadar y luego caminar por el bosque tropical°.
- **Teotihuacán** (México) Desde antes de la época° de los aztecas, aquí se celebra el equinoccio de primavera en la Pirámide del Sol.
- **Puerto Chicama** (Perú), con sus olas° de cuatro kilómetros de largo°, es un destino para surfistas expertos.
- **Tikal** (Guatemala) Aquí puedes ver las maravillas de la selva° y ruinas de la civilización maya.
- **Las playas de Rincón** (Puerto Rico) Son ideales para descansar y observar ballenas°.

ofrecen *offer* bosque tropical *rainforest*
Desde antes de la época *Since before the time* olas *waves*
de largo *in length* selva *jungle* ballenas *whales*

PERFIL
Punta del Este

One of South America's largest and most fashionable beach resort towns is Uruguay's **Punta del Este**, a narrow strip of land containing twenty miles of pristine beaches. Its peninsular shape gives it two very different seascapes. **La Playa Mansa**, facing the bay and therefore the more protected side, has calm waters. Here, people practice water sports like swimming, water skiing, windsurfing, and diving. **La Playa Brava**, facing the east, receives the Atlantic Ocean's powerful, wave-producing winds, making it popular for surfing, body boarding, and kite surfing. Besides the beaches, posh shopping, and world-famous nightlife, **Punta** offers its 600,000 yearly visitors yacht and fishing clubs, golf courses, and excursions to observe sea lions at the **Isla de Lobos** nature reserve.

Conexión Internet

¿Cuáles son los sitios más populares para el turismo en Puerto Rico?

Use the Web to find more cultural information related to this **Cultura** section.

ACTIVIDADES

2 Comprensión Complete the sentences.
1. En las playas de Rincón puedes ver __ballenas__.
2. Cerca de 600.000 turistas visitan __Punta del Este__ cada año.
3. En el avión pides un __asiento de la ventanilla__ si te gusta ver el paisaje.
4. En Punta del Este, la gente prefiere nadar en la Playa __Mansa__.
5. El __ómnibus__ es un medio de transporte en Perú.

3 De vacaciones Spring break is coming up, and you want to go on a short vacation with your family. Decide which of the locations featured on these pages best suits your likes and interests. Come to an agreement about how you will get there, where you prefer to stay and for how long, and what each of you will do during your free time. Answers will vary.

5 estructura

5.1 Estar with conditions and emotions

ANTE TODO As you learned in **Lecciones 1** and **2**, the verb **estar** is used to talk about how you feel and to say where people, places, and things are located. **Estar** is also used with adjectives to talk about certain emotional and physical conditions.

▶ Use **estar** with adjectives to describe the physical condition of places and things.

La habitación **está** sucia.
The room is dirty.

La puerta **está** cerrada.
The door is closed.

▶ Use **estar** with adjectives to describe how people feel, both mentally and physically.

Yo estoy cansada.

¿Están listos para su viaje?

CONSULTA
To review the present tense of **estar**, see **Senderos 1A**, **Estructura 2.3**, p. 83.
• • •
To review the present tense of **ser**, see **Senderos 1A**, **Estructura 1.3**, p. 44.

▶ **¡Atención!** Two important expressions with **estar** that you can use to talk about conditions and emotions are **estar de buen humor** (*to be in a good mood*) and **estar de mal humor** (*to be in a bad mood*).

Adjectives that describe emotions and conditions

abierto/a	open	contento/a	content	listo/a	ready
aburrido/a	bored	desordenado/a	disorderly	nervioso/a	nervous
alegre	happy	enamorado/a (de)	in love (with)	ocupado/a	busy
avergonzado/a	embarrassed			ordenado/a	orderly
cansado/a	tired	enojado/a	angry	preocupado/a (por)	worried (about)
cerrado/a	closed	equivocado/a	wrong		
cómodo/a	comfortable	feliz	happy	seguro/a	sure
confundido/a	confused	limpio/a	clean	sucio/a	dirty
				triste	sad

¡INTÉNTALO! Provide the present tense forms of **estar**, and choose which adjective best completes the sentence.

1. La biblioteca ___está___ (cerrada / nerviosa) los domingos por la noche. cerrada
2. Nosotros ___estamos___ muy (ocupados / equivocados) todos los lunes. ocupados
3. Ellas ___están___ (alegres / confundidas) porque tienen vacaciones. alegres
4. Javier ___está___ (enamorado / ordenado) de Maribel. enamorado
5. Diana ___está___ (enojada / limpia) con su hermano. enojada
6. Yo ___estoy___ (nerviosa / abierta) por el viaje. nerviosa
7. La habitación siempre ___está___ (ordenada / segura) cuando vienen sus padres. ordenada
8. Ustedes no comprenden; ___están___ (equivocados / tristes). equivocados

Práctica y Comunicación

1 **¿Cómo están?** Complete Martín's statements about how he and other people are feeling. In the first blank, fill in the correct form of **estar**. In the second blank, fill in the adjective that best fits the context. *Some answers may vary.*

AYUDA
Make sure that there is agreement between:
- Subjects and verbs in person and number
- Nouns and adjectives in gender and number

Ellos no **están** enferm**os**.
They are not sick.

1. Yo __estoy__ un poco __nervioso__ porque tengo un examen mañana.
2. Mi hermana Patricia __está__ muy __contenta__ porque mañana va a hacer una excursión al campo.
3. Mis hermanos Juan y José salen de la casa a las cinco de la mañana. Por la noche, siempre __están__ muy __cansados__.
4. Mi amigo Ramiro __está__ __enamorado__; su novia se llama Adela.
5. Mi papá y sus colegas __están__ muy __ocupados__ hoy. ¡Hay mucho trabajo!
6. Patricia y yo __estamos__ un poco __preocupados__ por ellos porque trabajan mucho.
7. Mi amiga Mónica __está__ un poco __triste/enojada__ porque sus amigos no pueden salir esta noche.
8. Esta clase no es muy interesante. ¿Tú __estás__ __aburrido/a__ también?

2 **Describir** Describe these people and places. *Answers will vary. Sample answers:*

1. Anabela
Está contenta/alegre/feliz.

2. Juan y Luisa
Están enojados.

3. la habitación de Teresa
Está ordenada/limpia.

4. la habitación de César
Está desordenada/sucia.

3 **Situaciones** With a partner, use **estar** to talk about how you feel in these situations. *Answers will vary.*

1. Cuando hace sol…
2. Cuando tomas un examen…
3. Cuando viajas en avión…
4. Cuando llueve…
5. Cuando ves una película con tu actor/actriz favorito/a…

4 **Emociones** Write an e-mail to a friend explaining what you do when you feel a certain way. Use five adjectives of emotion. *Answers will vary.*

> **modelo**
> Cuando estoy preocupado, hablo por teléfono con mi madre.
> Cuando estoy aburrido, miro la televisión…

Section Goals

In **Estructura 5.2**, students will learn:
- the present progressive of regular and irregular verbs
- the present progressive versus the simple present tense in Spanish

 Comparisons 4.1

Teacher Resources
Read the front matter for suggestions on how to incorporate all the program's components. See pages 61A–61B for a detailed listing of Teacher Resources online.

In-Class Tips
- Use regular verbs to ask questions about things students are not doing. Ex: **¿Estás comiendo pizza? (No, no estoy comiendo pizza.)**
- Explain the formation of the present progressive, writing examples on the board.
- Add a visual aspect to this grammar presentation. Use photos to elicit sentences with the present progressive. Ex: **¿Qué está haciendo el hombre alto? (Está sacando fotos.)** Include present participles ending in –**yendo** as well as those with stem changes.
- Point out that the present progressive is rarely used with the verbs **ir**, **poder**, and **venir** since they already imply an action in progress.

5.2 The present progressive

ANTE TODO Both Spanish and English use the present progressive, which consists of the present tense of the verb *to be* and the present participle of another verb (the *-ing* form in English).

Las chicas están hablando con el empleado del hotel.

¿Estás estudiando en la playa?

▶ Form the present progressive with the present tense of **estar** and a present participle.

FORM OF ESTAR + PRESENT PARTICIPLE	FORM OF ESTAR + PRESENT PARTICIPLE
Estoy pescando.	**Estamos** comiendo.
I am fishing.	*We are eating.*

▶ The present participle of regular **-ar**, **-er**, and **-ir** verbs is formed as follows:

INFINITIVE	STEM	ENDING	PRESENT PARTICIPLE
hablar	habl-	-ando	hablando
comer	com-	-iendo	comiendo
escribir	escrib-	-iendo	escribiendo

▶ **¡Atención!** When the stem of an **-er** or **-ir** verb ends in a vowel, the present participle ends in **-yendo**.

INFINITIVE	STEM	ENDING	PRESENT PARTICIPLE
leer	le-	-yendo	leyendo
oír	o-	-yendo	oyendo
traer	tra-	-yendo	trayendo

▶ **Ir**, **poder**, and **venir** have irregular present participles (**yendo**, **pudiendo**, **viniendo**). Several other verbs have irregular present participles that you will need to learn.

▶ **-Ir** stem-changing verbs have a stem change in the present participle.

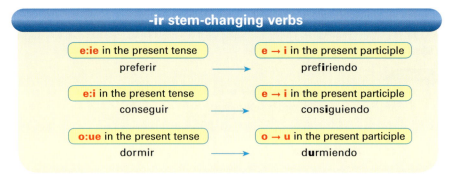

-ir stem-changing verbs

e:ie in the present tense	e → i in the present participle
preferir	prefiriendo

e:i in the present tense	e → i in the present participle
conseguir	consiguiendo

o:ue in the present tense	o → u in the present participle
dormir	durmiendo

TEACHING OPTIONS

TPR Divide the class into three groups. Appoint leaders and give them a list of verbs. Leaders call out a verb and a subject (Ex: **seguir/yo**), then toss a ball to someone in the group. That student says the appropriate present progressive form of the verb (Ex: **estoy siguiendo**) and tosses the ball back. Leaders should use all the verbs on the list and be sure to toss the ball to each member of the group.

TPR Play charades. In groups of four, have students take turns miming actions for the rest of the group to guess. Ex: Student pretends to read a newspaper. (**Estás leyendo el periódico.**) For incorrect guesses, the student should respond negatively. Ex: **No, no estoy estudiando.**

Las vacaciones

COMPARE & CONTRAST

The use of the present progressive is much more restricted in Spanish than in English. In Spanish, the present progressive is mainly used to emphasize that an action is in progress at the time of speaking.

Maru **está escuchando** música latina **ahora mismo**.
Maru is listening to Latin music right now.

Felipe y su amigo **todavía están jugando** al fútbol.
Felipe and his friend are still playing soccer.

In English, the present progressive is often used to talk about situations and actions that occur over an extended period of time or in the future. In Spanish, the simple present tense is often used instead.

Xavier **estudia** computación este semestre.
Xavier is studying computer science this semester.

Marissa **sale** mañana para los Estados Unidos.
Marissa is leaving tomorrow for the United States.

¿Está pensando en su futuro?
Nosotros, sí.

Preparándolo para el mañana

¡INTÉNTALO! Create complete sentences by putting the verbs in the present progressive.

1. mis amigos / descansar en la playa — Mis amigos están descansando en la playa.
2. nosotros / practicar deportes — Estamos practicando deportes.
3. Carmen / comer en casa — Carmen está comiendo en casa.
4. nuestro equipo / ganar el partido — Nuestro equipo está ganando el partido.
5. yo / leer el periódico — Estoy leyendo el periódico.
6. él / pensar comprar una bicicleta — Está pensando comprar una bicicleta.
7. ustedes / jugar a las cartas — Ustedes están jugando a las cartas.
8. José y Francisco / dormir — José y Francisco están durmiendo.
9. Marisa / leer correo electrónico — Marisa está leyendo correo electrónico.
10. yo / preparar sándwiches — Estoy preparando sándwiches.
11. Carlos / tomar fotos — Carlos está tomando fotos.
12. ¿dormir / tú? — ¿Estás durmiendo?

In-Class Tips
- Discuss each point in the **Compare & Contrast** box.
- Write these statements on the board and ask students if they would use the present or the present progressive in Spanish for each item. 1. I'm going on vacation tomorrow. 2. She's packing her suitcase right now. 3. They are fishing in Puerto Rico this week. 4. Roberto is still working. Then ask students to translate the items. (**1. Voy de vacaciones mañana. 2. Está haciendo la maleta ahora mismo. 3. Pescan en Puerto Rico esta semana. 4. Roberto todavía está trabajando.**)
- In this lesson, students learn **todavía** to mean *still* in the present progressive tense. You may want to point out that **todavía** also means *yet*. They will be able to use that meaning in later lessons as they learn the past tenses.
- Have students rewrite the sentences in the **¡Inténtalo!** activity using the simple present. Ask volunteers to explain how the sentences change depending on whether the verb is in the present progressive or the simple present.

Middle School Activity Pack
Give students extra practice with **¡A la pizarra!** in Resources online (Lección 5/Middle School Activity Pack/Grammar 5.2 Activity 1).

TEACHING OPTIONS

Pairs Have students write eight sentences in Spanish modeled after the examples in the **Compare & Contrast** box. There should be two sentences modeled after each example. Ask students to replace the verbs with blanks. Then, have students exchange papers with a partner and complete the sentences.

Extra Practice For homework, ask students to find five photos from a magazine or create five simple drawings of people performing different activities. For each image, have them write one sentence telling where the people are, one explaining what they are doing, and one describing how they feel. Ex: **Juan está en la biblioteca. Está estudiando. Está cansado.**

Práctica

1 Completar Alfredo's Spanish class is preparing to travel to Puerto Rico. Use the present progressive of the verb in parentheses to complete Alfredo's description of what everyone is doing.

1. Yo _estoy investigando_ (investigar) la situación política de la isla (*island*).
2. La esposa del profesor _está haciendo_ (hacer) las maletas.
3. Marta y José Luis _están buscando_ (buscar) información sobre San Juan en Internet.
4. Enrique y yo _estamos leyendo_ (leer) un correo electrónico de nuestro amigo puertorriqueño.
5. Javier _está aprendiendo_ (aprender) mucho sobre la cultura puertorriqueña.
6. Y tú _estás practicando_ (practicar) el español, ¿verdad?

2 ¿Qué están haciendo? María and her friends are vacationing at a resort in San Juan, Puerto Rico. Complete her description of what everyone is doing right now.

CONSULTA
For more information about Puerto Rico, see **Panorama**, pp. 96–97.

1. Yo estoy escribiendo una carta.

2. Javier está buceando en el mar.

3. Alejandro y Rebeca están jugando a las cartas.

4. Celia y yo estamos tomando el sol.

5. Samuel está escuchando música.

6. Lorenzo está durmiendo.

3 Personajes famosos Say what these celebrities are doing right now, using the cues provided. *Answers will vary.*

modelo
Shakira
Shakira está cantando una canción ahora mismo.

A		B	
Isabel Allende	Nelly Furtado	bailar	hacer
Rachael Ray	Dwight Howard	cantar	jugar
James Cameron	Las Rockettes de	correr	preparar
Venus y Serena	Nueva York	escribir	¿?
Williams	¿?	hablar	¿?
Joey Votto	¿?		

AYUDA
Isabel Allende: **novelas**
Rachael Ray: **televisión, negocios** (*business*)
James Cameron: **cine**
Venus y Serena Williams: **tenis**
Joey Votto: **béisbol**
Nelly Furtado: **canciones**
Dwight Howard: **baloncesto**
Las Rockettes de Nueva York: **baile**

Comunicación

4 Las vacaciones Read Elena's description of her family vacation. Then indicate whether these conclusions are **lógico** or **ilógico**, based on what you read.

> Está lloviendo. Mis tres hermanos están jugando a las cartas. Mi hermana está leyendo una revista. Mi madre está buscando la llave de la habitación. Mi padre está durmiendo. ¿Y yo? Estoy escribiendo este mensaje electrónico...

	Lógico	Ilógico
1. Hace mal tiempo.	✓	○
2. La familia es pequeña.	○	✓
3. La madre está contenta.	○	✓
4. El padre está en la cama.	✓	○
5. La familia está en un hotel.	✓	○

5 Preguntar Answer your partner's questions about what you are doing at these times. *Answers will vary.*

modelo
8:00 a.m.
Estudiante 1: Son las ocho de la mañana. ¿Qué estás haciendo?
Estudiante 2: Estoy desayunando.

1. 5:00 a.m.
2. 9:30 a.m.
3. 11:00 a.m.
4. 12:00 p.m.
5. 2:00 p.m.
6. 5:00 p.m.
7. 9:00 p.m.
8. 11:30 p.m.

6 Describir Use the present progressive to write a description of what is happening in this Spanish beach scene. *Answers will vary.*

NOTA CULTURAL
Nearly 60 million tourists travel to Spain every year, many of them drawn by the warm climate and beautiful coasts. Tourists wanting a beach vacation go mostly to the **Costa del Sol** or the Balearic Islands, in the Mediterranean.

Síntesis

7 ¿Qué están haciendo? With a partner, take turns asking each other what people are doing right now. You could ask about other students, professors, or even celebrities. *Answers will vary.*

| bailar | comer | escribir | estudiar | leer |
| cantar | enseñar | escuchar | jugar | mirar |

TEACHING OPTIONS

Video Show the **Fotonovela** episode again, pausing after each exchange. Ask students to describe what each person in the shot is doing at that moment.
TPR Write sentences with the present progressive on strips of paper. Call on volunteers to draw papers out of a hat to act out. The class should guess what the sentences are. Ex: **Yo estoy durmiendo en la cama.**

Pairs Add an auditory aspect to this grammar practice. Ask students to write a short paragraph using the present progressive. Students should try to make their sentences as complex as possible. Have students dictate their sentences to a partner. After pairs have finished dictating their sentences, have them exchange papers to check for accuracy. Circulate around the room and look over students' work.

5.3 Ser and estar

ANTE TODO You have already learned that **ser** and **estar** both mean *to be* but are used for different purposes. These charts summarize the key differences in usage between **ser** and **estar**.

Uses of ser

1. Nationality and place of origin . . . . Juan Carlos **es** argentino.
   Es de Buenos Aires.
2. Profession or occupation . . . . Adela **es** agente de viajes.
   Francisco **es** médico.
3. Characteristics of people and things . . . José y Clara **son** simpáticos.
   El clima de Puerto Rico **es** agradable.
4. Generalizations . . . . ¡**Es** fabuloso viajar!
   Es difícil estudiar a la una de la mañana.
5. Possession . . . . **Es** la pluma de Jimena.
   Son las llaves del señor Díaz.
6. What something is made of . . . . La bicicleta **es** de metal.
   Los pasajes **son** de papel.
7. Time and date . . . . Hoy **es** martes. **Son** las dos.
   Hoy **es** el primero de julio.
8. Where or when an event takes place . . . El partido **es** en el estadio Santa Fe.
   La conferencia **es** a las siete.

¡ATENCIÓN!
Ser de expresses not only origin (**Es de Buenos Aires.**) and possession (**Es la pluma de Maru.**), but also what material something is made of (**La bicicleta es de metal.**).

Ellos son mis amigos.

Miguel está enojado conmigo.

Uses of estar

1. Location or spatial relationships . . . . . El aeropuerto **está** lejos de la ciudad.
   Tu habitación **está** en el tercer piso.
2. Health . . . . ¿Cómo **estás**?
   Estoy bien, gracias.
3. Physical states and conditions . . . . . . El profesor **está** ocupado.
   Las ventanas **están** abiertas.
4. Emotional states . . . . Marissa **está** feliz hoy.
   Estoy muy enojado con Maru.
5. Certain weather expressions . . . . **Está** lloviendo.
   Está nublado.
6. Ongoing actions (progressive tenses) . . **Estamos** estudiando para un examen.
   Ana **está** leyendo una novela.

Ser and estar with adjectives

▶ With many descriptive adjectives, **ser** and **estar** can both be used, but the meaning will change.

Juan **es** delgado.
Juan is thin.

Juan **está** más delgado hoy.
Juan looks thinner today.

Ana **es** nerviosa.
Ana is a nervous person.

Ana **está** nerviosa por el examen.
Ana is nervous because of the exam.

▶ In the examples above, the statements with **ser** are general observations about the inherent qualities of Juan and Ana. The statements with **estar** describe conditions that are variable.

▶ Here are some adjectives that change in meaning when used with **ser** and **estar**.

With ser

El chico **es listo**.
The boy is smart.

La profesora **es mala**.
The professor is bad.

Jaime **es aburrido**.
Jaime is boring.

Las peras **son verdes**.
Pears are green.

El gato **es muy vivo**.
The cat is very clever.

Iván **es un hombre seguro**.
Iván is a confident man.

With estar

El chico **está listo**.
The boy is ready.

La profesora **está mala**.
The professor is sick.

Jaime **está aburrido**.
Jaime is bored.

Las peras **están verdes**.
The pears are not ripe.

El gato **está vivo**.
The cat is alive.

Iván no **está seguro**.
Iván is not sure.

¡ATENCIÓN!
When referring to objects, **ser seguro/a** means *to be safe*.
El puente es seguro.
The bridge is safe.

¡INTÉNTALO! Form complete sentences by using the correct form of **ser** or **estar** and making any other necessary changes.

1. Alejandra / cansado
   Alejandra está cansada.
2. ellos / pelirrojo
   Ellos son pelirrojos.
3. Carmen / alto
   Carmen es alta.
4. yo / la clase de español
   Estoy en la clase de español.
5. película / a las once
   La película es a las once.
6. hoy / viernes
   Hoy es viernes.
7. nosotras / enojado
   Nosotras estamos enojadas.
8. Antonio / médico
   Antonio es médico.
9. Romeo y Julieta / enamorado
   Romeo y Julieta están enamorados.
10. libros / de Ana
    Los libros son de Ana.
11. Marisa y Juan / estudiando
    Marisa y Juan están estudiando.
12. partido de baloncesto / gimnasio
    El partido de baloncesto es en el gimnasio.

Communication 1.1
Comparisons 4.1

1 In-Class Tip Have students identify the use(s) of **ser** or **estar** for each item.

1 Expansion To challenge students, ask them to use each adjective in a sentence. If the adjective can take both verbs, have them provide two sentences.

2 In-Class Tip To simplify, ask students to point out context clues that will help them determine whether to use **ser** or **estar**. Ex: The word **hoy** in line 2 suggests that **guapo** is a variable physical state.

2 Expansion Have pairs write a continuation of the conversation and then present it to the class.

3 In-Class Tip Use the **Lección 5 Estructura** online Resources to assist with the presentation of this activity.

3 Expansion Add another visual aspect to this grammar practice. Bring in photos or magazine pictures that show many different people performing a variety of activities. Have students use **ser** and **estar** to write short descriptions of the scenes.

Middle School Activity Pack
Find an alternative way to practice **Ser** and **estar** with **¡Caligrama!** in Resources online (Lección 5/Middle School Activity Pack/Grammar 5.3 Activity 1).

Práctica

1 **¿Ser o estar?** Indicate whether each adjective takes **ser** or **estar**. **¡Ojo!** Three of them can take both verbs.

	ser	estar			ser	estar
1. delgada	✓	✓	5. seguro	✓	✓
2. canadiense	✓	○	6. enojada	○	✓
3. enamorado	○	✓	7. importante	✓	○
4. lista	✓	✓	8. avergonzada	○	✓

2 **Completar** Complete this conversation with the appropriate forms of **ser** and **estar**.

EDUARDO ¡Hola, Ceci! ¿Cómo (1) _estás_?
CECILIA Hola, Eduardo. Bien, gracias. ¡Qué guapo (2) _estás_ hoy!
EDUARDO Gracias. (3) _Eres_ muy amable. Oye, ¿qué (4) _estás_ haciendo? (5)¿_Estás_ ocupada?
CECILIA No, sólo le (6) _estoy_ escribiendo una carta a mi prima Pilar.
EDUARDO ¿De dónde (7) _es_ ella?
CECILIA Pilar (8) _es_ de Ecuador. Su papá (9) _es_ médico en Quito. Pero ahora Pilar y su familia (10) _están_ de vacaciones en Ponce, Puerto Rico.
EDUARDO Y… ¿cómo (11) _es_ Pilar?
CECILIA (12) _Es_ muy lista. Y también (13) _es_ alta, rubia y muy bonita.

3 **En el parque** Describe the people in the drawing. Your descriptions should answer the questions provided. Answers will vary.

1. ¿Quiénes son?
2. ¿Dónde están?
3. ¿Cómo son?
4. ¿Cómo están?
5. ¿Qué están haciendo?
6. ¿Qué estación es?
7. ¿Qué tiempo hace?
8. ¿Quiénes están de vacaciones?

TEACHING OPTIONS

Extra Practice Have students write a paragraph about a close friend, including the person's physical appearance, general disposition, place of birth, birthday, profession, and where the friend is now. Ask volunteers to share their descriptions with the class.

Pairs Ask pairs to role-play this scenario: Student A is at the beach with some friends while Student B is at home. Student A calls Student B, trying to convince him or her to come to the beach. Students should try to employ as many uses of **ser** and **estar** in their scenario as possible. After acting out the scene once, have students switch roles.

Comunicación

4 Ponce Listen to Carolina's description of her vacation. Then indicate whether the following conclusions are **lógico** or **ilógico**, based on what you heard.

	Lógico	Ilógico
1. Carolina es una turista.	✓	○
2. Carolina prefiere acampar.	○	✓
3. A Carolina no le gusta ir a la playa.	○	✓
4. Carolina vive en Ponce.	○	✓
5. A Carolina le gustan los museos.	✓	○

5 Una persona famosa Describe a celebrity using these items as a guide. *Answers will vary.*

- descripción física
- cómo está ahora
- origen
- dónde está ahora
- qué está haciendo ahora
- profesión u ocupación

6 En el aeropuerto With a partner, take turns assuming the identity of a character from this drawing. Your partner will ask you questions using **ser** and **estar** to figure out who you are. *Answers will vary.*

modelo

Estudiante 2: ¿Dónde estás?
Estudiante 1: Estoy cerca de la puerta.
Estudiante 2: ¿Qué estás haciendo?
Estudiante 1: Estoy escuchando a otra persona.
Estudiante 2: ¿Eres uno de los pasajeros?
Estudiante 1: No, soy empleado del aeropuerto.
Estudiante 2: ¿Eres Camilo?

Síntesis

7 Un hotel magnífico Write a radio ad for a vacation resort somewhere in the Spanish-speaking world. Use **ser** and **estar** in as many different ways as you can. *Answers will vary.*

TEACHING OPTIONS

Small Groups Have students work in small groups to write a television commercial for a vacation resort in the Spanish-speaking world. Ask them to employ as many uses of **ser** and **estar** as they can. If possible, after they have written the commercial, have them tape it to show to the class.

TPR Call on a volunteer and whisper the name of a celebrity in his or her ear. The volunteer acts out verbs and characteristics and uses props to elicit descriptions from the class. Ex: The volunteer points to the U.S. on a map. (**Es de los Estados Unidos.**) He or she then indicates a tall, thin man. (**Es un hombre atlético y delgado.**) He or she acts out swimming. (**Está nadando. ¿Es Michael Phelps?**)

Communication 1.1, 1.2

4 In-Class Tip Have students listen to the audio once and ask for the global idea of the text (Ex: **Se trata de Carolina, una turista que está de vacaciones en la ciudad de Ponce**). Then, ask more specific questions, such as: **¿Qué va a hacer Carolina en Ponce? ¿Cómo se llama el museo que va a visitar?**

4 Script *See the script for this activity on Interleaf page 61B.*

5 In-Class Tip Have students work in pairs and take turns describing the celebrity without mentioning names. Model the activity for the class and tell students to use **una persona** to create ambiguity in their descriptions. Ex: **Es una persona alta…**

6 In-Class Tip Use the online Resources (Lección 5/ Digital Image Bank/ Estructura 5.3 **Ser** and **estar**) to assist with the presentation of this activity.

6 Expansion Have students pick one of the individuals pictured and write a one-paragraph description, employing as many different uses of **ser** and **estar** as possible.

6 Partner Chat Available online.

Communication 1.3
Cultures 2.1
Comparisons 4.1, 4.2

7 Expansion Have students record their radio ads, and listen to them in class.

The Affective Dimension
Encourage students to consider pair and group activities as a cooperative venture in which group members support and motivate each other.

Section Goals

In **Estructura 5.4**, students will study:
- direct object nouns
- the personal **a**
- direct object pronouns

 Comparisons 4.1

Teacher Resources
Read the front matter for suggestions on how to incorporate all the program's components. See pages 61A–61B for a detailed listing of Teacher Resources online.

In-Class Tips
- Write these sentences on the board: —**¿Quién tiene el pasaporte?** —**Juan lo tiene.** Underline **pasaporte** and explain that it is a direct object noun. Then underline **lo** and explain that it is the masculine singular direct object pronoun. Translate both sentences. Continue with: —**¿Quién saca fotos?** —**Simón las saca.** —**¿Quién tiene la llave?** —**Pilar la tiene.**
- Read this exchange aloud: —**¿Haces las maletas?** —**No, no hago las maletas.** —**¿Por qué no haces las maletas?** —**No hago las maletas porque las maletas no están aquí.** Ask students if the exchange sounds natural to them. Then write it on the board and ask students to use direct object pronouns to avoid repetition. If students try to say **no las están** in the last sentence, point out that direct object pronouns cannot replace the subject of a verb. The only option is to eliminate the subject: **no están.**
- Ask individuals questions to elicit the personal **a**: **¿Visitas a tu abuela los fines de semana? ¿Llamas a tu padre los sábados?**
- Ask questions to elicit third-person direct object pronouns. Ex: **¿Quién ve el lápiz de Marcos? ¿Quién quiere estos diccionarios?**

5.4 Direct object nouns and pronouns

▶ A direct object noun receives the action of the verb directly and generally follows the verb. In the example above, the direct object noun answers the question *What are Juan Carlos and Jimena taking?*

▶ When a direct object noun in Spanish is a person or a pet, it is preceded by the word **a**. This is called the personal **a**; there is no English equivalent for this construction.

Mariela mira **a** Carlos.
Mariela is watching Carlos.

Mariela mira televisión.
Mariela is watching TV.

▶ In the first sentence above, the personal **a** is required because the direct object is a person. In the second sentence, the personal **a** is not required because the direct object is a thing, not a person.

Miguel no me perdona.

No tenemos tablas de windsurf.

El botones las puede conseguir para ustedes.

▶ Direct object pronouns are words that replace direct object nouns. Like English, Spanish uses a direct object pronoun to avoid repeating a noun already mentioned.

	DIRECT OBJECT		DIRECT OBJECT PRONOUN	
Maribel hace	las maletas.	Maribel	las	hace.
Felipe compra	el sombrero.	Felipe	lo	compra.
Vicky tiene	la llave.	Vicky	la	tiene.

Direct object pronouns

SINGULAR		PLURAL	
me	*me*	nos	*us*
te	*you* (fam.)	os	*you* (fam.)
lo	*you* (m., form.)	los	*you* (m.)
	him; it (m.)		*them* (m.)
la	*you* (f., form.)	las	*you* (f.)
	her; it (f.)		*them* (f.)

TEACHING OPTIONS

TPR Call out a series of sentences with direct object nouns, some of which require the personal **a** and some of which do not. Ex: **Visito muchos museos. Visito a mis tíos.** Have students raise their hands if the personal **a** is used.

Extra Practice Write six sentences on the board that have direct object nouns. Use two verbs in the simple present tense, two in the present progressive, and two using **ir a** + [*infinitive*]. Draw a line through the direct objects as students call them out. Have students state which pronouns to write to replace them. Then, draw an arrow from each pronoun to where it goes in the sentence, as indicated by students.

▶ In affirmative sentences, direct object pronouns generally appear before the conjugated verb. In negative sentences, the pronoun is placed between the word **no** and the verb.

Adela practica **el tenis**.	Gabriela no tiene **las llaves**.
Adela **lo** practica.	Gabriela **no las** tiene.
Carmen compra **los pasajes**.	Diego no hace **las maletas**.
Carmen **los** compra.	Diego **no las** hace.

▶ When the verb is an infinitive construction, such as **ir a** + [*infinitive*], the direct object pronoun can be placed before the conjugated form or attached to the infinitive.

Ellos van a escribir **unas postales**.
— Ellos **las** van a escribir.
— Ellos van a escribir**las**.

Lidia quiere ver **una película**.
— Lidia **la** quiere ver.
— Lidia quiere ver**la**.

▶ When the verb is in the present progressive, the direct object pronoun can be placed before the conjugated form or attached to the present participle. **¡Atención!** When a direct object pronoun is attached to the present participle, an accent mark is added to maintain the proper stress.

Gerardo está leyendo **la lección**.
— Gerardo **la** está leyendo.
— Gerardo está leyéndo**la**.

Toni está mirando **el partido**.
— Toni **lo** está mirando.
— Toni está mirándo**lo**.

CONSULTA
To learn more about accents, see **Lección 4, Pronunciación**, p. 33.

¡INTÉNTALO!   Choose the correct direct object pronoun for each sentence.

1. Tienes el libro de español. *c*
   a. La tienes.   b. Los tienes.   c. Lo tienes.
2. Voy a ver el partido de baloncesto. *a*
   a. Voy a verlo.   b. Voy a verte.   c. Voy a vernos.
3. El artista quiere dibujar a Luisa y a su mamá. *c*
   a. Quiere dibujarme.   b. Quiere dibujarla.   c. Quiere dibujarlas.
4. Marcos busca la llave. *b*
   a. Me busca.   b. La busca.   c. Las busca.
5. Rita me lleva al aeropuerto y también lleva a Tomás. *a*
   a. Nos lleva.   b. Las lleva.   c. Te lleva.
6. Puedo oír a Gerardo y a Miguel. *b*
   a. Puedo oírte.   b. Puedo oírlos.   c. Puedo oírlo.
7. Quieren estudiar la gramática. *c*
   a. Quieren estudiarnos.   b. Quieren estudiarlo.   c. Quieren estudiarla.
8. ¿Practicas los verbos irregulares? *a*
   a. ¿Los practicas?   b. ¿Las practicas?   c. ¿Lo practicas?
9. Ignacio ve la película. *a*
   a. La ve.   b. Lo ve.   c. Las ve.
10. Sandra va a invitar a Mario a la excursión. También me va a invitar a mí. *c*
    a. Los va a invitar.   b. Lo va a invitar.   c. Nos va a invitar.

| Comparisons 4.1 | 86 ochenta y seis | Lección 5 |

Práctica

1 Simplificar Professor Vega's class is planning a trip to Costa Rica. Describe their preparations by changing the direct object nouns into direct object pronouns.

> **modelo**
> La profesora Vega tiene su pasaporte.
> La profesora Vega lo tiene.

1. Gustavo y Héctor confirman las reservaciones. *Gustavo y Héctor las confirman.*
2. Nosotros leemos los folletos (*brochures*). *Nosotros los leemos.*
3. Ana María estudia el mapa. *Ana María lo estudia.*
4. Yo aprendo los nombres de los monumentos de San José. *Yo los aprendo.*
5. Alicia escucha a la profesora. *Alicia la escucha.*
6. Miguel escribe las instrucciones para ir al hotel. *Miguel las escribe.*
7. Esteban busca el pasaje. *Esteban lo busca.*
8. Nosotros planeamos una excursión. *Nosotros la planeamos.*

¡LENGUA VIVA!
There are many Spanish words that correspond to *ticket*. **Billete** and **pasaje** usually refer to a ticket for travel, such as an airplane ticket. **Entrada** refers to a ticket to an event, such as a concert or a movie. **Boleto** can be used in either case.

2 Vacaciones Ramón is going to San Juan, Puerto Rico, with his friends, Javier and Marcos. Express his thoughts more succinctly using direct object pronouns.

> **modelo**
> Quiero hacer una excursión.
> Quiero hacerla./La quiero hacer.

1. Voy a hacer mi maleta. *Voy a hacerla./La voy a hacer.*
2. Necesitamos llevar los pasaportes. *Necesitamos llevarlos./Los necesitamos llevar.*
3. Marcos está pidiendo el folleto turístico. *Marcos está pidiéndolo./Marcos lo está pidiendo.*
4. Javier debe llamar a sus padres. *Javier debe llamarlos./Javier los debe llamar.*
5. Ellos desean visitar el Viejo San Juan. *Ellos desean visitarlo./Ellos lo desean visitar.*
6. Puedo llamar a Javier por la mañana. *Puedo llamarlo./Lo puedo llamar.*
7. Prefiero llevar mi cámara. *Prefiero llevarla./La prefiero llevar.*
8. No queremos perder nuestras reservaciones de hotel. *No queremos perderlas./No las queremos perder.*

NOTA CULTURAL
Puerto Rico is a U.S. territory, so people do not need travel documents when traveling to and from Puerto Rico from the U.S. mainland. However, everyone must meet all requirements for entering the U.S. when traveling directly to Puerto Rico from abroad.

3 ¿Quién? The Garza family is preparing to go on a vacation to Puerto Rico. Based on the clues, answer the questions. Use direct object pronouns in your answers.

> **modelo**
> ¿Quién hace las reservaciones para el hotel? (el Sr. Garza)
> El Sr. Garza las hace.

1. ¿Quién compra los pasajes para el vuelo (*flight*)? (la Sra. Garza)
   La Sra. Garza los compra.
2. ¿Quién tiene que hacer las maletas de los niños? (María)
   María tiene que hacerlas./María las tiene que hacer.
3. ¿Quiénes buscan los pasaportes? (Antonio y María)
   Antonio y María los buscan.
4. ¿Quién va a confirmar las reservaciones de hotel? (la Sra. Garza)
   La Sra. Garza va a confirmarlas./La Sra. Garza las va a confirmar.
5. ¿Quién busca la cámara? (María)
   María la busca.
6. ¿Quién compra un mapa de Puerto Rico? (Antonio)
   Antonio lo compra.

Comunicación

4 Escuchar Listen to Mercedes and Gabriel, two students in Chicago, talk about their winter break. Then indicate whether the following conclusions are **lógico** or **ilógico**, based on what you heard.

	Lógico	Ilógico
1. Gabriel va a la playa.	✓	
2. Gabriel está listo para salir.		✓
3. Va a hacer frío en Chicago.	✓	
4. Gabriel viaja a España.		✓
5. Mercedes va a viajar también.		✓

5 Entrevista Answer your partner's questions. Use direct object pronouns. *Answers will vary.*

1. ¿Ves mucho la televisión?
2. ¿Cuándo vas a ver tu programa favorito?
3. ¿Quién prepara la comida (*food*) en tu casa?
4. ¿Te visita mucho tu familia?
5. ¿Visitas mucho a tus abuelos?
6. ¿Nos entienden nuestros padres a nosotros?
7. ¿Cuándo ves a tus amigos/as?
8. ¿Cuándo te llaman tus amigos/as?

6 De mal humor The weather has ruined your plans to go to the beach. Using words from the list, your partner offers some suggestions to cheer you up. Use direct object pronouns in your responses. *Answers will vary.*

modelo
Estudiante 1: ¿Quieres ver la película de Ryan Gosling?
Estudiante 2: No la quiero ver.

| computadora | fotos | libro |
| película | revista | videojuegos |

Síntesis

7 Adivinanzas Write five riddles with descriptions of people, places, or things. Follow the model. Then see whether your teacher can solve your riddles. *Answers will vary.*

modelo
Lo uso para (*I use it to*) escribir en mi cuaderno.
No es muy grande y tiene borrador. ¿Qué es?

TEACHING OPTIONS

Game Play a game of **20 Preguntas**. Divide the class into two teams. Think of an object in the room and alternate calling on teams to ask questions. Once a team knows the answer, the team captain should raise his or her hand. If right, the team gets a point. If wrong, the team loses a point. Play until one team has earned five points.

Pairs Have students create five questions that include the direct object pronouns **me, te**, and **nos**. Then have them ask their partners the questions on their list. Ex: —¿Quién te llama mucho? —Mi mejor amiga me llama mucho. —¿Quién nos escucha cuando hacemos preguntas en español? —El/La profesor(a) y los estudiantes nos escuchan.

Recapitulación

RESUMEN GRAMATICAL

Review the grammar concepts you have learned in this lesson by completing these activities.

1 Completar
Complete the chart with the correct present participle of these verbs. **16 pts.**

Infinitive	Present participle	Infinitive	Present participle
hacer	haciendo	estar	estando
acampar	acampando	ser	siendo
tener	teniendo	vivir	viviendo
venir	viniendo	estudiar	estudiando

2 Vacaciones en París
Complete this paragraph about Julia's trip to Paris with the correct form of **ser** or **estar**. **24 pts.**

Hoy (1) **es** (es/está) el 3 de julio y voy a París por tres semanas. (Yo) (2) **Estoy** (Soy/Estoy) muy feliz porque voy a ver a mi mejor amiga. Ella (3) **es** (es/está) de Puerto Rico, pero ahora (4) **está** (es/está) viviendo en París. También (yo) (5) **estoy** (soy/estoy) un poco nerviosa porque (6) **es** (es/está) mi primer viaje a Francia. El vuelo (*flight*) (7) **es** (es/está) hoy por la tarde, pero ahora (8) **está** (es/está) lloviendo. Por eso (9) **estamos** (somos/estamos) preocupadas, porque probablemente el avión va a salir tarde. Mi equipaje ya (10) **está** (es/está) listo. (11) **Es** (Es/Está) tarde y me tengo que ir. ¡Va a (12) **ser** (ser/estar) un viaje fenomenal!

3 ¿Qué hacen?
Respond to these questions by indicating what people do with the items mentioned. Use direct object pronouns. **20 pts.**

modelo
¿Qué hacen ellos con la película? (ver)
La ven.

1. ¿Qué haces tú con el libro de viajes? (leer) **Lo leo.**
2. ¿Qué hacen los turistas en la ciudad? (explorar) **La exploran.**
3. ¿Qué hace el botones con el equipaje? (llevar) **Lo lleva (a la habitación).**
4. ¿Qué hace la agente con las reservaciones? (confirmar) **Las confirma.**
5. ¿Qué hacen ustedes con los pasaportes? (mostrar) **Los mostramos.**

5.1 Estar with conditions and emotions *p. 74*
- Yo **estoy** aburrido/a, feliz, nervioso/a.
- El cuarto **está** desordenado, limpio, ordenado.
- Estos libros **están** abiertos, cerrados, sucios.

5.2 The present progressive *pp. 76–77*
- The present progressive is formed with the present tense of estar plus the present participle.

Forming the present participle

infinitive	stem	ending	present participle
hablar	habl-	-ando	hablando
comer	com-	-iendo	comiendo
escribir	escrib-	-iendo	escribiendo

-ir stem-changing verbs

	infinitive	present participle
e:ie	preferir	prefiriendo
e:i	conseguir	consiguiendo
o:ue	dormir	durmiendo

- Irregular present participles: yendo (ir), pudiendo (poder), viniendo (venir)

5.3 Ser and estar *pp. 80–81*
- Uses of **ser**: nationality, origin, profession or occupation, characteristics, generalizations, possession, what something is made of, time and date, time and place of events
- Uses of **estar**: location, health, physical states and conditions, emotional states, weather expressions, ongoing actions
- Many adjectives can be used with both **ser** and **estar**, but the meaning of the adjectives will change.

Juan **es** delgado.   Juan **está** más delgado hoy.
Juan is thin.   *Juan looks thinner today.*

Las vacaciones

ochenta y nueve   89

4 Opuestos Complete these sentences with the appropriate form of the verb **estar** and an antonym for the underlined adjective. **20 pts.**

> **modelo**
> Mis respuestas están <u>bien</u>, pero las de Susana _están mal_.

1. Las tiendas están <u>abiertas</u>, pero la agencia de viajes _está_ _cerrada_.
2. No me gustan las habitaciones <u>desordenadas</u>. Incluso (*Even*) mi habitación de hotel _está ordenada_.
3. Nosotras estamos <u>tristes</u> cuando trabajamos. Hoy comienzan las vacaciones y _estamos contentas/alegres/felices_
4. En esta ciudad los autobuses están <u>sucios</u>, pero los taxis _están_ _limpios_.
5. —El avión sale a las 5:30, ¿verdad? —No, estás <u>confundida</u>. Yo _estoy_ _seguro/a_ de que el avión sale a las 5:00.

5.4 Direct object nouns and pronouns   *pp. 84–85*

Direct object pronouns

Singular		Plural	
me	lo	nos	los
te	la	os	las

In affirmative sentences:
Adela practica **el tenis**. → Adela **lo** practica.

In negative sentences: Adela no **lo** practica.

With an infinitive:
Adela **lo** va a practicar./Adela va a practicar**lo**.

With the present progressive:
Adela **lo** está practicando./Adela está practicándo**lo**.

5 En la playa Describe what these people are doing. Complete the sentences using the present progressive tense. **16 pts.**

1. El Sr. Camacho _está pescando_.
2. Felicia _está paseando en barco_.
3. Leo _está montando a caballo_.
4. Nosotros _estamos jugando a las cartas_.

6 Refrán Complete this Spanish saying by filling in the missing present participles. Refer to the translation and the drawing. **4 pts.**

"Se consigue más _haciendo_ que _diciendo_."

(*You can accomplish more by doing than by saying.*)

5 adelante

Lectura

Antes de leer

Estrategia

Scanning

Scanning involves glancing over a document in search of specific information. For example, you can scan a document to identify its format, to find cognates, to locate visual clues about the document's content, or to find specific facts. Scanning allows you to learn a great deal about a text without having to read it word for word.

Examinar el texto

Scan the reading selection for cognates and write down a few of them. Answers will vary.

1. _____   4. _____
2. _____   5. _____
3. _____   6. _____

Based on the cognates you found, what do you think this document is about?
_____

Preguntas

Read these questions. Then scan the document again to look for answers. Answers will vary.

1. What is the format of the reading selection?
_____
2. Which place is the document about?
_____
3. What are some of the visual cues this document provides? What do they tell you about the content of the document?
_____
4. Who produced the document, and what do you think it is for?
_____

Turismo ecológico en Puerto Rico

Hotel Vistahermosa
~ Lajas, Puerto Rico ~

- 40 habitaciones individuales
- 15 habitaciones dobles
- Teléfono/TV por cable/Internet
- Aire acondicionado
- Restaurante (Bar)
- Piscina
- Área de juegos
- Cajero automático°

El hotel está situado en Playa Grande, un pequeño pueblo de pescadores del mar Caribe. Es el lugar perfecto para el viajero que viene de vacaciones. Las playas son seguras y limpias, ideales para tomar el sol, descansar, tomar fotografías y nadar. Está abierto los 365 días del año. Hay una rebaja° especial para estudiantes universitarios.

DIRECCIÓN: Playa Grande 406, Lajas, PR 00667, cerca del Parque Nacional Foresta.

Cajero automático *ATM*   rebaja *discount*

Atracciones cercanas

Playa Grande ¿Busca la playa perfecta? Playa Grande es la playa que está buscando. Usted puede pescar, sacar fotos, nadar y pasear en bicicleta. Playa Grande es un paraíso para el turista que quiere practicar deportes acuáticos. El lugar es bonito e interesante y usted va a tener muchas oportunidades para descansar y disfrutar en familia.

Valle Niebla Ir de excursión, tomar café, montar a caballo, caminar, hacer picnics. Más de cien lugares para acampar.

Bahía Fosforescente Sacar fotos, salidas de noche, excursión en barco. Una maravillosa experiencia llena de luz°.

Arrecifes de Coral Sacar fotos, bucear, explorar. Es un lugar único en el Caribe.

Playa Vieja Tomar el sol, pasear en bicicleta, jugar a las cartas, escuchar música. Ideal para la familia.

Parque Nacional Foresta Sacar fotos, visitar el Museo de Arte Nativo. Reserva Mundial de la Biosfera.

Santuario de las Aves Sacar fotos, observar aves°, seguir rutas de excursión.

llena de luz *full of light*   aves *birds*

Después de leer

Listas
Which amenities of Hotel Vistahermosa would most interest these potential guests? Explain your choices.

1. dos padres con un hijo de seis años y una hija de ocho años
   _____
2. un hombre y una mujer en su luna de miel (*honeymoon*)
   _____
3. una persona en un viaje de negocios (*business trip*)
   _____

Conversaciones
Answer your partner's questions.

1. ¿Quieres visitar el Hotel Vistahermosa? ¿Por qué?
2. Tienes tiempo de visitar sólo tres de las atracciones turísticas que están cerca del hotel. ¿Cuáles vas a visitar? ¿Por qué?
3. ¿Qué prefieres hacer en Valle Niebla? ¿En Playa Vieja? ¿En el Parque Nacional Foresta?

Situaciones
You have just arrived at Hotel Vistahermosa. Your partner is the concierge. Use the phrases below to express your interests and ask for suggestions about where to go.

1. montar a caballo
2. bucear
3. pasear en bicicleta
4. pescar
5. observar aves

Contestar
Answer these questions.

1. ¿Quieres visitar Puerto Rico? Explica tu respuesta.
   _____
2. ¿Adónde quieres ir de vacaciones el verano que viene? Explica tu respuesta.
   _____

Section Goals

In **Escritura**, students will:
- write a brochure for a hotel or resort
- integrate travel-related vocabulary and structures taught in **Lección 5**

 Communication 1.3

 Pre-AP®

Interpersonal Writing: Estrategia
Explain that outlines are a great way for a writer to think about what a piece of writing will be like before actually expending much time and effort on writing. An outline is also a great way of keeping a writer on track while composing the piece and helps the person keep the whole project in mind as he or she focuses on a specific part.

Tema Discuss the hotel or resort brochure students are to write. Go over the list of information that they might include. You might indicate a specific number of the points that should be included in the brochure. Tell students that the brochure for **Hotel Vistahermosa** in **Lectura**, pages 90–91, can serve as a model for their writing. Remind them that they are writing with the purpose of attracting guests to the hotel or resort. Suggest that, as they begin to think about writing, students should brainstorm as many details as they can remember about the hotel they are going to describe. Tell them to do this in Spanish.

In-Class Tip Have students write each of the individual items of their brainstorm lists on index cards so that they can arrange and rearrange them into different idea maps as they plan their brochures.

Escritura

Estrategia
Making an outline

When we write to share information, an outline can serve to separate topics and subtopics, providing a framework for the presentation of data. Consider the following excerpt from an outline of the tourist brochure on pages 90–91.

IV. Descripción del sitio (con foto)
   A. Playa Grande
      1. Playas seguras y limpias
      2. Ideal para tomar el sol, descansar, tomar fotografías, nadar
   B. El hotel
      1. Abierto los 365 días del año
      2. Rebaja para estudiantes universitarios

Mapa de ideas
Idea maps can be used to create outlines. The major sections of an idea map correspond to the Roman numerals in an outline. The minor idea map sections correspond to the outline's capital letters, and so on. Examine the idea map that led to the outline above.

Tema
Escribir un folleto

Write a tourist brochure for a hotel or resort you have visited. If you wish, you may write about an imaginary location. You may want to include some of this information in your brochure:

▶ the name of the hotel or resort
▶ phone and fax numbers that tourists can use to make contact
▶ the hotel website that tourists can consult
▶ an e-mail address that tourists can use to request information
▶ a description of the exterior of the hotel or resort
▶ a description of the interior of the hotel or resort, including facilities and amenities
▶ a description of the surrounding area, including its climate
▶ a listing of nearby scenic natural attractions
▶ a listing of nearby cultural attractions
▶ a listing of recreational activities that tourists can pursue in the vicinity of the hotel or resort

EVALUATION: Folleto

Criteria	Scale
Appropriate details	1 2 3 4 5
Organization	1 2 3 4 5
Use of vocabulary	1 2 3 4 5
Grammatical accuracy	1 2 3 4 5

Scoring	
Excellent	18–20 points
Good	14–17 points
Satisfactory	10–13 points
Unsatisfactory	< 10 points

Escuchar

> **Estrategia**
>
> **Listening for key words**
>
> By listening for key words or phrases, you can identify the subject and main ideas of what you hear, as well as some of the details.
>
> 🔊 To practice this strategy, you will now listen to a short paragraph. As you listen, jot down the key words that help you identify the subject of the paragraph and its main ideas.

Preparación

Based on the illustration, who do you think Hernán Jiménez is, and what is he doing? What key words might you listen for to help you understand what he is saying?

Ahora escucha

Now you are going to listen to a weather report by Hernán Jiménez. Note which phrases are correct according to the key words and phrases you hear.

Santo Domingo

1. hace sol ✔
2. va a hacer frío
3. una mañana de mal tiempo
4. va a estar nublado ✔
5. buena tarde para tomar el sol
6. buena mañana para la playa ✔

San Francisco de Macorís

1. hace frío ✔
2. hace sol
3. va a nevar
4. va a llover ✔
5. hace calor
6. mal día para excursiones ✔

Comprensión

¿Cierto o falso?

Indicate whether each statement is **cierto** or **falso**, based on the weather report. Correct the false statements.

1. Según el meteorólogo, la temperatura en Santo Domingo es de 26 grados.
   Cierto.
2. La temperatura máxima en Santo Domingo hoy va a ser de 30 grados.
   Cierto.
3. Está lloviendo ahora en Santo Domingo.
   Falso. Hace sol.
4. En San Francisco de Macorís la temperatura mínima de hoy va a ser de 20 grados.
   Falso. La temperatura mínima va a ser de 18 grados.
5. Va a llover mucho hoy en San Francisco de Macorís.
   Cierto.

Preguntas

Answer these questions about the weather report.

1. ¿Hace viento en Santo Domingo ahora?
   Sí, hace viento en Santo Domingo.
2. ¿Está nublado en Santo Domingo ahora?
   No, no está nublado ahora en Santo Domingo.
3. ¿Está nevando ahora en San Francisco de Macorís?
   No, no está nevando ahora en San Francisco de Macorís.
4. ¿Qué tiempo hace en San Francisco de Macorís?
   Hace frío.

Section Goals

In **En pantalla**, students will:
- read about airline travel in Latin America
- watch an ad for **LANPASS**, a Chilean airline loyalty program

 Communication 1.1, 1.2, 1.3
Cultures 2.2
Connections 3.2
Comparisons 4.2
Communities 5.2

Teacher Resources
Read the front matter for suggestions on how to incorporate all the program's components. See pages 61A–61B for a detailed listing of Teacher Resources online.

El arte de viajar Check comprehension: 1. How will airline travel evolve in Latin America by the year 2034? 2. What is LAN? 3. What is LANPASS and what is its goal?

Pre-AP®

Audiovisual Interpretive Communication
Antes de ver **Strategy**
Remind students to focus first on familiar words to identify the purpose of the video.

Comprensión Once students have marked the items they hear in the ad, ask them to make a list of other ways everyday life is different when we travel.

Aplicación Encourage students to use photos or videos of their own family trips when presenting their ad to the class.

Anuncio de **Santander LANPASS**

Con lo que realmente nos importa°.

Preparación
Answer these questions in Spanish. Answers will vary.
1. ¿Te gusta viajar? ¿Por qué? ¿Adónde te gusta viajar?
2. ¿Qué te gusta hacer cuando estás de vacaciones?
3. ¿Qué modo de transporte prefieres usar? ¿Por qué?

El arte de viajar
Millions of people travel on airlines every year for business and pleasure. The number of airline passengers is expected to double between 2014 and 2034 worldwide. This is true for Latin America, too, as airlines are looking at how to attract all those customers to their planes. The airline of Chile, LAN, has partnered with the international bank Santander to create the loyalty program LANPASS to encourage frequent travel on LAN. What does an airline say to travelers that captures their attention and makes their business seem like your pleasure?

importa *matters*

Vocabulario útil

arena	sand
cambiar	to change
destino	destination
medir	to measure
mismo/a	itself
piel	skin
puestas de sol	sunsets
recuerdos	memories
sentirse	to feel
sino	but

Comprensión
Mark an X next to the phrases you hear in the ad.
Irse es volver a….

- x cambiar de piel
- x desconectarnos
- __ estudiar mucho
- x un mundo sin Internet
- __ trabajar
- x castillos de arena
- __ destinos exóticos
- x la esencia de todo
- __ la oficina
- x sentirse vivo
- x las siestas
- __ tiempo en familia

Conversación
Answers will vary.
Answer these questions with a classmate.
1. Según el anuncio, ¿cuáles son algunas cosas positivas de viajar?
2. ¿Cuáles de estas cosas positivas son importantes para ti? ¿Por qué?
3. Para tener experiencias positivas, ¿a dónde viajas tú? ¿A dónde viaja tu familia? ¿Y tus amigos?

Aplicación
With a classmate, prepare an ad inviting other people to travel to a special place. Explain why it is a perfect or ideal place. What evocative words and images will you use? Present your ad to the class. Answers will vary.

EXPANSION

Culture Note Although airline travel is becoming more popular throughout Latin America, in some countries people still use other means of transportation for their trips, especially intercity buses. This is in part a custom and in part due to the high costs of airline tickets. However, low-cost airlines have recently started operations in some countries.

Small Groups Have small groups of students research and create an oral presentation about other big airline companies in the Spanish-speaking world. Encourage them to include information on the alliances they have with other companies and the way they attract customers.

Las vacaciones

¡Vacaciones en Perú!

Between 1438 and 1533, when the vast and powerful Incan Empire was at its height, the Incas built an elaborate network of **caminos** (*trails*) that traversed the Andes Mountains and converged on the empire's capital, Cuzco. Today, hundreds of thousands of tourists come to Peru annually to walk the surviving trails and enjoy the spectacular scenery. The most popular trail, **el Camino Inca**, leads from Cuzco to **Intipunku** (*Sun Gate*), the entrance to the ancient mountain city of Machu Picchu.

Vocabulario útil

ciudadela	citadel
de cultivo	farming
el/la guía	guide
maravilla	wonder
quechua	Quechua (indigenous Peruvian)
sector (urbano)	(urban) sector

Preparación
Have you ever visited an archeological or historic site? Where? Why did you go there? *Answers will vary.*

Completar
Complete these sentences. Make the necessary changes.

1. Las ruinas de Machu Picchu son una antigua ___ciudadela___ inca.
2. La ciudadela estaba (*was*) dividida en tres sectores: ___urbano___, religioso y de cultivo.
3. Cada año los ___guías___ reciben a cientos (*hundreds*) de turistas de diferentes países.
4. Hoy en día, la cultura ___quechua___ está presente en las comunidades andinas (*Andean*) de Perú.

Machu Picchu [...] se encuentra aislada sobre° esta montaña...

... siempre he querido° venir [...] Me encantan° las civilizaciones antiguas°.

Somos una familia francesa [...] Perú es un país muy, muy bonito de verdad.

se encuentra aislada sobre *it is isolated on* siempre he querido *I have always wanted* Me encantan *I love* antiguas *ancient*

Section Goal

In **Panorama**, students will read about the geography, history, and culture of Puerto Rico.

Communication 1.3
Cultures 2.1, 2.2
Connections 3.1, 3.2
Comparisons 4.2

Teacher Resources
Read the front matter for suggestions on how to incorporate all the program's components. See pages 61A–61B for a detailed listing of Teacher Resources online.

In-Class Tips
- Use the **Lección 5 Panorama** online Resources to assist with this presentation.
- Discuss Puerto Rico's location in relation to the U.S. mainland and the other Caribbean islands. Encourage students to describe what they see in the photos on this page.

El país en cifras After reading **Puertorriqueños célebres**, ask volunteers who are familiar with these individuals to tell a little more about each one. For example, **José Rivera** is a playwright and screenwriter who was nominated for an Academy Award for his screenplay of *Diarios de motocicleta* (2004). You might also mention **Rita Moreno**, the only Hispanic female performer to have won an Oscar, a Tony, an Emmy, and a Grammy, and novelist **Rosario Ferré**, whose *House on the Lagoon* (**La casa de la laguna**) gives a fictional portrait of a large part of Puerto Rican history.

¡Increíble pero cierto! The **río Camuy** caves are actually a series of karstic sinkholes, formed by water sinking into and eroding limestone. Another significant cave in this system is **Cueva Clara**, located in the **Parque de las Cavernas del Río Camuy**.

---

5 | panorama

Puerto Rico

El país en cifras

▶ **Área:** 8.959 km² (3.459 millas²) menor° que el área de Connecticut
▶ **Población:** 3.667.084
Puerto Rico es una de las islas más densamente pobladas° del mundo. Más de la mitad de la población vive en San Juan, la capital.
▶ **Capital:** San Juan—2.730.000
▶ **Ciudades principales:** Arecibo, Bayamón, Fajardo, Mayagüez, Ponce
▶ **Moneda:** dólar estadounidense
▶ **Idiomas:** español (oficial); inglés (oficial)
Aproximadamente la cuarta parte de la población puertorriqueña habla inglés, pero en las zonas turísticas este porcentaje es mucho más alto. El uso del inglés es obligatorio para documentos federales.

Bandera de Puerto Rico

Puertorriqueños célebres
▶ **Raúl Juliá,** actor (1940–1994)
▶ **Roberto Clemente,** beisbolista (1934–1972)
▶ **Julia de Burgos,** escritora (1914–1953)
▶ **Benicio del Toro,** actor y productor (1967–)
▶ **Rosie Pérez,** actriz y bailarina (1964–)
▶ **José Rivera,** dramaturgo y guionista (1955–)

menor *less* pobladas *populated* río subterráneo *underground river* más largo *longest* cuevas *caves* bóveda *vault* fortaleza *fort* caber *fit*

¡Increíble pero cierto!
El río Camuy es el tercer río subterráneo° más largo° del mundo y tiene el sistema de cuevas° más grande del hemisferio occidental. La Cueva de los Tres Pueblos es una gigantesca bóveda°, tan grande que toda la fortaleza° del Morro puede caber° en su interior.

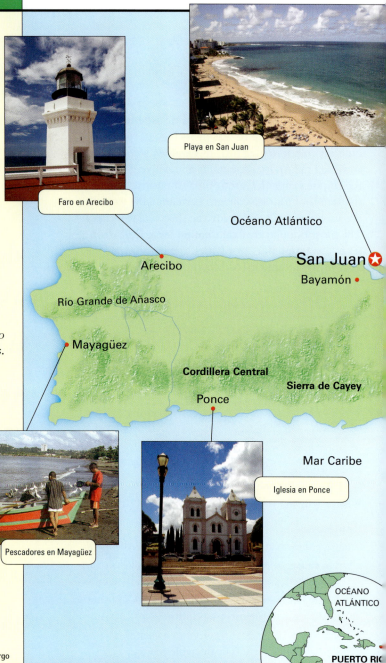

TEACHING OPTIONS

Heritage Speakers Encourage heritage speakers of Puerto Rican descent who have visited or lived on the island to share their impressions of it with the class. Ask them to describe people they knew or met, places they saw, and experiences they had. Have the class ask follow-up questions.
El béisbol Baseball is a popular sport in Puerto Rico, home of the Winter League. **Roberto Clemente**, a player with the Pittsburgh Pirates who died tragically in a plane crash, was the first Latino to be inducted into the Baseball Hall of Fame. He is venerated all over the island with buildings and monuments. There are numerous Major League Baseball players that were born in Puerto Rico, such as **Carlos Beltrán, Iván Rodríguez, Jorge Posada, Carlos Delgado,** and **Yadier Molina.**

Lugares • El Morro
El Morro es una fortaleza que se construyó para proteger° la bahía° de San Juan desde principios del siglo° XVI hasta principios del siglo XX. Hoy día muchos turistas visitan este lugar, convertido en un museo. Es el sitio más fotografiado de Puerto Rico. La arquitectura de la fortaleza es impresionante. Tiene misteriosos túneles, oscuras mazmorras° y vistas fabulosas de la bahía.

Artes • Salsa

La salsa, un estilo musical de origen puertorriqueño y cubano, nació° en el barrio latino de la ciudad de Nueva York. Dos de los músicos de salsa más famosos son Tito Puente y Willie Colón, los dos de Nueva York. Las estrellas° de la salsa en Puerto Rico son Felipe Rodríguez y Héctor Lavoe. Hoy en día, Puerto Rico es el centro internacional de este estilo musical. El Gran Combo de Puerto Rico es una de las orquestas de salsa más famosas del mundo°.

Ciencias • El Observatorio de Arecibo

El Observatorio de Arecibo tiene uno de los radiotelescopios más grandes del mundo. Gracias a este telescopio, los científicos° pueden estudiar las propiedades de la Tierra°, la Luna° y otros cuerpos celestes. También pueden analizar fenómenos celestiales como los quasares y pulsares, y detectar emisiones de radio de otras galaxias, en busca de inteligencia extraterrestre.

Historia • Relación con los Estados Unidos
Puerto Rico pasó a ser° parte de los Estados Unidos después de° la guerra° de 1898 y se hizo° un estado libre asociado en 1952. Los puertorriqueños, ciudadanos° estadounidenses desde° 1917, tienen representación política en el Congreso, pero no votan en las elecciones presidenciales y no pagan impuestos° federales. Hay un debate entre los puertorriqueños: ¿debe la isla seguir como estado libre asociado, hacerse un estado como los otros° o volverse° independiente?

¿Qué aprendiste? Contesta las preguntas con una oración completa.
1. ¿Cuál es la moneda de Puerto Rico? La moneda de Puerto Rico es el dólar estadounidense.
2. ¿Qué idiomas se hablan (*are spoken*) en Puerto Rico? Se hablan español e inglés en Puerto Rico.
3. ¿Cuál es el sitio más fotografiado de Puerto Rico? El Morro es el sitio más fotografiado de Puerto Rico.
4. ¿Qué es el Gran Combo? Es una orquesta de Puerto Rico.
5. ¿Qué hacen los científicos en el Observatorio de Arecibo? Los científicos estudian las propiedades de la Tierra y la Luna y detectan emisiones de otras galaxias.

Conexión Internet Investiga estos temas en Internet.
1. Describe a dos puertorriqueños famosos. ¿Cómo son? ¿Qué hacen? ¿Dónde viven? ¿Por qué son célebres?
2. Busca información sobre lugares en los que se puede hacer ecoturismo en Puerto Rico.

---

proteger *protect* bahía *bay* siglo *century* mazmorras *dungeons* nació *was born* estrellas *stars* mundo *world* científicos *scientists* Tierra *Earth* Luna *Moon* pasó a ser *became* después de *after* guerra *war* se hizo *became* ciudadanos *citizens* desde *since* pagan impuestos *pay taxes* otros *others* volverse *to become*

5 vocabulario

Comparisons 4.1

Teacher Resources
Read the front matter for suggestions on how to incorporate all the program's components. See pages 61A–61B for a detailed listing of Teacher Resources online.

In-Class Tip Ask students to prepare a list of the three products or perspectives they learned about in this lesson to share with the class. You may ask them to focus specifically on the **Cultura** and **Panorama** sections.

Los viajes y las vacaciones

acampar	to camp
confirmar una reservación	to confirm a reservation
estar de vacaciones (*f. pl.*)	to be on vacation
hacer las maletas	to pack (one's suitcases)
hacer un viaje	to take a trip
hacer (wind)surf	to (wind)surf
ir de compras (*f. pl.*)	to go shopping
ir de vacaciones	to go on vacation
ir en autobús (*m.*), auto(móvil) (*m.*), avión (*m.*), barco (*m.*), moto(cicleta) (*f.*), taxi (*m.*)	to go by bus, car, plane, boat, motorcycle, taxi
jugar a las cartas	to play cards
montar a caballo (*m.*)	to ride a horse
pescar	to fish
sacar/tomar fotos (*f. pl.*)	to take photos
el/la agente de viajes	travel agent
el/la inspector(a) de aduanas	customs inspector
el/la viajero/a	traveler
el aeropuerto	airport
la agencia de viajes	travel agency
el campo	countryside
el equipaje	luggage
la estación de autobuses, del metro, de tren	bus, subway, train station
la llegada	arrival
el mar	sea
el paisaje	landscape
el pasaje (de ida y vuelta)	(round-trip) ticket
el pasaporte	passport
la playa	beach
la salida	departure; exit
la tabla de (wind)surf	surfboard/sailboard

El hotel

el ascensor	elevator
la cama	bed
el/la empleado/a	employee
la habitación individual, doble	single, double room
el hotel	hotel
el/la huésped	guest
la llave	key
el piso	floor (of a building)
la planta baja	ground floor

Adjetivos

abierto/a	open
aburrido/a	bored; boring
alegre	happy
amable	nice; friendly
avergonzado/a	embarrassed
cansado/a	tired
cerrado/a	closed
cómodo/a	comfortable
confundido/a	confused
contento/a	content
desordenado/a	disorderly
enamorado/a (de)	in love (with)
enojado/a	angry
equivocado/a	wrong
feliz	happy
limpio/a	clean
listo/a	ready; smart
nervioso/a	nervous
ocupado/a	busy
ordenado/a	orderly
preocupado/a (por)	worried (about)
seguro/a	sure; safe; confident
sucio/a	dirty
triste	sad

Los números ordinales

primer, primero/a	first
segundo/a	second
tercer, tercero/a	third
cuarto/a	fourth
quinto/a	fifth
sexto/a	sixth
séptimo/a	seventh
octavo/a	eighth
noveno/a	ninth
décimo/a	tenth

Palabras adicionales

ahora mismo	right now
el año	year
¿Cuál es la fecha (de hoy)?	What is the date (today)?
de buen/mal humor	in a good/bad mood
la estación	season
el mes	month
todavía	yet; still

Seasons, months, and dates	See page 64.
Weather expressions	See page 64.
Direct object pronouns	See page 84.
Expresiones útiles	See page 69.

Lección 6: Teacher Resources

There is a wealth of resources online to support instruction using **Senderos**. For details on how to integrate these Teacher Resources into your lessons, see the front matter of this Teacher's Edition on pages T14 to T48.

Presentation	Practice & Communicate	Assess*	Scripts and Translations	

• Digital Images:
  • ¡De compras!
  • Los colores
	• Information Gap Activity*
	• Activity Pack Practice Activities (with Answer Key): Contextos
	• Additional Vocabulary (**Más vocabulario para ir de compras**)
	• Digital Image Bank (Shopping)
		• Vocabulary Quiz (with Answer Key)		contextos

		• Fotonovela Optional Testing Sections (with Answer Key)	• **Fotonovela** Videoscript • **Fotonovela** English Translation	fotonovela
• **Estructura 6.1** Grammar Slides	• Information Gap Activity* • Activity Pack Practice Activities (with Answer Key): **Saber** and **conocer** • Surveys: Worksheet for survey	• Grammar 6.1 Quiz (with Answer Key)	• Tutorial Script: **Saber** and **conocer**	estructura
• **Estructura 6.2** Grammar Slides	• Activity Pack Practice Activities (with Answer Key): Indirect object pronouns • Surveys: Worksheet for classroom survey	• Grammar 6.2 Quiz (with Answer Key)	• Tutorial Script: Indirect object pronouns	
• **Estructura 6.3** Grammar Slides	• Activity Pack Practice Activities (with Answer Key): Preterite tense of regular verbs	• Grammar 6.3 Quiz (with Answer Key)	• Tutorial Script: Preterite tense of regular verbs	
• **Estructura 6.4** Grammar Slides	• Activity Pack Practice Activities (with Answer Key): Demonstrative adjectives and pronouns	• Grammar 6.4 Quiz (with Answer Key)	• Tutorial Script: Demonstrative adjectives and pronouns	
			• **En pantalla** Videoscript • **En pantalla** English Translation	adelante / En pantalla
		• **Flash cultura** Optional Testing Sections (with Answer Key)	• **Flash cultura** Videoscript • **Flash cultura** English Translation	Flash cultura
Digital Images: • **Cuba**		• **Panorama** Optional Testing Sections (with Answer Key) • **Panorama cultural** (video)	• **Panorama cultural** Videoscript • **Panorama cultural** English Translation	Panorama

*Can also be assigned online.

Lección 6: Teacher Resources

Pulling It All Together

Practice and Communicate
- Role-plays
- Activity Pack Practice Activities (¡A repasar!) (with Answer Key)

Assessment

Tests and Exams*
- **Prueba A** with audio
- **Prueba B** with audio
- **Prueba C** with audio
- **Prueba D** with audio
- **Prueba E** with audio
- **Prueba F** with audio
- Tests Answer Key
- Oral Testing Suggestions
- **Examen A** with audio (lessons 4-6)
- **Examen B** with audio (lessons 4-6)
- Exams Answer Key

Audioscripts
- Tests and Exams Audioscripts
- Alternative Listening Sections Audioscript

Additional Tools for Planning and Teaching
- Essential Questions
- I Can Worksheets
- IPAs & Rubrics
- Lesson Plans
- Middle School Activity Pack
- Pacing Guides

Audio MP3s for Classroom Activities
- **Contextos.** Activities 1 and 2 (p. 101)
- **Contextos.** Comunicación: Activity 7 (p. 103)
- **Estructura 6.1. Comunicación:** Activity 3 (p. 111)
- **Estructura 6.3. Comunicación:** Activity 4 (p. 119)
- **Estructura 6.4. Comunicación:** Activity 4 (p. 123)
- **Escuchar** (p. 129)

Script for Comunicación: Actividad 7 (p. 103)

Juan Manuel	¿Quieres ir al gimnasio ahora?
Victoria	Ahora no puedo. Tengo que ir a la tienda a comprar unos regalos para mi familia. ¡Hoy hay rebaja!
Juan Manuel	¿Qué piensas comprar?
Victoria	A mi mamá le voy a comprar un traje de baño y a mi papá le voy a comprar una corbata.
Juan Manuel	¿Y a tu hermano qué le vas a comprar?
Victoria	No estoy segura.
Juan Manuel	¿Tiene pasatiempos?
Victoria	¡Sí! Juega al tenis los fines de semana.

Script for Comunicación: Actividad 3 (p. 111)

Conozco a Laura, mi mejor amiga, desde el primer día de escuela. Es una chica genial porque sabe hacer muchas cosas. Sabe cantar y bailar y habla español, francés e inglés. A Laura le gusta ir de compras, especialmente cuando hay rebajas. ¡Sabe regatear y siempre encuentra las mejores gangas! Y ella también practica muchos deportes. Sabe esquiar y patinar en línea. Para ella es fácil conocer gente nueva y hacer amigos.

Script for Comunicación: Actividad 4 (p. 119)

Matilde	Hola, Hernán. ¿Ya estás listo para tu viaje a Cuba?
Hernán	Sí, Matilde, creo que sí.
Matilde	Vamos a ver… ¿Ya compraste el pasaje de avión?
Hernán	Sí, Matilde. Lo compré la semana pasada.
Matilde	Bueno. ¿Confirmaste la reservación para el hotel?
Hernán	No, voy a hablar con la agente de viajes esta tarde.
Matilde	¿Ya encontraste tu pasaporte?
Hernán	Acabo de encontrarlo.
Matilde	¿Ya preparaste la maleta?
Hernán	Sí, la preparé anoche.
Matilde	¿Decidiste llevar tu mochila o no?
Hernán	Decidí no llevarla.
Matilde	¿Leíste tu libro sobre Cuba?
Hernán	No. Pienso leerlo en el avión.

Script for Comunicación: Actividad 4 (p. 123)

Alejandra	Me gusta esta falda azul.
Dependienta	Sí, es muy elegante. Acaba de llegar al almacén.
Alejandra	No es muy cara… La voy a comprar.
Dependienta	¿Y le gusta esta blusa blanca? Hace juego con la falda.
Alejandra	Tengo muchas blusas blancas. Pero… ¿y esa blusa gris? ¿Cuánto cuesta?
Dependienta	¿Esta blusa gris? Cuesta treinta pesos. Es una blusa muy bonita.
Alejandra	También necesito un cinturón. ¿Cuánto cuesta aquél negro?
Dependienta	Sólo cuesta diez pesos.
Alejandra	Voy a comprar el cinturón también, pero ya no quiero ver más cosas porque voy a gastar mucho dinero.

*Tests and Exams can also be assigned online.

¡De compras!

6 Communicative Goals

You will learn how to:
- Talk about and describe clothing
- Express preferences in a store
- Negotiate and pay for items you buy

pages 100–103 — contextos
- Clothing and shopping
- Negotiating a price and buying
- Colors
- More adjectives

pages 104–107 — fotonovela
The friends are back in Mérida where they go to the market to do some shopping. Who will get the best deal?

pages 108–109 — cultura
- Open-air markets
- Carolina Herrera

pages 110–125 — estructura
- Saber and conocer
- Indirect object pronouns
- Preterite tense of regular verbs
- Demonstrative adjectives and pronouns
- Recapitulación

pages 126–133 — adelante
Lectura: An advertisement for a store sale
Escritura: A report for the school newspaper
Escuchar: A conversation about clothes
En pantalla
Flash cultura
Panorama: Cuba

A PRIMERA VISTA
- ¿Está comprando algo la chica?
- ¿Crees que busca una maleta o una blusa?
- ¿Está contenta o enojada?
- ¿Cómo es la chica?

Lesson Goals

In **Lección 6**, students will be introduced to the following:
- terms for clothing and shopping
- colors
- open-air markets
- Venezuelan clothing designer **Carolina Herrera**
- the verbs **saber** and **conocer**
- indirect object pronouns
- preterite tense of regular verbs
- demonstrative adjectives and pronouns
- skimming a document
- how to report an interview
- writing a report
- listening for linguistic cues
- a television commercial for the Spanish toy store **Juguettos**
- a video about open-air markets
- cultural, geographic, economic, and historical information about Cuba

A primera vista Here are some additional questions you can ask to personalize the photo: ¿Te gusta ir de compras? ¿Por qué? ¿Estás de buen humor cuando vas de compras? ¿Piensas ir de compras este fin de semana? ¿Adónde? ¿Qué compras cuando estás de vacaciones?

Teaching Tip Look for these icons for additional communicative practice:

→👤←	Interpretive communication
↔👤	Presentational communication
👤↔👤	Interpersonal communication

SUPPORT FOR BACKWARD DESIGN

Lección 6 Essential Questions
1. How do people talk about shopping and describe clothing?
2. How do people talk about events in the past?
3. What types of markets are common in the Spanish-speaking world and why?

Lección 6 Integrated Performance Assessment
Before teaching this chapter, review the Integrated Performance Assessment (IPA) and its accompanying scoring rubric. Use the IPA to assess students' progress toward proficiency targets at the end of the chapter.
IPA Context: You are traveling to Colombia. Two of your friends have given you money to bring back clothing for them because they are interested in getting something unique from the Spanish-speaking world. Each of your friends, one male and one female, has given you $25, so you'll need to check the current exchange rate to find out how many pesos you have to spend.

 Voice boards online allow you and your students to record and share up to five minutes of audio. Use voice boards for presentations, oral assessments, discussions, directions, etc.

6 contextos

Section Goals
In **Contextos**, students will learn and practice:
- clothing vocabulary
- vocabulary to use while shopping
- colors

 Communication 1.2
Comparisons 4.1

Teacher Resources
Read the front matter for suggestions on how to incorporate all the program's components. See pages 99A–99B for a detailed listing of Teacher Resources online.

In-Class Tips
- Use the **Lección 6 Contextos** vocabulary presentation online or the digital images in the Resources online to assist with this presentation.
- Ask volunteers about shopping preferences and habits. Ex: **¿Qué te gusta comprar? ¿Música? ¿Libros? ¿Ropa?** (Point to your own clothing.) **¿Adónde vas para comprar esas cosas? ¿Las compras en una tienda o en Internet?** (Pretend to reach in your pocket and pay for something.) **¿Cuánto dinero gastas normalmente?** Ask another student: **¿Adónde va de compras ____? (Va a ____.) ¿Y qué compra allí? (Compra ____.)**
- Have students guess the meanings of **damas** and **caballeros**. As they refer to the scene, make true/false statements. Ex: **El hombre paga con tarjeta de crédito. (Cierto.) No venden zapatos en la tienda. (Falso.) Se puede regatear en el almacén. (Falso.)** Use as many clothing items and verbs from **Más vocabulario** as you can.

Note: At this point you may want to present *Vocabulario adicional: Más vocabulario para ir de compras* from the online Resources.

¡De compras!

Más vocabulario

el abrigo	coat
los calcetines (el calcetín)	sock(s)
el cinturón	belt
las gafas (de sol)	(sun)glasses
los guantes	gloves
el impermeable	raincoat
la ropa	clothes
la ropa interior	underwear
las sandalias	sandals
el traje	suit
el vestido	dress
los zapatos de tenis	sneakers
el regalo	gift
el almacén	department store
el centro comercial	shopping mall
el mercado (al aire libre)	(open-air) market
el precio (fijo)	(fixed; set) price
la rebaja	sale
la tienda	store
costar (o:ue)	to cost
gastar	to spend (money)
pagar	to pay
regatear	to bargain
vender	to sell
hacer juego (con)	to match (with)
llevar	to wear; to take
usar	to wear; to use

Variación léxica

calcetines ↔ medias (*Amér. L.*)
cinturón ↔ correa (*Col., Venez.*)
gafas/lentes ↔ espejuelos (*Cuba, P.R.*), anteojos (*Arg., Chile*)
zapatos de tenis ↔ zapatillas de deporte (*Esp.*), zapatillas (*Arg., Perú*)

TEACHING OPTIONS

TPR Call out a list of clothing items at random. Have students raise their right hand if they hear an item they associate with summer (Ex: **los pantalones cortos**), their left hand if they associate the item with winter (Ex: **el abrigo**), or both hands if the item can be worn in both seasons (Ex: **el cinturón**).
Variación léxica Point out that, although terms for clothing vary widely throughout the Spanish-speaking world, speakers in different regions can mutually understand each other.
TPR Have students stand in a circle. Name a sport, place, or activity and toss a ball to a student, who has three seconds to name a clothing item that goes with it. That student then names another sport, place, or activity and tosses the ball to another student. If a student cannot think of an item in time, he or she is eliminated. The last person standing wins.

Práctica

1 Escuchar Listen to Juanita and Vicente talk about what they're packing for their vacations. Indicate who is packing each item. If both are packing an item, write both names. If neither is packing an item, write an **X**.

1. abrigo _Vicente_
2. zapatos de tenis _Juanita, Vicente_
3. impermeable _X_
4. chaqueta _Vicente_
5. sandalias _Juanita_
6. bluejeans _Juanita, Vicente_
7. gafas de sol _Vicente_
8. camisetas _Juanita, Vicente_
9. traje de baño _Juanita_
10. botas _Vicente_
11. pantalones cortos _Juanita_
12. suéter _Vicente_

2 ¿Lógico o ilógico? Listen to Guillermo and Ana talk about vacation destinations. Indicate whether each statement is **lógico** or **ilógico**.

1. _ilógico_
2. _lógico_
3. _ilógico_
4. _lógico_

3 Completar Anita is talking about going shopping. Complete each sentence with the correct word(s), adding definite or indefinite articles when necessary.

caja	medias	tarjeta de crédito
centro comercial	par	traje de baño
dependientas	ropa	vendedores

1. Hoy voy a ir de compras al _centro comercial_.
2. Voy a ir a la tienda de ropa para mujeres. Siempre hay muchas rebajas y las _dependientas_ son muy simpáticas.
3. Necesito comprar _un par_ de zapatos.
4. Y tengo que comprar _un traje de baño_ porque el sábado voy a la playa con mis amigos.
5. También voy a comprar unas _medias_ para mi mamá.
6. Voy a pagar todo (*everything*) en _la caja_.
7. Pero hoy no tengo dinero. Voy a tener que usar mi _tarjeta de crédito_.
8. Mañana voy al mercado al aire libre. Me gusta regatear con los _vendedores_.

4 Escoger Choose the item in each group that does not belong.

1. almacén • centro comercial • mercado • (sombrero)
2. camisa • camiseta • blusa • (botas)
3. jeans • (bolsa) • falda • pantalones
4. abrigo • suéter • (corbata) • chaqueta
5. mercado • tienda • almacén • (cartera)
6. (pagar) • llevar • hacer juego (con) • usar
7. botas • sandalias • zapatos • (traje)
8. vender • regatear • (ropa interior) • gastar

Los colores

amarillo/a · anaranjado/a · azul
blanco/a · gris · marrón, café · morado/a · negro/a
rojo/a · rosado/a · verde

¡LENGUA VIVA!
The names of colors vary throughout the Spanish-speaking world. For example, in some countries, **anaranjado/a** may be referred to as **naranja**, **morado/a** as **púrpura**, and **rojo/a** as **colorado/a**.
Other terms that will prove helpful include **claro** (*light*) and **oscuro** (*dark*): **azul claro, azul oscuro**.

Adjetivos

barato/a	cheap
bueno/a	good
cada	each
caro/a	expensive
corto/a	short (in length)
elegante	elegant
hermoso/a	beautiful
largo/a	long
loco/a	crazy
nuevo/a	new
otro/a	other; another
pobre	poor
rico/a	rich

5 Contrastes Complete each phrase with the opposite of the underlined word.

1. una corbata <u>barata</u> • unas camisas… caras
2. unas vendedoras <u>malas</u> • unos dependientes… buenos
3. un vestido <u>corto</u> • una falda… larga
4. un hombre muy <u>pobre</u> • una mujer muy… rica
5. una cartera <u>nueva</u> • un cinturón… viejo
6. unos trajes <u>hermosos</u> • unos jeans… feos
7. un impermeable <u>caro</u> • unos suéteres… baratos
8. unos calcetines <u>blancos</u> • unas medias… negras

6 Preguntas Answer these questions.

1. ¿De qué color es la rosa de Texas? Es amarilla.
2. ¿De qué color es la bandera (*flag*) de Canadá? Es roja y blanca.
3. ¿De qué color es la casa donde vive el presidente de los EE.UU.? Es blanca.
4. ¿De qué color es el océano Atlántico? Es azul.
5. ¿De qué color es la nieve? Es blanca.
6. ¿De qué color es el café? Es marrón./Es café.
7. ¿De qué color es el dólar de los EE.UU.? Es verde y blanco.
8. ¿De qué color es la cebra (*zebra*)? Es negra y blanca.

CONSULTA
Like other adjectives you have seen, colors must agree in gender and number with the nouns they modify.
Ex: **las camisas verdes, el vestido amarillo**.
For a review of descriptive adjectives, see **Senderos 1A, Estructura 3.1**, pp. 112–113.

Comunicación

7 Los regalos Listen to the conversation between Victoria and her friend Juan Manuel. Then indicate whether the following conclusions are **lógico** or **ilógico**, based on what you heard.

	Lógico	Ilógico
1. Juan Manuel quiere ir de compras.	○	✓
2. A la mamá de Victoria le gusta nadar.	✓	○
3. El papá de Victoria usa camisas.	✓	○
4. Victoria va a regatear.	○	✓
5. Victoria le va a comprar a su hermano unas botas.	○	✓

8 Preferencias Answer your partner's questions. *Answers will vary.*

1. ¿Adónde vas a comprar ropa? ¿Por qué?
2. ¿Qué tipo de ropa prefieres? ¿Por qué?
3. ¿Cuáles son tus colores favoritos?
4. En tu opinión, ¿es importante comprar ropa nueva frecuentemente? ¿Por qué?
5. ¿Gastas mucho dinero en ropa cada mes? ¿Buscas rebajas?
6. ¿Regateas cuando compras ropa? ¿Usas tarjetas de crédito?

9 El viaje Write an e-mail to a relative about a trip you are taking with your family this summer. Include where you are going, what the weather is going to be like, what activities you are going to do, and what clothes you are taking. *Answers will vary.*

10 Las maletas With a partner, take turns asking questions about the drawings. Include the topics from the list to talk about Carmela's vacation and Pepe's trip to Bariloche. *Answers will vary.*

- ropa
- color
- lugar
- tiempo
- actividades

NOTA CULTURAL

Bariloche is a popular resort for skiing in South America. Located in Argentina's Patagonia region, the town is also known for its chocolate factories and its beautiful lakes, mountains, and forests.

CONSULTA

To review weather, see **Lección 5, Contextos**, p. 64.

Section Goals

In **Fotonovela**, students will:
- receive comprehensible input from free-flowing discourse
- learn functional phrases involving clothing and how much things cost

 Communication 1.2
Cultures 2.1, 2.2

Teacher Resources
Read the front matter for suggestions on how to incorporate all the program's components. See pages 99A–99B for a detailed listing of Teacher Resources online.

Video Recap: Lección 5
Before doing this **Fotonovela** section, review the previous episode with these questions:
1. ¿Qué problema hay cuando hablan con el empleado? (El empleado no encuentra la reservación.)
2. ¿Qué piensa Felipe del hotel? (Piensa que no está nada mal; es limpio y cómodo.)
3. ¿Qué deporte quieren hacer Miguel y Maru en la playa? (Quieren hacer windsurf.)
4. ¿Quién consigue las tablas de windsurf para Maru y Miguel? (El botones las consigue.)
5. ¿Quiénes nadan? (Juan Carlos y Jimena nadan.)

Video Synopsis
The friends are back in **Mérida** where they go to the market to do some shopping. They split into two teams, the boys versus the girls, to see who is better at bargaining. Who will get the best deal?

In-Class Tips
- Have students scan the **Fotonovela** captions for vocabulary related to clothing or colors.
- Point out the clothing that a few individual students are wearing and ask them some questions about it.
  Ex: **Me gusta esa camisa azul. ¿Es de algodón? ¿Dónde la compraste?**

6 | fotonovela

En el mercado

Los chicos van de compras al mercado. ¿Quién hizo la mejor compra?

PERSONAJES FELIPE   JUAN CARLOS

MARISSA Oigan, vamos al mercado.
JUAN CARLOS ¡Sí! Los chicos en un equipo y las chicas en otro.
FELIPE Tenemos dos horas para ir de compras.
MARU Y don Guillermo decide quién gana.

JIMENA Esta falda azul es muy elegante.
MARISSA ¡Sí! Además, este color está de moda.
MARU Éste rojo es de algodón.

(*Las chicas encuentran unas bolsas.*)
VENDEDOR Ésta de rayas cuesta 190 pesos, ésta 120 pesos y ésta 220 pesos.

MARISSA ¿Me das aquella blusa rosada? Me parece que hace juego con esta falda, ¿no? ¿No tienen otras tallas?
JIMENA Sí, aquí. ¿Qué talla usas?
MARISSA Uso talla 4.
JIMENA La encontré. ¡Qué ropa más bonita!

(*En otra parte del mercado*)
FELIPE Juan Carlos compró una camisa de muy buena calidad.
MIGUEL (*a la vendedora*) ¿Puedo ver ésos, por favor?
VENDEDORA Sí, señor. Le doy un muy buen precio.

VENDEDOR Son 530 por las tres bolsas. Pero como ustedes son tan bonitas, son 500 pesos.
MARU Señor, no somos turistas ricas. Somos estudiantes pobres.
VENDEDOR Bueno, son 480 pesos.

TEACHING OPTIONS

Video Tips General suggestions for using video clips in the classroom can be found in the front matter of this Teacher's Edition.

En el mercado Photocopy the **Fotonovela** Videoscript (Supersite) and white out 7–10 words in order to create a master for a cloze activity. Distribute photocopies of the master and have students fill in the missing words as they watch the **En el mercado** episode. You may want students to work in small groups and help each other fill in any gaps.

MARISSA JIMENA MARU MIGUEL DON GUILLERMO VENDEDORA VENDEDOR

JUAN CARLOS Miren, mi nueva camisa. Elegante, ¿verdad?
FELIPE A ver, Juan Carlos... te queda bien.

MARU ¿Qué compraste?
MIGUEL Sólo esto.
MARU ¡Qué bonitos aretes! Gracias, mi amor.

JUAN CARLOS Y ustedes, ¿qué compraron?
JIMENA Bolsas.
MARU Acabamos de comprar tres bolsas por sólo 480 pesos. ¡Una ganga!

FELIPE Don Guillermo, usted tiene que decidir quién gana. ¿Los chicos o las chicas?
DON GUILLERMO El ganador es... Miguel. ¡Porque no compró nada para él, sino para su novia!

Expresiones útiles

Talking about clothing
¡Qué ropa más bonita!
What nice clothing!
Esta falda azul es muy elegante.
This blue skirt is very elegant.
Está de moda.
It's in style.
Éste rojo es de algodón/lana.
This red one is cotton/wool.
Ésta de rayas/lunares/cuadros es de seda.
This striped / polka-dotted / plaid one is silk.
Es de muy buena calidad.
It's very good quality.
¿Qué talla usas/llevas?
What size do you wear?
Uso/Llevo talla 4.
I wear a size 4.
¿Qué número calza?
What size shoe do you wear?
Yo calzo siete.
I wear a size seven.

Negotiating a price
¿Cuánto cuesta?
How much does it cost?
Demasiado caro/a.
Too expensive.
Es una ganga.
It's a bargain.

Saying what you bought
¿Qué compraste?/¿Qué compró usted?
What did you buy?
Sólo compré esto.
I only bought this.
¡Qué bonitos aretes!
What beautiful earrings!
Y ustedes, ¿qué compraron?
And you guys, what did you buy?

Additional vocabulary
híjole *wow*

¿Qué pasó?

1 ¿Cierto o falso? Indicate whether each sentence is **cierto** or **falso**. Correct the false statements.

	Cierto	Falso
1. Jimena dice que la falda azul no es elegante.	○	● Jimena dice que la falda azul es muy elegante.
2. Juan Carlos compra una camisa.	●	○
3. Marissa dice que el azul es un color que está de moda.	●	○
4. Miguel compra unas sandalias para Maru.	○	● Miguel compra unos aretes para Maru.

NOTA CULTURAL

Las guayaberas are a popular men's shirt worn in hot climates. They are usually made of cotton, linen, or silk and decorated with pleats, pockets, and sometimes embroidery. They can be worn instead of a jacket to formal occasions or as everyday clothing.

2 Identificar Provide the first initial of the person who would make each statement.

MARU

FELIPE

JIMENA

- _M_ 1. ¿Te gusta cómo se me ven mis nuevos aretes?
- _F_ 2. Juan Carlos compró una camisa de muy buena calidad.
- _M_ 3. No podemos pagar 500, señor, eso es muy caro.
- _J_ 4. Aquí tienen ropa de muchas tallas.
- _J_ 5. Esta falda me gusta mucho, el color azul es muy elegante.
- _F_ 6. Hay que darnos prisa, sólo tenemos dos horas para ir de compras.

3 Completar Answer the questions using the information in the **Fotonovela**.

1. ¿Qué talla es Marissa? Marissa usa talla 4.
2. ¿Cuánto les pide el vendedor por las tres bolsas? Las bolsas cuestan 500 pesos.
3. ¿Cuál es el precio que pagan las tres amigas por las bolsas? El precio que pagan es 480 pesos.
4. ¿Qué dice Juan Carlos sobre su nueva camisa? Juan Carlos dice que su nueva camisa es elegante.
5. ¿Quién ganó al hacer las compras? ¿Por qué? Ganó Miguel porque le compró unos aretes a su novia.

AYUDA

When discussing prices, it's important to keep in mind singular and plural forms of verbs.

La **camisa cuesta** diez dólares.
Las **botas cuestan** sesenta dólares.
El **precio** de las botas **es** sesenta dólares.
Los **precios** de la ropa **son** altos.

4 Conversar With a partner, role-play a conversation between a customer and a salesperson in an open-air market. Use these expressions and also look at **Expresiones útiles** on the previous page. Answers will vary.

¿Qué desea?	Estoy buscando...	Prefiero el/la rojo/a.
What would you like?	I'm looking for...	I prefer the red one.

Cliente/a
- Say good afternoon.
- Explain that you are looking for a particular item of clothing.
- Discuss colors and sizes.
- Ask for the price and begin bargaining.
- Settle on a price and purchase the item.

Vendedor(a)
- Greet the customer and ask what he/she would like.
- Show him/her some items and ask what he/she prefers.
- Discuss colors and sizes.
- Tell him/her a price. Negotiate a price.
- Accept a price and say thank you.

Pronunciación
The consonants d and t

| ¿**D**ón**d**e? | ven**d**er | na**d**ar | ver**d**a**d** |

Like **b** and **v**, the Spanish **d** can have a hard sound or a soft sound, depending on which letters appear next to it.

| **D**on | **d**inero | tien**d**a | fal**d**a |

At the beginning of a phrase and after **n** or **l**, the letter **d** is pronounced with a hard sound. This sound is similar to the English *d* in *dog*, but a little softer and duller. The tongue should touch the back of the upper teeth, not the roof of the mouth.

| me**d**ias | ver**d**e | vesti**d**o | huéspe**d** |

In all other positions, **d** has a soft sound. It is similar to the English *th* in *there*, but a little softer.

Don **D**iego no tiene el **d**iccionario

When **d** begins a word, its pronunciation depends on the previous word. At the beginning of a phrase or after a word that ends in **n** or **l**, it is pronounced as a hard **d**.

Doña **D**olores es **d**e la capital

Words that begin with **d** are pronounced with a soft **d** if they appear immediately after a word that ends in a vowel or any consonant other than **n** or **l**.

| **t**raje | pan**t**alones | **t**arje**t**a | **t**ien**d**a |

When pronouncing the Spanish **t**, the tongue should touch the back of the upper teeth, not the roof of the mouth. Unlike the English *t*, no air is expelled from the mouth.

Práctica Read these phrases aloud to practice the **d** and the **t**.
1. Hasta pronto.
2. De nada.
3. Mucho gusto.
4. Lo siento.
5. No hay de qué.
6. ¿De dónde es usted?
7. ¡Todos a bordo!
8. No puedo.
9. Es estupendo.
10. No tengo computadora.
11. ¿Cuándo vienen?
12. Son las tres y media.

Oraciones Read these sentences aloud to practice the **d** and the **t**.
1. Don Teodoro tiene una tienda en un almacén en La Habana.
2. Don Teodoro vende muchos trajes, vestidos y zapatos todos los días.
3. Un día un turista, Federico Machado, entra en la tienda para comprar un par de botas.
4. Federico regatea con don Teodoro y compra las botas y también un par de sandalias.

Refranes Read these sayings aloud to practice the **d** and the **t**.

En la variedad está el gusto.¹

Aunque la mona se vista de seda, mona se queda.²

¹ Variety is the spice of life.
² You can't make a silk purse out of a sow's ear.

Section Goals

In **Cultura**, students will:
- read about open-air markets
- learn clothing-related terms
- read about Venezuelan clothing designer **Carolina Herrera**
- read about the fashions of Hispanic designers

Communication 1.1, 1.2
Cultures 2.1, 2.2
Connections 3.1, 3.2
Comparisons 4.2

En detalle
Antes de leer
Lead a discussion about open-air markets, such as a flea market. Have students share their experiences, including the market's location, goods sold there, and prices.

Lectura
- Explain that open-air markets that specialize in second-hand or low-priced goods are often referred to as **mercados de pulgas** (*flea markets*).
- Point out that many local artists take advantage of open-air markets to sell their pieces or display new works.
- Explain that **la ñapa** can be considered similar to the Anglo tradition of a baker's dozen.

Después de leer Ask students what facts are new or surprising to them.

1 Expansion Give students these statements as items 9–11: 9. The **Tianguis Cultural del Chopo** is not a good place to go if you are interested in Mexican crafts and art. (**Falso.** The **Tianguis Cultural del Chopo** has crafts and art.) 10. Market stands are referred to as **puestos**. (**Cierto**.) 11. Bargaining often raises the price of an item significantly. (**Falso.** It usually lowers the price significantly.)

6 cultura

EN DETALLE

Los mercados al aire libre

Mercados al aire libre are an integral part of commerce and culture in the Spanish-speaking world. Whether they take place daily or weekly, these markets are an important forum where tourists, locals, and vendors interact. People come to the marketplace to shop, socialize, taste local foods, and watch street performers. Wandering from one **puesto** (*stand*) to the next, one can browse for fresh fruits and vegetables, clothing, CDs and DVDs, and **artesanías** (*crafts*). Some markets offer a mix of products, while others specialize in food, fashion, or used merchandise, such as antiques and books.

When shoppers see an item they like, they can bargain with the vendor. Friendly bargaining is an expected ritual and may result in a significantly lower price. When selling food, vendors may give the customer a little extra of what they purchase; this free addition is known as **la ñapa**.

Many open-air markets are also tourist attractions. The market in Otavalo, Ecuador, is world-famous and has taken place every Saturday since pre-Incan times. This market is well-known for the colorful textiles woven by the **otavaleños**, the indigenous people of the area. One can also find leather goods and wood carvings from nearby towns. Another popular market is **El Rastro**, held every Sunday in Madrid, Spain. Sellers set up **puestos** along the streets to display their wares, which range from local artwork and antiques to inexpensive clothing and electronics.

Mercado de Otavalo

Otros mercados famosos

Mercado	Lugar	Productos
Feria Artesanal de Recoleta	Buenos Aires, Argentina	artesanías
Mercado Central	Santiago, Chile	mariscos°, pescado°, frutas, verduras°
Tianguis Cultural del Chopo	Ciudad de México, México	ropa, música, revistas, libros, arte, artesanías
El mercado de Chichicastenango	Chichicastenango, Guatemala	frutas y verduras, flores°, cerámica, textiles

mariscos *seafood* pescado *fish* verduras *vegetables* flores *flowers*

ACTIVIDADES

1 **¿Cierto o falso?** Indicate whether these statements are cierto or falso. Correct the false statements.

1. Generally, open-air markets specialize in one type of goods. **Falso.** They sell a variety of goods.
2. Bargaining is commonplace at outdoor markets. **Cierto.**
3. Only new goods can be found at open-air markets. **Falso.** They sell both new and used goods.
4. A Spaniard in search of antiques could search at **El Rastro**. **Cierto.**
5. If you are in Guatemala and want to buy ceramics, you can go to Chichicastenango. **Cierto.**
6. A **ñapa** is a tax on open-air market goods. **Falso.** A **ñapa** is a free addition sometimes given to customers.
7. The **otavaleños** weave colorful textiles to sell on Saturdays. **Cierto.**
8. Santiago's **Mercado Central** is known for books and music. **Falso.** It's known for seafood, fish, fruits, and vegetables.

TEACHING OPTIONS

TPR Create a series of true/false statements about goods one can purchase at the open-air markets mentioned in **En detalle**. Tell students to raise their right hand if a statement is true or their left hand if it is false. Ex: **Compro mariscos en El Rastro.** (left hand) **Compro flores en el mercado de Chichicastenango.** (right hand)

Small Groups Have students work in groups of three. For homework, have them research another famous open-air market in the Spanish-speaking world. Ex: **Pisac** (Peru), **La Romana** (Dominican Republic), **La Cancha** (Bolivia). In class, have each group present the location of the market, how often it takes place, what is sold, and any other significant information. Encourage students to bring in photos.

ASÍ SE DICE
La ropa

la chamarra (Méx.)	la chaqueta
de manga corta/larga	short/long-sleeved
los mahones (P. Rico);	los bluejeans
el pantalón de mezclilla (Méx.);	
los tejanos (Esp.);	
los vaqueros (Arg., Cuba, Esp., Uru.)	
la marca	brand
la playera (Méx.);	la camiseta
la remera (Arg.)	

EL MUNDO HISPANO
Diseñadores de moda

- **Adolfo Domínguez** (España) Su ropa tiene un estilo minimalista y práctico. Usa telas° naturales y cómodas en sus diseños.

- **Silvia Tcherassi** (Colombia) Los colores vivos y las líneas asimétricas de sus vestidos y trajes muestran influencias tropicales.

- **Óscar de la Renta** (República Dominicana) Diseñó ropa opulenta para la mujer clásica.

- **Narciso Rodríguez** (EE.UU.) En sus diseños delicados y finos predominan los colores blanco y negro. Hizo° el vestido de boda° de Carolyn Bessette Kennedy. También diseñó varios vestidos para Michelle Obama.

telas *fabrics* Hizo *He made* de boda *wedding*

PERFIL
Carolina Herrera

In 1980, at the urging of some friends, **Carolina Herrera** created a fashion collection as a "test." The Venezuelan designer received such a favorable response that within one year she moved her family from Caracas to New York City and created her own label, Carolina Herrera, Ltd.

"I love elegance and intricacy, but whether it is in a piece of clothing or a fragrance, the intricacy must appear as simplicity," Herrera once stated. She quickly found that many sophisticated women agreed; from the start, her sleek and glamorous designs have been in constant demand. Over the years, Herrera has grown her brand into a veritable fashion empire that encompasses her fashion and bridal collections, cosmetics, perfume, and accessories that are sold around the globe.

Conexión Internet

¿Qué marcas de ropa son populares en el mundo hispano?

Use the Web to find more cultural information related to this **Cultura** section.

ACTIVIDADES

2 Comprensión Complete these sentences.
1. Adolfo Domínguez usa telas __naturales__ y __cómodas__ en su ropa.
2. Si hace fresco en el D.F., puedes llevar una __chamarra__.
3. La diseñadora __Carolina Herrera__ hace ropa, perfumes y más.
4. La ropa de __Silvia Tcherassi__ muestra influencias tropicales.
5. Los __mahones__ son una ropa casual en Puerto Rico.

3 Mi ropa favorita Write a brief description of your favorite article of clothing. Mention what store it is from, the brand, colors, fabric, style, and any other information.

Answers will vary.

Section Goals

In **Estructura 6.1**, students will learn:
- the uses of **saber** and **conocer**
- more uses of the personal **a**
- other verbs conjugated like **conocer**

 Comparisons 4.1

Teacher Resources
Read the front matter for suggestions on how to incorporate all the program's components. See pages 99A–99B for a detailed listing of Teacher Resources online.

In-Class Tips
- Use the **Lección 6** Grammar Presentation Slides to assist with this presentation.
- Point out the irregular **yo** forms of **saber** and **conocer**.
- Divide the board into two columns with the headings **saber** and **conocer**. In the first column, write the uses of **saber** and model them by asking individuals what they know how to do and what factual information they know. Ex: ____, ¿sabes bailar salsa? ¿Sabes mi número de teléfono? In the second column, write the uses of **conocer** and model them by asking individuals about people and places they know. Ex: ____, ¿conoces Cuba? ¿Conoces a Yasiel Puig?
- Further distinguish the uses of **saber** and **conocer** by making statements such as: **Sé quién es el presidente de este país, pero no lo conozco.**
- Point out the first **¡Atención!** bullet. Ask volunteers to write the full conjugation of these verbs on the board.
- Point out the similar **yo** form for **conocer, parecer, ofrecer, conducir,** and **traducir**.
- Ask questions using the new verbs. Ex: ¿Quiénes conducen? ¿Qué carro conduces?

6 estructura

6.1 Saber and conocer

ANTE TODO Spanish has two verbs that mean *to know*: **saber** and **conocer**. They cannot be used interchangeably. Note the irregular **yo** forms.

The verbs saber and conocer

		saber *(to know)*	**conocer** *(to know)*
SINGULAR FORMS	yo	sé	conozco
	tú	sabes	conoces
	Ud./él/ella	sabe	conoce
PLURAL FORMS	nosotros/as	sabemos	conocemos
	vosotros/as	sabéis	conocéis
	Uds./ellos/ellas	saben	conocen

▶ **Saber** means *to know a fact or piece(s) of information* or *to know how to do something*.

No **sé** tu número de teléfono.
I don't know your telephone number.

Mi hermana **sabe** hablar francés.
My sister knows how to speak French.

▶ **Conocer** means *to know* or *be familiar/acquainted* with a person, place, or thing.

¿**Conoces** la ciudad de Nueva York?
Do you know New York City?

No **conozco** a tu amigo Esteban.
I don't know your friend Esteban.

▶ When the direct object of **conocer** is a person or pet, the personal **a** is used.

¿Conoces La Habana?   *but*   ¿Conoces **a** Celia Cruz?
Do you know Havana?   *Do you know Celia Cruz?*

▶ **¡Atención!** **Parecer** *(to seem)* and **ofrecer** *(to offer)* are conjugated like **conocer**.

▶ **¡Atención!** **Conducir** *(to drive)* and **traducir** *(to translate)* also have an irregular **yo** form, but since they are -ir verbs, they are conjugated differently from **conocer**.

| conducir traducir | | **conduzco**, condu**ces**, condu**ce**, condu**cimos**, condu**cís**, condu**cen**
traduzco, tradu**ces**, tradu**ce**, tradu**cimos**, tradu**cís**, tradu**cen** |

NOTA CULTURAL
Cuban singer **Celia Cruz** (1925–2003), known as the "Queen of Salsa," recorded many albums over her long career. Adored by her fans, she was famous for her colorful and lively on-stage performances.

¡INTÉNTALO!

Provide the appropriate forms of these verbs.

saber
1. José no _sabe_ la hora.
2. Sara y yo _sabemos_ jugar al tenis.
3. ¿Por qué no _sabes_ tú estos verbos?
4. Mis padres _saben_ hablar japonés.
5. Yo _sé_ a qué hora es la clase.
6. Usted no _sabe_ dónde vivo.
7. Mi hermano no _sabe_ nadar.
8. Nosotros _sabemos_ muchas cosas.

conocer
1. Usted y yo _conocemos_ bien Miami.
2. ¿Tú _conoces_ a mi amigo Manuel?
3. Sergio y Taydé _conocen_ mi pueblo.
4. Emiliano _conoce_ a mis padres.
5. Yo _conozco_ muy bien el centro.
6. ¿Ustedes _conocen_ la tienda Gigante?
7. Nosotras _conocemos_ una playa hermosa.
8. ¿Usted _conoce_ a mi profesora?

TEACHING OPTIONS

TPR Divide the class into two teams, **saber** and **conocer**, and have them line up. Indicate the first member of each team and call out a sentence in English that uses *to know*. (Ex: We know the answer.) The team member whose verb corresponds to the English sentence has to step forward and provide the Spanish translation.

Extra Practice Ask students to jot down three things they know how to do well (**saber** + [*infinitive*] + **bien**). Collect the papers, shuffle them, and read the sentences aloud. Have the rest of the class guess who wrote the sentences.

110   Teacher's Edition • Lesson Six

Práctica y Comunicación

1 Completar Indicate the correct verb for each sentence.
1. Mis hermanos (conocen/**saben**) conducir, pero yo no (**sé**/conozco).
2. —¿(Conocen/**Saben**) ustedes dónde está el estadio? —No, no lo (conocemos/**sabemos**).
3. —¿(**Conoces**/Sabes) a Lady Gaga? —Bueno, (**sé**/conozco) quién es, pero no la (**conozco**/sé).
4. Mi profesora (sabe/**conoce**) Cuba y también (conoce/**sabe**) bailar salsa.

2 Combinar Combine elements from each column to create sentences. *Answers will vary.*

A	B	C
Shakira	(no) conocer	Jimmy Fallon
los Yankees	(no) saber	cantar y bailar
el primer ministro de Canadá		La Habana Vieja
mis amigos y yo		muchas personas importantes
tú		hablar dos lenguas extranjeras
		jugar al béisbol

3 Mi mejor amiga Listen as Jennifer describes her best friend. Then indicate whether the following conclusions are **lógico** or **ilógico**, based on what you heard.

	Lógico	Ilógico
1. Jennifer y Laura son amigas.	✓	
2. Laura es antipática.		✓
3. A Laura le gustan las lenguas extranjeras.	✓	
4. Laura prefiere comprar ropa cara.		✓
5. Laura no tiene pasatiempos.		✓
6. Laura conoce a muchas personas.	✓	

4 Preguntas Answer your partner's questions. Use complete sentences. *Answers will vary.*
1. ¿Conoces a un(a) cantante famoso/a? ¿Te gusta cómo canta?
2. En tu familia, ¿quién sabe cantar bien? ¿Tu opinión es objetiva?
3. Y tú, ¿conduces bien o mal? ¿Y tus amigos?
4. Si un(a) amigo/a no conduce muy bien, ¿le ofreces crítica constructiva?
5. ¿Cómo parecen estar tus amigos hoy?

5 Conocimientos Tell about three things you know how to do, three places you are familiar with, and three people you know. *Answers will vary.*

6 Anuncio Write an advertisement using two examples each of **saber** and **conocer**. *Answers will vary.*

Section Goals

In **Estructura 6.2**, students will learn:
- to identify an indirect object noun
- how to use indirect object pronouns

Comparisons 4.1

Teacher Resources

Read the front matter for suggestions on how to incorporate all the program's components. See pages 99A–99B for a detailed listing of Teacher Resources online.

In-Class Tips

- Write on the board: **Mi primo me escribe un mensaje de texto.** Ask students what the direct object of the verb is. Then tell them that an indirect object answers the questions *to whom* or *for whom*.
- Write the indirect object pronouns on the board. Ask how their forms differ from those of direct object pronouns.
- Ask volunteers to read aloud the video-still captions, and have the class identify the indirect object pronoun in each.
- Point out that the redundant use of both an indirect object pronoun and an indirect object noun is common in Spanish and that, unlike in English, it is the indirect object noun that is optional, not the pronoun.

6.2 Indirect object pronouns

ANTE TODO In **Lección 5**, you learned that a direct object receives the action of the verb directly. In contrast, an indirect object receives the action of the verb indirectly.

SUBJECT	I.O. PRONOUN	VERB	DIRECT OBJECT	INDIRECT OBJECT
Roberto	**le**	presta	cien pesos	**a Luisa**.
Roberto		lends	100 pesos	to Luisa.

An indirect object is a noun or pronoun that answers the question *to whom* or *for whom* an action is done. In the preceding example, the indirect object answers this question: *¿A quién le presta Roberto cien pesos?* *To whom does Roberto lend 100 pesos?*

Indirect object pronouns

Singular forms		Plural forms	
me	(to, for) *me*	nos	(to, for) *us*
te	(to, for) *you* (fam.)	os	(to, for) *you* (fam.)
le	(to, for) *you* (form.)	les	(to, for) *you*
	(to, for) *him; her*		(to, for) *them*

▶ **¡Atención!** The forms of indirect object pronouns for the first and second persons (**me, te, nos, os**) are the same as the direct object pronouns. Indirect object pronouns agree in number with the corresponding nouns, but not in gender.

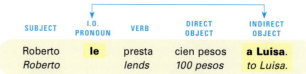

Bueno, le doy un descuento.

Acabo de mostrarles que sí sabemos regatear.

Using indirect object pronouns

▶ Spanish speakers commonly use both an indirect object pronoun and the noun to which it refers in the same sentence. This is done to emphasize and clarify to whom the pronoun refers.

I.O. PRONOUN		INDIRECT OBJECT	I.O. PRONOUN		INDIRECT OBJECT
Ella **le**	vende la ropa	**a Elena**.	**Les** prestamos	el dinero	**a Inés y a Álex**.

▶ Indirect object pronouns are also used without the indirect object noun when the person for whom the action is being done is known.

Ana **le** presta la falda **a Elena**.
Ana lends her skirt to Elena.

También **le** presta unos jeans.
She also lends her a pair of jeans.

TEACHING OPTIONS

Extra Practice Write sentences like these on the board:
1. Ana te prepara unos tacos. 2. Le presto dinero a Luisa. 3. Les compramos unos regalos a los niños. Ask students to come to the board and underline the direct objects and circle the indirect objects.

Small Groups Have students work in groups of three. Have Student A "lend" an object to Student B and say: **Te presto mi...** Student B responds: **Me prestas tu...** Student C says: **____ le presta a ____ su...** Have groups practice until each member has begun the chain twice. Practice plural pronouns by having two groups join together and two students "lend" something to two other students.

¡De compras!

▶ Indirect object pronouns are usually placed before the conjugated form of the verb. In negative sentences the pronoun is placed between **no** and the conjugated verb.

> Martín **me** compra un regalo.
> *Martín is buying me a gift.*

> Eva **no me** escribe cartas.
> *Eva doesn't write me letters.*

CONSULTA
For more information on accents, see **Lección 4, Pronunciación**, p. 33.

▶ When a conjugated verb is followed by an infinitive or the present progressive, the indirect object pronoun may be placed before the conjugated verb or attached to the infinitive or present participle. **¡Atención!** When an indirect object pronoun is attached to a present participle, an accent mark is added to maintain the proper stress.

> Él no quiere **pagarte**./
> Él no **te** quiere pagar.
> *He does not want to pay you.*

> Él está **escribiéndole** una postal a ella./
> Él **le** está escribiendo una postal a ella.
> *He is writing a postcard to her.*

▶ Because the indirect object pronouns **le** and **les** have multiple meanings, Spanish speakers often clarify to whom the pronouns refer with the preposition **a** + [*pronoun*] or **a** + [*noun*].

UNCLARIFIED STATEMENTS	CLARIFIED STATEMENTS
Yo **le** compro un abrigo.	Yo **le** compro un abrigo **a usted/él/ella**.
Ella **le** describe un libro.	Ella **le** describe un libro **a Juan**.

UNCLARIFIED STATEMENTS	CLARIFIED STATEMENTS
Él **les** vende unos sombreros.	Él **les** vende unos sombreros **a ustedes/ellos/ellas**.
Ellos **les** hablan muy claro.	Ellos **les** hablan muy claro **a los clientes**.

▶ The irregular verbs **dar** (*to give*) and **decir** (*to say; to tell*) are often used with indirect object pronouns.

The verbs dar and decir

Singular forms			Plural forms		
	dar	**decir**		**dar**	**decir**
yo	doy	digo	nosotros/as	damos	decimos
tú	das	dices	vosotros/as	dais	decís
Ud./él/ella	da	dice	Uds./ellos/ellas	dan	dicen

Me dan una fiesta cada año.
They give (throw) me a party every year.

Voy a **darle** consejos.
I'm going to give her advice.

Te digo la verdad.
I'm telling you the truth.

No **les digo** mentiras a mis padres.
I don't tell lies to my parents.

¡INTÉNTALO! Use the cues in parentheses to provide the correct indirect object pronoun for each sentence.

1. Juan __le__ quiere dar un regalo. (*to Elena*)
2. María __nos__ prepara un café. (*for us*)
3. Beatriz y Felipe __me__ escriben desde (*from*) Cuba. (*to me*)
4. Marta y yo __les__ compramos unos guantes. (*for them*)
5. Los vendedores __te__ venden ropa. (*to you, fam. sing.*)
6. La dependienta __nos__ muestra los guantes. (*to us*)

Práctica

1 Completar Fill in the blanks with the correct pronouns to complete Mónica's description of her family's holiday shopping.

1. Juan y yo __le__ damos una blusa a nuestra hermana Gisela.
2. Mi tía __nos__ da a nosotros una mesa para la casa.
3. Gisela __le__ da dos corbatas a su papá.
4. A mi mamá yo __le__ doy un par de guantes negros.
5. A mi profesora __le__ doy dos libros de José Martí.
6. Juan __les__ da un regalo a mis padres.
7. Mis padres __me__ dan un traje nuevo a mí.
8. Y a ti, yo __te__ doy un regalo también. ¿Quieres verlo?

NOTA CULTURAL

Cuban writer and patriot **José Martí** (1853–1895) was born in **La Habana Vieja**, the old colonial center of Havana. Founded by Spanish explorers in the early 1500s, Havana, along with San Juan, Puerto Rico, served as a major stopping point for Spaniards traveling to Mexico and South America.

2 En La Habana Describe what happens on Pascual's trip to Cuba based on the cues provided.

1. ellos / cantar / canción / (mí)
Ellos me cantan una canción (a mí).

2. él / comprar / libros / (sus hijos) / Plaza de Armas
Él les compra libros (a sus hijos) en la Plaza de Armas.

3. yo / preparar el almuerzo (*lunch*) / (ti)
Yo te preparo el almuerzo (a ti).

4. él / explicar cómo llegar / (conductor)
Él le explica cómo llegar (al conductor).

5. mi novia / sacar / foto / (nosotros)
Mi novia nos saca una foto (a nosotros).

6. el guía (*guide*) / mostrar / catedral de San Cristóbal / (ustedes)
El guía les muestra la catedral de San Cristóbal (a ustedes).

NOTA CULTURAL

La Habana Vieja, Cuba, is the site of another well-known outdoor market. Located in the **Plaza de la Catedral**, it is a place where Cuban painters, artists, and sculptors sell their work, and other vendors offer handmade crafts and clothing.

3 Combinar Use an item from each column and an indirect object pronoun to create logical sentences. Answers will vary.

 modelo
Mis padres les dan regalos a mis primos.

A	B	C	D
yo	comprar	mensajes electrónicos	mí
el dependiente	dar	corbata	ustedes
el profesor Arce	decir	dinero en efectivo	clienta
la vendedora	escribir	tarea	novia
mis padres	explicar	problemas	primos
tú	pagar	regalos	ti
nosotros/as	prestar	ropa	nosotros
¿?	vender	¿?	¿?

TEACHING OPTIONS

Heritage Speakers Ask heritage speakers to share any typical words or phrases that one would hear in a radio ad. Then have students work in pairs to create a radio commercial for their favorite clothing store. Have them tell customers what they can buy, for whom, and at what price.
Pairs Ask students to write five questions that elicit indirect object pronouns. In pairs, have students ask their questions and write down their partner's answers. Then ask pairs to review the questions and answers for accuracy.
Pairs Brainstorm on the board a list of things that parents tell high school-age or college-age children they should or should not do. Then have pairs ask each other if their parents tell them these things and summarize their findings for the class. Ex: **Nuestros padres nos dicen que no debemos tomar mucho café.**

Comunicación

4 Días locos Gabriela is e-mailing her friend Sandra about her semester. Indicate whether the following conclusions are **lógico** or **ilógico**, based on what you read.

De: Gabriela
Para: Sandra
Asunto: Días locos

Los profesores nos dan mucha tarea. ¡Vivo en la biblioteca! Mi mamá me escribe mensajes electrónicos cada dos horas. Obviamente, yo no tengo tiempo de contestarle, pero ¡ella no me entiende! Rodrigo, el hermano menor de Ana, viene a visitarme todo el tiempo y me da regalos. ¡También me canta! Le tengo que decir la verdad: ¡No quiero su atención!

	Lógico	Ilógico
1. Gabriela tiene muchos ratos libres.	○	●
2. La mamá de Gabriela está enojada con ella.	●	○
3. Rodrigo está enamorado de Gabriela.	●	○
4. Gabriela está enamorada de Rodrigo.	○	●
5. Rodrigo le debe dar más regalos a Gabriela.	○	●

5 Entrevista Answer your partner's questions. *Answers will vary.*

1. ¿Qué tiendas, almacenes o centros comerciales prefieres?
2. ¿A quién le compras regalos cuando hay rebajas?
3. ¿A quién le prestas dinero cuando lo necesita?
4. ¿Me explicas cómo regatear?
5. ¿Te dan tus padres su tarjeta de crédito cuando vas de compras?

6 ¡Somos ricos! You and another student chipped in on a lottery ticket and you won! Now you want to spend money on your loved ones. Write a paragraph telling what you plan to buy for your family and your friends. *Answers will vary.*

> **modelo**
> Quiero comprarle un vestido de Carolina Herrera a mi madre...

Síntesis

7 Minidrama With a partner, role-play a conversation between a customer and a clerk in a clothing store. The customer should talk about the clothes he/she is looking for and for whom he/she is buying the clothes. The clerk should recommend different items based on the customer's descriptions. Use these expressions and also look at **Expresiones útiles** on page 105. *Answers will vary.*

Me queda grande/pequeño.	¿Está en rebaja?
It's big/small on me.	*Is it on sale?*
¿Tiene otro color?	También estoy buscando...
Do you have another color?	*I'm also looking for...*

Section Goals

In **Estructura 6.3**, students will learn:
- the preterite of regular verbs
- spelling changes in the preterite for different verbs
- words commonly used with the preterite tense

Comparisons 4.1

Teacher Resources
Read the front matter for suggestions on how to incorporate all the program's components. See pages 99A–99B for a detailed listing of Teacher Resources online.

In-Class Tips
- Introduce the preterite by describing some things you did yesterday, using the first-person preterite of known regular verbs. Use adverbs that signal the preterite (page 117). Ex: **Ayer compré una chaqueta nueva. Bueno, entré en el almacén y compré una. Y de repente, vi un sombrero. Decidí comprarlo también.** Each time you introduce a preterite form, write it on the board.
- After you have used several regular first-person preterites, expand by asking students questions. Ex: **Ayer compré un sombrero. Y tú, ____, ¿qué compraste ayer? (Compré un libro.)** Ask other students about their classmates' answers. Ex: **¿Qué compró ____ ayer? (Compró un libro.)**

Middle School Activity Pack
Have students play the game **Categorías** in Resources online (Lección 6/Middle School Activity Pack/Grammar 6.3 Activity 2).

6.3 Preterite tense of regular verbs

ANTE TODO In order to talk about events in the past, Spanish uses two simple tenses: the preterite and the imperfect. In this lesson, you will learn how to form the preterite tense, which is used to express actions or states completed in the past.

▶ **¡Atención!** The **yo** and **Ud./él/ella** forms of all three conjugations have written accents on the last syllable to show that it is stressed.

▶ As the chart shows, the endings for regular **-er** and **-ir** verbs are identical in the preterite.

¿Qué compraste?

Compré estos aretes.

▶ Note that the **nosotros/as** forms of regular **-ar** and **-ir** verbs in the preterite are identical to the present tense forms. Context will help you determine which tense is being used.

En invierno **compramos** ropa.
In the winter, we buy clothes.

Anoche **compramos** unos zapatos.
Last night we bought some shoes.

▶ **-Ar** and **-er** verbs that have a stem change in the present tense are regular in the preterite. They do *not* have a stem change.

	PRESENT	PRETERITE
cerrar (e:ie)	La tienda **cierra** a las seis.	La tienda **cerró** a las seis.
volver (o:ue)	Carlitos **vuelve** tarde.	Carlitos **volvió** tarde.
jugar (u:ue)	Él **juega** al fútbol.	Él **jugó** al fútbol.

▶ **¡Atención!** **-Ir** verbs that have a stem change in the present tense also have a stem change in the preterite.

TEACHING OPTIONS

Extra Practice For practice with discrimination between preterite forms, call out preterite forms of regular verbs and point to individuals to provide the corresponding subject pronoun. Ex: **comimos** (nosotros/as), **creyeron** (ustedes/ellos/ellas), **llegué** (yo), **leíste** (tú).
Pairs Tell students to have a conversation about what they did last weekend. Make sure they include things they did by themselves and with others. Then, in groups of four, have them share their partner's weekend activities.
Small Groups Give each group of five a list of verbs, including some with spelling changes. Student A chooses a verb from the list and gives the **yo** form. Student B gives the **tú** form, and so on. Students work their way down the list, alternating who begins the conjugation chain.

▶ Verbs that end in **-car**, **-gar**, and **-zar** have a spelling change in the first person singular (**yo** form) in the preterite.

bus**car**	bus**c-**	**qu-**	yo bus**qué**
lle**gar**	lle**g-**	**gu-**	yo lle**gué**
empe**zar**	empe**z-**	**c-**	yo empe**cé**

▶ Except for the **yo** form, all other forms of **-car**, **-gar**, and **-zar** verbs are regular in the preterite.

▶ Three other verbs—**creer**, **leer**, and **oír**—have spelling changes in the preterite. The **i** of the verb endings of **creer**, **leer**, and **oír** carries an accent in the **yo**, **tú**, **nosotros/as**, and **vosotros/as** forms, and changes to **y** in the **Ud./él/ella** and **Uds./ellos/ellas forms**.

creer	cre-	cre**í**, cre**í**ste, cre**yó**, cre**í**mos, cre**í**steis, cre**yeron**
leer	le-	le**í**, le**í**ste, le**yó**, le**í**mos, le**í**steis, le**yeron**
oír	o-	o**í**, o**í**ste, o**yó**, o**í**mos, o**í**steis, o**yeron**

▶ **Ver** is regular in the preterite, but none of its forms has an accent.

ver → vi, viste, vio, vimos, visteis, vieron

Words commonly used with the preterite

anoche	last night	pasado/a (*adj.*)	last; past
anteayer	the day before yesterday	el año pasado	last year
ayer	yesterday	la semana pasada	last week
de repente	suddenly	una vez	once
desde… hasta…	from… until…	dos veces	twice
		ya	already

Ayer llegué a Santiago de Cuba.
Yesterday I arrived in Santiago de Cuba.

Anoche oí un ruido extraño.
Last night I heard a strange noise.

▶ **Acabar de** + [*infinitive*] is used to say that something has just occurred. Note that **acabar** is in the present tense in this construction.

Acabo de comprar una falda.
I just bought a skirt.

Acabas de ir de compras.
You just went shopping.

¡INTÉNTALO! Provide the appropriate preterite forms of the verbs.

	comer	salir	comenzar	leer
1. ellas	comieron	salieron	comenzaron	leyeron
2. tú	comiste	saliste	comenzaste	leíste
3. usted	comió	salió	comenzó	leyó
4. nosotros	comimos	salimos	comenzamos	leímos
5. yo	comí	salí	comencé	leí

In-Class Tips

- Point out that verbs ending in **-car** and **-gar** are regular and have logical spelling changes in the **yo** form in order to preserve the hard **c** and **g** sounds.
- Provide sentence starters using the present indicative and have students complete them in a logical manner. Ex: **Todos los días los estudiantes llegan temprano, pero anteayer…** (llegaron tarde.)
- Practice verbs with spelling changes in the preterite by asking students about things they read, heard, and saw yesterday. Ex: **¿Leíste las noticias ayer? ¿Quiénes vieron el pronóstico del tiempo? Yo oí que va a llover hoy. ¿Qué oyeron ustedes?**
- Add a visual aspect to this grammar presentation. Use magazine pictures to demonstrate **acabar de**. Ex: **¿Quién acaba de ganar?** (Serena Williams acaba de ganar.) **¿Qué acaban de ver ellos?** (Acaban de ver una película.)

Middle School Activity Pack
Have students play the game **Descarta** in Resources online (Lección 6/Middle School Activity Pack/Grammar 6.3 Activity 3).

TEACHING OPTIONS

Game Divide the class into teams of six and have them sit in rows. Call out the infinitive of a verb. The first person writes the preterite **yo** form on a sheet of paper and passes it to the second person, who writes the **tú** form, and so on. The sixth checks spelling. If all forms are correct, the team gets a point. Continue play, having team members rotate positions for each round. The team with the most points after six rounds wins.

Extra Practice Have students write down five things they did yesterday. Ask students questions about what they did to elicit as many different conjugations as possible. Ex: ____ , **¿leíste las noticias ayer? ¿Quién más leyó las noticias ayer?…** ____ **y** ____ , **ustedes dos leyeron las noticias ayer, ¿verdad? ¿Quiénes leyeron las noticias ayer?**

Communication 1.1
Comparisons 4.1

1 In-Class Tip To simplify, tell students to read through the items once and circle the correct infinitive for each sentence. Then ask them to read the sentences a second time and underline the subject for each verb. Finally, have them conjugate the infinitives.

1 Expansion
Ask questions about **Andrea's** weekend. Have students answer with complete sentences. Ex: **¿Quién asistió a una reunión? ¿Qué compraron los amigos?**

2 Expansion Have students repeat the activity, using **ustedes** as the subject of the questions and **nosotros** in the answers.

2 Partner Chat
Available online.

3 In-Class Tips
- To simplify, have students work with a partner to quickly review the preterite forms of the verbs in the activity.
- After students have completed item 7, discuss **las tres bes**. Ask students which one is most important to them when they go shopping.

3 Expansion
Have students share their responses with a partner, who will ask follow-up questions. Ex: —**Mis padres vieron una película la semana pasada.** —**¿Qué película vieron?** —**Vieron** *Gravity*. —**¿Qué les pareció?** —**Les pareció muy buena.**

---

118 ciento dieciocho **Lección 6**

Práctica

1 Completar Andrea is talking about what happened last weekend. Complete each sentence by choosing the correct verb and putting it in the preterite.

1. El viernes a las cuatro de la tarde, la profesora Mora __asistió__ (asistir, costar, usar) a una reunión (*meeting*) de profesores.
2. A la una, yo __llegué__ (llegar, bucear, llevar) a la tienda con mis amigos.
3. Mis amigos y yo __compramos__ (comprar, regatear, gastar) dos o tres cosas.
4. Yo __compré__ (costar, comprar, escribir) unos pantalones negros y mi amigo Mateo __compró__ (gastar, pasear, comprar) una camisa azul.
5. Después, nosotros __comimos__ (llevar, vivir, comer) cerca de un mercado.
6. A las tres, Pepe __habló__ (hablar, pasear, nadar) con su amiga por teléfono.
7. El sábado por la tarde, mi mamá __escribió__ (escribir, beber, vivir) una carta.
8. El domingo mi tía __decidió__ (decidir, salir, escribir) comprarme un traje.
9. A las cuatro de la tarde, mi tía __encontró__ (beber, salir, encontrar) el traje y después nosotras __vimos__ (acabar, ver, salir) una película.

2 Preguntas Imagine that you have a pesky friend who keeps asking you questions. Respond that you already did or have just done what he/she asks. Make sure you and your partner take turns playing the role of the pesky friend and responding to his/her questions.

modelo
leer la lección
Estudiante 1: ¿Leíste la lección?
Estudiante 2: Sí, ya la leí./Sí, acabo de leerla.

1. escribir el mensaje electrónico
2. lavar (*to wash*) la ropa
3. oír las noticias (*news*)
4. comprar pantalones cortos
5. practicar los verbos
6. pagar la cuenta (*bill*)
7. empezar la composición
8. ver la película *Diarios de motocicleta*

1. E1: ¿Escribiste el mensaje electrónico?
   E2: Sí, ya lo escribí./Acabo de escribirlo.
2. E1: ¿Lavaste la ropa?
   E2: Sí, ya la lavé./Acabo de lavarla.
3. E1: ¿Oíste las noticias?
   E2: Sí, ya las oí./Acabo de oírlas.
4. E1: ¿Compraste pantalones cortos?
   E2: Sí, ya los compré./Acabo de comprarlos.
5. E1: ¿Practicaste los verbos?
   E2: Sí, ya los practiqué./Acabo de practicarlos.
6. F1: ¿Pagaste la cuenta?
   E2: Sí, ya la pagué./Acabo de pagarla.
7. E1: ¿Empezaste la composición?
   E2: Sí, ya la empecé./Acabo de empezarla.
8. E1: ¿Viste la película *Diarios de motocicleta*?
   E2: Sí, ya la vi./Acabo de verla.

NOTA CULTURAL
Based on Ernesto "Che" Guevara's diaries, *Diarios de motocicleta* (2004) traces the road trip of Che (played by Gael García Bernal) with his friend Alberto Granado (played by Rodrigo de la Serna) through Argentina, Chile, Peru, Colombia, and Venezuela.

3 ¿Cuándo? Use the time expressions from the word bank to talk about when you and others did the activities listed. Answers will vary.

| anoche | anteayer | el mes pasado | una vez |
| ayer | la semana pasada | el año pasado | dos veces |

1. mi maestro/a: llegar tarde a clase
2. mi mejor (*best*) amigo/a: salir con un(a) chico/a guapo/a
3. mis padres: ver una película
4. yo: llevar un traje/vestido
5. el presidente/primer ministro de mi país: asistir a una conferencia internacional
6. mis amigos y yo: comer en un restaurante
7. ¿?: comprar algo (*something*) bueno, bonito y barato

TEACHING OPTIONS

TPR Have students stand in a circle. Begin by tossing a ball to a student and naming an infinitive and subject pronoun (Ex: **cerrar/tú**). The student who catches the ball has four seconds to provide the correct preterite form, toss the ball to another student, and name another infinitive and pronoun.
Extra Practice Ask students to imagine they have just visited an open-air market for the first time. Have them write a letter to a friend describing what they saw and did there. Then, ask students to exchange their letters with a classmate, who will respond.
Small Groups In groups of three, have students write down three sentences using verbs in the preterite. Then ask each group to act out its sentences for the class. When someone guesses the action, the group writes the sentence on the board.

Comunicación

4 **¿Estás listo?** Listen to the conversation between Matilde and Hernán. Then indicate whether the following conclusions are **lógico** or **ilógico**, based on what you heard.

	Lógico	Ilógico
1. Hernán compró un pasaje de ida y vuelta.	●	○
2. Matilde va a viajar con Hernán.	○	●
3. Hernán buscó su pasaporte.	●	○
4. Los documentos personales de Hernán están en su mochila.	○	●
5. Hernán tiene mucho equipaje.	○	●

5 **Ayer** Tell your partner at what time you did these activities yesterday. *Answers will vary.*

1. desayunar
2. salir de la casa
3. almorzar
4. ver a un(a) amigo/a
5. volver a la casa
6. cenar

6 **Las vacaciones** Imagine that you took these photos on a vacation with friends. Use the pictures to describe the trip. *Answers will vary.*

7 **Mi última compra** Write a short paragraph describing the last time you went shopping. Use at least four verbs in the preterite tense. *Answers will vary.*

Síntesis

8 **Conversación** With a partner, talk about what you did last week. Don't forget to include school activities, shopping, and pastimes. *Answers will vary.*

TEACHING OPTIONS

Large Group Have students stand up. Tell them to create a story chain about a student who had a very bad day. Begin the story by saying: **Ayer, Rigoberto pasó un día desastroso.** In order to sit down, students must contribute to the story. Call on a student to tell how **Rigoberto** began his day. The second person tells what happened next, and so on, until only one student remains. That person must conclude the story.

Extra Practice For homework, have students make a "to do" list at the beginning of their day. Then, ask students to return to their lists at the end of the day and write sentences stating which activities they completed. Ex: **limpiar mi habitación; No, no limpié mi habitación.**

6.4 Demonstrative adjectives and pronouns

Demonstrative adjectives

ANTE TODO In Spanish, as in English, demonstrative adjectives are words that "demonstrate" or "point out" nouns. Demonstrative adjectives precede the nouns they modify and, like other Spanish adjectives you have studied, agree with them in gender and number. Observe these examples and then study the chart below.

esta camisa	**ese** vendedor	**aquellos** zapatos
this shirt	that salesman	those shoes (over there)

Demonstrative adjectives

Singular		Plural		
MASCULINE	FEMININE	MASCULINE	FEMININE	
este	esta	estos	estas	this; these
ese	esa	esos	esas	that; those
aquel	aquella	aquellos	aquellas	that; those (over there)

▶ There are three sets of demonstrative adjectives. To determine which one to use, you must establish the relationship between the speaker and the noun(s) being pointed out.

▶ The demonstrative adjectives **este**, **esta**, **estos**, and **estas** are used to point out things that are close to the speaker and the listener.

Me gustan estos zapatos.

▶ The demonstrative adjectives **ese**, **esa**, **esos**, and **esas** are used to point out things that are not close in space and time to the speaker. They may, however, be close to the listener.

Prefiero esos zapatos.

¡De compras!

▸ The demonstrative adjectives **aquel**, **aquella**, **aquellos**, and **aquellas** are used to point out things that are far away from the speaker and the listener.

Aquel auto es de mi hermana.

Demonstrative pronouns

▸ Demonstrative pronouns are identical to their corresponding demonstrative adjectives, with the exception that they traditionally carry an accent mark on the stressed vowel. The **Real Academia** no longer requires this accent, but it is still commonly used.

Demonstrative pronouns

Singular		Plural	
MASCULINE	FEMININE	MASCULINE	FEMININE
éste	ésta	éstos	éstas
ése	ésa	ésos	ésas
aquél	aquélla	aquéllos	aquéllas

—¿Quieres comprar **este suéter**?
Do you want to buy this sweater?

—No, no quiero **éste**. Quiero **ése**.
No, I don't want this one. I want that one.

—¿Vas a leer **estas revistas**?
Are you going to read these magazines?

—Sí, voy a leer **éstas**. También voy a leer **aquéllas**.
Yes, I'm going to read these. I'll also read those (over there).

▸ **¡Atención!** Like demonstrative adjectives, demonstrative pronouns agree in gender and number with the corresponding noun.

Este libro es de Pablito.   **Éstos** son de Juana.

▸ There are three neuter demonstrative pronouns: **esto**, **eso**, and **aquello**. These forms refer to unidentified or unspecified things, situations, ideas, and concepts. They do not change in gender or number and never carry an accent mark.

—¿Qué es **esto**? —**Eso** es interesante. —**Aquello** es bonito.
What's this? *That's interesting.* *That's pretty.*

¡INTÉNTALO! Provide the correct form of the demonstrative adjective for these nouns.

1. la falda / este __esta falda__
2. los estudiantes / este __estos estudiantes__
3. los países / aquel __aquellos países__
4. la ventana / ese __esa ventana__
5. los periodistas / ese __esos periodistas__
6. el chico / aquel __aquel chico__
7. las sandalias / este __estas sandalias__
8. las chicas / aquel __aquellas chicas__

Práctica

1 Cambiar Make the singular sentences plural and the plural sentences singular.

> **modelo**
> Estas camisas son blancas.
> Esta camisa es blanca.

1. Aquellos sombreros son muy elegantes. *Aquel sombrero es muy elegante.*
2. Ese abrigo es muy caro. *Esos abrigos son muy caros.*
3. Estos cinturones son hermosos. *Este cinturón es hermoso.*
4. Esos precios son muy buenos. *Ese precio es muy bueno.*
5. Estas faldas son muy cortas. *Esta falda es muy corta.*
6. ¿Quieres ir a aquel almacén? *¿Quieres ir a aquellos almacenes?*
7. Esas blusas son baratas. *Esa blusa es barata.*
8. Esta corbata hace juego con mi traje. *Estas corbatas hacen juego con mis trajes.*

2 Completar Here are some things people might say while shopping. Complete the sentences with the correct demonstrative pronouns.

1. No me gustan esos zapatos. Voy a comprar __éstos__. (*these*)
2. ¿Vas a comprar ese traje o __éste__? (*this one*)
3. Esta guayabera es bonita, pero prefiero __ésa__. (*that one*)
4. Estas corbatas rojas son muy bonitas, pero __ésas__ son fabulosas. (*those*)
5. Estos cinturones cuestan demasiado. Prefiero __aquéllos__. (*those over there*)
6. ¿Te gustan esas botas o __éstas__? (*these*)
7. Esa bolsa roja es bonita, pero prefiero __aquélla__. (*that one over there*)
8. No voy a comprar estas botas; voy a comprar __aquéllas__. (*those over there*)
9. ¿Prefieres estos pantalones o __ésos__? (*those*)
10. Me gusta este vestido, pero voy a comprar __ése__. (*that one*)
11. Me gusta ese almacén, pero __aquél__ es mejor (*better*). (*that one over there*)
12. Esa blusa es bonita, pero cuesta demasiado. Voy a comprar __ésta__. (*this one*)

3 Describir Look for two items that are one of these colors: **amarillo**, **azul**, **blanco**, **marrón**, **negro**, **verde**, **rojo**. Point them out, first using demonstrative adjectives, and then demonstrative pronouns. *Answers will vary.*

> **modelo**
> azul
> Esta silla es azul. Aquella mochila es azul.
> Ésta es azul. Aquélla es azul.

Comunicación

4 **De compras** Listen to the conversation between Alejandra and a clerk. Then indicate whether the following conclusions are **lógico** or **ilógico**, based on what you heard.

	Lógico	Ilógico
1. A Alejandra no le gusta llevar faldas.	○	●
2. Alejandra va a comprar la blusa blanca.	○	●
3. La dependienta trabaja en un almacén.	●	○
4. A Alejandra le gustan los colores azul y gris.	●	○
5. El cinturón negro es muy caro.	○	●
6. Alejandra va a comprar una cartera también.	○	●

5 **En una tienda** Imagine that you and a partner are in Madrid shopping at Zara. Study the floor plan, then have a conversation about your surroundings. Use demonstrative adjectives and pronouns.

Answers will vary.

modelo
Estudiante 1: Me gusta este suéter azul.
Estudiante 2: Yo prefiero aquella chaqueta.

NOTA CULTURAL

Zara is an international clothing company based in Spain. Its innovative processes take a product from the design room to the manufacturing shelves in less than a month. This means that the merchandise is constantly changing to keep up with the most current trends.

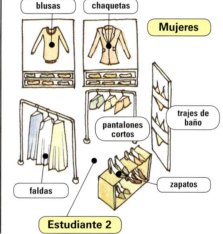

Síntesis

6 **En el café** Write a conversation between two people sitting at a busy sidewalk café. Use as many demonstrative adjectives and pronouns as possible to describe the people and things around them.

Answers will vary.

modelo
Carmen: Esa corbata es fea, ¿no?
Susana: Sí. No me gustan las corbatas rosadas y verdes. Y ese traje...

Recapitulación

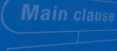

RESUMEN GRAMATICAL

Review the grammar concepts you have learned in this lesson by completing these activities.

1 Completar Complete the chart with the correct preterite or infinitive form of the verbs. **30 pts.**

Infinitive	yo	ella	ellos
tomar	tomé	tomó	**tomaron**
abrir	abrí	**abrió**	abrieron
comprender	comprendí	comprendió	comprendieron
leer	**leí**	leyó	leyeron
pagar	pagué	pagó	pagaron

2 En la tienda Look at the drawing and complete the conversation with demonstrative adjectives and pronouns. **14 pts.**

CLIENTE Buenos días, señorita. Deseo comprar (1) _esta_ corbata.

VENDEDORA Muy bien, señor. ¿No le interesa mirar (2) _aquellos_ trajes que están allá? Hay unos que hacen juego con la corbata.

CLIENTE (3) _Aquéllos_ de allá son de lana, ¿no? Prefiero ver (4) _ese_ traje marrón que está detrás de usted.

VENDEDORA Estupendo. Como puede ver, es de seda. Cuesta seiscientos cincuenta dólares.

CLIENTE Ah… eh… no, creo que sólo voy a comprar la corbata, gracias.

VENDEDORA Bueno… si busca algo más económico, hay rebaja en (5) _aquellos_ sombreros. Cuestan sólo treinta dólares.

CLIENTE ¡Magnífico! Me gusta (6) _aquél_, el blanco que está hasta arriba (*at the top*). Y quiero pagar todo con (7) _esta_ tarjeta.

VENDEDORA Sí, señor. Ahora mismo le traigo el sombrero.

6.1 Saber and conocer *p. 110*

saber	conocer
sé	conozco
sabes	conoces
sabe	conoce
sabemos	conocemos
sabéis	conocéis
saben	conocen

▶ **saber** = to know facts/how to do something
▶ **conocer** = to know a person, place, or thing

6.2 Indirect object pronouns *pp. 112–113*

Indirect object pronouns

Singular	Plural
me	nos
te	os
le	les

▶ **dar** = doy, das, da, damos, dais, dan
▶ **decir (e:i)** = digo, dices, dice, decimos, decís, dicen

6.3 Preterite tense of regular verbs *pp. 116–117*

comprar	vender	escribir
compré	vendí	escribí
compraste	vendiste	escribiste
compró	vendió	escribió
compramos	vendimos	escribimos
comprasteis	vendisteis	escribisteis
compraron	vendieron	escribieron

Verbs with spelling changes in the preterite

▶ **-car:** buscar → yo busqué
▶ **-gar:** llegar → yo llegué
▶ **-zar:** empezar → yo empecé
▶ **creer:** creí, creíste, creyó, creímos, creísteis, creyeron
▶ **leer:** leí, leíste, leyó, leímos, leísteis, leyeron
▶ **oír:** oí, oíste, oyó, oímos, oísteis, oyeron
▶ **ver:** vi, viste, vio, vimos, visteis, vieron

¡De compras!

ciento veinticinco 125

3 **¿Saber o conocer?** Complete each dialogue with the correct form of **saber** or **conocer**. **20 pts.**

1. —¿Qué __sabes__ hacer tú?
   —(Yo) __Sé__ jugar al fútbol.
2. —¿__Conoces__ tú esta tienda de ropa?
   —No, (yo) no la __conozco__. ¿Es buena?
3. —¿Tus amigos no __conocen__ a tu hermana?
   —No, ¡ellos no __saben__ que tengo una hermana!
4. —Mi maestra todavía no me __conoce__ bien.
   —Y tú, ¿la quieres __conocer__ a ella?
5. —¿__Saben__ ustedes dónde está el mercado?
   —No, nosotros no __conocemos__ bien esta ciudad.

6.4 Demonstrative adjectives and pronouns pp. 120–121

Demonstrative adjectives

Singular		Plural	
Masc.	Fem.	Masc.	Fem.
este	esta	estos	estas
ese	esa	esos	esas
aquel	aquella	aquellos	aquellas

Demonstrative pronouns

Singular		Plural	
Masc.	Fem.	Masc.	Fem.
éste	ésta	éstos	éstas
ése	ésa	ésos	ésas
aquél	aquélla	aquéllos	aquéllas

4 **Oraciones** Form complete sentences using the information provided. Use indirect object pronouns and the present tense of the verbs. **32 pts.**

1. Javier / prestar / el abrigo / a Maripili
   Javier le presta el abrigo a Maripili.
2. nosotros / vender / ropa / a los clientes
   Nosotros les vendemos ropa a los clientes.
3. el vendedor / traer / las camisetas / a mis amigos y a mí
   El vendedor nos trae las camisetas (a mis amigos y a mí).
4. yo / querer dar / consejos / a ti
   Yo quiero darte consejos (a ti)./Yo te quiero dar consejos (a ti).
5. ¿tú / ir a comprar / un regalo / a mí?
   ¿Tú vas a comprarme un regalo (a mí)?/¿Tú me vas a comprar un regalo (a mí)?
6. el dependiente / mostrar / las corbatas / a Santiago
   El dependiente le muestra las corbatas a Santiago.
7. los hijos / pedir / dinero / a sus padres
   Los hijos les piden dinero a sus padres.
8. la profesora / escribir / mensajes electrónicos / a nosotros
   La profesora nos escribe mensajes electrónicos (a nosotros).

5 **Poema** Write the missing words to complete the excerpt from the poem *Romance sonámbulo* by Federico García Lorca. **4 pts.**

> "Verde que __te__ quiero verde.
> Verde viento. Verdes ramas°.
> El barco sobre la mar
> y el caballo en la montaña, [...]
> Verde que te quiero __verde__ (*green*)."

ramas *branches*

6 adelante

Section Goals

In **Lectura**, students will:
- learn to skim a text
- use what they know about text format to predict a document's content
- read a text rich in cognates and recognizable format elements

 Communication 1.1, 1.2, 1.3
Cultures 2.1, 2.2
Connections 3.1, 3.2
Comparisons 4.2

 Pre-AP®

Interpretive Reading: Estrategia
Tell students that they can often predict the content of an unfamiliar document in Spanish by skimming it and looking for recognizable format elements.

Examinar el texto Point out the cognate **Liquidación** and the series of percentages. Ask them to predict what type of document it is. (It is an advertisement for a liquidation sale.) Then ask students to scan the rest of the ad.

Buscar cognados Ask volunteers to point out cognates.

Impresiones generales
Ask students to sum up their general impression of the document by answering the three questions at the bottom.

In-Class Tips
- Remind students that many store hours are given using the 24-hour clock.
- Remind students that, for these prices, periods are used where one would see a comma in English.
- Point out the shoe sizes and explain that they are European sizes. Then point out clothing sizes and ask students to guess what **P, M, G,** and **XG** stand for.

Lectura

Antes de leer

Estrategia
Skimming

Skimming involves quickly reading through a document to absorb its general meaning. This allows you to understand the main ideas without having to read word for word. When you skim a text, you might want to look at its title and subtitles. You might also want to read the first sentence of each paragraph.

Examinar el texto
Look at the format of the reading selection. How is it organized? What does the organization of the document tell you about its content?

Buscar cognados
Scan the reading selection to locate at least five cognates. Based on the cognates, what do you think the reading selection is about? *Answers will vary. Suggested answers for 1–5: elegancia, blusas, accesorios, pantalones, precio.*

1. _____   4. _____
2. _____   5. _____
3. _____

The reading selection is about ___*a sale in a store*___.

Impresiones generales
Now skim the reading selection to understand its general meaning. Jot down your impressions. What new information did you learn about the document by skimming it? Based on all the information you now have, answer these questions in Spanish.

1. Who created this document? *un almacén/una tienda*
2. What is its purpose? *vender ropa*
3. Who is its intended audience? *gente que quiere comprar ropa*

http://corona.cl

Corona
¡Corona tiene las ofertas más locas del verano!

La tienda más elegante de la ciudad con precios increíbles

niños | **mujeres** | casa | baño | equipaje

Faldas largas
ROPA BONITA
Algodón. De distintos colores
Talla mediana
Precio especial: 8.000 pesos

Blusas de seda
BAMBÚ
De cuadros y de lunares
Ahora: 21.000 pesos
40% de rebaja

Vestido de algodón
PANAMÁ
Colores blanco, azul y verde
Ahora: 18.000 pesos
30% de rebaja

Accesorios
BELLEZA
Cinturones, gafas de sol, sombreros, medias
Diversos estilos
Todos con un 40% de rebaja

Carteras
ELEGANCIA
Colores anaranjado, blanco, rosado y amarillo
Ahora: 15.000 pesos
50% de rebaja

Sandalias de playa
GINO
Números del 35 al 38
A sólo 12.000 pesos
50% de descuento

Lunes a sábado de 9 a 21 horas.
Domingo de 10 a 14 horas.

TEACHING OPTIONS

Large Groups Ask students to create an ad for one or two items of clothing. Then, in groups, have them combine their ads into a "catalogue." Have groups exchange catalogues and discuss what items they would like to buy.

Small Groups Have small groups of students work together to write a cloze paragraph about shopping for clothing, modeled on the **Completar** paragraph. Ask each group member to contribute two sentences to the paragraph. Then have the group make a clean copy, omitting several words or phrases, and writing the omitted words and phrases below the paragraph. Have groups exchange paragraphs and complete them.

Real° Liquidación°
¡La rebaja está de moda en Corona!
¡Grandes rebajas!
y con la tarjeta de crédito más conveniente del mercado.

bebé | **hombres** | jardín | joyas | electrónica

Chaquetas CASINO
Microfibra. Colores negro, café y gris
Tallas: P, M, G, XG
Ahora: 22.500 pesos

Traje inglés GALES
Modelos originales
Ahora: 105.000 pesos
30% de rebaja

Pantalones OCÉANO
Colores negro, gris y café
Ahora: 11.500 pesos
30% de rebaja

Accesorios GUAPO
Gafas de sol, corbatas, cinturones, calcetines
Diversos estilos
Todos con un 40% de rebaja

Zapatos COLOR
Italianos y franceses
Números del 40 al 45
A sólo 20.000 pesos

Ropa interior ATLÁNTICO
Tallas: P, M, G
Colores blanco, negro y gris
40% de rebaja

Real *Royal* Liquidación *Clearance sale*

Por la compra de 40.000 pesos, puede llevar un regalo gratis.
- Un hermoso cinturón de mujer
- Un par de calcetines
- Una corbata de seda
- Una bolsa para la playa
- Una mochila
- Unas medias

Después de leer

Completar
Complete this paragraph about the reading selection with the correct forms of the words from the word bank.

almacén	hacer juego	tarjeta de crédito
caro	increíble	tienda
dinero	pantalones	verano
falda	rebaja	zapato

En este anuncio, el __almacén__ Corona anuncia la liquidación de __verano__ con grandes __rebajas__. Con muy poco __dinero__ usted puede conseguir ropa fina y elegante. Si no tiene dinero en efectivo, puede utilizar su __tarjeta de crédito__ y pagar luego. Para el caballero con gustos refinados, hay __zapatos__ importados de París y Roma. La señora elegante puede encontrar blusas de seda que __hacen juego__ con todo tipo de __pantalones/faldas__ o __faldas/pantalones__. Los precios de esta liquidación son realmente __increíbles__.

¿Cierto o falso?
Indicate whether each statement is **cierto** or **falso**. Correct the false statements.

1. Hay sandalias de playa. Cierto.
2. Las corbatas tienen una rebaja del 30%. Falso. Tienen una rebaja del 40%.
3. El almacén Corona tiene un departamento de zapatos. Cierto.
4. Normalmente las sandalias cuestan 22.000 pesos. Falso. Normalmente cuestan 24.000 pesos.
5. Cuando gastas 30.000 pesos en la tienda, llevas un regalo gratis. Falso. Cuando gastas 40.000 pesos en la tienda, llevas un regalo gratis.
6. Tienen carteras amarillas. Cierto.

Preguntas
Answer these questions. Answers will vary.

1. Imagina que vas a ir a la tienda Corona. ¿Qué departamentos vas a visitar? ¿El departamento de ropa para señoras, el departamento de ropa para caballeros…?
2. ¿Qué vas a buscar en Corona?
3. ¿Hay tiendas similares a la tienda Corona en tu pueblo o ciudad? ¿Cómo se llaman? ¿Tienen muchas gangas?

Escritura

Estrategia
How to report an interview

There are several ways to prepare a written report about an interview. For example, you can transcribe the interview verbatim, you can simply summarize it, or you can summarize it but quote the speakers occasionally. In any event, the report should begin with an interesting title and a brief introduction, which may include the five Ws (*what, where, when, who, why*) and the H (*how*) of the interview. The report should end with an interesting conclusion. Note that when you transcribe dialogue in Spanish, you should pay careful attention to format and punctuation.

Writing dialogue in Spanish

- If you need to transcribe an interview verbatim, you can use speakers' names to indicate a change of speaker.

    CARMELA ¿Qué compraste? ¿Encontraste muchas gangas?

    ROBERTO Sí, muchas. Compré un suéter, una camisa y dos corbatas. Y tú, ¿qué compraste?

    CARMELA Una blusa y una falda muy bonitas. ¿Cuánto costó tu camisa?

    ROBERTO Sólo diez dólares. ¿Cuánto costó tu blusa?

    CARMELA Veinte dólares.

- You can also use a dash (*raya*) to mark the beginning of each speaker's words.

    —¿Qué compraste?

    —Un suéter y una camisa muy bonitos. Y tú, ¿encontraste muchas gangas?

    —Sí… compré dos blusas, tres camisetas y un par de zapatos.

    —¡A ver!

Tema
Escribe un informe

Write a report for the school newspaper about an interview you conducted with a student about his or her shopping habits and clothing preferences. First, brainstorm a list of interview questions. Then conduct the interview using the questions below as a guide, but feel free to ask other questions as they occur to you.

Examples of questions:

▸ ¿Cuándo vas de compras?

▸ ¿Adónde vas de compras?

▸ ¿Con quién vas de compras?

▸ ¿Qué tiendas, almacenes o centros comerciales prefieres?

▸ ¿Compras ropa de catálogos o por Internet?

▸ ¿Prefieres comprar ropa cara o barata? ¿Por qué? ¿Te gusta buscar gangas?

▸ ¿Qué ropa llevas cuando vas a clase?

▸ ¿Qué ropa llevas cuando sales a bailar?

▸ ¿Qué ropa llevas cuando practicas un deporte?

▸ ¿Cuáles son tus colores favoritos? ¿Compras mucha ropa de esos colores?

▸ ¿Les das ropa a tu familia o a tus amigos/as?

Escuchar

Estrategia
Listening for linguistic cues

You can enhance your listening comprehension by listening for specific linguistic cues. For example, if you listen for the endings of conjugated verbs, or for familiar constructions, such as **acabar de** + [*infinitive*] or **ir a** + [*infinitive*], you can find out whether an event already took place, is taking place now, or will take place in the future. Verb endings also give clues about who is participating in the action.

 To practice listening for linguistic cues, you will now listen to four sentences. As you listen, note whether each sentence refers to a past, present, or future action. Also jot down the subject of each sentence.

Preparación

Based on the photograph, what do you think Marisol has recently done? What do you think Marisol and Alicia are talking about? What else can you guess about their conversation from the visual clues in the photograph?

Ahora escucha

Now you are going to hear Marisol and Alicia's conversation. Make a list of the clothing items that each person mentions. Then put a check mark after the item if the person actually purchased it.

Marisol	Alicia
1. pantalones ✔	1. falda
2. blusa ✔	2. blusa
3. _____	3. zapatos
4. _____	4. cinturón

Comprensión

¿Cierto o falso?
Indicate whether each statement is **cierto** or **falso**. Then correct the false statements.

1. Marisol y Alicia acaban de ir de compras juntas (*together*). Falso. Marisol acaba de ir de compras.
2. Marisol va a comprar unos pantalones y una blusa mañana. Falso. Marisol ya los compró.
3. Marisol compró una blusa de cuadros. Cierto.
4. Alicia compró unos zapatos nuevos hoy. Falso. Alicia va a comprar unos zapatos nuevos.
5. Alicia y Marisol van a ir al café. Cierto.
6. Marisol gastó todo el dinero de la semana en ropa nueva. Cierto.

Preguntas
Answer the following questions. Be sure to explain your answers. Answers will vary.

1. ¿Crees que Alicia y Marisol son buenas amigas? ¿Por qué?
2. ¿Cuál de las dos estudiantes es más ahorradora (*frugal*)? ¿Por qué?
3. ¿Crees que a Alicia le gusta la ropa que Marisol compró?
4. ¿Crees que la moda es importante para Alicia? ¿Para Marisol? ¿Por qué?
5. ¿Es importante para ti estar a la moda? ¿Por qué?

Section Goals
In **Escuchar**, students will:
- listen for specific linguistic cues in oral sentences
- answer questions based on a recorded conversation

Communication 1.2

Estrategia
Script 1. Acabamos de pasear por la ciudad y encontramos unos monumentos fenomenales. 2. Estoy haciendo las maletas. 3. Carmen y Alejandro decidieron ir a un restaurante. 4. Mi familia y yo vamos a ir a la playa.

In-Class Tip Ask students to look at the photo of **Marisol** and **Alicia** and predict what they are talking about.

Ahora escucha
Script MARISOL: Oye, Alicia, ¿qué estás haciendo?
ALICIA: Estudiando no más. ¿Qué hay de nuevo?
M: Acabo de comprarme esos pantalones que andaba buscando.
A: ¿Los encontraste en el centro comercial? ¿Y cuánto te costaron?
M: Míralos. ¿Te gustan? En el almacén Melo tienen tremenda rebaja. Como estaban baratos me compré una blusa también. Es de cuadros, pero creo que hace juego con los pantalones por el color rojo. ¿Qué piensas?
A: Es de los mismos colores que la falda y la blusa que llevaste cuando fuimos al cine anoche. La verdad es que te quedan muy bien esos colores. ¿No encontraste unos zapatos y un cinturón para completar el juego?
M: No lo digas ni de chiste. Mi tarjeta de crédito está que no aguanta más. Y trabajé poco la semana pasada. ¡Acabo de gastar todo el dinero para la semana!

(Script continues at far left in the bottom panels.)

A: ¡Ay, chica! Fui al centro comercial el mes pasado y encontré unos zapatos muy, pero muy de moda. Muy caros… pero buenos. No me los compré porque no los tenían en mi número. Voy a comprarlos cuando lleguen más… el vendedor me va a llamar.

M: Ajá… ¿Y va a invitarte a salir con él?
A: ¡Ay! ¡No seas así! Ven, vamos al café. Te ves muy bien y no hay que gastar eso aquí.
M: De acuerdo. Vamos.

Section Goals

In **En pantalla**, students will:
- read about a toy store in Spain
- watch a television commercial for **Juguettos**, a Spanish toy store

Communication 1.1, 1.2, 1.3
Cultures 2.1, 2.2
Connections 3.1, 3.2
Comparisons 4.2

Teacher Resources
Read the front matter for suggestions on how to incorporate all the program's components. See pages 99A–99B for a detailed listing of Teacher Resources online.

Vocabulario útil
Guide students to identify the infinitives **ser** and **pedir** in the phrases **sean como sean** and **pidan lo que pidan**. Then ask them what is different about how they are conjugated. Briefly share that this "unexpected grammar" signals a mood of possibility called the subjunctive.

 Pre-AP®

Audiovisual Interpretive Communication
Antes de ver **Strategy**
- Read through the **Vocabulario útil** with students. Model the pronunciation.
- Have students predict what is happening based on the photo.

Aplicación Have students do their own quote exploration using such key search phrases as **citas sobre la imaginación** and **citas sobre las posesiones**. Which ones do they find especially provocative or insightful? How might they restate the quotes in their own words, illustrate them, or act them out?

Anuncio de juguetería Juguettos

Me lo pido.

Preparación
Answer these questions in Spanish. *Answers will vary.*
1. ¿Cómo eres? Escribe tres adjetivos que te describan.
2. ¿Qué actividades ilustran (*illustrates*) tu personalidad?

El País de Siempre Jugar
Juguettos, first established in Villena (Comunidad de Valencia), Spain, in the 1980s, now has chain stores all over the country. Juguettos offers both brand-name toys you would recognize (and maybe own) and those that specifically cater to a child's life and cultural experiences in Spain. When children dreaming of the perfect toy look in a Juguettos catalog, they may be looking for Legos® but also for Nenittos® or Hazlo tú®. But children's toys, like their imaginations, are very similar throughout the world. Indeed, the company declares it has founded its own "country," el País de Siempre Jugar.

Vocabulario útil
copionas	copycats
despistado/a	distracted
sean	they may be
pidan	they may ask for

Comprensión
Match the personality trait with its visual representation in the ad.

- _e_ 1. valiente
- _c_ 2. galáctico/a
- _d_ 3. artista
- _b_ 4. generoso/a
- _a_ 5. intrépido/a

a. Tienen una batalla (*battle*) imaginaria.
b. Le compra juguetes a su mascota (*pet*).
c. Está en un cartón con forma de nave espacial (*spaceship*).
d. Hacen música con parte de una basurera (*trashcan*).
e. Imagina que puede volar (*fly*).

Conversación
Answer these questions with a classmate. *Answers will vary.*
1. ¿Qué quieres hacer ahora en tu vida que no haces? ¿Por qué lo quieres hacer?
2. ¿Por qué es importante la imaginación en la vida de los niños?
3. ¿Qué importancia tiene la imaginación en la vida de los adultos?

Aplicación
The Spanish poet Gustavo Adolfo Bécquer wrote, **"Él que tiene imaginación, con qué facilidad saca de la nada un mundo."** Working with a partner, discuss your understanding of the quote. Then prepare and present a skit in Spanish that illustrates its point.
Answers will vary.

TEACHING OPTIONS

Discussion While being aware of your students' diverse economic situations, ask questions that explore the relationship between possessions and identity. Examples: **¿Cómo te describen tus posesiones? ¿Cómo se relacionan nuestra identidad y nuestras posesiones? ¿Es posible tener demasiadas posesiones? ¿Por qué? ¿Cómo se relacionan la imaginación y las posesiones?**

Heritage Learners Invite heritage students to share about toys in their cultures of origin. Where do children get the toys they play with? What are the roles of special stores and places dedicated to children's play? What similarities and differences do they see in the role of toys between their culture of origin and the United States? What about the role of imagination in play?

¡De compras!

Comprar en los mercados

In the Spanish-speaking world, most city dwellers shop at large supermarkets and little stores that specialize in just one item, such as a butcher shop (**carnicería**), vegetable market (**verdulería**), perfume shop (**perfumería**), or hat shop (**sombrerería**). In small towns where supermarkets are less common, many people rely exclusively on specialty shops. This requires shopping more frequently—often every day or every other day for perishable items—but also means that the foods they consume are fresher and the goods are usually locally produced. Each neighborhood generally has its own shops, so people don't have to walk far to find fresh bread (at a **panadería**) for the midday meal.

Vocabulario útil

colones (pl.)	currency from Costa Rica
¿Cuánto vale?	¿Cuánto cuesta?
descuento	discount
disculpe	excuse me
¿Dónde queda...?	Where is... located?
los helados	ice cream
el regateo	bargaining

Preparación

Have you ever been to an open-air market? What did you buy? Have you ever negotiated a price? What did you say? Answers will vary.

Comprensión

Select the option that best summarizes this episode.

a. Randy Cruz va al mercado al aire libre para comprar papayas. Luego va al Mercado Central. Él les pregunta a varios clientes qué compran, prueba (*tastes*) platos típicos y busca la heladería.

b. Randy Cruz va al mercado al aire libre para comprar papayas y pedir un descuento. Luego va al Mercado Central para preguntarles a los clientes qué compran en los mercados.

Trescientos colones.

... pero me hace un buen descuento.

¿Qué compran en el Mercado Central?

TEACHING OPTIONS

Pairs Have pairs of students write a series of true/false statements about what happened in this episode. Then have pairs exchange papers and complete the activity. They should correct the false statements.

Extra Practice Tell students to imagine that they are at one of the markets featured in the video. Ask them to jot down what they would like to buy there. Then have them write a dialogue of the conversation they would have in order to bargain for the goods they want to buy. Ask volunteers to role-play their dialogues for the class.

Section Goal
In **Panorama**, students will read about the geography, culture, history, and economy of Cuba.

- Communication 1.2, 1.3
- Cultures 2.1, 2.2
- Connections 3.1, 3.2
- Comparisons 4.2

Teacher Resources
Read the front matter for suggestions on how to incorporate all the program's components. See pages 99A–99B for a detailed listing of Teacher Resources online.

In-Class Tips
- Use the **Lección 6** online Resources to assist with this presentation.
- Ask students to look at the map. Ask volunteers to read the captions on each call-out photo. Then discuss the photos with the class.

The Affective Dimension
Some students may have strong feelings about Cuba. Encourage students to discuss their points of view.

El país en cifras
- After reading about **La Habana Vieja**, show students images of this part of the city.
- Draw attention to the design and colors of the Cuban flag. Compare the Cuban flag to the Puerto Rican flag (page 96). Explain that Puerto Rico and Cuba, the last Spanish colonies in the western hemisphere, both gained their independence from Spain in 1898, in part through the intervention of the U.S.

¡Increíble pero cierto! Due to the patterns of evolution and adaptation common to islands, Cuba has many examples of unique flora and fauna. Have students research other examples.

---

6 panorama

Cuba

El país en cifras

- **Área:** 110.860 km² (42.803 millas²), aproximadamente el área de Pensilvania
- **Población:** 11.061.886
- **Capital:** La Habana—2.116.000

La Habana Vieja fue declarada° Patrimonio° Cultural de la Humanidad por la UNESCO en 1982. Este distrito es uno de los lugares más fascinantes de Cuba. En La Plaza de Armas, se puede visitar el majestuoso Palacio de Capitanes Generales, que ahora es un museo. En la calle° Obispo, frecuentada por el autor Ernest Hemingway, hay hermosos cafés, clubes nocturnos y tiendas elegantes.

- **Ciudades principales:** Santiago de Cuba; Camagüey; Holguín; Guantánamo
- **Moneda:** peso cubano
- **Idiomas:** español (oficial)

Bandera de Cuba

Cubanos célebres
- **Carlos Finlay,** doctor y científico (1833–1915)
- **José Martí,** político y poeta (1853–1895)
- **Fidel Castro,** ex primer ministro, ex comandante en jefe° de las fuerzas armadas (1926–)
- **Zoé Valdés,** escritora (1959–)
- **Ibrahim Ferrer,** músico (1927–2005)
- **Carlos Acosta,** bailarín (1973–)

fue declarada *was declared* Patrimonio *Heritage* calle *street* comandante en jefe *commander in chief* liviano *light* colibrí abeja *bee hummingbird* ave *bird* mundo *world* miden *measure* pesan *weigh*

¡Increíble pero cierto!
Pequeño y liviano°, el colibrí abeja° de Cuba es una de las más de 320 especies de colibrí y es también el ave° más pequeña del mundo°. Menores que muchos insectos, estas aves minúsculas miden° 5 centímetros y pesan° sólo 1,95 gramos.

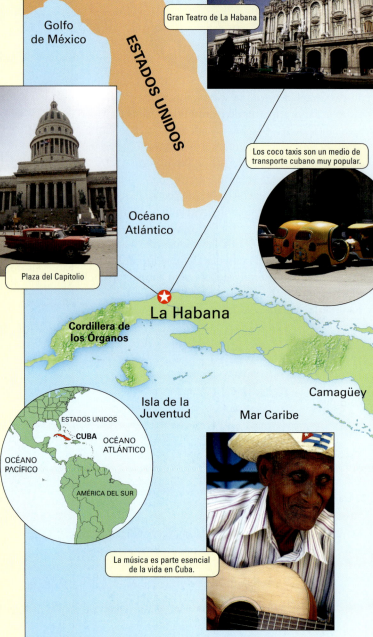

Gran Teatro de La Habana

Golfo de México

ESTADOS UNIDOS

Los coco taxis son un medio de transporte cubano muy popular.

Plaza del Capitolio

Océano Atlántico

Cordillera de los Órganos

La Habana

Isla de la Juventud

Camagüey

Mar Caribe

La música es parte esencial de la vida en Cuba.

TEACHING OPTIONS

Variación léxica An item of clothing that you will see everywhere if you visit Cuba (or the Caribbean in general) is the **guayabera**. A loose-fitting, short-sleeved shirt made of natural fibers, the **guayabera** is perfect for hot, humid climates. **Guayaberas** generally have large pockets and may be decorated with embroidery. They are worn open at the neck and never tucked in.

Extra Practice Give students two stanzas of the first poem from José Martí's collection **Versos sencillos**. Some students may recognize these as verses from the song **Guantanamera**.

*Yo soy un hombre sincero
de donde crece la palma;
y, antes de morirme, quiero
echar mis versos del alma.*

*Yo vengo de todas partes,
y hacia todas partes voy;
arte soy entre las artes;
en los montes, monte soy.*

Baile • Ballet Nacional de Cuba
La bailarina Alicia Alonso fundó el Ballet Nacional de Cuba en 1948, después de° convertirse en una estrella° internacional en el Ballet de Nueva York y en Broadway. El Ballet Nacional de Cuba es famoso en todo el mundo por su creatividad y perfección técnica.

Economía • La caña de azúcar y el tabaco
La caña de azúcar° es el producto agrícola° que más se cultiva en la isla y su exportación es muy importante para la economía del país. El tabaco, que se usa para fabricar los famosos puros° cubanos, es otro cultivo° de mucha importancia.

Gente • Población
La población cubana tiene raíces° muy heterogéneas. La inmigración a la isla fue determinante° desde la colonia hasta mediados° del siglo° XX. Los cubanos de hoy son descendientes de africanos, europeos, chinos y antillanos, entre otros.

Música • Buena Vista Social Club
En 1997 nace° el fenómeno musical conocido como *Buena Vista Social Club*. Este proyecto reúne° a un grupo de importantes músicos de Cuba, la mayoría ya mayores, con una larga trayectoria interpretando canciones clásicas del son° cubano. Ese mismo año ganaron un *Grammy*. Hoy en día estos músicos son conocidos en todo el mundo, y personas de todas las edades bailan al ritmo° de su música.

¿Qué aprendiste? Responde a las preguntas con una oración completa.
1. ¿Qué autor está asociado con la Habana Vieja? Ernest Hemingway está asociado con la Habana Vieja.
2. ¿Por qué es famoso el Ballet Nacional de Cuba? Es famoso por su creatividad y perfección técnica.
3. ¿Cuáles son los dos cultivos más importantes para la economía cubana? Los cultivos más importantes son la caña de azúcar y el tabaco.
4. ¿Qué fabrican los cubanos con la planta del tabaco? Los cubanos fabrican puros.
5. ¿De dónde son muchos de los inmigrantes que llegaron a Cuba? Son de África, de Europa, de China y de las Antillas, entre otros lugares.
6. ¿En qué año ganó un *Grammy* el disco *Buena Vista Social Club*? Ganó un *Grammy* en 1997.

Conexión Internet Investiga estos temas en Internet.
1. Busca información sobre un(a) cubano/a célebre. ¿Por qué es célebre? ¿Qué hace? ¿Todavía vive en Cuba?
2. Busca información sobre una de las ciudades principales de Cuba. ¿Qué atracciones hay en esta ciudad?

después de *after* estrella *star* caña de azúcar *sugar cane* agrícola *farming* puros *cigars* cultivo *crop* raíces *roots* determinante *deciding* mediados *halfway through* siglo *century* nace *is born* reúne *gets together* son *Cuban musical genre* ritmo *rhythm*

vocabulario

La ropa

el abrigo	coat
los (blue)jeans	jeans
la blusa	blouse
la bolsa	purse; bag
la bota	boot
los calcetines (el calcetín)	sock(s)
la camisa	shirt
la camiseta	t-shirt
la cartera	wallet
la chaqueta	jacket
el cinturón	belt
la corbata	tie
la falda	skirt
las gafas (de sol)	(sun)glasses
los guantes	gloves
el impermeable	raincoat
las medias	pantyhose; stockings
los pantalones	pants
los pantalones cortos	shorts
la ropa	clothes
la ropa interior	underwear
las sandalias	sandals
el sombrero	hat
el suéter	sweater
el traje	suit
el traje de baño	bathing suit
el vestido	dress
los zapatos de tenis	sneakers

Verbos

conducir	to drive
conocer	to know; to be acquainted with
dar	to give
ofrecer	to offer
parecer	to seem
saber	to know; to know how
traducir	to translate

Ir de compras

el almacén	department store
la caja	cash register
el centro comercial	shopping mall
el/la cliente/a	customer
el/la dependiente/a	clerk
el dinero	money
(en) efectivo	cash
el mercado (al aire libre)	(open-air) market
un par (de zapatos)	a pair (of shoes)
el precio (fijo)	(fixed; set) price
la rebaja	sale
el regalo	gift
la tarjeta de crédito	credit card
la tienda	store
el/la vendedor(a)	salesperson
costar (o:ue)	to cost
gastar	to spend (money)
hacer juego (con)	to match (with)
llevar	to wear; to take
pagar	to pay
regatear	to bargain
usar	to wear; to use
vender	to sell

Adjetivos

barato/a	cheap
bueno/a	good
cada	each
caro/a	expensive
corto/a	short (in length)
elegante	elegant
hermoso/a	beautiful
largo/a	long
loco/a	crazy
nuevo/a	new
otro/a	other; another
pobre	poor
rico/a	rich

Los colores

el color	color
amarillo/a	yellow
anaranjado/a	orange
azul	blue
blanco/a	white
gris	gray
marrón, café	brown
morado/a	purple
negro/a	black
rojo/a	red
rosado/a	pink
verde	green

Palabras adicionales

acabar de (+ *inf.*)	to have just done something
anoche	last night
anteayer	the day before yesterday
ayer	yesterday
de repente	suddenly
desde	from
dos veces	twice
hasta	until
pasado/a (*adj.*)	last; past
el año pasado	last year
la semana pasada	last week
prestar	to lend; to loan
una vez	once
ya	already

Indirect object pronouns	See page 112.
Demonstrative adjectives and pronouns	See page 120.
Expresiones útiles	See page 105.

Consulta

Vocabulario
Spanish–English pages A-2–17
English–Spanish pages A-18–33

References
pages A-34–45

Credits
pages A-46

Índice
pages A-47–48

Vocabulario

Guide to Vocabulary

Note on alphabetization

For purposes of alphabetization, **ch** and **ll** are not treated as separate letters, but **ñ** follows **n**. Therefore, in this glossary you will find that **año**, for example, appears after **anuncio**.

Abbreviations used in this glossary

adj.	adjective	*form.*	formal	*pl.*	plural
adv.	adverb	*indef.*	indefinite	*poss.*	possessive
art.	article	*interj.*	interjection	*prep.*	preposition
conj.	conjunction	*i.o.*	indirect object	*pron.*	pronoun
def.	definite	*m.*	masculine	*ref.*	reflexive
d.o.	direct object	*n.*	noun	*sing.*	singular
f.	feminine	*obj.*	object	*sub.*	subject
fam.	familiar	*p.p.*	past participle	*v.*	verb

Spanish–English

A

a *prep.* at; to 1.1
   ¿A qué hora...? At what time...? 1.1
   a bordo aboard
   a dieta on a diet 3.3
   a la derecha de to the right of 1.2
   a la izquierda de to the left of 1.2
   a la plancha grilled 2.2
   a la(s) + *time* at + *time* 1.1
   a menos que *conj.* unless 3.1
   a menudo *adv.* often 2.4
   a nombre de in the name of 1.5
   a plazos in installments 3.2
   A sus órdenes. At your service.
   a tiempo *adv.* on time 2.4
   a veces *adv.* sometimes 2.4
   a ver let's see
abeja *f.* bee
abierto/a *adj.* open 1.5, 3.2
abogado/a *m., f.* lawyer 3.4
abrazar(se) *v.* to hug; to embrace (each other) 2.5
abrazo *m.* hug
abrigo *m.* coat 1.6
abril *m.* April 1.5
abrir *v.* to open 1.3
abuelo/a *m., f.* grandfather/ grandmother 1.3
abuelos *pl.* grandparents 1.3
aburrido/a *adj.* bored; boring 1.5
aburrir *v.* to bore 2.1
aburrirse *v.* to get bored 3.5
acabar de (+ *inf.***)** *v.* to have just done something 1.6
acampar *v.* to camp 1.5
accidente *m.* accident 2.4
acción *f.* action 3.5
   de acción action (genre) 3.5

aceite *m.* oil 2.2
aceptar: ¡Acepto casarme contigo! I'll marry you! 3.5
acompañar *v.* to accompany 3.2
aconsejar *v.* to advise 2.6
acontecimiento *m.* event 3.6
acordarse (de) (o:ue) *v.* to remember 2.1
acostarse (o:ue) *v.* to go to bed 2.1
activo/a *adj.* active 3.3
actor *m.* actor 3.4
actriz *f.* actress 3.4
actualidades *f., pl.* news; current events 3.6
adelgazar *v.* to lose weight; to slim down 3.3
además (de) *adv.* furthermore; besides 2.4
adicional *adj.* additional
adiós *m.* goodbye 1.1
adjetivo *m.* adjective
administración de empresas *f.* business administration 1.2
adolescencia *f.* adolescence 2.3
¿adónde? *adv.* where (to)? (destination) 1.2
aduana *f.* customs
aeróbico/a *adj.* aerobic 3.3
aeropuerto *m.* airport 1.5
afectado/a *adj.* affected 3.1
afeitarse *v.* to shave 2.1
aficionado/a *m., f.* fan 1.4
afirmativo/a *adj.* affirmative
afuera *adv.* outside 1.5
afueras *f., pl.* suburbs; outskirts 2.6
agencia de viajes *f.* travel agency 1.5
agente de viajes *m., f.* travel agent 1.5
agosto *m.* August 1.5
agradable *adj.* pleasant
agua *f.* water 2.2
   agua mineral mineral water 2.2

aguantar *v.* to endure, to hold up 3.2
ahora *adv.* now 1.2
   ahora mismo right now 1.5
ahorrar *v.* to save (money) 3.2
ahorros *m., pl.* savings 3.2
aire *m.* air 3.1
ajo *m.* garlic 2.2
al (*contraction of* **a + el**) 1.4
   al aire libre open-air 1.6
   al contado in cash 3.2
   (al) este (to the) east 3.2
   al lado de next to; beside 1.2
   (al) norte (to the) north 3.2
   (al) oeste (to the) west 3.2
   (al) sur (to the) south 3.2
alcoba *f.* bedroom
alegrarse (de) *v.* to be happy 3.1
alegre *adj.* happy; joyful 1.5
alegría *f.* happiness 2.3
alemán, alemana *adj.* German 1.3
alérgico/a *adj.* allergic 2.4
alfombra *f.* carpet; rug 2.6
algo *pron.* something; anything 2.1
algodón *m.* cotton 1.6
alguien *pron.* someone; somebody; anyone 2.1
algún, alguno/a(s) *adj.* any; some 2.1
alimento *m.* food
   alimentación *f.* diet
aliviar *v.* to reduce 3.3
   aliviar el estrés/la tensión to reduce stress/tension 3.3
allá *adv.* over there 1.2
allí *adv.* there 1.2
alma *f.* soul 2.3
almacén *m.* department store 1.6
almohada *f.* pillow 2.6
almorzar (o:ue) *v.* to have lunch 1.4
almuerzo *m.* lunch 1.4, 2.2

Vocabulario

aló *interj.* hello (*on the telephone*) 2.5
alquilar *v.* to rent 2.6
alquiler *m.* rent (payment) 2.6
altar *m.* altar 2.3
altillo *m.* attic 2.6
alto/a *adj.* tall 1.3
aluminio *m.* aluminum 3.1
ama de casa *m., f.* housekeeper; caretaker 2.6
amable *adj.* nice; friendly 1.5
amarillo/a *adj.* yellow 1.6
amigo/a *m., f.* friend 1.3
amistad *f.* friendship 2.3
amor *m.* love 2.3
    amor a primera vista love at first sight 2.3
anaranjado/a *adj.* orange 1.6
ándale *interj.* come on 3.2
andar *v.* **en patineta** to skateboard 1.4
ángel *m.* angel 2.3
anillo *m.* ring 3.5
animal *m.* animal 3.1
aniversario (de bodas) *m.* (wedding) anniversary 2.3
anoche *adv.* last night 1.6
anteayer *adv.* the day before yesterday 1.6
antes *adv.* before 2.1
    antes (de) que *conj.* before 3.1
    antes de *prep.* before 2.1
antibiótico *m.* antibiotic 2.4
antipático/a *adj.* unpleasant 1.3
anunciar *v.* to announce; to advertise 3.6
anuncio *m.* advertisement 3.4
año *m.* year 1.5
    año pasado last year 1.6
apagar *v.* to turn off 2.5
aparato *m.* appliance
apartamento *m.* apartment 2.6
apellido *m.* last name 1.3
apenas *adv.* hardly; scarcely 2.4
aplaudir *v.* to applaud 3.5
aplicación *f.* app 2.5
apreciar *v.* to appreciate 3.5
aprender (a + *inf.*) *v.* to learn 1.3
apurarse *v.* to hurry; to rush 3.3
aquel, aquella *adj.* that (over there) 1.6
aquél, aquélla *pron.* that (over there) 1.6
aquello *neuter, pron.* that; that thing; that fact 1.6
aquellos/as *pl. adj.* those (over there) 1.6
aquéllos/as *pl. pron.* those (ones) (over there) 1.6
aquí *adv.* here 1.1
    Aquí está(n)... Here is/are... 1.5
árbol *m.* tree 3.1
archivo *m.* file 2.5
arete *m.* earring 1.6
argentino/a *adj.* Argentine 1.3
armario *m.* closet 2.6
arqueología *f.* archeology 1.2

arqueólogo/a *m., f.* archeologist 3.4
arquitecto/a *m., f.* architect 3.4
arrancar *v.* to start (*a car*) 2.5
arreglar *v.* to fix; to arrange 2.5; to neaten; to straighten up 2.6
arreglarse *v.* to get ready 2.1; to fix oneself (*clothes, hair, etc. to go out*) 2.1
arroba *f.* @ symbol 2.5
arroz *m.* rice 2.2
arte *m.* art 1.2
artes *f., pl.* arts 3.5
artesanía *f.* craftsmanship; crafts 3.5
artículo *m.* article 3.6
artista *m., f.* artist 1.3
artístico/a *adj.* artistic 3.5
arveja *f.* pea 2.2
asado/a *adj.* roast 2.2
ascenso *m.* promotion 3.4
ascensor *m.* elevator 1.5
así *adv.* like this; so (*in such a way*) 2.4
asistir (a) *v.* to attend 1.3
aspiradora *f.* vacuum cleaner 2.6
aspirante *m., f.* candidate; applicant 3.4
aspirina *f.* aspirin 2.4
atún *m.* tuna 2.2
aumentar *v.* to grow; to get bigger 3.1
aumentar *v.* **de peso** to gain weight 3.3
aumento *m.* increase
    aumento de sueldo pay raise 3.4
aunque although
autobús *m.* bus 1.1
automático/a *adj.* automatic
auto(móvil) *m.* auto(mobile) 1.5
autopista *f.* highway 2.5
ave *f.* bird 3.1
avenida *f.* avenue
aventura *f.* adventure 3.5
    de aventuras adventure (genre) 3.5
avergonzado/a *adj.* embarrassed 1.5
avión *m.* airplane 1.5
¡Ay! *interj.* Oh!
    ¡Ay, qué dolor! Oh, what pain!
ayer *adv.* yesterday 1.6
ayudar(se) *v.* to help (each other) 2.5
azúcar *m.* sugar 2.2
azul *adj. m., f.* blue 1.6

B

bailar *v.* to dance 1.2
bailarín/bailarina *m., f.* dancer 3.5
baile *m.* dance 3.5
bajar(se) de *v.* to get off of/out of (a vehicle) 2.5
bajo/a *adj.* short (*in height*) 1.3

balcón *m.* balcony 2.6
balde *m.* bucket 1.5
ballena *f.* whale 3.1
baloncesto *m.* basketball 1.4
banana *f.* banana 2.2
banco *m.* bank 3.2
banda *f.* band 3.5
bandera *f.* flag
bañarse *v.* to bathe; to take a bath 2.1
baño *m.* bathroom 2.1
barato/a *adj.* cheap 1.6
barco *m.* boat 1.5
barrer *v.* to sweep 2.6
    barrer el suelo *v.* to sweep the floor 2.6
barrio *m.* neighborhood 2.6
bastante *adv.* enough; rather 2.4
basura *f.* trash 2.6
baúl *m.* trunk 2.5
beber *v.* to drink 1.3
bebida *f.* drink 2.2
béisbol *m.* baseball 1.4
bellas artes *f., pl.* fine arts 3.5
belleza *f.* beauty 3.2
beneficio *m.* benefit 3.4
besar(se) *v.* to kiss (each other) 2.5
beso *m.* kiss 2.3
biblioteca *f.* library 1.2
bicicleta *f.* bicycle 1.4
bien *adv.* well 1.1
bienestar *m.* well-being 3.3
bienvenido(s)/a(s) *adj.* welcome 1.1
billete *m.* paper money; ticket
billón *m.* trillion
biología *f.* biology 1.2
bisabuelo/a *m., f.* great-grandfather/great-grandmother 1.3
bistec *m.* steak 2.2
blanco/a *adj.* white 1.6
blog *m.* blog 2.5
(blue)jeans *m., pl.* jeans 1.6
blusa *f.* blouse 1.6
boca *f.* mouth 2.4
boda *f.* wedding 2.3
boleto *m.* ticket 1.2, 3.5
bolsa *f.* purse, bag 1.6
bombero/a *m., f.* firefighter 3.4
bonito/a *adj.* pretty 1.3
borrador *m.* eraser 1.2
borrar *v.* to erase
bosque *m.* forest 3.1
    bosque tropical tropical forest; rain forest 3.1
bota *f.* boot 1.6
botella *f.* bottle 2.3
botones *m., f. sing.* bellhop 1.5
brazo *m.* arm 2.4
brindar *v.* to toast (*drink*) 2.3
bucear *v.* to scuba dive 1.4
buen, bueno/a *adj.* good 1.3, 1.6
    buena forma good shape (*physical*) 3.3

Vocabulario — Spanish-English

Buenas noches. Good evening; Good night. 1.1
Buenas tardes. Good afternoon. 1.1
Bueno. Hello. *(on telephone)* 2.5
Buenos días. Good morning. 1.1
bulevar *m.* boulevard
buscador *m.* browser 2.5
buscar *v.* to look for 1.2
buzón *m.* mailbox 3.2

C

caballero *m.* gentleman, sir 2.2
caballo *m.* horse 1.5
cabe: no cabe duda de there's no doubt 3.1
cabeza *f.* head 2.4
cada *adj. m., f.* each 1.6
caerse *v.* to fall (down) 2.4
café *m.* café 1.4; *adj. m., f.* brown 1.6; *m.* coffee 2.2
cafeína *f.* caffeine 3.3
cafetera *f.* coffee maker 2.6
cafetería *f.* cafeteria 1.2
caído/a *p.p.* fallen 3.2
caja *f.* cash register 1.6
cajero/a *m., f.* cashier
   cajero automático *m.* ATM 3.2
calavera de azúcar *f.* skull made out of sugar 2.3
calcetín (calcetines) *m.* sock(s) 1.6
calculadora *f.* calculator 1.2
calentamiento global *m.* global warming 3.1
calentarse (e:ie) *v.* to warm up 3.3
calidad *f.* quality 1.6
calle *f.* street 2.5
calor *m.* heat
caloría *f.* calorie 3.3
calzar *v.* to take size... shoes 1.6
cama *f.* bed 1.5
cámara de video *f.* video camera 2.5
cámara digital *f.* digital camera 2.5
camarero/a *m., f.* waiter/waitress 2.2
camarón *m.* shrimp 2.2
cambiar (de) *v.* to change 2.3
cambio: de cambio in change 1.2
cambio *m.* **climático** climate change 3.1
cambio *m.* **de moneda** currency exchange
caminar *v.* to walk 1.2
camino *m.* road
camión *m.* truck; bus
camisa *f.* shirt 1.6
camiseta *f.* t-shirt 1.6
campo *m.* countryside 1.5
canadiense *adj.* Canadian 1.3

canal *m.* (TV) channel 2.5; 3.5
canción *f.* song 3.5
candidato/a *m., f.* candidate 3.6
canela *f.* cinnamon 2.4
cansado/a *adj.* tired 1.5
cantante *m., f.* singer 3.5
cantar *v.* to sing 1.2
capital *f.* capital city
capó *m.* hood 2.5
cara *f.* face 2.1
caramelo *m.* caramel 2.3
cargador *m.* charger 2.5
carne *f.* meat 2.2
   carne de res *f.* beef 2.2
carnicería *f.* butcher shop 3.2
caro/a *adj.* expensive 1.6
carpintero/a *m., f.* carpenter 3.4
carrera *f.* career 3.4
carretera *f.* highway; (main) road 2.5
carro *m.* car; automobile 2.5
carta *f.* letter 1.4; *(playing)* card 1.5
cartel *m.* poster 2.6
cartera *f.* wallet 1.4, 1.6
cartero *m.* mail carrier 3.2
casa *f.* house; home 1.2
casado/a *adj.* married 2.3
casarse (con) *v.* to get married (to) 2.3
casi *adv.* almost 2.4
catorce fourteen 1.1
cazar *v.* to hunt 3.1
cebolla *f.* onion 2.2
cederrón *m.* CD-ROM
celebrar *v.* to celebrate 2.3
cementerio *m.* cemetery 2.3
cena *f.* dinner 2.2
cenar *v.* to have dinner 1.2
centro *m.* downtown 1.4
   centro comercial shopping mall 1.6
cepillarse los dientes/el pelo *v.* to brush one's teeth/one's hair 2.1
cerámica *f.* pottery 3.5
cerca de *prep.* near 1.2
cerdo *m.* pork 2.2
cereales *m., pl.* cereal; grains 2.2
cero *m.* zero 1.1
cerrado/a *adj.* closed 1.5
cerrar (e:ie) *v.* to close 1.4
césped *m.* grass
ceviche *m.* marinated fish dish 2.2
   ceviche de camarón *m.* lemon-marinated shrimp 2.2
chaleco *m.* vest
champiñón *m.* mushroom 2.2
champú *m.* shampoo 2.1
chaqueta *f.* jacket 1.6
chatear *v.* to chat 2.5
chau *fam. interj.* bye 1.1
cheque *m.* (bank) check 3.2
   cheque (de viajero) *m.* (traveler's) check 3.2
chévere *adj., fam.* terrific

chico/a *m., f.* boy/girl 1.1
chino/a *adj.* Chinese 1.3
chocar (con) *v.* to run into
chocolate *m.* chocolate 2.3
choque *m.* collision 3.6
chuleta *f.* chop *(food)* 2.2
   chuleta de cerdo *f.* pork chop 2.2
cibercafé *m.* cybercafé 2.5
ciclismo *m.* cycling 1.4
cielo *m.* sky 3.1
cien(to) one hundred 1.2
ciencias *f., pl.* sciences 1.2
   ciencias ambientales environmental science 1.2
   de ciencia ficción *f.* science fiction (genre) 3.5
científico/a *m., f.* scientist 3.4
cierto/a *adj.* certain 3.1
   es cierto it's certain 3.1
   no es cierto it's not certain 3.1
cima *f.* top, peak 3.3
cinco five 1.1
cincuenta fifty 1.2
cine *m.* movie theater 1.4
cinta *f.* (audio)tape
cinta caminadora *f.* treadmill 3.3
cinturón *m.* belt 1.6
circulación *f.* traffic 2.5
cita *f.* date; appointment 2.3
ciudad *f.* city
ciudadano/a *m., f.* citizen 3.6
Claro (que sí). *fam.* Of course.
clase *f.* class 1.2
   clase de ejercicios aeróbicos *f.* aerobics class 3.3
clásico/a *adj.* classical 3.5
cliente/a *m., f.* customer 1.6
clínica *f.* clinic 2.4
cobrar *v.* to cash (a check) 3.2
coche *m.* car; automobile 2.5
cocina *f.* kitchen; stove 2.3, 2.6
cocinar *v.* to cook 2.6
cocinero/a *m., f.* cook, chef 3.4
cofre *m.* hood 3.2
cola *f.* line 3.2
colesterol *m.* cholesterol 3.3
color *m.* color 1.6
comedia *f.* comedy; play 3.5
comedor *m.* dining room 2.6
comenzar (e:ie) *v.* to begin 1.4
comer *v.* to eat 1.3
comercial *adj.* commercial; business-related 3.4
comida *f.* food; meal 1.4, 2.2
como like; as 2.2
¿cómo? what?; how? 1.1, 1.2
   ¿Cómo es...? What's... like?
   ¿Cómo está usted? *form.* How are you? 1.1
   ¿Cómo estás? *fam.* How are you? 1.1
   ¿Cómo se llama usted? *(form.)* What's your name? 1.1
   ¿Cómo te llamas? *fam.* What's your name? 1.1

Vocabulario

Spanish-English

cómoda *f.* chest of drawers 2.6
cómodo/a *adj.* comfortable 1.5
compañero/a de clase *m., f.* classmate 1.2
compañero/a de cuarto *m., f.* roommate 1.2
compañía *f.* company; firm 3.4
compartir *v.* to share 1.3
compositor(a) *m., f.* composer 3.5
comprar *v.* to buy 1.2
compras *f., pl.* purchases
  ir de compras to go shopping 1.5
comprender *v.* to understand 1.3
comprobar *v.* to check
comprometerse (con) *v.* to get engaged (to) 2.3
computación *f.* computer science 1.2
computadora *f.* computer 1.1
computadora portátil *f.* portable computer; laptop 2.5
comunicación *f.* communication 3.6
comunicarse (con) *v.* to communicate (with) 3.6
comunidad *f.* community 1.1
con *prep.* with 1.2
  Con él/ella habla. Speaking. (*on telephone*) 2.5
  con frecuencia *adv.* frequently 2.4
  Con permiso. Pardon me; Excuse me. 1.1
  con tal (de) que *conj.* provided (that) 3.1
concierto *m.* concert 3.5
concordar *v.* to agree
concurso *m.* game show; contest 3.5
conducir *v.* to drive 1.6, 2.5
conductor(a) *m., f.* driver 1.1
conexión *f.* **inalámbrica** wireless connection 2.5
confirmar *v.* to confirm 1.5
confirmar *v.* **una reservación** *f.* to confirm a reservation 1.5
confundido/a *adj.* confused 1.5
congelador *m.* freezer 2.6
congestionado/a *adj.* congested; stuffed-up 2.4
conmigo *pron.* with me 1.4, 2.3
conocer *v.* to know; to be acquainted with 1.6
conocido/a *adj.; p.p.* known
conseguir (e:i) *v.* to get; to obtain 1.4
consejero/a *m., f.* counselor; advisor 3.4
consejo *m.* advice
conservación *f.* conservation 3.1
conservar *v.* to conserve 3.1
construir *v.* to build
consultorio *m.* doctor's office 2.4
consumir *v.* to consume 3.3
contabilidad *f.* accounting 1.2
contador(a) *m., f.* accountant 3.4

contaminación *f.* pollution 3.1
  contaminación del aire/del agua air/water pollution 3.1
contaminado/a *adj.* polluted 3.1
contaminar *v.* to pollute 3.1
contar (o:ue) *v.* to count; to tell 1.4
contento/a *adj.* content 1.5
contestadora *f.* answering machine
contestar *v.* to answer 1.2
contigo *fam. pron.* with you 1.5, 2.3
contratar *v.* to hire 3.4
control *m.* **remoto** remote control 2.5
controlar *v.* to control 3.1
conversación *f.* conversation 1.1
conversar *v.* to converse, to chat 1.2
corazón *m.* heart 2.4
corbata *f.* tie 1.6
corredor(a) *m., f.* **de bolsa** stockbroker 3.4
correo *m.* mail; post office 3.2
  correo de voz *m.* voice mail 2.5
  correo electrónico *m.* e-mail 1.4
correr *v.* to run 1.3
cortesía *f.* courtesy
cortinas *f., pl.* curtains 2.6
corto/a *adj.* short (*in length*) 1.6
cosa *f.* thing 1.1
costar (o:ue) *v.* to cost 1.6
costarricense *adj.* Costa Rican 1.3
cráter *m.* crater 3.1
creer *v.* to believe 1.3, 3.1
  creer (en) *v.* to believe (in) 1.3
  no creer *v.* not to believe 3.1
creído/a *adj., p.p.* believed 3.2
crema de afeitar *f.* shaving cream 1.5, 2.1
crimen *m.* crime; murder 3.6
cruzar *v.* to cross 3.2
cuaderno *m.* notebook 1.1
cuadra *f.* (city) block 3.2
¿cuál(es)? which?; which one(s)? 1.2
  ¿Cuál es la fecha de hoy? What is today's date? 1.5
cuadro *m.* picture 2.6
cuando *conj.* when 2.1; 3.1
¿cuándo? when? 1.2
¿cuánto(s)/a(s)? how much/how many? 1.1, 1.2
  ¿Cuánto cuesta...? How much does... cost? 1.6
  ¿Cuántos años tienes? How old are you?
cuarenta forty 1.2
cuarto de baño *m.* bathroom 2.1
cuarto *m.* room 1.2; 2.1
cuarto/a *adj.* fourth 1.5
  menos cuarto quarter to (*time*) 1.1
  y cuarto quarter after (*time*) 1.1
cuatro four 1.1
cuatrocientos/as four hundred 1.2
cubano/a *adj.* Cuban 1.3

cubiertos *m., pl.* silverware
cubierto/a *p.p.* covered
cubrir *v.* to cover
cuchara *f.* (table or large) spoon 2.6
cuchillo *m.* knife 2.6
cuello *m.* neck 2.4
cuenta *f.* bill 2.2; account 3.2
  cuenta corriente *f.* checking account 3.2
  cuenta de ahorros *f.* savings account 3.2
cuento *m.* short story 3.5
cuerpo *m.* body 2.4
cuidado *m.* care
cuidar *v.* to take care of 3.1
cultura *f.* culture 1.2, 3.5
cumpleaños *m., sing.* birthday 2.3
cumplir años *v.* to have a birthday
cuñado/a *m., f.* brother-in-law/sister-in-law 1.3
currículum *m.* résumé 3.4
curso *m.* course 1.2

D

danza *f.* dance 3.5
dañar *v.* to damage; to break down 2.4
dar *v.* to give 1.6
  dar un consejo *v.* to give advice
  darse con *v.* to bump into; to run into (something) 2.4
  darse prisa *v.* to hurry; to rush 3.3
de *prep.* of; from 1.1
  ¿De dónde eres? *fam.* Where are you from? 1.1
  ¿De dónde es usted? *form.* Where are you from? 1.1
  ¿De parte de quién? Who is speaking/calling? (*on telephone*) 2.5
  ¿de quién...? whose...? (*sing.*) 1.1
  ¿de quiénes...? whose...? (*pl.*) 1.1
  de algodón (made) of cotton 1.6
  de aluminio (made) of aluminum 3.1
  de buen humor in a good mood 1.5
  de compras shopping 1.5
  de cuadros plaid 1.6
  de excursión hiking 1.4
  de hecho in fact
  de ida y vuelta roundtrip 1.5
  de la mañana in the morning; A.M. 1.1
  de la noche in the evening; at night; P.M. 1.1
  de la tarde in the afternoon; in the early evening; P.M. 1.1
  de lana (made) of wool 1.6
  de lunares polka-dotted 1.6
  de mal humor in a bad mood 1.5
  de moda in fashion 1.6

De nada. You're welcome. 1.1
de niño/a as a child 2.4
de parte de on behalf of 2.5
de plástico (made) of plastic 3.1
de rayas striped 1.6
de repente suddenly 1.6
de seda (made) of silk 1.6
de vaqueros western (genre) 3.5
de vez en cuando from time to time 2.4
de vidrio (made) of glass 3.1
debajo de *prep.* below; under 1.2
deber (+ *inf.*) *v.* should; must; ought to 1.3
deber *m.* responsibility; obligation 3.6
debido a due to (the fact that)
débil *adj.* weak 3.3
decidir (+ *inf.*) *v.* to decide 1.3
décimo/a *adj.* tenth 1.5
decir (e:i) *v.* **(que)** to say (that); to tell (that) 1.4
   decir la respuesta to say the answer 1.4
   decir la verdad to tell the truth 1.4
   decir mentiras to tell lies 1.4
declarar *v.* to declare; to say 3.6
dedo *m.* finger 2.4
dedo del pie *m.* toe 2.4
deforestación *f.* deforestation 3.1
dejar *v.* to let; to quit; to leave behind 3.4
   dejar de (+ *inf.*) *v.* to stop (*doing something*) 3.1
   dejar una propina *v.* to leave a tip
del (*contraction of* **de + el**) of the; from the 1.1
delante de *prep.* in front of 1.2
delgado/a *adj.* thin; slender 1.3
delicioso/a *adj.* delicious 2.2
demás *adj.* the rest
demasiado *adv.* too much 1.6
dentista *m., f.* dentist 2.4
dentro de (diez años) within (ten years) 3.4; inside
dependiente/a *m., f.* clerk 1.6
deporte *m.* sport 1.4
deportista *m.* sports person
deportivo/a *adj.* sports-related 1.4
depositar *v.* to deposit 3.2
derecha *f.* right 1.2
   a la derecha de to the right of 1.2
derecho *adv.* straight (ahead) 3.2
derechos *m., pl.* rights 3.6
desarrollar *v.* to develop 3.1
desastre (natural) *m.* (natural) disaster 3.6
desayunar *v.* to have breakfast 1.2
desayuno *m.* breakfast 2.2
descafeinado/a *adj.* decaffeinated 3.3
descansar *v.* to rest 1.2

descargar *v.* to download 2.5
descompuesto/a *adj.* not working; out of order 2.5
describir *v.* to describe 1.3
descrito/a *p.p.* described 3.2
descubierto/a *p.p.* discovered 3.2
descubrir *v.* to discover 3.1
desde *prep.* from 1.6
desear *v.* to wish; to desire 1.2
desempleo *m.* unemployment 3.6
desierto *m.* desert 3.1
desigualdad *f.* inequality 3.6
desordenado/a *adj.* disorderly 1.5
despacio *adv.* slowly 2.4
despedida *f.* farewell; goodbye
despedir (e:i) *v.* to fire 3.4
despedirse (de) (e:i) *v.* to say goodbye (to) 3.6
despejado/a *adj.* clear (*weather*)
despertador *m.* alarm clock 2.1
despertarse (e:ie) *v.* to wake up 2.1
después *adv.* afterwards; then 2.1
   después de after 2.1
   después de que *conj.* after 3.1
destruir *v.* to destroy 3.1
detrás de *prep.* behind 1.2
día *m.* day 1.1
   día de fiesta holiday 2.3
diario *m.* diary 1.1; newspaper 3.6
diario/a *adj.* daily 2.1
dibujar *v.* to draw 1.2
dibujo *m.* drawing
   dibujos animados *m., pl.* cartoons 3.5
diccionario *m.* dictionary 1.1
dicho/a *p.p.* said 3.2
diciembre *m.* December 1.5
dictadura *f.* dictatorship 3.6
diecinueve nineteen 1.1
dieciocho eighteen 1.1
dieciséis sixteen 1.1
diecisiete seventeen 1.1
diente *m.* tooth 2.1
dieta *f.* diet 3.3
   comer una dieta equilibrada to eat a balanced diet 3.3
diez ten 1.1
difícil *adj.* difficult; hard 1.3
Diga. Hello. (*on telephone*) 2.5
diligencia *f.* errand 3.2
dinero *m.* money 1.6
dirección *f.* address 3.2
   dirección electrónica *f.* e-mail address 2.5
director(a) *m., f.* director; (*musical*) conductor 3.5
dirigir *v.* to direct 3.5
disco compacto compact disc (CD) 2.5
discriminación *f.* discrimination 3.6
discurso *m.* speech 3.6
diseñador(a) *m., f.* designer 3.4
diseño *m.* design

disfraz *m.* costume 2.3
disfrutar (de) *v.* to enjoy; to reap the benefits (of) 3.3
disminuir *v.* to reduce 3.4
diversión *f.* fun activity; entertainment; recreation 1.4
divertido/a *adj.* fun
divertirse (e:ie) *v.* to have fun 2.3
divorciado/a *adj.* divorced 2.3
divorciarse (de) *v.* to get divorced (from) 2.3
divorcio *m.* divorce 2.3
doblar *v.* to turn 3.2
doble *adj.* double 1.5
doce twelve 1.1
doctor(a) *m., f.* doctor 1.3; 2.4
documental *m.* documentary 3.5
documentos de viaje *m., pl.* travel documents
doler (o:ue) *v.* to hurt 2.4
dolor *m.* ache; pain 2.4
   dolor de cabeza *m.* headache 2.4
doméstico/a *adj.* domestic 2.6
domingo *m.* Sunday 1.2
don *m.* Mr.; sir 1.1
doña *f.* Mrs.; ma'am 1.1
donde *adv.* where
   ¿Dónde está...? Where is...? 1.2
   ¿dónde? where? 1.1, 1.2
dormir (o:ue) *v.* to sleep 1.4
dormirse (o:ue) *v.* to go to sleep; to fall asleep 2.1
dormitorio *m.* bedroom 2.6
dos two 1.1
   dos veces *f.* twice; two times 1.6
doscientos/as two hundred 1.2
drama *m.* drama; play 3.5
dramático/a *adj.* dramatic 3.5
dramaturgo/a *m., f.* playwright 3.5
ducha *f.* shower 2.1
ducharse *v.* to shower; to take a shower 2.1
duda *f.* doubt 3.1
dudar *v.* to doubt 3.1
   no dudar *v.* not to doubt 3.1
dueño/a *m., f.* owner 2.2
dulces *m., pl.* sweets; candy 2.3
durante *prep.* during 2.1
durar *v.* to last 3.6

E

e *conj.* (*used instead of* **y** *before words beginning with* **i** *and* **hi**) and
echar *v.* to throw
   echar (una carta) al buzón *v.* to put (a letter) in the mailbox; to mail 3.2
ecología *f.* ecology 3.1
ecológico/a *adj.* ecological 3.1
ecologista *m., f.* ecologist 3.1
economía *f.* economics 1.2
ecoturismo *m.* ecotourism 3.1

ecuatoriano/a *adj.* Ecuadorian 1.3
edad *f.* age 2.3
edificio *m.* building 2.6
   edificio de apartamentos apartment building 2.6
(en) efectivo *m.* cash 1.6
ejercer *v.* to practice/exercise (a degree/profession) 3.4
ejercicio *m.* exercise 3.3
   ejercicios aeróbicos aerobic exercises 3.3
   ejercicios de estiramiento stretching exercises 3.3
ejército *m.* army 3.6
el *m., sing., def. art.* the 1.1
él *sub. pron.* he 1.1; *obj. pron.* him
elecciones *f., pl.* election 3.6
electricista *m., f.* electrician 3.4
electrodoméstico *m.* electric appliance 2.6
elegante *adj. m., f.* elegant 1.6
elegir (e:i) *v.* to elect 3.6
ella *sub. pron.* she 1.1; *obj. pron.* her
ellos/as *sub. pron.* they 1.1; *obj. pron.* them
embarazada *adj.* pregnant 2.4
emergencia *f.* emergency 2.4
emitir *v.* to broadcast 3.6
emocionante *adj. m., f.* exciting
empezar (e:ie) *v.* to begin 1.4
empleado/a *m., f.* employee 1.5
empleo *m.* job; employment 3.4
empresa *f.* company; firm 3.4
en *prep.* in; on 1.2
   en casa at home
   en caso (de) que *conj.* in case (that) 3.1
   en cuanto *conj.* as soon as 3.1
   en efectivo in cash 3.2
   en exceso in excess; too much 3.3
   en línea in-line 1.4
   en punto on the dot; exactly; sharp (*time*) 1.1
   en qué in what; how
   ¿En qué puedo servirles? How can I help you? 1.5
   en vivo live 2.1
enamorado/a (de) *adj.* in love (with) 1.5
enamorarse (de) *v.* to fall in love (with) 2.3
encantado/a *adj.* delighted; pleased to meet you 1.1
encantar *v.* to like very much; to love (*inanimate objects*) 2.1
encima de *prep.* on top of 1.2
encontrar (o:ue) *v.* to find 1.4
encontrar(se) (o:ue) *v.* to meet (each other); to run into (each other) 2.5
   encontrarse con to meet up with 2.1
encuesta *f.* poll; survey 3.6
energía *f.* energy 3.1

energía nuclear nuclear energy 3.1
energía solar solar energy 3.1
enero *m.* January 1.5
enfermarse *v.* to get sick 2.4
enfermedad *f.* illness 2.4
enfermero/a *m., f.* nurse 2.4
enfermo/a *adj.* sick 2.4
enfrente de *adv.* opposite; facing 3.2
engordar *v.* to gain weight 3.3
enojado/a *adj.* angry 1.5
enojarse (con) *v.* to get angry (with) 2.1
ensalada *f.* salad 2.2
ensayo *m.* essay 1.3
enseguida *adv.* right away
enseñar *v.* to teach 1.2
ensuciar *v.* to get (something) dirty 2.6
entender (e:ie) *v.* to understand 1.4
enterarse *v.* to find out 3.4
entonces *adv.* so, then 1.5, 2.1
entrada *f.* entrance 2.6; ticket
entre *prep.* between; among 1.2
entregar *v.* to hand in 2.5
entremeses *m., pl.* hors d'oeuvres; appetizers 2.2
entrenador(a) *m., f.* trainer 3.3
entrenarse *v.* to practice; to train 3.3
entrevista *f.* interview 3.4
entrevistador(a) *m., f.* interviewer 3.4
entrevistar *v.* to interview 3.4
envase *m.* container 3.1
enviar *v.* to send; to mail 3.2
equilibrado/a *adj.* balanced 3.3
equipaje *m.* luggage 1.5
equipo *m.* team 1.4
equivocado/a *adj.* wrong 1.5
eres *fam.* you are 1.1
es he/she/it is 1.1
   Es bueno que... It's good that... 2.6
   es cierto it's certain 3.1
   es extraño it's strange 3.1
   es igual it's the same 1.5
   Es importante que... It's important that... 2.6
   es imposible it's impossible 3.1
   es improbable it's improbable 3.1
   Es malo que... It's bad that... 2.6
   Es mejor que... It's better that... 2.6
   Es necesario que... It's necessary that... 2.6
   es obvio it's obvious 3.1
   es posible it's possible 3.1
   es probable it's probable 3.1
   es ridículo it's ridiculous 3.1
   es seguro it's certain 3.1
   es terrible it's terrible 3.1
   es triste it's sad 3.1

   Es urgente que... It's urgent that... 2.6
   Es la una. It's one o'clock. 1.1
   es una lástima it's a shame 3.1
   es verdad it's true 3.1
esa(s) *f., adj.* that; those 1.6
ésa(s) *f., pron.* that (one); those (ones) 1.6
escalar *v.* to climb 1.4
   escalar montañas to climb mountains 1.4
escalera *f.* stairs; stairway 2.6
escalón *m.* step 3.3
escanear *v.* to scan 2.5
escoger *v.* to choose 2.2
escribir *v.* to write 1.3
   escribir un mensaje electrónico to write an e-mail 1.4
   escribir una carta to write a letter 1.4
escrito/a *p.p.* written 3.2
escritor(a) *m., f.* writer 3.5
escritorio *m.* desk 1.2
escuchar *v.* to listen (to) 1.2
   escuchar la radio to listen to the radio 1.2
   escuchar música to listen to music 1.2
escuela *f.* school 1.1
esculpir *v.* to sculpt 3.5
escultor(a) *m., f.* sculptor 3.5
escultura *f.* sculpture 3.5
ese *m., sing., adj.* that 1.6
ése *m., sing., pron.* that one 1.6
eso *neuter, pron.* that; that thing 1.6
esos *m., pl., adj.* those 1.6
ésos *m., pl., pron.* those (ones) 1.6
España *f.* Spain
español *m.* Spanish (*language*) 1.2
español(a) *adj. m., f.* Spanish 1.3
espárragos *m., pl.* asparagus 2.2
especialidad: las especialidades del día today's specials 2.2
especialización *f.* major 1.2
espectacular *adj.* spectacular
espectáculo *m.* show 3.5
espejo *m.* mirror 2.1
esperar *v.* to hope; to wish 3.1
   esperar (+ *inf.*) *v.* to wait (for); to hope 1.2
esposo/a *m., f.* husband/wife; spouse 1.3
esquí (acuático) *m.* (water) skiing 1.4
esquiar *v.* to ski 1.4
esquina *f.* corner 3.2
está he/she/it is, you are
   Está bien. That's fine.
   Está (muy) despejado. It's (very) clear. (*weather*)
   Está lloviendo. It's raining. 1.5
   Está nevando. It's snowing. 1.5
   Está (muy) nublado. It's (very) cloudy. (*weather*) 1.5
esta(s) *f., adj.* this; these 1.6

Vocabulario

esta noche tonight
ésta(s) *f., pron.* this (one); these (ones) 1.6
establecer *v.* to establish 3.4
estación *f.* station; season 1.5
   estación de autobuses bus station 1.5
   estación del metro subway station 1.5
   estación de tren train station 1.5
estacionamiento *m.* parking lot 3.2
estacionar *v.* to park 2.5
estadio *m.* stadium 1.2
estado civil *m.* marital status 2.3
Estados Unidos *m., pl.* (EE.UU.; E.U.) United States
estadounidense *adj. m., f.* from the United States 1.3
estampilla *f.* stamp 3.2
estante *m.* bookcase; bookshelves 2.6
estar *v.* to be 1.2
   estar a dieta to be on a diet 3.3
   estar aburrido/a to be bored 1.5
   estar afectado/a (por) to be affected (by) 3.1
   estar cansado/a to be tired 1.5
   estar contaminado/a to be polluted 3.1
   estar de acuerdo to agree 3.5
   Estoy de acuerdo. I agree. 3.5
   No estoy de acuerdo. I don't agree. 3.5
   estar de moda to be in fashion 1.6
   estar de vacaciones *f., pl.* to be on vacation 1.5
   estar en buena forma to be in good shape 3.3
   estar enfermo/a to be sick 2.4
   estar harto/a de... to be sick of... 3.6
   estar listo/a to be ready 1.5
   estar perdido/a to be lost 3.2
   estar roto/a to be broken
   estar seguro/a to be sure 1.5
   estar torcido/a to be twisted; to be sprained 2.4
   No está nada mal. It's not bad at all. 1.5
estatua *f.* statue 3.5
este *m.* east 3.2
este *m., sing., adj.* this 1.6
éste *m., sing., pron.* this (one) 1.6
estéreo *m.* stereo 2.5
estilo *m.* style
estiramiento *m.* stretching 3.3
esto *neuter pron.* this; this thing 1.6
estómago *m.* stomach 2.4
estornudar *v.* to sneeze 2.4
estos *m., pl., adj.* these 1.6

éstos *m., pl., pron.* these (ones) 1.6
estrella *f.* star 3.1
   estrella de cine *m., f.* movie star 3.5
estrés *m.* stress 3.3
estudiante *m., f.* student 1.1, 1.2
estudiantil *adj. m., f.* student 1.2
estudiar *v.* to study 1.2
estufa *f.* stove 2.6
estupendo/a *adj.* stupendous 1.5
etapa *f.* stage 2.3
evitar *v.* to avoid 3.1
examen *m.* test; exam 1.2
   examen médico physical exam 2.4
excelente *adj. m., f.* excellent 1.5
exceso *m.* excess 3.3
excursión *f.* hike; tour; excursion 1.4
excursionista *m., f.* hiker
éxito *m.* success
experiencia *f.* experience
explicar *v.* to explain 1.2
explorar *v.* to explore
expresión *f.* expression
extinción *f.* extinction 3.1
extranjero/a *adj.* foreign 3.5
extrañar *v.* to miss 3.4
extraño/a *adj.* strange 3.1

F

fábrica *f.* factory 3.1
fabuloso/a *adj.* fabulous 1.5
fácil *adj.* easy 1.3
falda *f.* skirt 1.6
faltar *v.* to lack; to need 2.1
familia *f.* family 1.3
famoso/a *adj.* famous
farmacia *f.* pharmacy 2.4
fascinar *v.* to fascinate 2.1
favorito/a *adj.* favorite 1.4
fax *m.* fax (machine)
febrero *m.* February 1.5
fecha *f.* date 1.5
¡Felicidades! Congratulations! 2.3
¡Felicitaciones! Congratulations! 2.3
feliz *adj.* happy 1.5
   ¡Feliz cumpleaños! Happy birthday! 2.3
fenomenal *adj.* great, phenomenal 1.5
feo/a *adj.* ugly 1.3
festival *m.* festival 3.5
fiebre *f.* fever 2.4
fiesta *f.* party 2.3
fijo/a *adj.* fixed, set 1.6
fin *m.* end 1.4
   fin de semana weekend 1.4
finalmente *adv.* finally
firmar *v.* to sign (*a document*) 3.2
física *f.* physics 1.2
flan (de caramelo) *m.* baked (caramel) custard 2.3

flexible *adj.* flexible 3.3
flor *f.* flower 3.1
folclórico/a *adj.* folk; folkloric 3.5
folleto *m.* brochure
forma *f.* shape 3.3
formulario *m.* form 3.2
foto(grafía) *f.* photograph 1.1
francés, francesa *adj. m., f.* French 1.3
frecuentemente *adv.* frequently
frenos *m., pl.* brakes
frente (frío) *m.* (cold) front 1.5
fresco/a *adj.* cool
frijoles *m., pl.* beans 2.2
frío/a *adj.* cold
frito/a *adj.* fried 2.2
fruta *f.* fruit 2.2
frutería *f.* fruit store 3.2
fuera *adv.* outside
fuerte *adj. m., f.* strong 3.3
fumar *v.* to smoke 3.3
   (no) fumar *v.* (not) to smoke 3.3
funcionar *v.* to work 2.5; to function
fútbol *m.* soccer 1.4
fútbol americano *m.* football 1.4
futuro/a *adj.* future
   en el futuro in the future

G

gafas (de sol) *f., pl.* (sun)glasses 1.6
gafas (oscuras) *f., pl.* (sun)glasses
galleta *f.* cookie 2.3
ganar *v.* to win 1.4; to earn (*money*) 3.4
ganga *f.* bargain 1.6
garaje *m.* garage; (mechanic's) repair shop 2.5; garage (*in a house*) 2.6
garganta *f.* throat 2.4
gasolina *f.* gasoline 2.5
gasolinera *f.* gas station 2.5
gastar *v.* to spend (*money*) 1.6
gato *m.* cat 3.1
gemelo/a *m., f.* twin 1.3
genial *adj.* great 3.4
gente *f.* people 1.3
geografía *f.* geography 1.2
gerente *m., f.* manager 2.2, 3.4
gimnasio *m.* gymnasium 1.4
gobierno *m.* government 3.1
golf *m.* golf 1.4
gordo/a *adj.* fat 1.3
grabar *v.* to record 2.5
gracias *f., pl.* thank you; thanks 1.1
   Gracias por invitarme. Thanks for inviting me. 2.3
graduarse (de/en) *v.* to graduate (from/in) 2.3
grande *adj.* big; large 1.3
grasa *f.* fat 3.3
gratis *adj. m., f.* free of charge 3.2
grave *adj.* grave; serious 2.4
gripe *f.* flu 2.4
gris *adj. m., f.* gray 1.6

Vocabulario — Spanish-English

gritar *v.* to scream, to shout
grito *m.* scream 1.5
guantes *m., pl.* gloves 1.6
guapo/a *adj.* handsome; good-looking 1.3
guardar *v.* to save (on a computer) 2.5
guerra *f.* war 3.6
guía *m., f.* guide
gustar *v.* to be pleasing to; to like 1.2
   Me gustaría... I would like...
gusto *m.* pleasure 1.1
   El gusto es mío. The pleasure is mine. 1.1
   Mucho gusto. Pleased to meet you. 1.1
   ¡Qué gusto verlo/la! *(form.)* How nice to see you! 3.6
   ¡Qué gusto verte! *(fam.)* How nice to see you! 3.6

H

haber *(auxiliar) v.* to have (done something) 3.3
habitación *f.* room 1.5
   habitación doble double room 1.5
   habitación individual single room 1.5
hablar *v.* to talk; to speak 1.2
hacer *v.* to do; to make 1.4
   Hace buen tiempo. The weather is good. 1.5
   Hace (mucho) calor. It's (very) hot. *(weather)* 1.5
   Hace fresco. It's cool. *(weather)* 1.5
   Hace (mucho) frío. It's (very) cold. *(weather)* 1.5
   Hace mal tiempo. The weather is bad. 1.5
   Hace (mucho) sol. It's (very) sunny. *(weather)* 1.5
   Hace (mucho) viento. It's (very) windy. *(weather)* 1.5
hacer cola to stand in line 3.2
hacer diligencias to run errands 3.2
hacer ejercicio to exercise 3.3
hacer ejercicios aeróbicos to do aerobics 3.3
hacer ejercicios de estiramiento to do stretching exercises 3.3
hacer el papel (de) to play the role (of) 3.5
hacer gimnasia to work out 3.3
hacer juego (con) to match (with) 1.6
hacer la cama to make the bed 2.6
hacer las maletas to pack (one's) suitcases 1.5
hacer quehaceres domésticos to do household chores 2.6
hacer (wind)surf to (wind)surf 1.5
hacer turismo to go sightseeing
hacer un viaje to take a trip 1.5
¿Me harías el honor de casarte conmigo? Would you do me the honor of marrying me? 3.5
hacia *prep.* toward 3.2
hambre *f.* hunger
hamburguesa *f.* hamburger 2.2
hasta *prep.* until 1.6; toward
   Hasta la vista. See you later. 1.1
   Hasta luego. See you later. 1.1
   Hasta mañana. See you tomorrow. 1.1
   Hasta pronto. See you soon. 1.1
hasta que *conj.* until 3.1
hay there is; there are 1.1
   Hay (mucha) contaminación. It's (very) smoggy.
   Hay (mucha) niebla. It's (very) foggy.
   Hay que It is necessary that
   No hay de qué. You're welcome. 1.1
   No hay duda de There's no doubt 3.1
hecho/a *p.p.* done 3.2
heladería *f.* ice cream shop 3.2
helado/a *adj.* iced 2.2
helado *m.* ice cream 2.3
hermanastro/a *m., f.* stepbrother/stepsister 1.3
hermano/a *m., f.* brother/sister 1.3
hermano/a mayor/menor *m., f.* older/younger brother/sister 1.3
hermanos *m., pl.* siblings (brothers and sisters) 1.3
hermoso/a *adj.* beautiful 1.6
hierba *f.* grass 3.1
hijastro/a *m., f.* stepson/stepdaughter 1.3
hijo/a *m., f.* son/daughter 1.3
   hijo/a único/a *m., f.* only child 1.3
hijos *m., pl.* children 1.3
híjole *interj.* wow 1.6
historia *f.* history 1.2; story 3.5
hockey *m.* hockey 1.4
hola *interj.* hello; hi 1.1
hombre *m.* man 1.1
   hombre de negocios *m.* businessman 3.4
hora *f.* hour 1.1; the time
horario *m.* schedule 1.2
horno *m.* oven 2.6
   horno de microondas *m.* microwave oven 2.6
horror *m.* horror 3.5
   de horror horror (genre) 3.5
hospital *m.* hospital 2.4
hotel *m.* hotel 1.5
hoy *adv.* today 1.2
   hoy día *adv.* nowadays
   Hoy es... Today is... 1.2
hueco *m.* hole 1.4
huelga *f.* strike (*labor*) 3.6
hueso *m.* bone 2.4
huésped *m., f.* guest 1.5
huevo *m.* egg 2.2
humanidades *f., pl.* humanities 1.2
huracán *m.* hurricane 3.6

I

ida *f.* one way (*travel*)
idea *f.* idea 3.6
iglesia *f.* church 1.4
igualdad *f.* equality 3.6
igualmente *adv.* likewise 1.1
impermeable *m.* raincoat 1.6
importante *adj. m., f.* important 1.3
importar *v.* to be important to; to matter 2.1
imposible *adj. m., f.* impossible 3.1
impresora *f.* printer 2.5
imprimir *v.* to print 2.5
improbable *adj. m., f.* improbable 3.1
impuesto *m.* tax 3.6
incendio *m.* fire 3.6
increíble *adj. m., f.* incredible 1.5
indicar cómo llegar *v.* to give directions 3.2
individual *adj.* single (*room*) 1.5
infección *f.* infection 2.4
informar *v.* to inform 3.6
informe *m.* report; paper (*written work*) 3.6
ingeniero/a *m., f.* engineer 1.3
inglés *m.* English (*language*) 1.2
inglés, inglesa *adj.* English 1.3
inodoro *m.* toilet 2.1
insistir (en) *v.* to insist (on) 2.6
inspector(a) de aduanas *m., f.* customs inspector 1.5
inteligente *adj. m., f.* intelligent 1.3
intento *m.* attempt 2.5
intercambiar *v.* to exchange
interesante *adj. m., f.* interesting 1.3
interesar *v.* to be interesting to; to interest 2.1
internacional *adj. m., f.* international 3.6
Internet Internet 2.5
inundación *f.* flood 3.6
invertir (e:ie) *v.* to invest 3.4
invierno *m.* winter 1.5
invitado/a *m., f.* guest 2.3
invitar *v.* to invite 2.3
inyección *f.* injection 2.4
ir *v.* to go 1.4
   ir a (+ *inf.*) to be going to do something 1.4
   ir de compras to go shopping 1.5
   ir de excursión (a las montañas) to go on a hike (in the mountains) 1.4
   ir de pesca to go fishing

Vocabulario

Spanish-English

ir de vacaciones to go on vacation 1.5
ir en autobús to go by bus 1.5
ir en auto(móvil) to go by auto(mobile); to go by car 1.5
ir en avión to go by plane 1.5
ir en barco to go by boat 1.5
ir en metro to go by subway
ir en moto(cicleta) to go by motorcycle 1.5
ir en taxi to go by taxi 1.5
ir en tren to go by train
irse *v.* to go away; to leave 2.1
italiano/a *adj.* Italian 1.3
izquierda *f.* left 1.2
   a la izquierda de to the left of 1.2

J

jabón *m.* soap 2.1
jamás *adv.* never; not ever 2.1
jamón *m.* ham 2.2
japonés, japonesa *adj.* Japanese 1.3
jardín *m.* garden; yard 2.6
jefe, jefa *m., f.* boss 3.4
jengibre *m.* ginger 2.4
joven *adj. m., f., sing.* (**jóvenes** *pl.*) young 1.3
   joven *m., f., sing.* (**jóvenes** *pl.*) young person 1.1
joyería *f.* jewelry store 3.2
jubilarse *v.* to retire (*from work*) 2.3
juego *m.* game
jueves *m., sing.* Thursday 1.2
jugador(a) *m., f.* player 1.4
jugar (u:ue) *v.* to play 1.4
   jugar a las cartas *f., pl.* to play cards 1.5
jugo *m.* juice 2.2
   jugo de fruta *m.* fruit juice 2.2
julio *m.* July 1.5
jungla *f.* jungle 3.1
junio *m.* June 1.5
juntos/as *adj.* together 2.3
juventud *f.* youth 2.3

K

kilómetro *m.* kilometer 2.5

L

la *f., sing., def. art.* the 1.1; *f., sing., d.o. pron.* her, it, *form.* you 1.5
laboratorio *m.* laboratory 1.2
lago *m.* lake 3.1
lámpara *f.* lamp 2.6
lana *f.* wool 1.6
langosta *f.* lobster 2.2
lápiz *m.* pencil 1.1
largo/a *adj.* long 1.6
las *f., pl., def. art.* the 1.1; *f., pl., d.o. pron.* them; you 1.5
lástima *f.* shame 3.1
lastimarse *v.* to injure oneself 2.4
   lastimarse el pie to injure one's foot 2.4
lata *f.* (*tin*) can 3.1
lavabo *m.* sink 2.1
lavadora *f.* washing machine 2.6
lavandería *f.* laundromat 3.2
lavaplatos *m., sing.* dishwasher 2.6
lavar *v.* to wash 2.6
   lavar (el suelo, los platos) to wash (the floor, the dishes) 2.6
lavarse *v.* to wash oneself 2.1
   lavarse la cara to wash one's face 2.1
   lavarse las manos to wash one's hands 2.1
le *sing., i.o. pron.* to/for him, her, *form.* you 1.6
   Le presento a... *form.* I would like to introduce you to (name). 1.1
lección *f.* lesson 1.1
leche *f.* milk 2.2
lechuga *f.* lettuce 2.2
leer *v.* to read 1.3
   leer el correo electrónico to read e-mail 1.4
   leer un periódico to read a newspaper 1.4
   leer una revista to read a magazine 1.4
leído/a *p.p.* read 3.2
lejos de *prep.* far from 1.2
lengua *f.* language 1.2
   lenguas extranjeras *f., pl.* foreign languages 1.2
lentes de contacto *m., pl.* contact lenses
   lentes (de sol) (sun)glasses
lento/a *adj.* slow 2.5
les *pl., i.o. pron.* to/for them, you 1.6
letrero *m.* sign 3.2
levantar *v.* to lift 3.3
   levantar pesas to lift weights 3.3
levantarse *v.* to get up 2.1
ley *f.* law 3.1
libertad *f.* liberty; freedom 3.6
libre *adj. m., f.* free 1.4
librería *f.* bookstore 1.2
libro *m.* book 1.2
licencia de conducir *f.* driver's license 2.5
limón *m.* lemon 2.2
limpiar *v.* to clean 2.6
   limpiar la casa *v.* to clean the house 2.6
limpio/a *adj.* clean 1.5
línea *f.* line 1.4
listo/a *adj.* ready; smart 1.5
literatura *f.* literature 1.2
llamar *v.* to call 2.5
   llamar por teléfono to call on the phone
llamarse *v.* to be called; to be named 2.1
llanta *f.* tire 2.5
llave *f.* key 1.5; wrench 2.5
llegada *f.* arrival 1.5
llegar *v.* to arrive 1.2
llenar *v.* to fill 2.5, 3.2
   llenar el tanque to fill the tank 2.5
   llenar (un formulario) to fill out (a form) 3.2
lleno/a *adj.* full 2.5
llevar *v.* to carry 1.2; to wear; to take 1.6
   llevar una vida sana to lead a healthy lifestyle 3.3
   llevarse bien/mal (con) to get along well/badly (with) 2.3
llorar *v.* to cry 3.3
llover (o:ue) *v.* to rain 1.5
Llueve. It's raining. 1.5
lluvia *f.* rain
lo *m., sing. d.o. pron.* him, it, *form.* you 1.5
   ¡Lo he pasado de película! I've had a fantastic time! 3.6
   lo mejor the best (thing)
   lo que that which; what 2.6
   Lo siento. I'm sorry. 1.1
loco/a *adj.* crazy 1.6
locutor(a) *m., f.* (TV or radio) announcer 3.6
lodo *m.* mud
los *m., pl., def. art.* the 1.1; *m. pl., d.o. pron.* them, you 1.5
luchar (contra/por) *v.* to fight; to struggle (against/for) 3.6
luego *adv.* then 2.1; later 1.1
lugar *m.* place 1.2, 1.4
luna *f.* moon 3.1
lunares *m.* polka dots
lunes *m., sing.* Monday 1.2
luz *f.* light; electricity 2.6

M

madrastra *f.* stepmother 1.3
madre *f.* mother 1.3
madurez *f.* maturity; middle age 2.3
maestro/a *m., f.* teacher 3.4
magnífico/a *adj.* magnificent 1.5
maíz *m.* corn 2.2
mal, malo/a *adj.* bad 1.3
maleta *f.* suitcase 1.1
mamá *f.* mom
mandar *v.* to order 2.6; to send; to mail 3.2
manejar *v.* to drive 2.5
manera *f.* way
mano *f.* hand 1.1
manta *f.* blanket 2.6
mantener *v.* to maintain 3.3
   mantenerse en forma to stay in shape 3.3
mantequilla *f.* butter 2.2
manzana *f.* apple 2.2

mañana *f.* morning, a.m. 1.1; tomorrow 1.1
mapa *m.* map 1.1, 1.2
maquillaje *m.* makeup 2.1
maquillarse *v.* to put on makeup 2.1
mar *m.* sea 1.5
maravilloso/a *adj.* marvelous 1.5
mareado/a *adj.* dizzy; nauseated 2.4
margarina *f.* margarine 2.2
mariscos *m., pl.* shellfish 2.2
marrón *adj. m., f.* brown 1.6
martes *m., sing.* Tuesday 1.2
marzo *m.* March 1.5
más *adv.* more 1.2
    más de (+ *number***)** more than 2.2
    más tarde later (on) 2.1
    más... que more... than 2.2
masaje *m.* massage 3.3
matemáticas *f., pl.* mathematics 1.2
materia *f.* course 1.2
matrimonio *m.* marriage 2.3
máximo/a *adj.* maximum 2.5
mayo *m.* May 1.5
mayonesa *f.* mayonnaise 2.2
mayor *adj.* older 1.3
    el/la mayor *adj.* oldest 2.2
me *sing., d.o. pron.* me 1.5; *sing. i.o. pron.* to/for me 1.6
    Me gusta... I like... 1.2
    Me gustaría(n)... I would like... 3.3
    Me llamo... My name is... 1.1
    Me muero por... I'm dying to (for)...
mecánico/a *m., f.* mechanic 2.5
mediano/a *adj.* medium
medianoche *f.* midnight 1.1
medias *f., pl.* pantyhose, stockings 1.6
medicamento *m.* medication 2.4
medicina *f.* medicine 2.4
médico/a *m., f.* doctor 1.3; *adj.* medical 2.4
medio/a *adj.* half 1.3
    medio ambiente *m.* environment 3.1
    medio/a hermano/a *m., f.* half-brother/half-sister 1.3
    mediodía *m.* noon 1.1
    medios de comunicación *m., pl.* means of communication; media 3.6
    y media thirty minutes past the hour (time) 1.1
mejor *adj.* better 2.2
    el/la mejor *m., f.* the best 2.2
mejorar *v.* to improve 3.1
melocotón *m.* peach 2.2
menor *adj.* younger 1.3
    el/la menor *m., f.* youngest 2.2
menos *adv.* less 2.4
    menos cuarto..., menos quince... quarter to... (*time*) 1.1
    menos de (+ *number***)** fewer than 2.2
    menos... que less... than 2.2
mensaje *m.* **de texto** text message 2.5
mensaje electrónico *m.* e-mail message 1.4
mentira *f.* lie 1.4
menú *m.* menu 2.2
mercado *m.* market 1.6
    mercado al aire libre open-air market 1.6
merendar (e:ie) *v.* to snack 2.2; to have an afternoon snack
merienda *f.* afternoon snack 3.3
mes *m.* month 1.5
mesa *f.* table 1.2
mesita *f.* end table 2.6
    mesita de noche night stand 2.6
meterse en problemas *v.* to get into trouble 3.1
metro *m.* subway 1.5
mexicano/a *adj.* Mexican 1.3
mí *pron., obj. of prep.* me 2.3
mi(s) *poss. adj.* my 1.3
microonda *f.* microwave 2.6
    horno de microondas *m.* microwave oven 2.6
miedo *m.* fear
miel *f.* honey 2.4
mientras *conj.* while 2.4
miércoles *m., sing.* Wednesday 1.2
mil *m.* one thousand 1.2
    mil millones billion
milla *f.* mile
millón *m.* million 1.2
millones (de) *m.* millions (of)
mineral *m.* mineral 3.3
minuto *m.* minute
mío(s)/a(s) *poss.* my; (of) mine 2.5
mirar *v.* to look (at); to watch 1.2
    mirar (la) televisión to watch television 1.2
mismo/a *adj.* same 1.3
mochila *f.* backpack 1.2
moda *f.* fashion 1.6
moderno/a *adj.* modern 3.5
molestar *v.* to bother; to annoy 2.1
monitor *m.* (computer) monitor 2.5
    monitor(a) *m., f.* trainer
mono *m.* monkey 3.1
montaña *f.* mountain 1.4
montar *v.* **a caballo** to ride a horse 1.5
montón: un montón de a lot of 1.4
monumento *m.* monument 1.4
morado/a *adj.* purple 1.6
moreno/a *adj.* brunet(te) 1.3
morir (o:ue) *v.* to die 2.2
mostrar (o:ue) *v.* to show 1.4
moto(cicleta) *f.* motorcycle 1.5
motor *m.* motor
muchacho/a *m., f.* boy/girl 1.3
mucho/a *adj.,* a lot of; much; many 1.3
    (Muchas) gracias. Thank you (very much); Thanks (a lot). 1.1
    muchas veces *adv.* a lot; many times 2.4
    Mucho gusto. Pleased to meet you. 1.1
mudarse *v.* to move (from one house to another) 2.6
muebles *m., pl.* furniture 2.6
muerte *f.* death 2.3
muerto/a *p.p.* died 3.2
mujer *f.* woman 1.1
    mujer de negocios *f.* business woman 3.4
    mujer policía *f.* female police officer
multa *f.* fine
mundial *adj. m., f.* worldwide
mundo *m.* world 2.2
muro *m.* wall 3.3
músculo *m.* muscle 3.3
museo *m.* museum 1.4
música *f.* music 1.2, 3.5
musical *adj. m., f.* musical 3.5
músico/a *m., f.* musician 3.5
muy *adv.* very 1.1
    (Muy) bien, gracias. (Very) well, thanks. 1.1

N

nacer *v.* to be born 2.3
nacimiento *m.* birth 2.3
nacional *adj. m., f.* national 3.6
nacionalidad *f.* nationality 1.1
nada nothing 1.1; not anything 2.1
    nada mal not bad at all 1.5
nadar *v.* to swim 1.4
nadie *pron.* no one, nobody, not anyone 2.1
naranja *f.* orange 2.2
nariz *f.* nose 2.4
natación *f.* swimming 1.4
natural *adj. m., f.* natural 3.1
naturaleza *f.* nature 3.1
navegador *m.* **GPS** GPS 2.5
navegar (en Internet) *v.* to surf (the Internet) 2.5
Navidad *f.* Christmas 2.3
necesario/a *adj.* necessary 2.6
necesitar (+ *inf.***)** *v.* to need 1.2
negar (e:ie) *v.* to deny 3.1
    no negar (e:ie) *v.* not to deny 3.1
negocios *m., pl.* business; commerce 3.4
negro/a *adj.* black 1.6
nervioso/a *adj.* nervous 1.5
nevar (e:ie) *v.* to snow 1.5
    Nieva. It's snowing. 1.5
ni...ni neither... nor 2.1
niebla *f.* fog

Vocabulario

Spanish-English

nieto/a *m., f.* grandson/granddaughter 1.3
nieve *f.* snow
ningún, ninguno/a(s) *adj.* no; none; not any 2.1
niñez *f.* childhood 2.3
niño/a *m., f.* child 1.3
no no; not 1.1
  ¿no? right? 1.1
  no cabe duda de there is no doubt 3.1
  no es seguro it's not certain 3.1
  no es verdad it's not true 3.1
  No está nada mal. It's not bad at all. 1.5
  no estar de acuerdo to disagree
  No estoy seguro. I'm not sure.
  no hay there is not; there are not 1.1
  No hay de qué. You're welcome. 1.1
  no hay duda de there is no doubt 3.1
  ¡No me diga(s)! You don't say!
  No me gustan nada. I don't like them at all. 1.2
  no muy bien not very well 1.1
  No quiero. I don't want to. 1.4
  No sé. I don't know.
  No te preocupes. (*fam.*) Don't worry. 2.1
  no tener razón to be wrong 1.3
noche *f.* night 1.1
nombre *m.* name 1.1
norte *m.* north 3.2
norteamericano/a *adj.* (North) American 1.3
nos *pl., d.o. pron.* us 1.5; *pl., i.o. pron.* to/for us 1.6
  Nos vemos. See you. 1.1
nosotros/as *sub. pron.* we 1.1; *obj. pron.* us
noticia *f.* news 2.5
noticias *f., pl.* news 3.6
noticiero *m.* newscast 3.6
novecientos/as nine hundred 1.2
noveno/a *adj.* ninth 1.5
noventa ninety 1.2
noviembre *m.* November 1.5
novio/a *m., f.* boyfriend/girlfriend 1.3
nube *f.* cloud 3.1
nublado/a *adj.* cloudy 1.5
  Está (muy) nublado. It's very cloudy. 1.5
nuclear *adj. m. f.* nuclear 3.1
nuera *f.* daughter-in-law 1.3
nuestro(s)/a(s) *poss. adj.* our 1.3; our, (of) ours 2.5
nueve nine 1.1
nuevo/a *adj.* new 1.6
número *m.* number 1.1; (shoe) size 1.6
nunca *adv.* never; not ever 2.1

nutrición *f.* nutrition 3.3
nutricionista *m., f.* nutritionist 3.3

O

o or 2.1
o... o; either... or 2.1
obedecer *v.* to obey 3.6
obra *f.* work (*of art, literature, music, etc.*) 3.5
  obra maestra *f.* masterpiece 3.5
obtener *v.* to obtain; to get 3.4
obvio/a *adj.* obvious 3.1
océano *m.* ocean
ochenta eighty 1.2
ocho eight 1.1
ochocientos/as eight hundred 1.2
octavo/a *adj.* eighth 1.5
octubre *m.* October 1.5
ocupación *f.* occupation 3.4
ocupado/a *adj.* busy 1.5
ocurrir *v.* to occur; to happen 3.6
odiar *v.* to hate 2.3
oeste *m.* west 3.2
oferta *f.* offer
oficina *f.* office 2.6
oficio *m.* trade 3.4
ofrecer *v.* to offer 1.6
oído *m.* (sense of) hearing; inner ear 2.4
oído/a *p.p.* heard 3.2
oír *v.* to hear 1.4
ojalá (que) *interj.* I hope (that); I wish (that) 3.1
ojo *m.* eye 2.4
olvidar *v.* to forget 2.4
once eleven 1.1
ópera *f.* opera 3.5
operación *f.* operation 2.4
ordenado/a *adj.* orderly 1.5
ordinal *adj.* ordinal (*number*)
oreja *f.* (outer) ear 2.4
organizarse *v.* to organize oneself 2.6
orquesta *f.* orchestra 3.5
ortografía *f.* spelling
ortográfico/a *adj.* spelling
os *fam., pl. d.o. pron.* you 1.5; *fam., pl. i.o. pron.* to/for you 1.6
otoño *m.* autumn 1.5
otro/a *adj.* other; another 1.6
  otra vez again

P

paciente *m., f.* patient 2.4
padrastro *m.* stepfather 1.3
padre *m.* father 1.3
padres *m., pl.* parents 1.3
pagar *v.* to pay 1.6
  pagar a plazos to pay in installments 3.2
  pagar al contado to pay in cash 3.2
  pagar en efectivo to pay in cash 3.2
  pagar la cuenta to pay the bill

página *f.* page 2.5
  página principal *f.* home page 2.5
país *m.* country 1.1
paisaje *m.* landscape 1.5
pájaro *m.* bird 3.1
palabra *f.* word 1.1
paleta helada *f.* popsicle 1.4
pálido/a *adj.* pale 3.2
pan *m.* bread 2.2
  pan tostado *m.* toasted bread 2.2
panadería *f.* bakery 3.2
pantalla *f.* screen 2.5
  pantalla táctil *f.* touch screen
pantalones *m., pl.* pants 1.6
  pantalones cortos *m., pl.* shorts 1.6
pantuflas *f.* slippers 2.1
papa *f.* potato 2.2
  papas fritas *f., pl.* fried potatoes; French fries 2.2
papá *m.* dad
  papás *m., pl.* parents
papel *m.* paper 1.2; role 3.5
papelera *f.* wastebasket 1.2
paquete *m.* package 3.2
par *m.* pair 1.6
  par de zapatos pair of shoes 1.6
para *prep.* for; in order to; by; used for; considering 2.5
  para que *conj.* so that 3.1
parabrisas *m., sing.* windshield 2.5
parar *v.* to stop 2.5
parecer *v.* to seem 1.6
pared *f.* wall 2.6
pareja *f.* (married) couple; partner 2.3
parientes *m., pl.* relatives 1.3
parque *m.* park 1.4
párrafo *m.* paragraph
parte: de parte de on behalf of 2.5
partido *m.* game; match (*sports*) 1.4
pasado/a *adj.* last; past 1.6
  pasado *p.p.* passed
pasaje *m.* ticket 1.5
  pasaje de ida y vuelta *m.* roundtrip ticket 1.5
pasajero/a *m., f.* passenger 1.1
pasaporte *m.* passport 1.5
pasar *v.* to go through
  pasar la aspiradora to vacuum 2.6
  pasar por la aduana to go through customs
  pasar tiempo to spend time
  pasarlo bien/mal to have a good/bad time 2.3
pasatiempo *m.* pastime; hobby 1.4
pasear *v.* to take a walk; to stroll 1.4
  pasear en bicicleta to ride a bicycle 1.4
  pasear por to walk around
pasillo *m.* hallway 2.6

pasta *f.* **de dientes** toothpaste 2.1
pastel *m.* cake; pie 2.3
   pastel de chocolate *m.* chocolate cake 2.3
   pastel de cumpleaños *m.* birthday cake
pastelería *f.* pastry shop 3.2
pastilla *f.* pill; tablet 2.4
patata *f.* potato 2.2
   patatas fritas *f., pl.* fried potatoes; French fries 2.2
patinar (en línea) *v.* to (inline) skate 1.4
patineta *f.* skateboard 1.4
patio *m.* patio; yard 2.6
pavo *m.* turkey 2.2
paz *f.* peace 3.6
pedir (e:i) *v.* to ask for; to request 1.4; to order (*food*) 2.2
   pedir prestado *v.* to borrow 3.2
   pedir un préstamo *v.* to apply for a loan 3.2
   Todos me dijeron que te pidiera una disculpa de su parte. They all told me to ask you to excuse them/forgive them. 3.6
peinarse *v.* to comb one's hair 2.1
película *f.* movie 1.4
peligro *m.* danger 3.1
peligroso/a *adj.* dangerous 3.6
pelirrojo/a *adj.* red-haired 1.3
pelo *m.* hair 2.1
pelota *f.* ball 1.4
peluquería *f.* beauty salon 3.2
peluquero/a *m., f.* hairdresser 3.4
penicilina *f.* penicillin
pensar (e:ie) *v.* to think 1.4
   pensar (+ *inf.*) *v.* to intend to; to plan to (*do something*) 1.4
   pensar en *v.* to think about 1.4
pensión *f.* boardinghouse
peor *adj.* worse 2.2
   el/la peor *adj.* the worst 2.2
pequeño/a *adj.* small 1.3
pera *f.* pear 2.2
perder (e:ie) *v.* to lose; to miss 1.4
perdido/a *adj.* lost 3.1, 3.2
Perdón. Pardon me.; Excuse me. 1.1
perezoso/a *adj.* lazy
perfecto/a *adj.* perfect 1.5
periódico *m.* newspaper 1.4
periodismo *m.* journalism 1.2
periodista *m., f.* journalist 1.3
permiso *m.* permission
pero *conj.* but 1.2
perro *m.* dog 3.1
persona *f.* person 1.3
personaje *m.* character 3.5
   personaje principal *m.* main character 3.5
pesas *f. pl.* weights 3.3
pesca *f.* fishing
pescadería *f.* fish market 3.2

pescado *m.* fish (*cooked*) 2.2
pescar *v.* to fish 1.5
peso *m.* weight 3.3
pez *m., sing.* (**peces** *pl.*) fish (*live*) 3.1
pie *m.* foot 2.4
piedra *f.* stone 3.1
pierna *f.* leg 2.4
pimienta *f.* black pepper 2.2
pintar *v.* to paint 3.5
pintor(a) *m., f.* painter 3.4
pintura *f.* painting; picture 2.6, 3.5
piña *f.* pineapple
piscina *f.* swimming pool 1.4
piso *m.* floor (*of a building*) 1.5
pizarra *f.* blackboard 1.2
placer *m.* pleasure
planchar la ropa *v.* to iron the clothes 2.6
planes *m., pl.* plans
planta *f.* plant 3.1
   planta baja *f.* ground floor 1.5
plástico *m.* plastic 3.1
plato *m.* dish (*in a meal*) 2.2; *m.* plate 2.6
   plato principal *m.* main dish 2.2
playa *f.* beach 1.5
plaza *f.* city or town square 1.4
plazos *m., pl.* periods; time 3.2
pluma *f.* pen 1.2
plumero *m.* duster 2.6
población *f.* population 3.1
pobre *adj. m., f.* poor 1.6
pobrecito/a *adj.* poor thing 1.3
pobreza *f.* poverty
poco *adv.* little 1.5, 2.4
poder (o:ue) *v.* to be able to; can 1.4
   ¿Podría pedirte algo? Could I ask you something? 3.5
   ¿Puedo dejar un recado? May I leave a message? 2.5
poema *m.* poem 3.5
poesía *f.* poetry 3.5
poeta *m., f.* poet 3.5
policía *f.* police (force) 2.5
política *f.* politics 3.6
político/a *m., f.* politician 3.4; *adj.* political 3.6
pollo *m.* chicken 2.2
   pollo asado *m.* roast chicken 2.2
poner *v.* to put; to place 1.4; to turn on (*electrical appliances*) 2.5
   poner la mesa to set the table 2.6
   poner una inyección to give an injection 2.4
   ponerle el nombre to name someone/something 2.3
ponerse (+ *adj.*) *v.* to become (+ *adj.*) 2.1; to put on 2.1
por *prep.* in exchange for; for; by; in; through; around; along; during; because of; on account of; on behalf of; in search of; by way of; by means of 2.5

por aquí around here 2.5
por ejemplo for example 2.5
por eso that's why; therefore 2.5
por favor please 1.1
por fin finally 2.5
por la mañana in the morning 2.1
por la noche at night 2.1
por la tarde in the afternoon 2.1
por lo menos *adv.* at least 2.4
¿por qué? why? 1.2
Por supuesto. Of course.
por teléfono by phone; on the phone
por último finally 2.1
porque *conj.* because 1.2
portátil *adj.* portable 2.5
portero/a *m., f.* doorman/doorwoman 1.1
porvenir *m.* future 3.4
   por el porvenir for/to the future 3.4
posesivo/a *adj.* possessive
posible *adj.* possible 3.1
   es posible it's possible 3.1
   no es posible it's not possible 3.1
postal *f.* postcard
postre *m.* dessert 2.3
practicar *v.* to practice 1.2
   practicar deportes *m., pl.* to play sports 1.4
precio (fijo) *m.* (fixed; set) price 1.6
preferir (e:ie) *v.* to prefer 1.4
pregunta *f.* question
preguntar *v.* to ask (*a question*) 1.2
premio *m.* prize; award 3.5
prender *v.* to turn on 2.5
prensa *f.* press 3.6
preocupado/a (por) *adj.* worried (about) 1.5
preocuparse (por) *v.* to worry (about) 2.1
preparar *v.* to prepare 1.2
preposición *f.* preposition
presentación *f.* introduction
presentar *v.* to introduce; to present 3.5; to put on (*a performance*) 3.5
   Le presento a... I would like to introduce you to (name). (*form.*) 1.1
   Te presento a... I would like to introduce you to (name). (*fam.*) 1.1
presiones *f., pl.* pressures 3.3
prestado/a *adj.* borrowed
préstamo *m.* loan 3.2
prestar *v.* to lend; to loan 1.6
primavera *f.* spring 1.5
primer, primero/a *adj.* first 1.5
primero *adv.* first 1.2
primo/a *m., f.* cousin 1.3
principal *adj. m., f.* main 2.2

prisa *f.* haste
  darse prisa *v.* to hurry; to rush 3.3
probable *adj. m., f.* probable 3.1
  es probable it's probable 3.1
  no es probable it's not probable 3.1
probar (o:ue) *v.* to taste; to try 2.2
probarse (o:ue) *v.* to try on 2.1
problema *m.* problem 1.1
profesión *f.* profession 1.3; 3.4
profesor(a) *m., f.* teacher 1.1, 1.2
programa *m.* program 1.1
  programa de computación *m.* software 2.5
  programa de entrevistas *m.* talk show 3.5
  programa de realidad *m.* reality show 3.5
programador(a) *m., f.* computer programmer 1.3
prohibir *v.* to prohibit 2.4; to forbid
pronombre *m.* pronoun
pronto *adv.* soon 2.4
propina *f.* tip 2.2
propio/a *adj.* own
proteger *v.* to protect 3.1
proteína *f.* protein 3.3
próximo/a *adj.* next 1.3, 3.4
proyecto *m.* project 2.5
prueba *f.* test; quiz 1.2
psicología *f.* psychology 1.2
psicólogo/a *m., f.* psychologist 3.4
publicar *v.* to publish 3.5
público *m.* audience 3.5
pueblo *m.* town
puerta *f.* door 1.2
puertorriqueño/a *adj.* Puerto Rican 1.3
pues *conj.* well
puesto *m.* position; job 3.4
puesto/a *p.p.* put 3.2
puro/a *adj.* pure 3.1

Q

que *pron.* that; which; who 2.6
  ¿En qué...? In which...?
  ¡Qué...! How...!
  ¡Qué dolor! What pain!
  ¡Qué ropa más bonita! What pretty clothes! 1.6
  ¡Qué sorpresa! What a surprise!
  ¿qué? what? 1.1, 1.2
  ¿Qué día es hoy? What day is it? 1.2
  ¿Qué hay de nuevo? What's new? 1.1
  ¿Qué hora es? What time is it? 1.1
  ¿Qué les parece? What do you *(pl.)* think?
  ¿Qué onda? What's up? 3.2

¿Qué pasa? What's happening? What's going on? 1.1
¿Qué pasó? What happened?
¿Qué precio tiene? What is the price?
¿Qué tal...? How are you?; How is it going? 1.1
¿Qué talla lleva/usa? What size do you wear? 1.6
¿Qué tiempo hace? How's the weather? 1.5
quedar *v.* to be left over; to fit *(clothing)* 2.1; to be located 3.2
quedarse *v.* to stay; to remain 2.1
quehaceres domésticos *m., pl.* household chores 2.6
quemar (un CD/DVD) *v.* to burn (a CD/DVD)
querer (e:ie) *v.* to want; to love 1.4
queso *m.* cheese 2.2
quien(es) *pron.* who; whom; that 2.6
¿quién(es)? who?; whom? 1.1, 1.2
  ¿Quién es...? Who is...? 1.1
  ¿Quién habla? Who is speaking/calling? *(telephone)* 2.5
química *f.* chemistry 1.2
quince fifteen 1.1
  menos quince quarter to *(time)* 1.1
  y quince quarter after *(time)* 1.1
quinceañera *f.* young woman celebrating her fifteenth birthday 2.3
quinientos/as five hundred 1.2
quinto/a *adj.* fifth 1.5
quisiera *v.* I would like
quitar el polvo *v.* to dust 2.6
quitar la mesa *v.* to clear the table 2.6
quitarse *v.* to take off 2.1
quizás *adv.* maybe 1.5

R

racismo *m.* racism 3.6
radio *f.* radio *(medium)* 1.2; *m.* radio (set) 2.5
radiografía *f.* X-ray 2.4
rápido *adv.* quickly 2.4
ratón *m.* mouse 2.5
ratos libres *m., pl.* spare (free) time 1.4
raya *f.* stripe
razón *f.* reason
rebaja *f.* sale 1.6
receta *f.* prescription 2.4
recetar *v.* to prescribe 2.4
recibir *v.* to receive 1.3
reciclaje *m.* recycling 3.1
reciclar *v.* to recycle 3.1
recién casado/a *m., f.* newlywed 2.3
recoger *v.* to pick up 3.1
recomendar (e:ie) *v.* to recommend 2.2, 2.6

recordar (o:ue) *v.* to remember 1.4
recorrer *v.* to tour an area
recorrido *m.* tour 3.1
recuperar *v.* to recover 2.5
recurso *m.* resource 3.1
  recurso natural *m.* natural resource 3.1
red *f.* network; Web 2.5
reducir *v.* to reduce 3.1
refresco *m.* soft drink 2.2
refrigerador *m.* refrigerator 2.6
regalar *v.* to give (a gift) 2.3
regalo *m.* gift 1.6
regatear *v.* to bargain 1.6
región *f.* region; area
regresar *v.* to return 1.2
regular *adv.* so-so; OK 1.1
reído *p.p.* laughed 3.2
reírse (e:i) *v.* to laugh 2.3
relaciones *f., pl.* relationships
relajarse *v.* to relax 2.3
reloj *m.* clock; watch 1.2
renovable *adj.* renewable 3.1
renunciar (a) *v.* to resign (from) 3.4
repetir (e:i) *v.* to repeat 1.4
reportaje *m.* report 3.6
reportero/a *m., f.* reporter 3.4
representante *m., f.* representative 3.6
reproductor de CD *m.* CD player 2.5
reproductor de DVD *m.* DVD player 2.5
reproductor de MP3 *m.* MP3 player 2.5
resfriado *m.* cold *(illness)* 2.4
residencia estudiantil *f.* dormitory 1.2
resolver (o:ue) *v.* to resolve; to solve 3.1
respirar *v.* to breathe 3.1
responsable *adj.* responsible 2.2
respuesta *f.* answer
restaurante *m.* restaurant 1.4
resuelto/a *p.p.* resolved 3.2
reunión *f.* meeting 3.4
revisar *v.* to check 2.5
  revisar el aceite *v.* to check the oil 2.5
revista *f.* magazine 1.4
rico/a *adj.* rich 1.6; *adj.* tasty; delicious 2.2
ridículo/a *adj.* ridiculous 3.1
río *m.* river 3.1
rodilla *f.* knee 2.4
rogar (o:ue) *v.* to beg; to plead 2.6
rojo/a *adj.* red 1.6
romántico/a *adj.* romantic 3.5
romper *v.* to break 2.4
  romperse la pierna *v.* to break one's leg 2.4
romper (con) *v.* to break up (with) 2.3
ropa *f.* clothing; clothes 1.6

ropa interior *f.* underwear 1.6
rosado/a *adj.* pink 1.6
roto/a *adj.* broken 3.2
rubio/a *adj.* blond(e) 1.3
ruso/a *adj.* Russian 1.3
rutina *f.* routine 2.1
  rutina diaria *f.* daily routine 2.1

S

sábado *m.* Saturday 1.2
saber *v.* to know; to know how 1.6
  saber a to taste like 2.2
sabrosísimo/a *adj.* extremely delicious 2.2
sabroso/a *adj.* tasty; delicious 2.2
sacar *v.* to take out
  sacar buenas notas to get good grades 1.2
  sacar fotos to take photos 1.5
  sacar la basura to take out the trash 2.6
  sacar(se) un diente to have a tooth removed 2.4
sacudir *v.* to dust 2.6
  sacudir los muebles to dust the furniture 2.6
sal *f.* salt 2.2
sala *f.* living room 2.6; room
  sala de emergencia(s) emergency room 2.4
salario *m.* salary 3.4
salchicha *f.* sausage 2.2
salida *f.* departure; exit 1.5
salir *v.* to leave 1.4; to go out
  salir con to go out with; to date 1.4, 2.3
  salir de to leave from 1.4
  salir para to leave for (*a place*) 1.4
salmón *m.* salmon 2.2
salón de belleza *m.* beauty salon 3.2
salud *f.* health 2.4
saludable *adj.* healthy 2.4
saludar(se) *v.* to greet (each other) 2.5
saludo *m.* greeting 1.1
  saludos a... greetings to... 1.1
sandalia *f.* sandal 1.6
sandía *f.* watermelon
sándwich *m.* sandwich 2.2
sano/a *adj.* healthy 2.4
se *ref. pron.* himself, herself, itself, *form.* yourself, themselves, yourselves 2.1
se *impersonal* one 2.4
  Se hizo... He/she/it became...
secadora *f.* clothes dryer 2.6
secarse *v.* to dry (oneself) 2.1
sección de (no) fumar *f.* (non) smoking section 2.2
secretario/a *m., f.* secretary 3.4
secuencia *f.* sequence
sed *f.* thirst

seda *f.* silk 1.6
sedentario/a *adj.* sedentary; related to sitting 3.3
seguir (e:i) *v.* to follow; to continue 1.4
según according to
segundo/a *adj.* second 1.5
seguro/a *adj.* sure; safe; confident 1.5
seis six 1.1
seiscientos/as six hundred 1.2
sello *m.* stamp 3.2
selva *f.* jungle 3.1
semáforo *m.* traffic light 3.2
semana *f.* week 1.2
  fin *m.* **de semana** weekend 1.4
  semana *f.* **pasada** last week 1.6
semestre *m.* semester 1.2
sendero *m.* trail; path 3.1
sentarse (e:ie) *v.* to sit down 2.1
sentir (e:ie) *v.* to be sorry; to regret 3.1
sentirse (e:ie) *v.* to feel 2.1
señor (Sr.); don *m.* Mr.; sir 1.1
señora (Sra.); doña *f.* Mrs.; ma'am 1.1
señorita (Srta.) *f.* Miss 1.1
separado/a *adj.* separated 2.3
separarse (de) *v.* to separate (from) 2.3
septiembre *m.* September 1.5
séptimo/a *adj.* seventh 1.5
ser *v.* to be 1.1
  ser aficionado/a (a) to be a fan (of)
  ser alérgico/a (a) to be allergic (to) 2.4
  ser gratis to be free of charge 3.2
serio/a *adj.* serious
servicio *m.* service 3.3
servilleta *f.* napkin 2.6
servir (e:i) *v.* to serve 2.2; to help 1.5
sesenta sixty 1.2
setecientos/as seven hundred 1.2
setenta seventy 1.2
sexismo *m.* sexism 3.6
sexto/a *adj.* sixth 1.5
sí *adv.* yes 1.1
si *conj.* if 1.4
SIDA *m.* AIDS 3.6
siempre *adv.* always 2.1
siete seven 1.1 **silla** *f.* seat 1.2
sillón *m.* armchair 2.6
similar *adj. m., f.* similar
simpático/a *adj.* nice; likeable 1.3
sin *prep.* without 3.1
  sin duda without a doubt
  sin embargo however
  sin que *conj.* without 3.1
sino but (rather) 2.1
síntoma *m.* symptom 2.4
sitio *m.* place 1.3
sitio *m.* **web** website 2.5

situado/a *p.p.* located
sobre *m.* envelope 3.2; *prep.* on; over 1.2
  sobre todo above all 3.1
(sobre)población *f.* (over)population 3.1
sobrino/a *m., f.* nephew/niece 1.3
sociología *f.* sociology 1.2
sofá *m.* couch; sofa 2.6
sol *m.* sun 3.1
solar *adj. m., f.* solar 3.1
soldado *m., f.* soldier 3.6
soleado/a *adj.* sunny
solicitar *v.* to apply (*for a job*) 3.4
solicitud (de trabajo) *f.* (job) application 3.4
sólo *adv.* only 1.6
solo/a *adj.* alone
soltero/a *adj.* single 2.3
solución *f.* solution 3.1
sombrero *m.* hat 1.6
Son las dos. It's two o'clock. 1.1
sonar (o:ue) *v.* to ring 2.5
sonreído *p.p.* smiled 3.2
sonreír (e:i) *v.* to smile 2.3
sopa *f.* soup 2.2
sorprender *v.* to surprise 2.3
sorpresa *f.* surprise 2.3
sótano *m.* basement; cellar 2.6
soy I am 1.1
  Soy de... I'm from... 1.1
su(s) *poss. adj.* his; her; its; *form.* your; their 1.3
subir(se) a *v.* to get on/into (*a vehicle*) 2.5
sucio/a *adj.* dirty 1.5
sudar *v.* to sweat 3.3
suegro/a *m., f.* father-in-law/mother-in-law 1.3
sueldo *m.* salary 3.4
suelo *m.* floor 2.6
sueño *m.* sleep
suerte *f.* luck
suéter *m.* sweater 1.6
sufrir *v.* to suffer 2.4
  sufrir muchas presiones to be under a lot of pressure 3.3
  sufrir una enfermedad to suffer an illness 2.4
sugerir (e:ie) *v.* to suggest 2.6
supermercado *m.* supermarket 3.2
suponer *v.* to suppose 1.4
sur *m.* south 3.2
sustantivo *m.* noun
suyo(s)/a(s) *poss.* (of) his/her; (of) hers; its; *form.* your, (of) yours, (of) theirs, their 2.5

T

tabla de (wind)surf *f.* surf board/sailboard 1.5
tal vez *adv.* maybe 1.5
talentoso/a *adj.* talented 3.5
talla *f.* size 1.6
  talla grande *f.* large

Vocabulario

taller *m.* **mecánico** garage; mechanic's repair shop 2.5
también *adv.* also; too 1.2; 2.1
tampoco *adv.* neither; not either 2.1
tan *adv.* so 1.5
    tan... como as... as 2.2
    tan pronto como *conj.* as soon as 3.1
tanque *m.* tank 2.5
tanto *adv.* so much
    tanto... como as much... as 2.2
tantos/as... como as many... as 2.2
tarde *adv.* late 2.1; *f.* afternoon; evening; P.M. 1.1
tarea *f.* homework 1.2
tarjeta *f.* (post) card
tarjeta de crédito *f.* credit card 1.6
tarjeta postal *f.* postcard
taxi *m.* taxi 1.5
taza *f.* cup 2.6
te *sing., fam., d.o. pron.* you 1.5; *sing., fam., i.o. pron.* to/for you 1.6
    Te presento a... *fam.* I would like to introduce you to (name). 1.1
    ¿Te gustaría? Would you like to?
    ¿Te gusta(n)...? Do you like...? 1.2
té *m.* tea 2.2
    té helado *m.* iced tea 2.2
teatro *m.* theater 3.5
teclado *m.* keyboard 2.5
técnico/a *m., f.* technician 3.4
tejido *m.* weaving 3.5
teleadicto/a *m., f.* couch potato 3.3
(teléfono) celular *m.* (cell) phone 2.5
telenovela *f.* soap opera 3.5
teletrabajo *m.* telecommuting 3.4
televisión *f.* television 1.2
televisión por cable *f.* cable television
televisor *m.* television set 2.5
temer *v.* to fear; to be afraid 3.1
temperatura *f.* temperature 2.4
temporada *f.* period of time 1.5
temprano *adv.* early 2.1
tenedor *m.* fork 2.6
tener *v.* to have 1.3
    tener... años to be... years old 1.3
    tener (mucho) calor to be (very) hot 1.3
    tener (mucho) cuidado to be (very) careful 1.3
    tener dolor to have pain 2.4
    tener éxito to be successful 3.4
    tener fiebre to have a fever 2.4
    tener (mucho) frío to be (very) cold 1.3

tener ganas de (+ *inf.***)** to feel like (doing something) 1.3
tener (mucha) hambre *f.* to be (very) hungry 1.3
tener (mucho) miedo (de) to be (very) afraid (of); to be (very) scared (of) 1.3
tener miedo (de) que to be afraid that
tener planes *m., pl.* to have plans
tener (mucha) prisa to be in a (big) hurry 1.3
tener que (+ *inf.***)** *v.* to have to (do something) 1.3
tener razón *f.* to be right 1.3
tener (mucha) sed *f.* to be (very) thirsty 1.3
tener (mucho) sueño to be (very) sleepy 1.3
tener (mucha) suerte to be (very) lucky 1.3
tener tiempo to have time 3.2
tener una cita to have a date; to have an appointment 2.3
tenis *m.* tennis 1.4
tensión *f.* tension 3.3
tercer, tercero/a *adj.* third 1.5
terco/a *adj.* stubborn 2.4
terminar *v.* to end; to finish 1.2
    terminar de (+ *inf.***)** *v.* to finish (doing something)
terremoto *m.* earthquake 3.6
terrible *adj. m., f.* terrible 3.1
ti *obj. of prep., fam.* you 2.3
tiempo *m.* time 3.2; weather 1.5
    tiempo libre free time
tienda *f.* store 1.6
tierra *f.* land; soil 3.1
tío/a *m., f.* uncle/aunt 1.3
tíos *m., pl.* aunts and uncles 1.3
título *m.* title 3.4
tiza *f.* chalk 1.2
toalla *f.* towel 2.1
tobillo *m.* ankle 2.4
tocar *v.* to play (*a musical instrument*) 3.5; to touch 3.5
todavía *adv.* yet; still 1.3, 1.5
todo *m.* everything 1.5
todo(s)/a(s) *adj.* all
todos *m., pl.* all of us; *m., pl.* everybody; everyone
todos los días *adv.* every day 2.4
tomar *v.* to take; to drink 1.2
    tomar clases *f., pl.* to take classes 1.2
    tomar el sol to sunbathe 1.4
    tomar en cuenta to take into account
    tomar fotos *f., pl.* to take photos 1.5
    tomar la temperatura to take someone's temperature 2.4
    tomar una decisión to make a decision 3.3
tomate *m.* tomato 2.2
tonto/a *adj.* foolish 1.3

torcerse (o:ue) (el tobillo) *v.* to sprain (one's ankle) 2.4
tormenta *f.* storm 3.6
tornado *m.* tornado 3.6
tortuga (marina) *f.* (sea) turtle 3.1
tos *f., sing.* cough 2.4
toser *v.* to cough 2.4
tostado/a *adj.* toasted 2.2
tostadora *f.* toaster 2.6
trabajador(a) *adj.* hard-working 1.3
trabajar *v.* to work 1.2
trabajo *m.* job; work 3.4
traducir *v.* to translate 1.6
traer *v.* to bring 1.4
tráfico *m.* traffic 2.5
tragedia *f.* tragedy 3.5
traído/a *p.p.* brought 3.2
traje *m.* suit 1.6
    traje de baño *m.* bathing suit 1.6
trajinera *f.* type of barge 1.3
tranquilo/a *adj.* calm; quiet 3.3
    Tranquilo/a. Relax. 2.1
    Tranquilo/a, cariño. Relax, sweetie. 2.5
transmitir *v.* to broadcast 3.6
tratar de (+ *inf.***)** *v.* to try (to do something) 3.3
trece thirteen 1.1
treinta thirty 1.1, 1.2
    y treinta thirty minutes past the hour (time) 1.1
tren *m.* train 1.5
tres three 1.1
trescientos/as three hundred 1.2
trimestre *m.* trimester; quarter 1.2
triste *adj.* sad 1.5
tú *fam. sub. pron.* you 1.1
tu(s) *fam. poss. adj.* your 1.3
turismo *m.* tourism
turista *m., f.* tourist 1.1
turístico/a *adj.* touristic
tuyo(s)/a(s) *fam. poss. pron.* your; (of) yours 2.5

U

Ud. *form. sing.* you 1.1
Uds. *pl.* you 1.1
último/a *adj.* last 2.1
    la última vez the last time 2.1
un, uno/a *indef. art.* a; one 1.1
    a la una at one o'clock 1.1
    una vez once 1.6
    una vez más one more time
uno one 1.1
único/a *adj.* only 1.3; unique 2.3
universidad *f.* university; college 1.2
unos/as *m., f., pl. indef. art.* some 1.1
urgente *adj.* urgent 2.6
usar *v.* to wear; to use 1.6

Vocabulario Spanish-English

usted (Ud.) *form. sing.* you 1.1
ustedes (Uds.) *pl.* you 1.1
útil *adj.* useful
uva *f.* grape 2.2

V

vaca *f.* cow 3.1
vacaciones *f. pl.* vacation 1.5
valle *m.* valley 3.1
vamos let's go 1.4
vaquero *m.* cowboy 3.5
   de vaqueros *m., pl.* western (genre) 3.5
varios/as *adj. m. f., pl.* various; several
vaso *m.* glass 2.6
veces *f., pl.* times 1.6
vecino/a *m., f.* neighbor 2.6
veinte twenty 1.1
veinticinco twenty-five 1.1
veinticuatro twenty-four 1.1
veintidós twenty-two 1.1
veintinueve twenty-nine 1.1
veintiocho twenty-eight 1.1
veintiséis twenty-six 1.1
veintisiete twenty-seven 1.1
veintitrés twenty-three 1.1
veintiún, veintiuno/a *adj.* twenty-one 1.1
veintiuno twenty-one 1.1
vejez *f.* old age 2.3
velocidad *f.* speed 2.5
   velocidad máxima *f.* speed limit 2.5
vencer *v.* to expire 3.2
vendedor(a) *m., f.* salesperson 1.6
vender *v.* to sell 1.6

venir *v.* to come 1.3
ventana *f.* window 1.2
ver *v.* to see 1.4
   a ver *v.* let's see
   ver películas *f., pl.* to see movies 1.4
verano *m.* summer 1.5
verbo *m.* verb
verdad *f.* truth 1.4
   (no) es verdad it's (not) true 3.1
   ¿verdad? right? 1.1
verde *adj., m. f.* green 1.6
verduras *pl., f.* vegetables 2.2
vestido *m.* dress 1.6
vestirse (e:i) *v.* to get dressed 2.1
vez *f.* time 1.6
viajar *v.* to travel 1.2
viaje *m.* trip 1.5
viajero/a *m., f.* traveler 1.5
vida *f.* life 2.3
video *m.* video 1.1
videoconferencia *f.* videoconference 3.4
videojuego *m.* video game 1.4
vidrio *m.* glass 3.1
viejo/a *adj.* old 1.3
viento *m.* wind
viernes *m., sing.* Friday 1.2
vinagre *m.* vinegar 2.2
violencia *f.* violence 3.6
visitar *v.* to visit 1.4
   visitar monumentos *m., pl.* to visit monuments 1.4
visto/a *p.p.* seen 3.2
vitamina *f.* vitamin 3.3
viudo/a *adj.* widower/widow 2.3
vivienda *f.* housing 2.6
vivir *v.* to live 1.3

vivo/a *adj.* clever; living
volante *m.* steering wheel 2.5
volcán *m.* volcano 3.1
vóleibol *m.* volleyball 1.4
volver (o:ue) *v.* to return 1.4
volver a ver(te, lo, la) *v.* to see (you, him, her) again
vos *pron.* you
vosotros/as *fam., pl.* you 1.1
votar *v.* to vote 3.6
vuelta *f.* return trip
vuelto/a *p.p.* returned 3.2
vuestro(s)/a(s) *poss. adj.* your 1.3; your, (of) yours *fam., pl.* 2.5

Y

y *conj.* and 1.1
   y cuarto quarter after (time) 1.1
   y media half-past (time) 1.1
   y quince quarter after (time) 1.1
   y treinta thirty (minutes past the hour) 1.1
   ¿Y tú? *fam.* And you? 1.1
   ¿Y usted? *form.* And you? 1.1
ya *adv.* already 1.6
yerno *m.* son-in-law 1.3
yo *sub. pron.* I 1.1
yogur *m.* yogurt 2.2

Z

zanahoria *f.* carrot 2.2
zapatería *f.* shoe store 3.2
zapatos de tenis *m., pl.* tennis shoes, sneakers 1.6

Vocabulario

English–Spanish

A

a **un/a** *m., f., sing.; indef. art.* 1.1
@ (*symbol*) **arroba** *f.* 2.5
a.m. **de la mañana** *f.* 1.1
able: be able to **poder (o:ue)** *v.* 1.4
aboard **a bordo**
above all **sobre todo** 3.1
accident **accidente** *m.* 2.4
accompany **acompañar** *v.* 3.2
account **cuenta** *f.* 3.2
 on account of **por** *prep.* 2.5
accountant **contador(a)** *m., f.* 3.4
accounting **contabilidad** *f.* 1.2
ache **dolor** *m.* 2.4
acquainted: be acquainted with
 conocer *v.* 1.6
action (genre) **de acción** *f.* 3.5
active **activo/a** *adj.* 3.3
actor **actor** *m.*, **actriz** *f.* 3.4
additional **adicional** *adj.*
address **dirección** *f.* 3.2
adjective **adjetivo** *m.*
adolescence **adolescencia** *f.* 2.3
adventure (genre) **de aventuras**
 f. 3.5
advertise **anunciar** *v.* 3.6
advertisement **anuncio** *m.* 3.4
advice **consejo** *m.*
 give advice **dar consejos** 1.6
advise **aconsejar** *v.* 2.6
advisor **consejero/a** *m., f.* 3.4
aerobic **aeróbico/a** *adj.* 3.3
 aerobics class **clase de
  ejercicios aeróbicos** 3.3
 to do aerobics **hacer ejercicios
  aeróbicos** 3.3
affected **afectado/a** *adj.* 3.1
 be affected (by) **estar** *v.*
  afectado/a (por) 3.1
affirmative **afirmativo/a** *adj.*
afraid: be (very) afraid (of) **tener
 (mucho) miedo (de)** 1.3
 be afraid that **tener miedo
  (de) que**
after **después de** *prep.* 2.1;
 después de que *conj.* 3.1
afternoon **tarde** *f.* 1.1
afterward **después** *adv.* 2.1
again **otra vez**
age **edad** *f.* 2.3
agree **concordar** *v.*
agree **estar** *v.* **de acuerdo** 3.5
 I agree. **Estoy de acuerdo.** 3.5
 I don't agree. **No estoy de
  acuerdo.** 3.5
agreement **acuerdo** *m.*
AIDS **SIDA** *m.* 3.6
air **aire** *m.* 3.1
 air pollution **contaminación
  del aire** 3.1
airplane **avión** *m.* 1.5
airport **aeropuerto** *m.* 1.5
alarm clock **despertador** *m.* 2.1
all **todo(s)/a(s)** *adj.*
 all of us **todos**

allergic **alérgico/a** *adj.* 2.4
 be allergic (to) **ser alérgico/a
  (a)** 2.4
alleviate **aliviar** *v.*
almost **casi** *adv.* 2.4
alone **solo/a** *adj.*
along **por** *prep.* 2.5
already **ya** *adv.* 1.6
also **también** *adv.* 1.2; 2.1
altar **altar** *m.* 2.3
aluminum **aluminio** *m.* 3.1
 (made) of aluminum **de
  aluminio** 3.1
always **siempre** *adv.* 2.1
American (*North*)
 norteamericano/a *adj.* 1.3
among **entre** *prep.* 1.2
amusement **diversión** *f.*
and **y** 1.1, **e** (*before words
 beginning with i or hi*)
 And you?**¿Y tú?** *fam.* 1.1;
  ¿Y usted? *form.* 1.1
angel **ángel** *m.* 2.3
angry **enojado/a** *adj.* 1.5
 get angry (with) **enojarse** *v.*
  (con) 2.1
animal **animal** *m.* 3.1
ankle **tobillo** *m.* 2.4
anniversary **aniversario** *m.* 2.3
 (wedding) anniversary
  aniversario *m.* **(de
  bodas)** 2.3
announce **anunciar** *v.* 3.6
announcer (*TV/radio*) **locutor(a)**
 m., f. 3.6
annoy **molestar** *v.* 2.1
another **otro/a** *adj.* 1.6
answer **contestar** *v.* 1.2;
 respuesta *f.*
answering machine **contestadora** *f.*
antibiotic **antibiótico** *m.* 2.4
any **algún, alguno/a(s)** *adj.* 2.1
anyone **alguien** *pron.* 2.1
anything **algo** *pron.* 2.1
apartment **apartamento** *m.* 2.6
apartment building **edificio de
 apartamentos** 2.6
app **aplicación** *f.* 2.5
appear **parecer** *v.*
appetizers **entremeses** *m., pl.* 2.2
applaud **aplaudir** *v.* 3.5
apple **manzana** *f.* 2.2
appliance (electric)
 electrodoméstico *m.* 2.6
applicant **aspirante** *m., f.* 3.4
application **solicitud** *f.* 3.4
 job application **solicitud de
  trabajo** 3.4
apply (*for a job*) **solicitar** *v.* 3.4
 apply for a loan **pedir (e:i)** *v.*
  un préstamo 3.2
appointment **cita** *f.* 2.3
 have an appointment **tener** *v.*
  una cita 2.3
appreciate **apreciar** *v.* 3.5
April **abril** *m.* 1.5
archeologist **arqueólogo/a**
 m., f. 3.4
archeology **arqueología** *f.* 1.2
architect **arquitecto/a** *m., f.* 3.4

area **región** *f.*
Argentine **argentino/a** *adj.* 1.3
arm **brazo** *m.* 2.4
armchair **sillón** *m.* 2.6
army **ejército** *m.* 3.6
around **por** *prep.* 2.5
 around here **por aquí** 2.5
arrange **arreglar** *v.* 2.5
arrival **llegada** *f.* 1.5
arrive **llegar** *v.* 1.2
art **arte** *m.* 1.2
 (fine) arts **bellas artes** *f.,
  pl.* 3.5
article **artículo** *m.* 3.6
artist **artista** *m., f.* 1.3
artistic **artístico/a** *adj.* 3.5
arts **artes** *f., pl.* 3.5
as **como** 2.2
 as a child **de niño/a** 2.4
 as... as **tan... como** 2.2
 as many... as **tantos/as...
  como** 2.2
 as much... as **tanto... como** 2.2
 as soon as **en cuanto** *conj.* 3.1;
  tan pronto como *conj.* 3.1
ask (*a question*) **preguntar** *v.* 1.2
ask for **pedir (e:i)** *v.* 1.4
asparagus **espárragos** *m., pl.* 2.2
aspirin **aspirina** *f.* 2.4
at **a** *prep.* 1.1; **en** *prep.* 1.2
 at + *time* **a la(s)** + *time* 1.1
 at home **en casa**
 at least **por lo menos** 2.4
 at night **por la noche** 2.1
 At what time...? **¿A qué
  hora...?** 1.1
 At your service. **A sus
  órdenes.**
ATM **cajero automático** *m.* 3.2
attempt **intento** *m.* 2.5
attend **asistir (a)** *v.* 1.3
attic **altillo** *m.* 2.6
audience **público** *m.* 3.5
August **agosto** *m.* 1.5
aunt **tía** *f.* 1.3
 aunts and uncles **tíos** *m., pl.* 1.3
automobile **automóvil** *m.* 1.5;
 carro *m.*; **coche** *m.* 2.5
autumn **otoño** *m.* 1.5
avenue **avenida** *f.*
avoid **evitar** *v.* 3.1
award **premio** *m.* 3.5

B

backpack **mochila** *f.* 1.2
bad **mal, malo/a** *adj.* 1.3
 It's bad that... **Es malo
  que...** 2.6
 It's not bad at all. **No está
  nada mal.** 1.5
bag **bolsa** *f.* 1.6
bakery **panadería** *f.* 3.2
balanced **equilibrado/a** *adj.* 3.3
 to eat a balanced diet **comer
  una dieta equilibrada** 3.3
balcony **balcón** *m.* 2.6
ball **pelota** *f.* 1.4
banana **banana** *f.* 2.2

Vocabulario — English-Spanish

band **banda** *f.* 3.5
bank **banco** *m.* 3.2
bargain **ganga** *f.* 1.6; **regatear** *v.* 1.6
baseball (*game*) **béisbol** *m.* 1.4
basement **sótano** *m.* 2.6
basketball (*game*) **baloncesto** *m.* 1.4
bathe **bañarse** *v.* 2.1
bathing suit **traje** *m.* **de baño** 1.6
bathroom **baño** *m.* 2.1; **cuarto de baño** *m.* 2.1
be **ser** *v.* 1.1; **estar** *v.* 1.2
   be… years old **tener… años** 1.3
   be sick of… **estar harto/a de…** 3.6
beach **playa** *f.* 1.5
beans **frijoles** *m., pl.* 2.2
beautiful **hermoso/a** *adj.* 1.6
beauty **belleza** *f.* 3.2
   beauty salon **peluquería** *f.* 3.2; **salón** *m.* **de belleza** 3.2
because **porque** *conj.* 1.2
   because of **por** *prep.* 2.5
become (+ *adj.*) **ponerse (+ adj.)** 2.1; **convertirse** *v.*
bed **cama** *f.* 1.5
   go to bed **acostarse (o:ue)** *v.* 2.1
bedroom **alcoba** *f.*, **recámara** *f.*; **dormitorio** *m.* 2.6
beef **carne de res** *f.* 2.2
before **antes** *adv.* 2.1; **antes de** *prep.* 2.1; **antes (de) que** *conj.* 3.1
beg **rogar (o:ue)** *v.* 2.6
begin **comenzar (e:ie)** *v.* 1.4; **empezar (e:ie)** *v.* 1.4
behalf: on behalf of **de parte de** 2.5
behind **detrás de** *prep.* 1.2
believe (in) **creer** *v.* **(en)** 1.3; **creer** *v.* 3.1
   not to believe **no creer** 3.1
believed **creído/a** *p.p.* 3.2
bellhop **botones** *m., f. sing.* 1.5
below **debajo de** *prep.* 1.2
belt **cinturón** *m.* 1.6
benefit **beneficio** *m.* 3.4
beside **al lado de** *prep.* 1.2
besides **además (de)** *adv.* 2.4
best **mejor** *adj.*
   the best **el/la mejor** *m., f.* 2.2 **lo mejor** *neuter*
better **mejor** *adj.* 2.2
   It's better that… **Es mejor que…** 2.6
between **entre** *prep.* 1.2
beverage **bebida** *f.* 2.2
bicycle **bicicleta** *f.* 1.4
big **grande** *adj.* 1.3
bill **cuenta** *f.* 2.2
billion **mil millones**
biology **biología** *f.* 1.2
bird **ave** *f.* 3.1; **pájaro** *m.* 3.1
birth **nacimiento** *m.* 2.3
birthday **cumpleaños** *m., sing.* 2.3
have a birthday **cumplir** *v.* **años**
black **negro/a** *adj.* 1.6
blackboard **pizarra** *f.* 1.2
blanket **manta** *f.* 2.6
block (*city*) **cuadra** *f.* 3.2
blog **blog** *m.* 2.5
blond(e) **rubio/a** *adj.* 1.3
blouse **blusa** *f.* 1.6
blue **azul** *adj. m., f.* 1.6
boarding house **pensión** *f.*
boat **barco** *m.* 1.5
body **cuerpo** *m.* 2.4
bone **hueso** *m.* 2.4
book **libro** *m.* 1.2
bookcase **estante** *m.* 2.6
bookshelves **estante** *m.* 2.6
bookstore **librería** *f.* 1.2
boot **bota** *f.* 1.6
bore **aburrir** *v.* 2.1
bored **aburrido/a** *adj.* 1.5
   be bored **estar** *v.* **aburrido/a** 1.5
   get bored **aburrirse** *v.* 3.5
boring **aburrido/a** *adj.* 1.5
born: be born **nacer** *v.* 2.3
borrow **pedir (e:i)** *v.* **prestado** 3.2
borrowed **prestado/a** *adj.*
boss **jefe** *m.*, **jefa** *f.* 3.4
bother **molestar** *v.* 2.1
bottle **botella** *f.* 2.3
bottom **fondo** *m.*
boulevard **bulevar** *m.*
boy **chico** *m.* 1.1; **muchacho** *m.* 1.3
boyfriend **novio** *m.* 1.3
brakes **frenos** *m., pl.*
bread **pan** *m.* 2.2
break **romper** *v.* 2.4
   break (one's leg) **romperse (la pierna)** 2.4
   break down **dañar** *v.* 2.4
   break up (with) **romper** *v.* **(con)** 2.3
breakfast **desayuno** *m.* 2.2
   have breakfast **desayunar** *v.* 1.2
breathe **respirar** *v.* 3.1
bring **traer** *v.* 1.4
broadcast **transmitir** *v.* 3.6; **emitir** *v.* 3.6
brochure **folleto** *m.*
broken **roto/a** *adj.* 3.2
   be broken **estar roto/a**
brother **hermano** *m.* 1.3
brother-in-law **cuñado** *m.* 1.3
brothers and sisters **hermanos** *m., pl.* 1.3
brought **traído/a** *p.p.* 3.2
brown **café** *adj.* 1.6; **marrón** *adj.* 1.6
browser **buscador** *m.* 2.5
brunet(te) **moreno/a** *adj.* 1.3
brush **cepillar(se)** *v.* 2.1
   brush one's hair **cepillarse el pelo** 2.1
   brush one's teeth **cepillarse los dientes** 2.1
bucket **balde** *m.* 1.5
build **construir** *v.*
building **edificio** *m.* 2.6
bump into (*something accidentally*) **darse con** 2.4; (*someone*) **encontrarse** *v.* 2.5
burn (a CD/DVD) **quemar** *v.* **(un CD/DVD)**
bus **autobús** *m.* 1.1
   bus station **estación** *f.* **de autobuses** 1.5
business **negocios** *m. pl.* 3.4
   business administration **administración** *f.* **de empresas** 1.2
   business-related **comercial** *adj.* 3.4
businessperson **hombre** *m.* **/ mujer** *f.* **de negocios** 3.4
busy **ocupado/a** *adj.* 1.5
but **pero** *conj.* 1.2; (*rather*) **sino** *conj.* (*in negative sentences*) 2.1
butcher shop **carnicería** *f.* 3.2
butter **mantequilla** *f.* 2.2
buy **comprar** *v.* 1.2
by **por** *prep.* 2.5; **para** *prep.* 2.5
   by means of **por** *prep.* 2.5
   by phone **por teléfono**
   by plane **en avión** 1.5
   by way of **por** *prep.* 2.5
bye **chau** *interj. fam.* 1.1

C

cable television **televisión** *f.* **por cable** *m.*
café **café** *m.* 1.4
cafeteria **cafetería** *f.* 1.2
caffeine **cafeína** *f.* 3.3
cake **pastel** *m.* 2.3
   chocolate cake **pastel de chocolate** *m.* 2.3
calculator **calculadora** *f.* 1.2
call **llamar** *v.* 2.5
   be called **llamarse** *v.* 2.1
   call on the phone **llamar por teléfono**
calm **tranquilo/a** *adj.* 3.3
calorie **caloría** *f.* 3.3
camera **cámara** *f.* 2.5
camp **acampar** *v.* 1.5
can (*tin*) **lata** *f.* 3.1
can **poder (o:ue)** *v.* 1.4
   Could I ask you something? **¿Podría pedirte algo?** 3.5
Canadian **canadiense** *adj.* 1.3
candidate **aspirante** *m., f.* 3.4; **candidato/a** *m., f.* 3.6
candy **dulces** *m., pl.* 2.3
capital city **capital** *f.*
car **coche** *m.* 2.5; **carro** *m.* 2.5; **auto(móvil)** *m.* 1.5
caramel **caramelo** *m.* 2.3
card **tarjeta** *f.*; (*playing*) **carta** *f.* 1.5

Vocabulario — English-Spanish

care **cuidado** *m.*
   take care of **cuidar** *v.* 3.1
career **carrera** *f.* 3.4
careful: be (very) careful **tener** *v.* **(mucho) cuidado** 1.3
caretaker **ama** *m., f.* **de casa** 2.6
carpenter **carpintero/a** *m., f.* 3.4
carpet **alfombra** *f.* 2.6
carrot **zanahoria** *f.* 2.2
carry **llevar** *v.* 1.2
cartoons **dibujos** *m, pl.* **animados** 3.5
case: in case (that) **en caso (de) que** 3.1
cash (a check) **cobrar** *v.* 3.2;
   cash **(en) efectivo** 1.6
   cash register **caja** *f.* 1.6
   pay in cash **pagar** *v.* **al contado** 3.2; **pagar en efectivo** 3.2
cashier **cajero/a** *m., f.*
cat **gato** *m.* 3.1
CD **disco compacto** *m.* 2.5
CD player **reproductor de CD** *m.* 2.5
CD-ROM **cederrón** *m.*
celebrate **celebrar** *v.* 2.3
celebration **celebración** *f.*
cellar **sótano** *m.* 2.6
(cell) phone **(teléfono) celular** *m.* 2.5
cemetery **cementerio** *m.* 2.3
cereal **cereales** *m., pl.* 2.2
certain **cierto/a** *adj.*; **seguro/a** *adj.* 3.1
   it's (not) certain **(no) es cierto/seguro** 3.1
chalk **tiza** *f.* 1.2
change **cambiar** *v.* **(de)** 2.3
change: in change **de cambio** 1.2
channel (*TV*) **canal** *m.* 2.5; 3.5
character (*fictional*) **personaje** *m.* 3.5
   (main) character *m.* **personaje (principal)** 3.5
charger **cargador** *m.* 2.5
chat **conversar** *v.* 1.2; **chatear** *v.* 2.5
cheap **barato/a** *adj.* 1.6
check **comprobar (o:ue)** *v.*; **revisar** *v.* 2.5; (*bank*) **cheque** *m.* 3.2
   check the oil **revisar el aceite** 2.5
checking account **cuenta** *f.* **corriente** 3.2
cheese **queso** *m.* 2.2
chef **cocinero/a** *m., f.* 3.4
chemistry **química** *f.* 1.2
chest of drawers **cómoda** *f.* 2.6
chicken **pollo** *m.* 2.2
child **niño/a** *m., f.* 1.3
childhood **niñez** *f.* 2.3
children **hijos** *m., pl.* 1.3
Chinese **chino/a** *adj.* 1.3
chocolate **chocolate** *m.* 2.3
   chocolate cake **pastel** *m.* **de chocolate** 2.3
cholesterol **colesterol** *m.* 3.3
choose **escoger** *v.* 2.2

chop (*food*) **chuleta** *f.* 2.2
Christmas **Navidad** *f.* 2.3
church **iglesia** *f.* 1.4
cinnamon **canela** *f.* 2.4
citizen **ciudadano/a** *m., f.* 3.6
city **ciudad** *f.*
class **clase** *f.* 1.2
   take classes **tomar clases** 1.2
classical **clásico/a** *adj.* 3.5
classmate **compañero/a** *m., f.* **de clase** 1.2
clean **limpio/a** *adj.* 1.5; **limpiar** *v.* 2.6
   clean the house *v.* **limpiar la casa** 2.6
clear (*weather*) **despejado/a** *adj.*
   clear the table **quitar la mesa** 2.6
   It's (very) clear. (*weather*) **Está (muy) despejado.**
clerk **dependiente/a** *m., f.* 1.6
climate change **cambio climático** *m.* 3.1
climb **escalar** *v.* 1.4
   climb mountains **escalar montañas** 1.4
clinic **clínica** *f.* 2.4
clock **reloj** *m.* 1.2
close **cerrar (e:ie)** *v.* 1.4
closed **cerrado/a** *adj.* 1.5
closet **armario** *m.* 2.6
clothes **ropa** *f.* 1.6
   clothes dryer **secadora** *f.* 2.6
clothing **ropa** *f.* 1.6
cloud **nube** *f.* 3.1
cloudy **nublado/a** *adj.* 1.5
   It's (very) cloudy. **Está (muy) nublado.** 1.5
coat **abrigo** *m.* 1.6
coffee **café** *m.* 2.2
   coffee maker **cafetera** *f.* 2.6
cold **frío** *m.* 1.5;
   (*illness*) **resfriado** *m.* 2.4
   be (*feel*) (very) cold **tener (mucho) frío** 1.3
   It's (very) cold. (*weather*) **Hace (mucho) frío.** 1.5
college **universidad** *f.* 1.2
collision **choque** *m.* 3.6
color **color** *m.* 1.6
comb one's hair **peinarse** *v.* 2.1
come **venir** *v.* 1.3
come on **ándale** *interj.* 3.2
comedy **comedia** *f.* 3.5
comfortable **cómodo/a** *adj.* 1.5
commerce **negocios** *m., pl.* 3.4
commercial **comercial** *adj.* 3.4
communicate (with) **comunicarse** *v.* **(con)** 3.6
communication **comunicación** *f.* 3.6
   means of communication **medios** *m. pl.* **de comunicación** 3.6
community **comunidad** *f.* 1.1
company **compañía** *f.* 3.4; **empresa** *f.* 3.4
comparison **comparación** *f.*
composer **compositor(a)** *m., f.* 3.5
computer **computadora** *f.* 1.1

computer disc **disco** *m.*
computer monitor **monitor** *m.* 2.5
computer programmer **programador(a)** *m., f.* 1.3
computer science **computación** *f.* 1.2
concert **concierto** *m.* 3.5
conductor (*musical*) **director(a)** *m., f.* 3.5
confident **seguro/a** *adj.* 1.5
confirm **confirmar** *v.* 1.5
   confirm a reservation **confirmar una reservación** 1.5
confused **confundido/a** *adj.* 1.5
congested **congestionado/a** *adj.* 2.4
Congratulations! **¡Felicidades!; ¡Felicitaciones!** *f., pl.* 2.3
conservation **conservación** *f.* 3.1
conserve **conservar** *v.* 3.1
considering **para** *prep.* 2.5
consume **consumir** *v.* 3.3
container **envase** *m.* 3.1
contamination **contaminación** *f.*
content **contento/a** *adj.* 1.5
contest **concurso** *m.* 3.5
continue **seguir (e:i)** *v.* 1.4
control **control** *m.*; **controlar** *v.* 3.1
conversation **conversación** *f.* 1.1
converse **conversar** *v.* 1.2
cook **cocinar** *v.* 2.6; **cocinero/a** *m., f.* 3.4
cookie **galleta** *f.* 2.3
cool **fresco/a** *adj.* 1.5
   It's cool. (*weather*) **Hace fresco.** 1.5
corn **maíz** *m.* 2.2
corner **esquina** *f.* 3.2
cost **costar (o:ue)** *v.* 1.6
Costa Rican **costarricense** *adj.* 1.3
costume **disfraz** *m.* 2.3
cotton **algodón** *f.* 1.6
   (made of) cotton **de algodón** 1.6
couch **sofá** *m.* 2.6
couch potato **teleadicto/a** *m., f.* 3.3
cough **tos** *f.* 2.4; **toser** *v.* 2.4
counselor **consejero/a** *m., f.* 3.4
count **contar (o:ue)** *v.* 1.4
country (*nation*) **país** *m.* 1.1
countryside **campo** *m.* 1.5
(married) couple **pareja** *f.* 2.3
course **curso** *m.* 1.2; **materia** *f.* 1.2
courtesy **cortesía** *f.*
cousin **primo/a** *m., f.* 1.3
cover **cubrir** *v.*
covered **cubierto/a** *p.p.*
cow **vaca** *f.* 3.1
crafts **artesanía** *f.* 3.5
craftsmanship **artesanía** *f.* 3.5
crater **cráter** *m.* 3.1
crazy **loco/a** *adj.* 1.6
create **crear** *v.*
credit **crédito** *m.* 1.6
   credit card **tarjeta** *f.* **de crédito** 1.6
crime **crimen** *m.* 3.6
cross **cruzar** *v.* 3.2

Vocabulario

English-Spanish

cry **llorar** *v.* 3.3
Cuban **cubano/a** *adj.* 1.3
culture **cultura** *f.* 1.2, 3.5
cup **taza** *f.* 2.6
currency exchange **cambio** *m.* **de moneda**
current events **actualidades** *f., pl.* 3.6
curtains **cortinas** *f., pl.* 2.6
custard (*baked*) **flan** *m.* 2.3
custom **costumbre** *f.*
customer **cliente/a** *m., f.* 1.6
customs **aduana** *f.*
    customs inspector **inspector(a)** *m., f.* **de aduanas** 1.5
cybercafé **cibercafé** *m.* 2.5
cycling **ciclismo** *m.* 1.4

D

dad **papá** *m.*
daily **diario/a** *adj.* 2.1
    daily routine **rutina** *f.* **diaria** 2.1
damage **dañar** *v.* 2.4
dance **bailar** *v.* 1.2; **danza** *f.* 3.5; **baile** *m.* 3.5
dancer **bailarín/bailarina** *m., f.* 3.5
danger **peligro** *m.* 3.1
dangerous **peligroso/a** *adj.* 3.6
date (*appointment*) **cita** *f.* 2.3; (*calendar*) **fecha** *f.* 1.5; (*someone*) **salir** *v.* **con (alguien)** 2.3
    have a date **tener una cita** 2.3
daughter **hija** *f.* 1.3
daughter-in-law **nuera** *f.* 1.3
day **día** *m.* 1.1
    day before yesterday **anteayer** *adv.* 1.6
death **muerte** *f.* 2.3
decaffeinated **descafeinado/a** *adj.* 3.3
December **diciembre** *m.* 1.5
decide **decidir** *v.* (**+ *inf.***) 1.3
declare **declarar** *v.* 3.6
deforestation **deforestación** *f.* 3.1
delicious **delicioso/a** *adj.* 2.2; **rico/a** *adj.* 2.2; **sabroso/a** *adj.* 2.2
delighted **encantado/a** *adj.* 1.1
dentist **dentista** *m., f.* 2.4
deny **negar (e:ie)** *v.* 3.1
    not to deny **no negar** 3.1
department store **almacén** *m.* 1.6
departure **salida** *f.* 1.5
deposit **depositar** *v.* 3.2
describe **describir** *v.* 1.3
described **descrito/a** *p.p.* 3.2
desert **desierto** *m.* 3.1
design **diseño** *m.*
designer **diseñador(a)** *m., f.* 3.4
desire **desear** *v.* 1.2
desk **escritorio** *m.* 1.2
dessert **postre** *m.* 2.3
destroy **destruir** *v.* 3.1
develop **desarrollar** *v.* 3.1

diary **diario** *m.* 1.1
dictatorship **dictadura** *f.* 3.6
dictionary **diccionario** *m.* 1.1
die **morir (o:ue)** *v.* 2.2
died **muerto/a** *p.p.* 3.2
diet **dieta** *f.* 3.3; **alimentación**
    balanced diet **dieta equilibrada** 3.3
    be on a diet **estar a dieta** 3.3
difficult **difícil** *adj. m., f.* 1.3
digital camera **cámara** *f.* **digital** 2.5
dining room **comedor** *m.* 2.6
dinner **cena** *f.* 2.2
    have dinner **cenar** *v.* 1.2
direct **dirigir** *v.* 3.5
director **director(a)** *m., f.* 3.5
dirty **ensuciar** *v.*; **sucio/a** *adj.* 1.5
    get (something) dirty **ensuciar** *v.* 2.6
disagree **no estar de acuerdo**
disaster **desastre** *m.* 3.6
discover **descubrir** *v.* 3.1
discovered **descubierto/a** *p.p.* 3.2
discrimination **discriminación** *f.* 3.6
dish **plato** *m.* 2.2, 2.6
    main dish *m.* **plato principal** 2.2
dishwasher **lavaplatos** *m., sing.* 2.6
disk **disco** *m.*
disorderly **desordenado/a** *adj.* 1.5
divorce **divorcio** *m.* 2.3
divorced **divorciado/a** *adj.* 2.3
    get divorced (from) **divorciarse** *v.* **(de)** 2.3
dizzy **mareado/a** *adj.* 2.4
do **hacer** *v.* 1.4
    do aerobics **hacer ejercicios aeróbicos** 3.3
    do household chores **hacer quehaceres domésticos** 2.6
    do stretching exercises **hacer ejercicios de estiramiento** 3.3
    (I) don't want to. **No quiero.** 1.4
doctor **doctor(a)** *m., f.* 1.3; 2.4; **médico/a** *m., f.* 1.3
documentary (*film*) **documental** *m.* 3.5
dog **perro** *m.* 3.1
domestic **doméstico/a** *adj.*
    domestic appliance **electrodoméstico** *m.*
done **hecho/a** *p.p.* 3.2
door **puerta** *f.* 1.2
doorman/doorwoman **portero/a** *m., f.* 1.1
dormitory **residencia** *f.* **estudiantil** 1.2
double **doble** *adj.* 1.5
    double room **habitación** *f.* **doble** 1.5
doubt **duda** *f.* 3.1; **dudar** *v.* 3.1
    not to doubt **no dudar** 3.1
    there is no doubt that **no cabe duda de** 3.1; **no hay duda de** 3.1
download **descargar** *v.* 2.5
downtown **centro** *m.* 1.4
drama **drama** *m.* 3.5

dramatic **dramático/a** *adj.* 3.5
draw **dibujar** *v.* 1.2
drawing **dibujo** *m.*
dress **vestido** *m.* 1.6
    get dressed **vestirse (e:i)** *v.* 2.1
drink **beber** *v.* 1.3; **bebida** *f.* 2.2; **tomar** *v.* 1.2
drive **conducir** *v.* 1.6; **manejar** *v.* 2.5
driver **conductor(a)** *m., f.* 1.1
dry (oneself) **secarse** *v.* 2.1
during **durante** *prep.* 2.1; **por** *prep.* 2.5
dust **sacudir** *v.* 2.6; **quitar** *v.* **el polvo** 2.6
    dust the furniture **sacudir los muebles** 2.6
duster **plumero** *m.* 2.6
DVD player **reproductor** *m.* **de DVD** 2.5

E

each **cada** *adj.* 1.6
ear (outer) **oreja** *f.* 2.4
early **temprano** *adv.* 2.1
earn **ganar** *v.* 3.4
earring **arete** *m.* 1.6
earthquake **terremoto** *m.* 3.6
ease **aliviar** *v.*
east **este** *m.* 3.2
    to the east **al este** 3.2
easy **fácil** *adj. m., f.* 1.3
eat **comer** *v.* 1.3
ecological **ecológico/a** *adj.* 3.1
ecologist **ecologista** *m., f.* 3.1
ecology **ecología** *f.* 3.1
economics **economía** *f.* 1.2
ecotourism **ecoturismo** *m.* 3.1
Ecuadorian **ecuatoriano/a** *adj.* 1.3
effective **eficaz** *adj. m., f.*
egg **huevo** *m.* 2.2
eight **ocho** 1.1
eight hundred **ochocientos/as** 1.2
eighteen **dieciocho** 1.1
eighth **octavo/a** 1.5
eighty **ochenta** 1.2
either... or **o... o** *conj.* 2.1
elect **elegir (e:i)** *v.* 3.6
election **elecciones** *f. pl.* 3.6
electric appliance **electrodoméstico** *m.* 2.6
electrician **electricista** *m., f.* 3.4
electricity **luz** *f.* 2.6
elegant **elegante** *adj. m., f.* 1.6
elevator **ascensor** *m.* 1.5
eleven **once** 1.1
e-mail **correo** *m.* **electrónico** 1.4
    e-mail address **dirección** *f.* **electrónica** 2.5
    e-mail message **mensaje** *m.* **electrónico** 1.4
    read e-mail **leer** *v.* **el correo electrónico** 1.4
embarrassed **avergonzado/a** *adj.* 1.5
embrace (each other) **abrazar(se)** *v.* 2.5

Vocabulario — English-Spanish

emergency **emergencia** *f.* 2.4
  emergency room **sala** *f.* **de emergencia(s)** 2.4
employee **empleado/a** *m., f.* 1.5
employment **empleo** *m.* 3.4
end **fin** *m.* 1.4; **terminar** *v.* 1.2
  end table **mesita** *f.* 2.6
endure **aguantar** *v.* 3.2
energy **energía** *f.* 3.1
engaged: get engaged (to) **comprometerse** *v.* **(con)** 2.3
engineer **ingeniero/a** *m., f.* 1.3
English (*language*) **inglés** *m.* 1.2; **inglés, inglesa** *adj.* 1.3
enjoy **disfrutar** *v.* **(de)** 3.3
enough **bastante** *adv.* 2.4
entertainment **diversión** *f.* 1.4
entrance **entrada** *f.* 2.6
envelope **sobre** *m.* 3.2
environment **medio ambiente** *m.* 3.1
environmental science **ciencias ambientales** 1.2
equality **igualdad** *f.* 3.6
erase **borrar** *v.* 2.5
eraser **borrador** *m.* 1.2
errand **diligencia** *f.* 3.2
essay **ensayo** *m.* 1.3
establish **establecer** *v.* 3.4
evening **tarde** *f.* 1.1
event **acontecimiento** *m.* 3.6
every day **todos los días** 2.4
everything **todo** *m.* 1.5
exactly **en punto** 1.1
exam **examen** *m.* 1.2
excellent **excelente** *adj.* 1.5
excess **exceso** *m.* 3.3
  in excess **en exceso** 3.3
exchange **intercambiar** *v.*
  in exchange for **por** 2.5
exciting **emocionante** *adj. m., f.*
excursion **excursión** *f.*
excuse **disculpar** *v.*
Excuse me. (*May I?*) **Con permiso.** 1.1; (*I beg your pardon.*) **Perdón.** 1.1
exercise **ejercicio** *m.* 3.3; **hacer** *v.* **ejercicio** 3.3; (*a degree/profession*) **ejercer** *v.* 3.4
exit **salida** *f.* 1.5
expensive **caro/a** *adj.* 1.6
experience **experiencia** *f.*
expire **vencer** *v.* 3.2
explain **explicar** *v.* 1.2
explore **explorar** *v.*
expression **expresión** *f.*
extinction **extinción** *f.* 3.1
eye **ojo** *m.* 2.4

F

fabulous **fabuloso/a** *adj.* 1.5
face **cara** *f.* 2.1
facing **enfrente de** *prep.* 3.2
fact: in fact **de hecho**
factory **fábrica** *f.* 3.1
fall (down) **caerse** *v.* 2.4
  fall asleep **dormirse (o:ue)** *v.* 2.1
fall in love (with) **enamorarse** *v.* **(de)** 2.3
fall (*season*) **otoño** *m.* 1.5
fallen **caído/a** *p.p.* 3.2
family **familia** *f.* 1.3
famous **famoso/a** *adj.*
fan **aficionado/a** *m., f.* 1.4
  be a fan (of) **ser aficionado/a (a)**
far from **lejos de** *prep.* 1.2
farewell **despedida** *f.*
fascinate **fascinar** *v.* 2.1
fashion **moda** *f.* 1.6
  be in fashion **estar de moda** 1.6
fast **rápido/a** *adj.*
fat **gordo/a** *adj.* 1.3; **grasa** *f.* 3.3
father **padre** *m.* 1.3
father-in-law **suegro** *m.* 1.3
favorite **favorito/a** *adj.* 1.4
fax (*machine*) **fax** *m.*
fear **miedo** *m.*; **temer** *v.* 3.1
February **febrero** *m.* 1.5
feel **sentir(se) (e:ie)** *v.* 2.1
  feel like (*doing something*) **tener ganas de (+** *inf.***)** 1.3
festival **festival** *m.* 3.5
fever **fiebre** *f.* 2.4
  have a fever **tener** *v.* **fiebre** 2.4
few **pocos/as** *adj. pl.*
  fewer than **menos de (+** *number***)** 2.2
field: major field of study **especialización** *f.*
fifteen **quince** 1.1
  fifteen-year-old girl celebrating her birthday **quinceañera** *f.*
fifth **quinto/a** 1.5
fifty **cincuenta** 1.2
fight (for/against) **luchar** *v.* **(por/contra)** 3.6
figure (*number*) **cifra** *f.*
file **archivo** *m.* 2.5
fill **llenar** *v.* 2.5
  fill out (a form) **llenar (un formulario)** 3.2
  fill the tank **llenar el tanque** 2.5
finally **finalmente** *adv.*; **por último** 2.1; **por fin** 2.5
find **encontrar (o:ue)** *v.* 1.4
  find (each other) **encontrar(se)**
  find out **enterarse** *v.* 3.4
fine **multa** *f.*
  That's fine. **Está bien.**
(fine) arts **bellas artes** *f., pl.* 3.5
finger **dedo** *m.* 2.4
finish **terminar** *v.* 1.2
  finish (*doing something*) **terminar** *v.* **de (+** *inf.***)**
fire **incendio** *m.* 3.6; **despedir (e:i)** *v.* 3.4
firefighter **bombero/a** *m., f.* 3.4
firm **compañía** *f.* 3.4; **empresa** *f.* 3.4
first **primer, primero/a** 1.2, 1.5

fish (*food*) **pescado** *m.* 2.2; **pescar** *v.* 1.5; (*live*) **pez** *m., sing.* (**peces** *pl.*) 3.1
fish market **pescadería** *f.* 3.2
fishing **pesca** *f.*
fit (*clothing*) **quedar** *v.* 2.1
five **cinco** 1.1
five hundred **quinientos/as** 1.2
fix (*put in working order*) **arreglar** *v.* 2.5; (*clothes, hair, etc. to go out*) **arreglarse** *v.* 2.1
fixed **fijo/a** *adj.* 1.6
flag **bandera** *f.*
flexible **flexible** *adj.* 3.3
flood **inundación** *f.* 3.6
floor (*of a building*) **piso** *m.* 1.5; **suelo** *m.* 2.6
  ground floor **planta baja** *f.* 1.5
  top floor **planta** *f.* **alta**
flower **flor** *f.* 3.1
flu **gripe** *f.* 2.4
fog **niebla** *f.*
folk **folclórico/a** *adj.* 3.5
follow **seguir (e:i)** *v.* 1.4
food **comida** *f.* 1.4, 2.2
foolish **tonto/a** *adj.* 1.3
foot **pie** *m.* 2.4
football **fútbol** *m.* **americano** 1.4
for **para** *prep.* 2.5; **por** *prep.* 2.5
  for example **por ejemplo** 2.5
  for me **para mí** 2.2
forbid **prohibir** *v.*
foreign **extranjero/a** *adj.* 3.5
  foreign languages **lenguas** *f., pl.* **extranjeras** 1.2
forest **bosque** *m.* 3.1
forget **olvidar** *v.* 2.4
fork **tenedor** *m.* 2.6
form **formulario** *m.* 3.2
forty **cuarenta** 1.2
four **cuatro** 1.1
four hundred **cuatrocientos/as** 1.2
fourteen **catorce** 1.1
fourth **cuarto/a** *m., f.* 1.5
free **libre** *adj. m., f.* 1.4
  be free (of charge) **ser gratis** 3.2
  free time **tiempo libre**; spare (free) time **ratos libres** 1.4
freedom **libertad** *f.* 3.6
freezer **congelador** *m.* 2.6
French **francés, francesa** *adj.* 1.3
  French fries **papas** *f., pl.* **fritas** 2.2; **patatas** *f., pl.* **fritas** 2.2
frequently **frecuentemente** *adv.*; **con frecuencia** *adv.* 2.4
Friday **viernes** *m., sing.* 1.2
fried **frito/a** *adj.* 2.2
  fried potatoes **papas** *f., pl.* **fritas** 2.2; **patatas** *f., pl.* **fritas** 2.2
friend **amigo/a** *m., f.* 1.3
friendly **amable** *adj. m., f.* 1.5

Vocabulario

English-Spanish

friendship **amistad** *f.* 2.3
from **de** *prep.* 1.1; **desde** *prep.* 1.6
   from the United States **estadounidense** *m., f. adj.* 1.3
   from time to time **de vez en cuando** 2.4
   I'm from… **Soy de…** 1.1
front: (cold) front **frente (frío)** *m.* 1.5
fruit **fruta** *f.* 2.2
   fruit juice **jugo** *m.* **de fruta** 2.2
   fruit store **frutería** *f.* 3.2
full **lleno/a** *adj.* 2.5
fun **divertido/a** *adj.*
   fun activity **diversión** *f.* 1.4
   have fun **divertirse (e:ie)** *v.* 2.3
function **funcionar** *v.*
furniture **muebles** *m., pl.* 2.6
furthermore **además (de)** *adv.* 2.4
future **porvenir** *m.* 3.4
   for/to the future **por el porvenir** 3.4
   in the future **en el futuro**

G

gain weight **aumentar** *v.* **de peso** 3.3; **engordar** *v.* 3.3
game **juego** *m.*; (*match*) **partido** *m.* 1.4
   game show **concurso** *m.* 3.5
garage (*in a house*) **garaje** *m.* 2.6; **garaje** *m.* 2.5; **taller (mecánico)** 2.5
garden **jardín** *m.* 2.6
garlic **ajo** *m.* 2.2
gas station **gasolinera** *f.* 2.5
gasoline **gasolina** *f.* 2.5
gentleman **caballero** *m.* 2.2
geography **geografía** *f.* 1.2
German **alemán, alemana** *adj.* 1.3
get **conseguir(e:i)** *v.* 1.4; **obtener** *v.* 3.4
   get along well/badly (with) **llevarse bien/mal (con)** 2.3
   get bigger **aumentar** *v.* 3.1
   get bored **aburrirse** *v.* 3.5
   get good grades **sacar buenas notas** 1.2
   get into trouble **meterse en problemas** *v.* 3.1
   get off of (a vehicle) **bajar(se)** *v.* **de** 2.5
   get on/into (a vehicle) **subir(se)** *v.* **a** 2.5
   get out of (a vehicle) **bajar(se)** *v.* **de** 2.5
   get ready **arreglarse** *v.* 2.1
   get up **levantarse** *v.* 2.1
gift **regalo** *m.* 1.6
ginger **jengibre** *m.* 2.4
girl **chica** *f.* 1.1; **muchacha** *f.* 1.3
girlfriend **novia** *f.* 1.3

give **dar** *v.* 1.6; (*as a gift*) **regalar** 2.3
   give directions **indicar cómo llegar** 3.2
glass (*drinking*) **vaso** *m.* 2.6; **vidrio** *m.* 3.1
   (made) of glass **de vidrio** 3.1
glasses **gafas** *f., pl.* 1.6
   sunglasses **gafas** *f., pl.* **de sol** 1.6
global warming **calentamiento global** *m.* 3.1
gloves **guantes** *m., pl.* 1.6
go **ir** *v.* 1.4
   go away **irse** 2.1
   go by boat **ir en barco** 1.5
   go by bus **ir en autobús** 1.5
   go by car **ir en auto(móvil)** 1.5
   go by motorcycle **ir en moto(cicleta)** 1.5
   go by plane **ir en avión** 1.5
   go by taxi **ir en taxi** 1.5
   go down **bajar(se)** *v.*
   go on a hike **ir de excursión** 1.4
   go out (with) **salir** *v.* **(con)** 2.3
   go up **subir** *v.*
   Let's go. **Vamos.** 1.4
goblet **copa** *f.* 2.6
going to: be going to (*do something*) **ir a (+ *inf.*)** 1.4
golf **golf** *m.* 1.4
good **buen, bueno/a** *adj.* 1.3, 1.6
   Good afternoon. **Buenas tardes.** 1.1
   Good evening. **Buenas noches.** 1.1
   Good morning. **Buenos días.** 1.1
   Good night. **Buenas noches.** 1.1
   It's good that… **Es bueno que…** 2.6
goodbye **adiós** *m.* 1.1
   say goodbye (to) **despedirse** *v.* **(de) (e:i)** 3.6
good-looking **guapo/a** *adj.* 1.3
government **gobierno** *m.* 3.1
GPS **navegador GPS** *m.* 2.5
graduate (from/in) **graduarse** *v.* **(de/en)** 2.3
grains **cereales** *m., pl.* 2.2
granddaughter **nieta** *f.* 1.3
grandfather **abuelo** *m.* 1.3
grandmother **abuela** *f.* 1.3
grandparents **abuelos** *m., pl.* 1.3
grandson **nieto** *m.* 1.3
grape **uva** *f.* 2.2
grass **hierba** *f.* 3.1
grave **grave** *adj.* 2.4
gray **gris** *adj. m., f.* 1.6
great **fenomenal** *adj. m., f.* 1.5; **genial** *adj.* 3.4
great-grandfather **bisabuelo** *m.* 1.3
great-grandmother **bisabuela** *f.* 1.3
green **verde** *adj. m., f.* 1.6
greet (each other) **saludar(se)** *v.* 2.5

greeting **saludo** *m.* 1.1
   Greetings to… **Saludos a…** 1.1
grilled **a la plancha** 2.2
ground floor **planta baja** *f.* 1.5
grow **aumentar** *v.* 3.1
guest (*at a house/hotel*) **huésped** *m., f.* 1.5 (*invited to a function*) **invitado/a** *m., f.* 2.3
guide **guía** *m., f.*
gymnasium **gimnasio** *m.* 1.4

H

hair **pelo** *m.* 2.1
hairdresser **peluquero/a** *m., f.* 3.4
half **medio/a** *adj.* 1.3
   half-brother **medio hermano** *m.* 1.3
   half-past… (*time*) **…y media** 1.1
   half-sister **media hermana** *f.* 1.3
hallway **pasillo** *m.* 2.6
ham **jamón** *m.* 2.2
hamburger **hamburguesa** *f.* 2.2
hand **mano** *f.* 1.1
hand in **entregar** *v.* 2.5
handsome **guapo/a** *adj.* 1.3
happen **ocurrir** *v.* 3.6
happiness **alegría** *v.* 2.3
Happy birthday! **¡Feliz cumpleaños!** 2.3
happy **alegre** *adj.* 1.5; **contento/a** *adj.* 1.5; **feliz** *adj. m., f.* 1.5
   be happy **alegrarse** *v.* **(de)** 3.1
hard **difícil** *adj. m., f.* 1.3
hard-working **trabajador(a)** *adj.* 1.3
hardly **apenas** *adv.* 2.4
hat **sombrero** *m.* 1.6
hate **odiar** *v.* 2.3
have **tener** *v.* 1.3
   have time **tener tiempo** 3.2
   have to (*do something*) **tener que (+ *inf.*)** 1.3
   have a tooth removed **sacar(se) un diente** 2.4
he **él** 1.1
head **cabeza** *f.* 2.4
headache **dolor** *m.* **de cabeza** 2.4
health **salud** *f.* 2.4
healthy **saludable** *adj. m., f.* 2.4; **sano/a** *adj.* 2.4
   lead a healthy lifestyle **llevar** *v.* **una vida sana** 3.3
hear **oír** *v.* 1.4
heard **oído/a** *p.p.* 3.2
hearing: sense of hearing **oído** *m.* 2.4
heart **corazón** *m.* 2.4
heat **calor** *m.*
Hello. **Hola.** 1.1; (*on the telephone*) **Aló.** 2.5; **Bueno.** 2.5; **Diga.** 2.5
help **ayudar** *v.*; **servir (e:i)** *v.* 1.5
   help each other **ayudarse** *v.* 2.5
her **su(s)** *poss. adj.* 1.3; (of) hers **suyo(s)/a(s)** *poss.* 2.5
   her **la** *f., sing., d.o. pron.* 1.5
   to/for her **le** *f., sing., i.o. pron.* 1.6

A-23

here **aquí** *adv.* 1.1
    Here is/are... **Aquí está(n)...** 1.5
Hi. **Hola.** 1.1
highway **autopista** *f.* 2.5; **carretera** *f.* 2.5
hike **excursión** *f.* 1.4
    go on a hike **ir de excursión** 1.4
hiker **excursionista** *m., f.*
hiking **de excursión** 1.4
him *m., sing., d.o. pron.* **lo** 1.5; to/for him **le** *m., sing., i.o. pron.* 1.6
hire **contratar** *v.* 3.4
his **su(s)** *poss. adj.* 1.3; (of) his **suyo(s)/a(s)** *poss. pron.* 2.5
history **historia** *f.* 1.2; 3.5
hobby **pasatiempo** *m.* 1.4
hockey **hockey** *m.* 1.4
hold up **aguantar** *v.* 3.2
hole **hueco** *m.* 1.4
holiday **día** *m.* **de fiesta** 2.3
home **casa** *f.* 1.2
    home page **página** *f.* **principal** 2.5
homework **tarea** *f.* 1.2
honey **miel** *f.* 2.4
hood **capó** *m.* 2.5; **cofre** *m.* 2.5
hope **esperar** *v.* (+ *inf.*) 1.2; **esperar** *v.* 3.1
    I hope (that) **ojalá (que)** 3.1
horror (genre) **de horror** *m.* 3.5
hors d'oeuvres **entremeses** *m., pl.* 2.2
horse **caballo** *m.* 1.5
hospital **hospital** *m.* 2.4
hot: be (*feel*) (very) hot **tener (mucho) calor** 1.3
    It's (very) hot. **Hace (mucho) calor.** 1.5
hotel **hotel** *m.* 1.5
hour **hora** *f.* 1.1
house **casa** *f.* 1.2
household chores **quehaceres** *m. pl.* **domésticos** 2.6
housekeeper **ama** *m., f.* **de casa** 2.6
housing **vivienda** *f.* 2.6
How...! **¡Qué...!**
    how **¿cómo?** *adv.* 1.1, 1.2
    How are you? **¿Qué tal?** 1.1
    How are you? **¿Cómo estás?** *fam.* 1.1
    How are you? **¿Cómo está usted?** *form.* 1.1
    How can I help you? **¿En qué puedo servirles?** 1.5
    How is it going? **¿Qué tal?** 1.1
    How is the weather? **¿Qué tiempo hace?** 1.5
    How much/many? **¿Cuánto(s)/a(s)?** 1.1
    How much does... cost? **¿Cuánto cuesta...?** 1.6
    How old are you? **¿Cuántos años tienes?** *fam.*
however **sin embargo**

hug (each other) **abrazar(se)** *v.* 2.5
humanities **humanidades** *f., pl.* 1.2
hundred **cien, ciento** 1.2
hunger **hambre** *f.*
hungry: be (very) hungry **tener** *v.* **(mucha) hambre** 1.3
hunt **cazar** *v.* 3.1
hurricane **huracán** *m.* 3.6
hurry **apurarse** *v.* 3.3; **darse prisa** *v.* 3.3
    be in a (big) hurry **tener** *v.* **(mucha) prisa** 1.3
hurt **doler (o:ue)** *v.* 2.4
husband **esposo** *m.* 1.3

I

I **yo** 1.1
    I hope (that) **Ojalá (que)** *interj.* 3.1
    I wish (that) **Ojalá (que)** *interj.* 3.1
ice cream **helado** *m.* 2.3
    ice cream shop **heladería** *f.* 3.2
iced **helado/a** *adj.* 2.2
    iced tea **té** *m.* **helado** 2.2
idea **idea** *f.* 3.6
if **si** *conj.* 1.4
illness **enfermedad** *f.* 2.4
important **importante** *adj.* 1.3
    be important to **importar** *v.* 2.1
    It's important that... **Es importante que...** 2.6
impossible **imposible** *adj.* 3.1
    it's impossible **es imposible** 3.1
improbable **improbable** *adj.* 3.1
    it's improbable **es improbable** 3.1
improve **mejorar** *v.* 3.1
in **en** *prep.* 1.2; **por** *prep.* 2.5
    in the afternoon **de la tarde** 1.1; **por la tarde** 2.1
    in a bad mood **de mal humor** 1.5
    in the direction of **para** *prep.* 2.5
    in the early evening **de la tarde** 1.1
    in the evening **de la noche** 1.1; **por la tarde** 2.1
    in a good mood **de buen humor** 1.5
    in the morning **de la mañana** 1.1; **por la mañana** 2.1
    in love (with) **enamorado/a (de)** 1.5
    in search of **por** *prep.* 2.5
in front of **delante de** *prep.* 1.2
increase **aumento** *m.*
incredible **increíble** *adj.* 1.5
inequality **desigualdad** *f.* 3.6
infection **infección** *f.* 2.4
inform **informar** *v.* 3.6
injection **inyección** *f.* 2.4
    give an injection *v.* **poner una inyección** 2.4

injure (oneself) **lastimarse** 2.4
    injure (one's foot) **lastimarse** *v.* **(el pie)** 2.4
inner ear **oído** *m.* 2.4
inside **dentro** *adv.*
insist (on) **insistir** *v.* **(en)** 2.6
installments: pay in installments **pagar** *v.* **a plazos** 3.2
intelligent **inteligente** *adj.* 1.3
intend to **pensar** *v.* (+ *inf.*) 1.4
interest **interesar** *v.* 2.1
interesting **interesante** *adj.* 1.3
    be interesting to **interesar** *v.* 2.1
international **internacional** *adj. m., f.* 3.6
Internet **Internet** 2.5
interview **entrevista** *f.* 3.4; interview **entrevistar** *v.* 3.4
interviewer **entrevistador(a)** *m., f.* 3.4
introduction **presentación** *f.*
    I would like to introduce you to (name). **Le presento a...** *form.* 1.1; **Te presento a...** *fam.* 1.1
invest **invertir (e:ie)** *v.* 3.4
invite **invitar** *v.* 2.3
iron (clothes) **planchar** *v.* **la ropa** 2.6
it **lo/la** *sing., d.o., pron.* 1.5
Italian **italiano/a** *adj.* 1.3
its **su(s)** *poss. adj.* 1.3; **suyo(s)/a(s)** *poss. pron.* 2.5
it's the same **es igual** 1.5

J

jacket **chaqueta** *f.* 1.6
January **enero** *m.* 1.5
Japanese **japonés, japonesa** *adj.* 1.3
jeans **(blue)jeans** *m., pl.* 1.6
jewelry store **joyería** *f.* 3.2
job **empleo** *m.* 3.4; **puesto** *m.* 3.4; **trabajo** *m.* 3.4
    job application **solicitud** *f.* **de trabajo** 3.4
jog **correr** *v.*
journalism **periodismo** *m.* 1.2
journalist **periodista** *m., f.* 1.3
joy **alegría** *f.* 2.3
juice **jugo** *m.* 2.2
July **julio** *m.* 1.5
June **junio** *m.* 1.5
jungle **selva, jungla** *f.* 3.1
just **apenas** *adv.*
    have just done something **acabar de** (+ *inf.*) 1.6

K

key **llave** *f.* 1.5
keyboard **teclado** *m.* 2.5
kilometer **kilómetro** *m.* 2.5

Vocabulario — English-Spanish

kiss **beso** *m.* 2.3
   kiss each other **besarse** *v.* 2.5
kitchen **cocina** *f.* 2.3, 2.6
knee **rodilla** *f.* 2.4
knife **cuchillo** *m.* 2.6
know **saber** *v.* 1.6; **conocer** *v.* 1.6
know how **saber** *v.* 1.6

L

laboratory **laboratorio** *m.* 1.2
lack **faltar** *v.* 2.1
lake **lago** *m.* 3.1
lamp **lámpara** *f.* 2.6
land **tierra** *f.* 3.1
landscape **paisaje** *m.* 1.5
language **lengua** *f.* 1.2
laptop (computer) **computadora** *f.* **portátil** 2.5
large **grande** *adj.* 1.3
large (*clothing size*) **talla grande**
last **durar** *v.* 3.6; **pasado/a** *adj.* 1.6; **último/a** *adj.* 2.1
   last name **apellido** *m.* 1.3
   last night **anoche** *adv.* 1.6
   last week **semana** *f.* **pasada** 1.6
   last year **año** *m.* **pasado** 1.6
   the last time **la última vez** 2.1
late **tarde** *adv.* 2.1
later (on) **más tarde** 2.1
   See you later. **Hasta la vista.** 1.1; **Hasta luego.** 1.1
laugh **reírse (e:i)** *v.* 2.3
laughed **reído** *p.p.* 3.2
laundromat **lavandería** *f.* 3.2
law **ley** *f.* 3.1
lawyer **abogado/a** *m., f.* 3.4
lazy **perezoso/a** *adj.*
learn **aprender** *v.* (**a** + *inf.*) 1.3
least, at **por lo menos** *adv.* 2.4
leave **salir** *v.* 1.4; **irse** *v.* 2.1
   leave a tip **dejar una propina**
   leave behind **dejar** *v.* 3.4
   leave for (*a place*) **salir para**
   leave from **salir de**
left **izquierda** *f.* 1.2
   be left over **quedar** *v.* 2.1
   to the left of **a la izquierda de** 1.2
leg **pierna** *f.* 2.4
lemon **limón** *m.* 2.2
lend **prestar** *v.* 1.6
less **menos** *adv.* 2.4
   less... than **menos... que** 2.2
   less than **menos de** (+ *number*)
lesson **lección** *f.* 1.1
let **dejar** *v.*
let's see **a ver**
letter **carta** *f.* 1.4, 3.2
lettuce **lechuga** *f.* 2.2
liberty **libertad** *f.* 3.6
library **biblioteca** *f.* 1.2
license (*driver's*) **licencia** *f.* **de conducir** 2.5

lie **mentira** *f.* 1.4
life **vida** *f.* 2.3
lifestyle: lead a healthy lifestyle **llevar una vida sana** 3.3
lift **levantar** *v.* 3.3
   lift weights **levantar pesas** 3.3
light **luz** *f.* 2.6
like **como** *prep.* 2.2; **gustar** *v.* 1.2
   I like... **Me gusta(n)...** 1.2
   like this **así** *adv.* 2.4
   like very much **encantar** *v.*; **fascinar** *v.* 2.1
   Do you like...? **¿Te gusta(n)...?** 1.2
likeable **simpático/a** *adj.* 1.3
likewise **igualmente** *adv.* 1.1
line **línea** *f.* 1.4; **cola** (*queue*) *f.* 3.2
listen (to) **escuchar** *v.* 1.2
   listen to music **escuchar música** 1.2
   listen to the radio **escuchar la radio** 1.2
literature **literatura** *f.* 1.2
little (*quantity*) **poco** *adv.* 2.4
live **vivir** *v.* 1.3; **en vivo** *adj.* 2.1
living room **sala** *f.* 2.6
loan **préstamo** *m.* 3.2; **prestar** *v.* 1.6, 3.2
lobster **langosta** *f.* 2.2
located **situado/a** *adj.*
   be located **quedar** *v.* 3.2
long **largo/a** *adj.* 1.6
look (at) **mirar** *v.* 1.2
look for **buscar** *v.* 1.2
lose **perder (e:ie)** *v.* 1.4
   lose weight **adelgazar** *v.* 3.3
lost **perdido/a** *adj.* 3.1, 3.2
   be lost **estar perdido/a** 3.2
lot, a **muchas veces** *adv.* 2.4
lot of, a **mucho/a** *adj.* 1.3; **un montón de** 1.4
love (*another person*) **querer (e:ie)** *v.* 1.4; (*inanimate objects*) **encantar** *v.* 2.1; **amor** *m.* 2.3
   in love **enamorado/a** *adj.* 1.5
   love at first sight **amor a primera vista** 2.3
luck **suerte** *f.*
lucky: be (very) lucky **tener (mucha) suerte** 1.3
luggage **equipaje** *m.* 1.5
lunch **almuerzo** *m.* 1.4, 2.2
   have lunch **almorzar (o:ue)** *v.* 1.4

M

ma'am **señora (Sra.)**; **doña** *f.* 1.1
mad **enojado/a** *adj.* 1.5
magazine **revista** *f.* 1.4
magnificent **magnífico/a** *adj.* 1.5
mail **correo** *m.* 3.2; **enviar** *v.*, **mandar** *v.* 3.2; **echar (una carta) al buzón** 3.2
   mail carrier **cartero** *m.* 3.2
mailbox **buzón** *m.* 3.2
main **principal** *adj. m., f.* 2.2

maintain **mantener** *v.* 3.3
major **especialización** *f.* 1.2
make **hacer** *v.* 1.4
   make a decision **tomar una decisión** 3.3
   make the bed **hacer la cama** 2.6
makeup **maquillaje** *m.* 2.1
   put on makeup **maquillarse** *v.* 2.1
man **hombre** *m.* 1.1
manager **gerente** *m., f.* 2.2, 3.4
many **mucho/a** *adj.* 1.3
   many times **muchas veces** 2.4
map **mapa** *m.* 1.1, 1.2
March **marzo** *m.* 1.5
margarine **margarina** *f.* 2.2
marinated fish **ceviche** *m.* 2.2
   lemon-marinated shrimp **ceviche** *m.* **de camarón** 2.2
marital status **estado** *m.* **civil** 2.3
market **mercado** *m.* 1.6
   open-air market **mercado al aire libre** 1.6
marriage **matrimonio** *m.* 2.3
married **casado/a** *adj.* 2.3
   get married (to) **casarse** *v.* **(con)** 2.3
   I'll marry you! **¡Acepto casarme contigo!** 3.5
marvelous **maravilloso/a** *adj.* 1.5
massage **masaje** *m.* 3.3
masterpiece **obra maestra** *f.* 3.5
match (*sports*) **partido** *m.* 1.4
match (with) **hacer** *v.* **juego (con)** 1.6
mathematics **matemáticas** *f., pl.* 1.2
matter **importar** *v.* 2.1
maturity **madurez** *f.* 2.3
maximum **máximo/a** *adj.* 2.5
May **mayo** *m.* 1.5
May I leave a message? **¿Puedo dejar un recado?** 2.5
maybe **tal vez** 1.5; **quizás** 1.5
mayonnaise **mayonesa** *f.* 2.2
me **me** *sing., d.o. pron.* 1.5
   to/for me **me** *sing., i.o. pron.* 1.6
meal **comida** *f.* 2.2
means of communication **medios** *m., pl.* **de comunicación** 3.6
meat **carne** *f.* 2.2
mechanic **mecánico/a** *m., f.* 2.5
   mechanic's repair shop **taller mecánico** 2.5
media **medios** *m., pl.* **de comunicación** 3.6
medical **médico/a** *adj.* 2.4
medication **medicamento** *m.* 2.4
medicine **medicina** *f.* 2.4
medium **mediano/a** *adj.*
meet (each other) **encontrar(se)** *v.* 2.5; **conocer(se)** *v.* 2.2
   meet up with **encontrarse con** 2.1
meeting **reunión** *f.* 3.4
menu **menú** *m.* 2.2

Vocabulario — English-Spanish

message **mensaje** *m.*
Mexican **mexicano/a** *adj.* 1.3
microwave **microonda** *f.* 2.6
   microwave oven **horno** *m.* **de microondas** 2.6
middle age **madurez** *f.* 2.3
midnight **medianoche** *f.* 1.1
mile **milla** *f.*
milk **leche** *f.* 2.2
million **millón** *m.* 1.2
   million of **millón de** 1.2
mine **mío(s)/a(s)** *poss.* 2.5
mineral **mineral** *m.* 3.3
   mineral water **agua** *f.* **mineral** 2.2
minute **minuto** *m.*
mirror **espejo** *m.* 2.1
Miss **señorita (Srta.)** *f.* 1.1
miss **perder (e:ie)** *v.* 1.4; **extrañar** *v.* 3.4
mistaken **equivocado/a** *adj.*
modern **moderno/a** *adj.* 3.5
mom **mamá** *f.*
Monday **lunes** *m., sing.* 1.2
money **dinero** *m.* 1.6
monitor **monitor** *m.* 2.5
monkey **mono** *m.* 3.1
month **mes** *m.* 1.5
monument **monumento** *m.* 1.4
moon **luna** *f.* 3.1
more **más** 1.2
   more… than **más… que** 2.2
   more than **más de (+ *number*)** 2.2
morning **mañana** *f.* 1.1
mother **madre** *f.* 1.3
mother-in-law **suegra** *f.* 1.3
motor **motor** *m.*
motorcycle **moto(cicleta)** *f.* 1.5
mountain **montaña** *f.* 1.4
mouse **ratón** *m.* 2.5
mouth **boca** *f.* 2.4
move (*from one house to another*) **mudarse** *v.* 2.6
movie **película** *f.* 1.4
   movie star **estrella** *f.* **de cine** 3.5
   movie theater **cine** *m.* 1.4
MP3 player **reproductor** *m.* **de MP3** 2.5
Mr. **señor (Sr.); don** *m.* 1.1
Mrs. **señora (Sra.); doña** *f.* 1.1
much **mucho/a** *adj.* 1.3
mud **lodo** *m.*
murder **crimen** *m.* 3.6
muscle **músculo** *m.* 3.3
museum **museo** *m.* 1.4
mushroom **champiñón** *m.* 2.2
music **música** *f.* 1.2, 3.5
musical **musical** *adj., m., f.* 3.5
musician **músico/a** *m., f.* 3.5
must **deber** *v.* (+ *inf.*) 1.3
my **mi(s)** *poss. adj.* 1.3; **mío(s)/a(s)** *poss. pron.* 2.5

N

name **nombre** *m.* 1.1
   be named **llamarse** *v.* 2.1
   in the name of **a nombre de** 1.5
   last name **apellido** *m.* 1.3
   My name is… **Me llamo…** 1.1
   name someone/something **ponerle el nombre** 2.3
napkin **servilleta** *f.* 2.6
national **nacional** *adj. m., f.* 3.6
nationality **nacionalidad** *f.* 1.1
natural **natural** *adj. m., f.* 3.1
   natural disaster **desastre** *m.* **natural** 3.6
   natural resource **recurso** *m.* **natural** 3.1
nature **naturaleza** *f.* 3.1
nauseated **mareado/a** *adj.* 2.4
near **cerca de** *prep.* 1.2
neaten **arreglar** *v.* 2.6
necessary **necesario/a** *adj.* 2.6
   It is necessary that… **Es necesario que…** 2.6
neck **cuello** *m.* 2.4
need **faltar** *v.* 2.1; **necesitar** *v.* (+ *inf.*) 1.2
neighbor **vecino/a** *m., f.* 2.6
neighborhood **barrio** *m.* 2.6
neither **tampoco** *adv.* 2.1
neither… nor **ni… ni** *conj.* 2.1
nephew **sobrino** *m.* 1.3
nervous **nervioso/a** *adj.* 1.5
network **red** *f.* 2.5
never **nunca** *adj.* 2.1; **jamás** 2.1
new **nuevo/a** *adj.* 1.6
newlywed **recién casado/a** *m., f.* 2.3
news **noticias** *f., pl.* 3.6; **actualidades** *f., pl.* 3.6; **noticia** *f.* 2.5
newscast **noticiero** *m.* 3.6
newspaper **periódico** 1.4; **diario** *m.* 3.6
next **próximo/a** *adj.* 1.3, 3.4
   next to **al lado de** *prep.* 1.2
nice **simpático/a** *adj.* 1.3; **amable** *adj.* 1.5
niece **sobrina** *f.* 1.3
night **noche** *f.* 1.1
   night stand **mesita** *f.* **de noche** 2.6
nine **nueve** 1.1
nine hundred **novecientos/as** 1.2
nineteen **diecinueve** 1.1
ninety **noventa** 1.2
ninth **noveno/a** 1.5
no **no** 1.1; **ningún, ninguno/a(s)** *adj.* 2.1
   no one **nadie** *pron.* 2.1
nobody **nadie** 2.1
none **ningún, ninguno/a(s)** *adj.* 2.1
noon **mediodía** *m.* 1.1
nor **ni** *conj.* 2.1
north **norte** *m.* 3.2
   to the north **al norte** 3.2
nose **nariz** *f.* 2.4
not **no** 1.1
   not any **ningún, ninguno/a(s)** *adj.* 2.1
   not anyone **nadie** *pron.* 2.1
   not anything **nada** *pron.* 2.1
   not bad at all **nada mal** 1.5
   not either **tampoco** *adv.* 2.1
   not ever **nunca** *adv.* 2.1; **jamás** *adv.* 2.1
   not very well **no muy bien** 1.1
   not working **descompuesto/a** *adj.* 2.5
notebook **cuaderno** *m.* 1.1
nothing **nada** 1.1; 2.1
noun **sustantivo** *m.*
November **noviembre** *m.* 1.5
now **ahora** *adv.* 1.2
nowadays **hoy día** *adv.*
nuclear **nuclear** *adj. m., f.* 3.1
   nuclear energy **energía nuclear** 3.1
number **número** *m.* 1.1
nurse **enfermero/a** *m., f.* 2.4
nutrition **nutrición** *f.* 3.3
nutritionist **nutricionista** *m., f.* 3.3

O

o'clock: It's… o'clock **Son las…** 1.1
   It's one o'clock. **Es la una.** 1.1
obey **obedecer** *v.* 3.6
obligation **deber** *m.* 3.6
obtain **conseguir (e:i)** *v.* 1.4; **obtener** *v.* 3.4
obvious **obvio/a** *adj.* 3.1
   it's obvious **es obvio** 3.1
occupation **ocupación** *f.* 3.4
occur **ocurrir** *v.* 3.6
October **octubre** *m.* 1.5
of **de** *prep.* 1.1
   Of course. **Claro que sí.; Por supuesto.**
offer **oferta** *f.*; **ofrecer (c:zc)** *v.* 1.6
office **oficina** *f.* 2.6
   doctor's office **consultorio** *m.* 2.4
often **a menudo** *adv.* 2.4
Oh! **¡Ay!**
oil **aceite** *m.* 2.2
OK **regular** *adj.* 1.1
   It's okay. **Está bien.**
old **viejo/a** *adj.* 1.3
old age **vejez** *f.* 2.3
older **mayor** *adj. m., f.* 1.3
   older brother, sister **hermano/a mayor** *m., f.* 1.3
oldest **el/la mayor** 2.2
on **en** *prep.* 1.2; **sobre** *prep.* 1.2

on behalf of **por** *prep.* 2.5
on the dot **en punto** 1.1
on time **a tiempo** 2.4
on top of **encima de** 1.2
once **una vez** 1.6
one **uno** 1.1
   one hundred **cien(to)** 1.2
   one million **un millón** *m.* 1.2
   one more time **una vez más**
   one thousand **mil** 1.2
   one time **una vez** 1.6
onion **cebolla** *f.* 2.2
only **sólo** *adv.* 1.6; **único/a** *adj.* 1.3
   only child **hijo/a único/a** *m., f.* 1.3
open **abierto/a** *adj.* 1.5, 3.2; **abrir** *v.* 1.3
open-air **al aire libre** 1.6
opera **ópera** *f.* 3.5
operation **operación** *f.* 2.4
opposite **enfrente de** *prep.* 3.2
or **o** *conj.* 2.1
orange **anaranjado/a** *adj.* 1.6; **naranja** *f.* 2.2
orchestra **orquesta** *f.* 3.5
order **mandar** 2.6; (*food*) **pedir (e:i)** *v.* 2.2
   in order to **para** *prep.* 2.5
orderly **ordenado/a** *adj.* 1.5
ordinal (*numbers*) **ordinal** *adj.*
organize oneself **organizarse** *v.* 2.6
other **otro/a** *adj.* 1.6
ought to **deber** *v.* (**+ *inf.***) *adj.* 1.3
our **nuestro(s)/a(s)** *poss. adj.* 1.3; *poss. pron.* 2.5
out of order **descompuesto/a** *adj.* 2.5
outside **afuera** *adv.* 1.5
outskirts **afueras** *f., pl.* 2.6
oven **horno** *m.* 2.6
over **sobre** *prep.* 1.2
(over)population **(sobre)población** *f.* 3.1
over there **allá** *adv.* 1.2
own **propio/a** *adj.*
owner **dueño/a** *m., f.* 2.2

P

p.m. **de la tarde, de la noche** *f.* 1.1
pack (one's suitcases) **hacer** *v.* **las maletas** 1.5
package **paquete** *m.* 3.2
page **página** *f.* 2.5
pain **dolor** *m.* 2.4
   have pain **tener** *v.* **dolor** 2.4
paint **pintar** *v.* 3.5
painter **pintor(a)** *m., f.* 3.4
painting **pintura** *f.* 2.6, 3.5
pair **par** *m.* 1.6
   pair of shoes **par** *m.* **de zapatos** 1.6
pale **pálido/a** *adj.* 3.2
pants **pantalones** *m., pl.* 1.6

pantyhose **medias** *f., pl.* 1.6
paper **papel** *m.* 1.2; (*report*) **informe** *m.* 3.6
Pardon me. (*May I?*) **Con permiso.** 1.1; (*Excuse me.*) Pardon me. **Perdón.** 1.1
parents **padres** *m., pl.* 1.3; **papás** *m., pl.*
park **estacionar** *v.* 2.5; **parque** *m.* 1.4
parking lot **estacionamiento** *m.* 3.2
partner (*one of a married couple*) **pareja** *f.* 2.3
party **fiesta** *f.* 2.3
passed **pasado/a** *p.p.*
passenger **pasajero/a** *m., f.* 1.1
passport **pasaporte** *m.* 1.5
past **pasado/a** *adj.* 1.6
pastime **pasatiempo** *m.* 1.4
pastry shop **pastelería** *f.* 3.2
path **sendero** *m.* 3.1
patient **paciente** *m., f.* 2.4
patio **patio** *m.* 2.6
pay **pagar** *v.* 1.6
   pay in cash **pagar** *v.* **al contado**; **pagar en efectivo** 3.2
   pay in installments **pagar** *v.* **a plazos** 3.2
   pay the bill **pagar la cuenta**
pea **arveja** *m.* 2.2
peace **paz** *f.* 3.6
peach **melocotón** *m.* 2.2
peak **cima** *f.* 3.3
pear **pera** *f.* 2.2
pen **pluma** *f.* 1.2
pencil **lápiz** *m.* 1.1
penicillin **penicilina** *f.*
people **gente** *f.* 1.3
pepper (*black*) **pimienta** *f.* 2.2
per **por** *prep.* 2.5
perfect **perfecto/a** *adj.* 1.5
period of time **temporada** *f.* 1.5
person **persona** *f.* 1.3
pharmacy **farmacia** *f.* 2.4
phenomenal **fenomenal** *adj.* 1.5
photograph **foto(grafía)** *f.* 1.1
physical (*exam*) **examen** *m.* **médico** 2.4
physician **doctor(a), médico/a** *m., f.* 1.3
physics **física** *f. sing.* 1.2
pick up **recoger** *v.* 3.1
picture **cuadro** *m.* 2.6; **pintura** *f.* 2.6
pie **pastel** *m.* 2.3
pill (*tablet*) **pastilla** *f.* 2.4
pillow **almohada** *f.* 2.6
pineapple **piña** *f.*
pink **rosado/a** *adj.* 1.6
place **lugar** *m.* 1.2, 1.4; **sitio** *m.* 1.3; **poner** *v.* 1.4
plaid **de cuadros** 1.6
plans **planes** *m., pl.*
   have plans **tener planes**
plant **planta** *f.* 3.1
plastic **plástico** *m.* 3.1
   (made) of plastic **de plástico** 3.1

plate **plato** *m.* 2.6
play **drama** *m.* 3.5; **comedia** *f.* 3.5 **jugar (u:ue)** *v.* 1.4; (*a musical instrument*) **tocar** *v.* 3.5; (*a role*) **hacer el papel de** 3.5; (*cards*) **jugar a (las cartas)** 1.5; (*sports*) **practicar deportes** 1.4
player **jugador(a)** *m., f.* 1.4
playwright **dramaturgo/a** *m., f.* 3.5
plead **rogar (o:ue)** *v.* 2.6
pleasant **agradable** *adj.*
please **por favor** 1.1
Pleased to meet you. **Mucho gusto.** 1.1; **Encantado/a.** *adj.* 1.1
pleasing: be pleasing to **gustar** *v.* 2.1
pleasure **gusto** *m.* 1.1; **placer** *m.*
   The pleasure is mine. **El gusto es mío.** 1.1
poem **poema** *m.* 3.5
poet **poeta** *m., f.* 3.5
poetry **poesía** *f.* 3.5
police (*force*) **policía** *f.* 2.5
political **político/a** *adj.* 3.6
politician **político/a** *m., f.* 3.4
politics **política** *f.* 3.6
polka-dotted **de lunares** 1.6
poll **encuesta** *f.* 3.6
pollute **contaminar** *v.* 3.1
polluted **contaminado/a** *m., f.* 3.1
   be polluted **estar contaminado/a** 3.1
pollution **contaminación** *f.* 3.1
pool **piscina** *f.* 1.4
poor **pobre** *adj., m., f.* 1.6
   poor thing **pobrecito/a** *adj.* 1.3
popsicle **paleta helada** *f.* 1.4
population **población** *f.* 3.1
pork **cerdo** *m.* 2.2
   pork chop **chuleta** *f.* **de cerdo** 2.2
portable **portátil** *adj.* 2.5
   portable computer **computadora** *f.* **portátil** 2.5
position **puesto** *m.* 3.4
possessive **posesivo/a** *adj.*
possible **posible** *adj.* 3.1
   it's (not) possible **(no) es posible** 3.1
post office **correo** *m.* 3.2
postcard **postal** *f.*
poster **cartel** *m.* 2.6
potato **papa** *f.* 2.2; **patata** *f.* 2.2
pottery **cerámica** *f.* 3.5
practice **entrenarse** *v.* 3.3; **practicar** *v.* 1.2; (*a degree/profession*) **ejercer** *v.* 3.4
prefer **preferir (e:ie)** *v.* 1.4
pregnant **embarazada** *adj. f.* 2.4
prepare **preparar** *v.* 1.2
preposition **preposición** *f.*
prescribe (*medicine*) **recetar** *v.* 2.4
prescription **receta** *f.* 2.4
present **regalo** *m.*; **presentar** *v.* 3.5

press **prensa** *f.* 3.6
pressure **presión** *f.*
  be under a lot of pressure **sufrir muchas presiones** 3.3
pretty **bonito/a** *adj.* 1.3
price **precio** *m.* 1.6
  (fixed, set) price **precio** *m.* **fijo** 1.6
print **imprimir** *v.* 2.5
printer **impresora** *f.* 2.5
prize **premio** *m.* 3.5
probable **probable** *adj.* 3.1
  it's (not) probable **(no) es probable** 3.1
problem **problema** *m.* 1.1
profession **profesión** *f.* 1.3; 3.4
professor **profesor(a)** *m., f.*
program **programa** *m.* 1.1
programmer **programador(a)** *m., f.* 1.3
prohibit **prohibir** *v.* 2.4
project **proyecto** *m.* 2.5
promotion (*career*) **ascenso** *m.* 3.4
pronoun **pronombre** *m.*
protect **proteger** *v.* 3.1
protein **proteína** *f.* 3.3
provided (that) **con tal (de) que** *conj.* 3.1
psychologist **psicólogo/a** *m., f.* 3.4
psychology **psicología** *f.* 1.2
publish **publicar** *v.* 3.5
Puerto Rican **puertorriqueño/a** *adj.* 1.3
purchases **compras** *f., pl.*
pure **puro/a** *adj.* 3.1
purple **morado/a** *adj.* 1.6
purse **bolsa** *f.* 1.6
put **poner** *v.* 1.4; **puesto/a** *p.p.* 3.2
  put (a letter) in the mailbox **echar (una carta) al buzón** 3.2
  put on (*a performance*) **presentar** *v.* 3.5
  put on (*clothing*) **ponerse** *v.* 2.1
  put on makeup **maquillarse** *v.* 2.1

Q

quality **calidad** *f.* 1.6
quarter (*academic*) **trimestre** *m.* 1.2
  quarter after (*time*) **y cuarto** 1.1; **y quince** 1.1
  quarter to (*time*) **menos cuarto** 1.1; **menos quince** 1.1
question **pregunta** *f.*
quickly **rápido** *adv.* 2.4
quiet **tranquilo/a** *adj.* 3.3
quit **dejar** *v.* 3.4
quiz **prueba** *f.* 1.2

R

racism **racismo** *m.* 3.6
radio (*medium*) **radio** *f.* 1.2
  radio (set) **radio** *m.* 2.5
rain **llover (o:ue)** *v.* 1.5; **lluvia** *f.*
  It's raining. **Llueve.** 1.5; **Está lloviendo.** 1.5
raincoat **impermeable** *m.* 1.6
rain forest **bosque** *m.* **tropical** 3.1
raise (*salary*) **aumento de sueldo** 3.4
rather **bastante** *adv.* 2.4
read **leer** *v.* 1.3; **leído/a** *p.p.* 3.2
  read e-mail **leer el correo electrónico** 1.4
  read a magazine **leer una revista** 1.4
  read a newspaper **leer un periódico** 1.4
ready **listo/a** *adj.* 1.5
reality show **programa de realidad** *m.* 3.5
reap the benefits (of) *v.* **disfrutar** *v.* **(de)** 3.3
receive **recibir** *v.* 1.3
recommend **recomendar (e:ie)** *v.* 2.2; 2.6
record **grabar** *v.* 2.5
recover **recuperar** *v.* 2.5
recreation **diversión** *f.* 1.4
recycle **reciclar** *v.* 3.1
recycling **reciclaje** *m.* 3.1
red **rojo/a** *adj.* 1.6
red-haired **pelirrojo/a** *adj.* 1.3
reduce **reducir** *v.* 3.1; **disminuir** *v.* 3.4
  reduce stress/tension **aliviar el estrés/la tensión** 3.3
refrigerator **refrigerador** *m.* 2.6
region **región** *f.*
regret **sentir (e:ie)** *v.* 3.1
relatives **parientes** *m., pl.* 1.3
relax **relajarse** *v.* 2.3
  Relax. **Tranquilo/a.** 2.1
  Relax, sweetie. **Tranquilo/a, cariño.** 2.5
remain **quedarse** *v.* 2.1
remember **acordarse (o:ue)** *v.* **(de)** 2.1; **recordar (o:ue)** *v.* 1.4
remote control **control remoto** *m.* 2.5
renewable **renovable** *adj.* 3.1
rent **alquilar** *v.* 2.6; (payment) **alquiler** *m.* 2.6
repeat **repetir (e:i)** *v.* 1.4
report **informe** *m.* 3.6; **reportaje** *m.* 3.6
reporter **reportero/a** *m., f.* 3.4
representative **representante** *m., f.* 3.6
request **pedir (e:i)** *v.* 1.4
reservation **reservación** *f.* 1.5
resign (from) **renunciar (a)** *v.* 3.4
resolve **resolver (o:ue)** *v.* 3.1
resolved **resuelto/a** *p.p.* 3.2
resource **recurso** *m.* 3.1
responsibility **deber** *m.* 3.6; **responsabilidad** *f.*
responsible **responsable** *adj.* 2.2
rest **descansar** *v.* 1.2
restaurant **restaurante** *m.* 1.4
résumé **currículum** *m.* 3.4
retire (from work) **jubilarse** *v.* 2.3
return **regresar** *v.* 1.2; **volver (o:ue)** *v.* 1.4
returned **vuelto/a** *p.p.* 3.2
rice **arroz** *m.* 2.2
rich **rico/a** *adj.* 1.6
ride a bicycle **pasear** *v.* **en bicicleta** 1.4
ride a horse **montar** *v.* **a caballo** 1.5
ridiculous **ridículo/a** *adj.* 3.1
  it's ridiculous **es ridículo** 3.1
right **derecha** *f.* 1.2
  be right **tener razón** 1.3
  right? (*question tag*) **¿no?** 1.1; **¿verdad?** 1.1
  right away **enseguida** *adv.*
  right now **ahora mismo** 1.5
  to the right of **a la derecha de** 1.2
rights **derechos** *m.* 3.6
ring **anillo** *m.* 3.5
ring (*a doorbell*) **sonar (o:ue)** *v.* 2.5
river **río** *m.* 3.1
road **carretera** *f.* 2.5; **camino** *m.*
roast **asado/a** *adj.* 2.2
roast chicken **pollo** *m.* **asado** 2.2
rollerblade **patinar en línea** *v.*
romantic **romántico/a** *adj.* 3.5
room **habitación** *f.* 1.5; **cuarto** *m.* 1.2; 2.1
  living room **sala** *f.* 2.6
roommate **compañero/a** *m., f.* **de cuarto** 1.2
roundtrip **de ida y vuelta** 1.5
  roundtrip ticket **pasaje** *m.* **de ida y vuelta** 1.5
routine **rutina** *f.* 2.1
rug **alfombra** *f.* 2.6
run **correr** *v.* 1.3
  run errands **hacer diligencias** 3.2
  run into (*have an accident*) **chocar (con)** *v.*; (*meet accidentally*) **encontrar(se) (o:ue)** *v.* 2.5; (*run into something*) **darse (con)** 2.4
  run into (each other) **encontrar(se) (o:ue)** *v.* 2.5
rush **apurarse, darse prisa** *v.* 3.3
Russian **ruso/a** *adj.* 1.3

S

sad **triste** adj. 1.5; 3.1
  it's sad **es triste** 3.1
safe **seguro/a** adj. 1.5
said **dicho/a** p.p. 3.2
sailboard **tabla de windsurf** f. 1.5
salad **ensalada** f. 2.2
salary **salario** m. 3.4; **sueldo** m. 3.4
sale **rebaja** f. 1.6
salesperson **vendedor(a)** m., f. 1.6
salmon **salmón** m. 2.2
salt **sal** f. 2.2
same **mismo/a** adj. 1.3
sandal **sandalia** f. 1.6
sandwich **sándwich** m. 2.2
Saturday **sábado** m. 1.2
sausage **salchicha** f. 2.2
save (*on a computer*) **guardar** v. 2.5; save (*money*) **ahorrar** v. 3.2
savings **ahorros** m. 3.2
  savings account **cuenta** f. **de ahorros** 3.2
say **decir** v. 1.4; **declarar** v. 3.6
say (that) **decir (que)** v. 1.4
  say the answer **decir la respuesta** 1.4
scan **escanear** v. 2.5
scarcely **apenas** adv. 2.4
scared: be (very) scared (of) **tener (mucho) miedo (de)** 1.3
schedule **horario** m. 1.2
school **escuela** f. 1.1
sciences f., pl. **ciencias** 1.2
science fiction (genre) **de ciencia ficción** 3.5
scientist **científico/a** m., f. 3.4
scream **grito** m. 1.5; **gritar** v.
screen **pantalla** f. 2.5
scuba dive **bucear** v. 1.4
sculpt **esculpir** v. 3.5
sculptor **escultor(a)** m., f. 3.5
sculpture **escultura** f. 3.5
sea **mar** m. 1.5
  (sea) turtle **tortuga (marina)** f. 3.1
season **estación** f. 1.5
seat **silla** f. 1.2
second **segundo/a** 1.5
secretary **secretario/a** m., f. 3.4
sedentary **sedentario/a** adj. 3.3
see **ver** v. 1.4
  see (you, him, her) again **volver a ver(te, lo, la)**
  see movies **ver películas** 1.4
  See you. **Nos vemos.** 1.1
  See you later. **Hasta la vista.** 1.1; **Hasta luego.** 1.1
  See you soon. **Hasta pronto.** 1.1
  See you tomorrow. **Hasta mañana.** 1.1
seem **parecer** v. 1.6
seen **visto/a** p.p. 3.2
sell **vender** v. 1.6
semester **semestre** m. 1.2
send **enviar; mandar** v. 3.2
separate (from) **separarse** v. **(de)** 2.3

separated **separado/a** adj. 2.3
September **septiembre** m. 1.5
sequence **secuencia** f.
serious **grave** adj. 2.4
serve **servir (e:i)** v. 2.2
service **servicio** m. 3.3
set (*fixed*) **fijo/a** adj. 1.6
  set the table **poner la mesa** 2.6
seven **siete** 1.1
seven hundred **setecientos/as** 1.2
seventeen **diecisiete** 1.1
seventh **séptimo/a** 1.5
seventy **setenta** 1.2
several **varios/as** adj. pl.
sexism **sexismo** m. 3.6
shame **lástima** f. 3.1
  it's a shame **es una lástima** 3.1
shampoo **champú** m. 2.1
shape **forma** f. 3.3
  be in good shape **estar en buena forma** 3.3
  stay in shape **mantenerse en forma** 3.3
share **compartir** v. 1.3
sharp (*time*) **en punto** 1.1
shave **afeitarse** v. 2.1
shaving cream **crema** f. **de afeitar** 1.5, 2.1
she **ella** 1.1
shellfish **mariscos** m., pl. 2.2
ship **barco** m.
shirt **camisa** f. 1.6
shoe **zapato** m. 1.6
  shoe size **número** m. 1.6
  shoe store **zapatería** f. 3.2
    tennis shoes **zapatos** m., pl. **de tenis** 1.6
shop **tienda** f. 1.6
shopping, to go **ir de compras** 1.5
  shopping mall **centro comercial** m. 1.6
short (*in height*) **bajo/a** adj. 1.3; (*in length*) **corto/a** adj. 1.6
short story **cuento** m. 3.5
shorts **pantalones cortos** m., pl. 1.6
should (*do something*) **deber** v. (+ *inf.*) 1.3
shout **gritar** v.
show **espectáculo** m. 3.5; **mostrar (o:ue)** v. 1.4
  game show **concurso** m. 3.5
shower **ducha** f. 2.1; **ducharse** v. 2.1
shrimp **camarón** m. 2.2
siblings **hermanos/as** pl. 1.3
sick **enfermo/a** adj. 2.4
  be sick **estar enfermo/a** 2.4
  get sick **enfermarse** v. 2.4
sign **firmar** v. 3.2; **letrero** m. 3.2
silk **seda** f. 1.6
  (made of) silk **de seda** 1.6
since **desde** prep.
sing **cantar** v. 1.2
singer **cantante** m., f. 3.5
single **soltero/a** adj. 2.3
  single room **habitación** f. **individual** 1.5
sink **lavabo** m. 2.1
sir **señor (Sr.), don** m. 1.1; **caballero** m. 2.2

sister **hermana** f. 1.3
sister-in-law **cuñada** f. 1.3
sit down **sentarse (e:ie)** v. 2.1
six **seis** 1.1
six hundred **seiscientos/as** 1.2
sixteen **dieciséis** 1.1
sixth **sexto/a** 1.5
sixty **sesenta** 1.2
size **talla** f. 1.6
  shoe size m. **número** 1.6
(in-line) skate **patinar (en línea)** 1.4
skateboard **andar en patineta** v. 1.4
ski **esquiar** v. 1.4
skiing **esquí** m. 1.4
  water-skiing **esquí** m. **acuático** 1.4
skirt **falda** f. 1.6
skull made out of sugar **calavera de azúcar** f. 2.3
sky **cielo** m. 3.1
sleep **dormir (o:ue)** v. 1.4; **sueño** m.
  go to sleep **dormirse (o:ue)** v. 2.1
sleepy: be (very) sleepy **tener (mucho) sueño** 1.3
slender **delgado/a** adj. 1.3
slim down **adelgazar** v. 3.3
slippers **pantuflas** f. 2.1
slow **lento/a** adj. 2.5
slowly **despacio** adv. 2.4
small **pequeño/a** adj. 1.3
smart **listo/a** adj. 1.5
smile **sonreír (e:i)** v. 2.3
smiled **sonreído** p.p. 3.2
smoggy: It's (very) smoggy. **Hay (mucha) contaminación.**
smoke **fumar** v. 3.3
  (not) to smoke **(no) fumar** 3.3
smoking section **sección** f. **de fumar** 2.2
  (non) smoking section f. **sección de (no) fumar** 2.2
snack **merendar (e:ie)** v. 2.2
  afternoon snack **merienda** f. 3.3
  have a snack **merendar** v. 2.2
sneakers **los zapatos de tenis** 1.6
sneeze **estornudar** v. 2.4
snow **nevar (e:ie)** v. 1.5; **nieve** f.
snowing: It's snowing. **Nieva.** 1.5; **Está nevando.** 1.5
so (*in such a way*) **así** adv. 2.4; **tan** adv. 1.5
  so much **tanto** adv.
  so-so **regular** 1.1
  so that **para que** conj. 3.1
soap **jabón** m. 2.1
soap opera **telenovela** f. 3.5
soccer **fútbol** m. 1.4
sociology **sociología** f. 1.2
sock(s) **calcetín (calcetines)** m. 1.6
sofa **sofá** m. 2.6
soft drink **refresco** m. 2.2
software **programa** m. **de computación** 2.5
soil **tierra** f. 3.1
solar **solar** adj., m., f. 3.1
  solar energy **energía solar** 3.1

Vocabulario

English-Spanish

soldier **soldado** *m., f.* 3.6
solution **solución** *f.* 3.1
solve **resolver (o:ue)** *v.* 3.1
some **algún, alguno/a(s)**
    adj. 2.1; **unos/as** *indef. art.* 1.1
somebody **alguien** *pron.* 2.1
someone **alguien** *pron.* 2.1
something **algo** *pron.* 2.1
sometimes **a veces** *adv.* 2.4
son **hijo** *m.* 1.3
song **canción** *f.* 3.5
son-in-law **yerno** *m.* 1.3
soon **pronto** *adv.* 2.4
    See you soon. **Hasta pronto.** 1.1
sorry: be sorry **sentir (e:ie)** *v.* 3.1
    I'm sorry. **Lo siento.** 1.1
soul **alma** *f.* 2.3
soup **sopa** *f.* 2.2
south **sur** *m.* 3.2
    to the south **al sur** 3.2
Spain **España** *f.*
Spanish (*language*) **español** *m.* 1.2; **español(a)** *adj.* 1.3
spare (free) time **ratos libres** 1.4
speak **hablar** *v.* 1.2
    Speaking. (*on the telephone*) **Con él/ella habla.** 2.5
special: today's specials **las especialidades del día** 2.2
spectacular **espectacular** *adj. m., f.*
speech **discurso** *m.* 3.6
speed **velocidad** *f.* 2.5
    speed limit **velocidad** *f.* **máxima** 2.5
spelling **ortografía** *f.*, **ortográfico/a** *adj.*
spend (*money*) **gastar** *v.* 1.6
spoon (*table or large*) **cuchara** *f.* 2.6
sport **deporte** *m.* 1.4
    sports-related **deportivo/a** *adj.* 1.4
spouse **esposo/a** *m., f.* 1.3
sprain (one's ankle) **torcerse (o:ue)** *v.* **(el tobillo)** 2.4
spring **primavera** *f.* 1.5
(city or town) square **plaza** *f.* 1.4
stadium **estadio** *m.* 1.2
stage **etapa** *f.* 2.3
stairs **escalera** *f.* 2.6
stairway **escalera** *f.* 2.6
stamp **estampilla** *f.* 3.2; **sello** *m.* 3.2
stand in line **hacer** *v.* **cola** 3.2
star **estrella** *f.* 3.1
start (*a vehicle*) **arrancar** *v.* 2.5
station **estación** *f.* 1.5
statue **estatua** *f.* 3.5
status: marital status **estado** *m.* **civil** 2.3
stay **quedarse** *v.* 2.1
    stay in shape **mantenerse en forma** 3.3
steak **bistec** *m.* 2.2
steering wheel **volante** *m.* 2.5
step **escalón** *m.* 3.3
stepbrother **hermanastro** *m.* 1.3

stepdaughter **hijastra** *f.* 1.3
stepfather **padrastro** *m.* 1.3
stepmother **madrastra** *f.* 1.3
stepsister **hermanastra** *f.* 1.3
stepson **hijastro** *m.* 1.3
stereo **estéreo** *m.* 2.5
still **todavía** *adv.* 1.5
stockbroker **corredor(a)** *m., f.* **de bolsa** 3.4
stockings **medias** *f., pl.* 1.6
stomach **estómago** *m.* 2.4
stone **piedra** *f.* 3.1
stop **parar** *v.* 2.5
    stop (*doing something*) **dejar de (+ *inf.*)** 3.1
store **tienda** *f.* 1.6
storm **tormenta** *f.* 3.6
story **cuento** *m.* 3.5; **historia** *f.* 3.5
stove **cocina, estufa** *f.* 2.6
straight **derecho** *adv.* 3.2
    straight (ahead) **derecho** 3.2
straighten up **arreglar** *v.* 2.6
strange **extraño/a** *adj.* 3.1
    it's strange **es extraño** 3.1
street **calle** *f.* 2.5
stress **estrés** *m.* 3.3
stretching **estiramiento** *m.* 3.3
    do stretching exercises **hacer ejercicios** *m. pl.* **de estiramiento** 3.3
strike (*labor*) **huelga** *f.* 3.6
striped **de rayas** 1.6
stroll **pasear** *v.* 1.4
strong **fuerte** *adj. m., f.* 3.3
struggle (for/against) **luchar** *v.* **(por/contra)** 3.6
student **estudiante** *m., f.* 1.1; 1.2; **estudiantil** *adj.* 1.2
study **estudiar** *v.* 1.2
stupendous **estupendo/a** *adj.* 1.5
style **estilo** *m.*
suburbs **afueras** *f., pl.* 2.6
subway **metro** *m.* 1.5
    subway station **estación** *f.* **del metro** 1.5
success **éxito** *m.*
successful: be successful **tener éxito** 3.4
such as **tales como**
suddenly **de repente** *adv.* 1.6
suffer **sufrir** *v.* 2.4
    suffer an illness **sufrir una enfermedad** 2.4
sugar **azúcar** *m.* 2.2
suggest **sugerir (e:ie)** *v.* 2.6
suit **traje** *m.* 1.6
suitcase **maleta** *f.* 1.1
summer **verano** *m.* 1.5
sun **sol** *m.* 3.1
sunbathe **tomar** *v.* **el sol** 1.4
Sunday **domingo** *m.* 1.2
(sun)glasses **gafas** *f., pl.* **(de sol)** 1.6
sunny: It's (very) sunny. **Hace (mucho) sol.** 1.5
supermarket **supermercado** *m.* 3.2

suppose **suponer** *v.* 1.4
sure **seguro/a** *adj.* 1.5
    be sure **estar seguro/a** 1.5
surf **hacer** *v.* **surf** 1.5; (*the Internet*) **navegar** *v.* **(en Internet)** 2.5
surfboard **tabla de surf** *f.* 1.5
surprise **sorprender** *v.* 2.3; **sorpresa** *f.* 2.3
survey **encuesta** *f.* 3.6
sweat **sudar** *v.* 3.3
sweater **suéter** *m.* 1.6
sweep the floor **barrer el suelo** 2.6
sweets **dulces** *m., pl.* 2.3
swim **nadar** *v.* 1.4
swimming **natación** *f.* 1.4
    swimming pool **piscina** *f.* 1.4
symptom **síntoma** *m.* 2.4

T

table **mesa** *f.* 1.2
tablespoon **cuchara** *f.* 2.6
tablet (*pill*) **pastilla** *f.* 2.4
take **tomar** *v.* 1.2; **llevar** *v.* 1.6
    take care of **cuidar** *v.* 3.1
    take someone's temperature **tomar** *v.* **la temperatura** 2.4
    take (*wear*) a shoe size **calzar** *v.* 1.6
    take a bath **bañarse** *v.* 2.1
    take a shower **ducharse** *v.* 2.1
    take off **quitarse** *v.* 2.1
    take out the trash *v.* **sacar la basura** 2.6
    take photos **tomar** *v.* **fotos** 1.5; **sacar** *v.* **fotos** 1.5
talented **talentoso/a** *adj.* 3.5
talk **hablar** *v.* 1.2
    talk show **programa** *m.* **de entrevistas** 3.5
tall **alto/a** *adj.* 1.3
tank **tanque** *m.* 2.5
taste **probar (o:ue)** *v.* 2.2
    taste like **saber a** 2.2
tasty **rico/a** *adj.* 2.2; **sabroso/a** *adj.* 2.2
tax **impuesto** *m.* 3.6
taxi **taxi** *m.* 1.5
tea **té** *m.* 2.2
teach **enseñar** *v.* 1.2
teacher **profesor(a)** *m., f.* 1.1, 1.2; **maestro/a** *m., f.* 3.4
team **equipo** *m.* 1.4
technician **técnico/a** *m., f.* 3.4
telecommuting **teletrabajo** *m.* 3.4
telephone **teléfono** 2.5
television **televisión** *f.* 1.2
    television set **televisor** *m.* 2.5
tell **contar** *v.* 1.4; **decir** *v.* 1.4
tell (that) **decir** *v.* **(que)** 1.4
    tell lies **decir mentiras** 1.4
    tell the truth **decir la verdad** 1.4
temperature **temperatura** *f.* 2.4
ten **diez** 1.1
tennis **tenis** *m.* 1.4

Vocabulario

English-Spanish

tennis shoes **zapatos** *m., pl.* **de tenis** 1.6
tension **tensión** *f.* 3.3
tent **tienda** *f.* **de campaña**
tenth **décimo/a** 1.5
terrible **terrible** *adj. m., f.* 3.1
   it's terrible **es terrible** 3.1
terrific **chévere** *adj.*
test **prueba** *f.* 1.2; **examen** *m.* 1.2
text message **mensaje** *m.* **de texto** 2.5
Thank you. **Gracias.** *f., pl.* 1.1
   Thank you (very much). **(Muchas) gracias.** 1.1
   Thanks (a lot). **(Muchas) gracias.** 1.1
   Thanks for inviting me. **Gracias por invitarme.** 2.3
that **que, quien(es)** *pron.* 2.6
   that (one) **ése, ésa, eso** *pron.* 1.6; **ese, esa,** *adj.* 1.6
   that (over there) **aquél, aquélla, aquello** *pron.* 1.6; **aquel, aquella** *adj.* 1.6
   that which **lo que** 2.6
   that's why **por eso** 2.5
the **el** *m.,* **la** *f. sing.,* **los** *m.,* **las** *f., pl.* 1.1
theater **teatro** *m.* 3.5
their **su(s)** *poss. adj.* 1.3; **suyo(s)/a(s)** *poss. pron.* 2.5
them **los/las** *pl., d.o. pron.* 1.5
   to/for them **les** *pl., i.o. pron.* 1.6
then (afterward) **después** *adv.* 2.1; (as a result) **entonces** *adv.* 1.5, 2.1; (next) **luego** *adv.* 2.1
there **allí** *adv.* 1.2
   There is/are... **Hay...** 1.1
   There is/are not... **No hay...** 1.1
therefore **por eso** 2.5
these **éstos, éstas** *pron.* 1.6; **estos, estas,** *adj.* 1.6
they **ellos** *m.,* **ellas** *f. pron.* 1.1
   They all told me to ask you to excuse them/forgive them. **Todos me dijeron que te pidiera una disculpa de su parte.** 3.6
thin **delgado/a** *adj.* 1.3
thing **cosa** *f.* 1.1
think **pensar (e:ie)** *v.* 1.4; (believe) **creer** *v.*
   think about **pensar en** *v.* 1.4
third **tercero/a** 1.5
thirst **sed** *f.*
thirsty: be (very) thirsty **tener (mucha) sed** 1.3
thirteen **trece** 1.1
thirty **treinta** 1.1; thirty (minutes past the hour) **y treinta; y media** 1.1
this **este, esta** *adj.;* **éste, ésta, esto** *pron.* 1.6
those **ésos, ésas** *pron.* 1.6; **esos, esas** *adj.* 1.6
those (over there) **aquéllos, aquéllas** *pron.* 1.6; **aquellos, aquellas** *adj.* 1.6
thousand **mil** *m.* 1.2
three **tres** 1.1
three hundred **trescientos/as** 1.2
throat **garganta** *f.* 2.4
through **por** *prep.* 2.5
Thursday **jueves** *m., sing.* 1.2
thus (in such a way) **así** *adv.*
ticket **boleto** *m.* 1.2, 3.5; **pasaje** *m.* 1.5
tie **corbata** *f.* 1.6
time **vez** *f.* 1.6; **tiempo** *m.* 3.2
   have a good/bad time **pasarlo bien/mal** 2.3
   I've had a fantastic time. **Lo he pasado de película.** 3.6
   What time is it? **¿Qué hora es?** 1.1
   (At) What time...? **¿A qué hora...?** 1.1
times **veces** *f., pl.* 1.6
   many times **muchas veces** 2.4
   two times **dos veces** 1.6
tip **propina** *f.* 2.2
tire **llanta** *f.* 2.5
tired **cansado/a** *adj.* 1.5
   be tired **estar cansado/a** 1.5
title **título** *m.* 3.4
to **a** *prep.* 1.1
toast (drink) **brindar** *v.* 2.3
   toast **pan** *m.* **tostado** 2.2
toasted **tostado/a** *adj.* 2.2
   toasted bread **pan tostado** *m.* 2.2
toaster **tostadora** *f.* 2.6
today **hoy** *adv.* 1.2
   Today is... **Hoy es...** 1.2
toe **dedo** *m.* **del pie** 2.4
together **juntos/as** *adj.* 2.3
toilet **inodoro** *m.* 2.1
tomato **tomate** *m.* 2.2
tomorrow **mañana** *f.* 1.1
   See you tomorrow. **Hasta mañana.** 1.1
tonight **esta noche** *adv.*
too **también** *adv.* 1.2; 2.1
   too much **demasiado** *adv.* 1.6; **en exceso** 3.3
tooth **diente** *m.* 2.1
toothpaste **pasta** *f.* **de dientes** 2.1
top **cima** *f.* 3.3
tornado **tornado** *m.* 3.6
touch **tocar** *v.* 3.5
touch screen **pantalla táctil** *f.*
tour **excursión** *f.* 1.4; **recorrido** *m.* 3.1
tour an area **recorrer** *v.*
tourism **turismo** *m.*
tourist **turista** *m., f.* 1.1; **turístico/a** *adj.*
toward **hacia** *prep.* 3.2; **para** *prep.* 2.5
towel **toalla** *f.* 2.1
town **pueblo** *m.*
trade **oficio** *m.* 3.4
traffic **circulación** *f.* 2.5; **tráfico** *m.* 2.5
   traffic light **semáforo** *m.* 3.2
tragedy **tragedia** *f.* 3.5
trail **sendero** *m.* 3.1
train **entrenarse** *v.* 3.3; **tren** *m.* 1.5
train station **estación** *f.* **de tren** *m.* 1.5
trainer **entrenador(a)** *m., f.* 3.3
translate **traducir** *v.* 1.6
trash **basura** *f.* 2.6
travel **viajar** *v.* 1.2
   travel agency **agencia** *f.* **de viajes** 1.5
   travel agent **agente** *m., f.* **de viajes** 1.5
traveler **viajero/a** *m., f.* 1.5
   (traveler's) check **cheque (de viajero)** 3.2
treadmill **cinta caminadora** *f.* 3.3
tree **árbol** *m.* 3.1
trillion **billón** *m.*
trimester **trimestre** *m.* 1.2
trip **viaje** *m.* 1.5
   take a trip **hacer un viaje** 1.5
tropical forest **bosque** *m.* **tropical** 3.1
true: it's (not) true **(no) es verdad** 3.1
trunk **baúl** *m.* 2.5
truth **verdad** *f.* 1.4
try **intentar** *v.;* **probar (o:ue)** *v.* 2.2
   try (to do something) **tratar de (+ inf.)** 3.3
   try on **probarse (o:ue)** *v.* 2.1
t-shirt **camiseta** *f.* 1.6
Tuesday **martes** *m., sing.* 1.2
tuna **atún** *m.* 2.2
turkey **pavo** *m.* 2.2
turn **doblar** *v.* 3.2
   turn off (electricity/appliance) **apagar** *v.* 2.5
   turn on (electricity/appliance) **poner** *v.* 2.5; **prender** *v.* 2.5
twelve **doce** 1.1
twenty **veinte** 1.1
twenty-eight **veintiocho** 1.1
twenty-five **veinticinco** 1.1
twenty-four **veinticuatro** 1.1
twenty-nine **veintinueve** 1.1
twenty-one **veintiuno** 1.1; **veintiún, veintiuno/a** *adj.* 1.1
twenty-seven **veintisiete** 1.1
twenty-six **veintiséis** 1.1
twenty-three **veintitrés** 1.1
twenty-two **veintidós** 1.1
twice **dos veces** 1.6
twin **gemelo/a** *m., f.* 1.3
two **dos** 1.1
   two hundred **doscientos/as** 1.2
   two times **dos veces** 1.6

U

ugly **feo/a** *adj.* 1.3
uncle **tío** *m.* 1.3
under **debajo de** *prep.* 1.2
understand **comprender** *v.* 1.3; **entender (e:ie)** *v.* 1.4
underwear **ropa interior** 1.6
unemployment **desempleo** *m.* 3.6

Vocabulario

English-Spanish

unique **único/a** *adj.* 2.3
United States **Estados Unidos (EE.UU.)** *m. pl.*
university **universidad** *f.* 1.2
unless **a menos que** *conj.* 3.1
unmarried **soltero/a** *adj.* 2.3
unpleasant **antipático/a** *adj.* 1.3
until **hasta** *prep.* 1.6; **hasta que** *conj.* 3.1
urgent **urgente** *adj.* 2.6
    It's urgent that… **Es urgente que…** 2.6
us **nos** *pl., d.o. pron.* 1.5
    to/for us **nos** *pl., i.o. pron.* 1.6
use **usar** *v.* 1.6
used for **para** *prep.* 2.5
useful **útil** *adj. m., f.*

V

vacation **vacaciones** *f., pl.* 1.5
    be on vacation **estar de vacaciones** 1.5
    go on vacation **ir de vacaciones** 1.5
vacuum **pasar** *v.* **la aspiradora** 2.6
    vacuum cleaner **aspiradora** *f.* 2.6
valley **valle** *m.* 3.1
various **varios/as** *adj. m., f. pl.*
vegetables **verduras** *pl., f.* 2.2
verb **verbo** *m.*
very **muy** *adv.* 1.1
    (Very) well, thank you. **(Muy) bien, gracias.** 1.1
video **video** *m.* 1.1
    video camera **cámara** *f.* **de video** 2.5
    video game **videojuego** *m.* 1.4
videoconference **videoconferencia** *f.* 3.4
vinegar **vinagre** *m.* 2.2
violence **violencia** *f.* 3.6
visit **visitar** *v.* 1.4
    visit monuments **visitar monumentos** 1.4
vitamin **vitamina** *f.* 3.3
voice mail **correo de voz** *m.* 2.5
volcano **volcán** *m.* 3.1
volleyball **vóleibol** *m.* 1.4
vote **votar** *v.* 3.6

W

wait (for) **esperar** *v.* **(+ *inf.*)** 1.2
waiter/waitress **camarero/a** *m., f.* 2.2
wake up **despertarse (e:ie)** *v.* 2.1
walk **caminar** *v.* 1.2
    take a walk **pasear** *v.* 1.4
    walk around **pasear por** 1.4
wall **pared** *f.* 2.6; **muro** *m.* 3.3
wallet **cartera** *f.* 1.4, 1.6

want **querer (e:ie)** *v.* 1.4
war **guerra** *f.* 3.6
warm up **calentarse (e:ie)** *v.* 3.3
wash **lavar** *v.* 2.6
    wash one's face/hands **lavarse la cara/las manos** 2.1
    wash (the floor, the dishes) **lavar (el suelo, los platos)** 2.6
    wash oneself **lavarse** *v.* 2.1
washing machine **lavadora** *f.* 2.6
wastebasket **papelera** *f.* 1.2
watch **mirar** *v.* 1.2; **reloj** *m.* 1.2
    watch television **mirar (la) televisión** 1.2
water **agua** *f.* 2.2
    water pollution **contaminación del agua** 3.1
    water-skiing **esquí** *m.* **acuático** 1.4
way **manera** *f.*
we **nosotros(as)** *m., f.* 1.1
weak **débil** *adj. m., f.* 3.3
wear **llevar** *v.* 1.6; **usar** *v.* 1.6
weather **tiempo** *m.*
    The weather is bad. **Hace mal tiempo.** 1.5
    The weather is good. **Hace buen tiempo.** 1.5
weaving **tejido** *m.* 3.5
Web **red** *f.* 2.5
website **sitio** *m.* **web** 2.5
wedding **boda** *f.* 2.3
Wednesday **miércoles** *m., sing.* 1.2
week **semana** *f.* 1.2
weekend **fin** *m.* **de semana** 1.4
weight **peso** *m.* 3.3
    lift weights **levantar** *v.* **pesas** *f., pl.* 3.3
welcome **bienvenido(s)/a(s)** *adj.* 1.1
well: (Very) well, thanks. **(Muy) bien, gracias.** 1.1
well-being **bienestar** *m.* 3.3
well organized **ordenado/a** *adj.* 1.5
west **oeste** *m.* 3.2
    to the west **al oeste** 3.2
western (*genre*) **de vaqueros** 3.5
whale **ballena** *f.* 3.1
what **lo que** *pron.* 2.6
what? **¿qué?** 1.1
    At what time…? **¿A qué hora…?** 1.1
    What a pleasure to…! **¡Qué gusto (+ *inf.*)…!** 3.6
    What day is it? **¿Qué día es hoy?** 1.2
    What do you guys think? **¿Qué les parece?**
    What happened? **¿Qué pasó?**
    What is today's date? **¿Cuál es la fecha de hoy?** 1.5
    What nice clothes! **¡Qué ropa más bonita!** 1.6
    What size do you wear? **¿Qué talla lleva (usa)?** 1.6

What time is it? **¿Qué hora es?** 1.1
What's going on? **¿Qué pasa?** 1.1
What's happening? **¿Qué pasa?** 1.1
What's… like? **¿Cómo es…?**
What's new? **¿Qué hay de nuevo?** 1.1
What's the weather like? **¿Qué tiempo hace?** 1.5
What's up? **¿Qué onda?** 3.2
What's wrong? **¿Qué pasó?**
What's your name? **¿Cómo se llama usted?** *form.* 1.1; **¿Cómo te llamas (tú)?** *fam.* 1.1
when **cuando** *conj.* 2.1; 3.1
When? **¿Cuándo?** 1.2
where **donde**
where (to)? (*destination*) **¿adónde?** 1.2; (*location*) **¿dónde?** 1.1, 1.2
    Where are you from? **¿De dónde eres (tú)?** (*fam.*) 1.1; **¿De dónde es (usted)?** (*form.*) 1.1
    Where is…? **¿Dónde está…?** 1.2
which **que** *pron.*, **lo que** *pron.* 2.6
which? **¿cuál?** 1.2; **¿qué?** 1.2
    In which…? **¿En qué…?**
    which one(s)? **¿cuál(es)?** 1.2
while **mientras** *conj.* 2.4
who **que** *pron.* 2.6; **quien(es)** *pron.* 2.6
who? **¿quién(es)?** 1.1, 1.2
Who is…? **¿Quién es…?** 1.1
    Who is speaking/calling? (*on telephone*) **¿De parte de quién?** 2.5
    Who is speaking? (*on telephone*) **¿Quién habla?** 2.5
whole **todo/a** *adj.*
whom **quien(es)** *pron.* 2.6
whose? **¿de quién(es)?** 1.1
why? **¿por qué?** 1.2
widower/widow **viudo/a** *adj.* 2.3
wife **esposa** *f.* 1.3
win **ganar** *v.* 1.4
wind **viento** *m.*
window **ventana** *f.* 1.2
windshield **parabrisas** *m., sing.* 2.5
windsurf **hacer** *v.* **windsurf** 1.5
windy: It's (very) windy. **Hace (mucho) viento.** 1.5
winter **invierno** *m.* 1.5
wireless connection **conexión inalámbrica** *f.* 2.5
wish **desear** *v.* 1.2; **esperar** *v.* 3.1
    I wish (that) **ojalá (que)** 3.1
with **con** *prep.* 1.2
    with me **conmigo** 1.4; 2.3
    with you **contigo** *fam.* 1.5, 2.3
within (ten years) **dentro de (diez años)** *prep.* 3.4
without **sin** *prep.* 1.2; **sin que** *conj.* 3.1
woman **mujer** *f.* 1.1

Vocabulario — English-Spanish

wool **lana** *f.* 1.6
  (made of) wool **de lana** 1.6
word **palabra** *f.* 1.1
work **trabajar** *v.* 1.2; **funcionar** *v.* 2.5; **trabajo** *m.* 3.4
  work (*of art, literature, music, etc.*) **obra** *f.* 3.5
  work out **hacer gimnasia** 3.3
world **mundo** *m.* 2.2
worldwide **mundial** *adj. m., f.*
worried (about) **preocupado/a (por)** *adj.* 1.5
worry (about) **preocuparse** *v.* **(por)** 2.1
  Don't worry. **No te preocupes.** *fam.* 2.1
worse **peor** *adj. m., f.* 2.2
worst **el/la peor** 2.2
Would you like to…? **¿Te gustaría…?** *fam.*
Would you do me the honor of marrying me? **¿Me harías el honor de casarte conmigo?** 3.5
wow **híjole** *interj.* 1.6
wrench **llave** *f.* 2.5
write **escribir** *v.* 1.3
  write a letter/an e-mail **escribir una carta/un mensaje electrónico** 1.4
writer **escritor(a)** *m., f* 3.5
written **escrito/a** *p.p.* 3.2
wrong **equivocado/a** *adj.* 1.5
  be wrong **no tener razón** 1.3

X

X-ray **radiografía** *f.* 2.4

Y

yard **jardín** *m.* 2.6; **patio** *m.* 2.6
year **año** *m.* 1.5
  be… years old **tener… años** 1.3
yellow **amarillo/a** *adj.* 1.6
yes **sí** *interj.* 1.1
yesterday **ayer** *adv.* 1.6
yet **todavía** *adv.* 1.5
yogurt **yogur** *m.* 2.2
you **tú** *fam.* **usted (Ud.)** *form. sing.* **vosotros/as** *m., f. fam. pl.* **ustedes (Uds.)** *pl.* 1.1; (to, for) you *fam. sing.* **te** *pl.* **os** 1.6; *form. sing.* **le** *pl.* **les** 1.6
you **te** *fam., sing.,* **lo/la** *form., sing.,* **os** *fam., pl.,* **los/las** *pl, d.o. pron.* 1.5
You don't say! **¡No me digas!** *fam.;* **¡No me diga!** *form.*
You're welcome. **De nada.** 1.1; **No hay de qué.** 1.1
young **joven** *adj., sing.* (**jóvenes** *pl.*) 1.3
  young person **joven** *m., f., sing.* (**jóvenes** *pl.*) 1.1
  young woman **señorita (Srta.)** *f.*
younger **menor** *adj. m., f.* 1.3
younger: younger brother, sister *m., f.* **hermano/a menor** 1.3
youngest **el/la menor** *m., f.* 2.2
your **su(s)** *poss. adj. form.* 1.3; **tu(s)** *poss. adj. fam. sing.* 1.3; **vuestro/a(s)** *poss. adj. fam. pl.* 1.3
your(s) *form.* **suyo(s)/a(s)** *poss. pron. form.* 2.5; **tuyo(s)/a(s)** *poss. fam. sing.* 2.5; **vuestro(s)/a(s)** *poss. fam.* 2.5
youth *f.* **juventud** 2.3

Z

zero **cero** *m.* 1.1

MATERIAS — ACADEMIC SUBJECTS

la administración de empresas	business administration
la agronomía	agriculture
el alemán	German
el álgebra	algebra
la antropología	anthropology
la arqueología	archaeology
la arquitectura	architecture
el arte	art
la astronomía	astronomy
la biología	biology
la bioquímica	biochemistry
la botánica	botany
el cálculo	calculus
el chino	Chinese
las ciencias políticas	political science
la computación	computer science
las comunicaciones	communications
la contabilidad	accounting
la danza	dance
el derecho	law
la economía	economics
la educación	education
la educación física	physical education
la enfermería	nursing
el español	Spanish
la filosofía	philosophy
la física	physics
el francés	French
la geografía	geography
la geología	geology
el griego	Greek
el hebreo	Hebrew
la historia	history
la informática	computer science
la ingeniería	engineering
el inglés	English
el italiano	Italian
el japonés	Japanese
el latín	Latin
las lenguas clásicas	classical languages
las lenguas romances	Romance languages
la lingüística	linguistics
la literatura	literature
las matemáticas	mathematics
la medicina	medicine
el mercadeo/ la mercadotecnia	marketing
la música	music
los negocios	business
el periodismo	journalism
el portugués	Portuguese
la psicología	psychology
la química	chemistry
el ruso	Russian
los servicios sociales	social services
la sociología	sociology
el teatro	theater
la trigonometría	trigonometry

LOS ANIMALES — ANIMALS

la abeja	bee
la araña	spider
la ardilla	squirrel
el ave (f.), el pájaro	bird
la ballena	whale
el burro	donkey
la cabra	goat
el caimán	alligator
el camello	camel
la cebra	zebra
el ciervo, el venado	deer
el cochino, el cerdo, el puerco	pig
el cocodrilo	crocodile
el conejo	rabbit
el coyote	coyote
la culebra, la serpiente, la víbora	snake
el elefante	elephant
la foca	seal
la gallina	hen
el gallo	rooster
el gato	cat
el gorila	gorilla
el hipopótamo	hippopotamus
la hormiga	ant
el insecto	insect
la jirafa	giraffe
el lagarto	lizard
el león	lion
el lobo	wolf
el loro, la cotorra, el papagayo, el perico	parrot
la mariposa	butterfly
el mono	monkey
la mosca	fly
el mosquito	mosquito
el oso	bear
la oveja	sheep
el pato	duck
el perro	dog
el pez	fish
la rana	frog
el ratón	mouse
el rinoceronte	rhinoceros
el saltamontes, el chapulín	grasshopper
el tiburón	shark
el tigre	tiger
el toro	bull
la tortuga	turtle
la vaca	cow
el zorro	fox

EL CUERPO HUMANO Y LA SALUD

THE HUMAN BODY AND HEALTH

El cuerpo humano / The human body

la barba	beard
el bigote	mustache
la boca	mouth
el brazo	arm
la cabeza	head
la cadera	hip
la ceja	eyebrow
el cerebro	brain
la cintura	waist
el codo	elbow
el corazón	heart
la costilla	rib
el cráneo	skull
el cuello	neck
el dedo	finger
el dedo del pie	toe
la espalda	back
el estómago	stomach
la frente	forehead
la garganta	throat
el hombro	shoulder
el hueso	bone
el labio	lip
la lengua	tongue
la mandíbula	jaw
la mejilla	cheek
el mentón, la barba, la barbilla	chin
la muñeca	wrist
el músculo	muscle
el muslo	thigh
las nalgas, el trasero, las asentaderas	buttocks
la nariz	nose
el nervio	nerve
el oído	(inner) ear
el ojo	eye
el ombligo	navel, belly button
la oreja	(outer) ear
la pantorrilla	calf
el párpado	eyelid
el pecho	chest
la pestaña	eyelash
el pie	foot
la piel	skin
la pierna	leg
el pulgar	thumb
el pulmón	lung
la rodilla	knee
la sangre	blood
el talón	heel
el tobillo	ankle
el tronco	torso, trunk
la uña	fingernail
la uña del dedo del pie	toenail
la vena	vein

Los cinco sentidos / The five senses

el gusto	taste
el oído	hearing
el olfato	smell
el tacto	touch
la vista	sight

La salud / Health

el accidente	accident
alérgico/a	allergic
el antibiótico	antibiotic
la aspirina	aspirin
el ataque cardiaco, el ataque al corazón	heart attack
el cáncer	cancer
la cápsula	capsule
la clínica	clinic
congestionado/a	congested
el consultorio	doctor's office
la curita	adhesive bandage
el/la dentista	dentist
el/la doctor(a), el/la médico/a	doctor
el dolor (de cabeza)	(head)ache, pain
embarazada	pregnant
la enfermedad	illness, disease
el/la enfermero/a	nurse
enfermo/a	ill, sick
la erupción	rash
el examen médico	physical exam
la farmacia	pharmacy
la fiebre	fever
la fractura	fracture
la gripe	flu
la herida	wound
el hospital	hospital
la infección	infection
el insomnio	insomnia
la inyección	injection
el jarabe	(cough) syrup
mareado/a	dizzy, nauseated
el medicamento	medication
la medicina	medicine
las muletas	crutches
la operación	operation
el/la paciente	patient
el/la paramédico/a	paramedic
la pastilla, la píldora	pill, tablet
los primeros auxilios	first aid
la pulmonía	pneumonia
los puntos	stitches
la quemadura	burn
el quirófano	operating room
la radiografía	x-ray
la receta	prescription
el resfriado	cold (illness)
la sala de emergencia(s)	emergency room
saludable	healthy, healthful
sano/a	healthy
el seguro médico	medical insurance
la silla de ruedas	wheelchair
el síntoma	symptom
el termómetro	thermometer
la tos	cough
la transfusión	transfusion

la vacuna	vaccination	la hoja de actividades	activity sheet
la venda	bandage	el horario de clases	class schedule
el virus	virus	la oración, las oraciones	sentence(s)
		el párrafo	paragraph
cortar(se)	to cut (oneself)	la persona	person
curar	to cure, to treat	presente	present
desmayar(se)	to faint	la prueba	test, quiz
enfermarse	to get sick	siguiente	following
enyesar	to put in a cast	la tarea	homework
estornudar	to sneeze		
guardar cama	to stay in bed	**Expresiones útiles**	**Useful expressions**
hinchar(se)	to swell	Abra(n) su(s) libro(s).	Open your book(s).
internar(se) en el hospital	to check into the hospital	Cambien de papel.	Change roles.
lastimarse (el pie)	to hurt (one's foot)	Cierre(n) su(s) libro(s).	Close your book(s).
mejorar(se)	to get better; to improve	¿Cómo se dice ___ en español?	How do you say ___ in Spanish?
operar	to operate	¿Cómo se escribe ___ en español?	How do you write ___ in Spanish?
quemar(se)	to burn	¿Comprende(n)?	Do you understand?
respirar (hondo)	to breathe (deeply)	(No) comprendo.	I (don't) understand.
romperse (la pierna)	to break (one's leg)	Conteste(n) las preguntas.	Answer the questions.
sangrar	to bleed	Continúe(n), por favor.	Continue, please.
sufrir	to suffer	Escriba(n) su nombre.	Write your name.
tomarle la presión a alguien	to take someone's blood pressure	Escuche(n) el audio.	Listen to the audio.
tomarle el pulso a alguien	to take someone's pulse	Estudie(n) la Lección tres.	Study Lesson three.
torcerse (el tobillo)	to sprain (one's ankle)	Haga(n) la actividad (el ejercicio) número cuatro.	Do activity (exercise) number four.
vendar	to bandage	Lea(n) la oración en voz alta.	Read the sentence aloud.

EXPRESIONES ÚTILES PARA LA CLASE / USEFUL CLASSROOM EXPRESSIONS

Palabras útiles	**Useful words**		
ausente	absent	Levante(n) la mano.	Raise your hand(s).
el departamento	department	Más despacio, por favor.	Slower, please.
el dictado	dictation	No sé.	I don't know.
la conversación, las conversaciones	conversation(s)	Páse(n)me los exámenes.	Pass me the tests.
		¿Qué significa ___?	What does ___ mean?
la expresión, las expresiones	expression(s)	Repita(n), por favor.	Repeat, please.
		Siénte(n)se, por favor.	Sit down, please.
el examen, los exámenes	test(s), exam(s)	Siga(n) las instrucciones.	Follow the instructions.
la frase	sentence	¿Tiene(n) alguna pregunta?	Do you have any questions?
		Vaya(n) a la página dos.	Go to page two.

COUNTRIES & NATIONALITIES / PAÍSES Y NACIONALIDADES

North America / Norteamérica

Canada	**Canadá**	*canadiense*
Mexico	**México**	*mexicano/a*
United States	**Estados Unidos**	*estadounidense*

Central America / Centroamérica

Belize	**Belice**	*beliceño/a*
Costa Rica	**Costa Rica**	*costarricense*
El Salvador	**El Salvador**	*salvadoreño/a*
Guatemala	**Guatemala**	*guatemalteco/a*
Honduras	**Honduras**	*hondureño/a*
Nicaragua	**Nicaragua**	*nicaragüense*
Panama	**Panamá**	*panameño/a*

References

The Caribbean
Cuba
Dominican Republic
Haiti
Puerto Rico

South America
Argentina
Bolivia
Brazil
Chile
Colombia
Ecuador
Paraguay
Peru
Uruguay
Venezuela

Europe
Armenia
Austria
Belgium
Bosnia
Bulgaria
Croatia
Czech Republic
Denmark
England
Estonia
Finland
France
Germany
Great Britain (United Kingdom)
Greece
Hungary
Iceland
Ireland
Italy
Latvia
Lithuania
Netherlands (Holland)
Norway
Poland
Portugal
Romania
Russia
Scotland
Serbia
Slovakia
Slovenia
Spain
Sweden
Switzerland
Ukraine
Wales

Asia
Bangladesh
Cambodia
China
India
Indonesia
Iran
Iraq

El Caribe
Cuba
República Dominicana
Haití
Puerto Rico

Suramérica
Argentina
Bolivia
Brasil
Chile
Colombia
Ecuador
Paraguay
Perú
Uruguay
Venezuela

Europa
Armenia
Austria
Bélgica
Bosnia
Bulgaria
Croacia
República Checa
Dinamarca
Inglaterra
Estonia
Finlandia
Francia
Alemania
Gran Bretaña (Reino Unido)
Grecia
Hungría
Islandia
Irlanda
Italia
Letonia
Lituania
Países Bajos (Holanda)
Noruega
Polonia
Portugal
Rumania
Rusia
Escocia
Serbia
Eslovaquia
Eslovenia
España
Suecia
Suiza
Ucrania
Gales

Asia
Bangladés
Camboya
China
India
Indonesia
Irán
Iraq, Irak

cubano/a
dominicano/a
haitiano/a
puertorriqueño/a

argentino/a
boliviano/a
brasileño/a
chileno/a
colombiano/a
ecuatoriano/a
paraguayo/a
peruano/a
uruguayo/a
venezolano/a

armenio/a
austríaco/a
belga
bosnio/a
búlgaro/a
croata
checo/a
danés, danesa
inglés, inglesa
estonio/a
finlandés, finlandesa
francés, francesa
alemán, alemana
británico/a
griego/a
húngaro/a
islandés, islandesa
irlandés, irlandesa
italiano/a
letón, letona
lituano/a
holandés, holandesa
noruego/a
polaco/a
portugués, portuguesa
rumano/a
ruso/a
escocés, escocesa
serbio/a
eslovaco/a
esloveno/a
español(a)
sueco/a
suizo/a
ucraniano/a
galés, galesa

bangladesí
camboyano/a
chino/a
indio/a
indonesio/a
iraní
iraquí

Israel	Israel	israelí
Japan	Japón	japonés, japonesa
Jordan	Jordania	jordano/a
Korea	Corea	coreano/a
Kuwait	Kuwait	kuwaití
Lebanon	Líbano	libanés, libanesa
Malaysia	Malasia	malasio/a
Pakistan	Pakistán	pakistaní
Russia	Rusia	ruso/a
Saudi Arabia	Arabia Saudí	saudí
Singapore	Singapur	singapurés, singapuresa
Syria	Siria	sirio/a
Taiwan	Taiwán	taiwanés, taiwanesa
Thailand	Tailandia	tailandés, tailandesa
Turkey	Turquía	turco/a
Vietnam	Vietnam	vietnamita

Africa / África

Algeria	Argelia	argelino/a
Angola	Angola	angoleño/a
Cameroon	Camerún	camerunés, camerunesa
Congo	Congo	congolés, congolesa
Egypt	Egipto	egipcio/a
Equatorial Guinea	Guinea Ecuatorial	ecuatoguineano/a
Ethiopia	Etiopía	etíope
Ivory Coast	Costa de Marfil	marfileño/a
Kenya	Kenia, Kenya	keniano/a, keniata
Libya	Libia	libio/a
Mali	Malí	maliense
Morocco	Marruecos	marroquí
Mozambique	Mozambique	mozambiqueño/a
Nigeria	Nigeria	nigeriano/a
Rwanda	Ruanda	ruandés, ruandesa
Somalia	Somalia	somalí
South Africa	Sudáfrica	sudafricano/a
Sudan	Sudán	sudanés, sudanesa
Tunisia	Tunicia, Túnez	tunecino/a
Uganda	Uganda	ugandés, ugandesa
Zambia	Zambia	zambiano/a
Zimbabwe	Zimbabue	zimbabuense

Australia and the Pacific / Australia y el Pacífico

Australia	Australia	australiano/a
New Zealand	Nueva Zelanda	neozelandés, neozelandesa
Philippines	Filipinas	filipino/a

MONEDAS DE LOS PAÍSES HISPANOS / CURRENCIES OF HISPANIC COUNTRIES

País / Country	Moneda / Currency
Argentina	el peso
Bolivia	el boliviano
Chile	el peso
Colombia	el peso
Costa Rica	el colón
Cuba	el peso
Ecuador	el dólar estadounidense
El Salvador	el dólar estadounidense
España	el euro
Guatemala	el quetzal
Guinea Ecuatorial	el franco
Honduras	el lempira
México	el peso
Nicaragua	el córdoba
Panamá	el balboa, el dólar estadounidense
Paraguay	el guaraní
Perú	el nuevo sol
Puerto Rico	el dólar estadounidense
República Dominicana	el peso
Uruguay	el peso
Venezuela	el bolívar

EXPRESIONES Y REFRANES / EXPRESSIONS AND SAYINGS

Expresiones y refranes con partes del cuerpo / Expressions and sayings with parts of the body

A cara o cruz	Heads or tails
A corazón abierto	Open heart
A ojos vistas	Clearly, visibly
Al dedillo	Like the back of one's hand
¡Choca/Vengan esos cinco!	Put it there!/Give me five!
Codo con codo	Side by side
Con las manos en la masa	Red-handed
Costar un ojo de la cara	To cost an arm and a leg
Darle a la lengua	To chatter/To gab
De rodillas	On one's knees
Duro de oído	Hard of hearing
En cuerpo y alma	In body and soul
En la punta de la lengua	On the tip of one's tongue
En un abrir y cerrar de ojos	In a blink of the eye
Entrar por un oído y salir por otro	In one ear and out the other
Estar con el agua al cuello	To be up to one's neck with/in
Estar para chuparse los dedos	To be delicious/To be finger-licking good
Hablar entre dientes	To mutter/To speak under one's breath
Hablar por los codos	To talk a lot/To be a chatterbox
Hacer la vista gorda	To turn a blind eye on something
Hombro con hombro	Shoulder to shoulder
Llorar a lágrima viva	To sob/To cry one's eyes out
Metérsele (a alguien) algo entre ceja y ceja	To get an idea in your head
No pegar ojo	Not to sleep a wink
No tener corazón	Not to have a heart
No tener dos dedos de frente	Not to have an ounce of common sense
Ojos que no ven, corazón que no siente	Out of sight, out of mind
Perder la cabeza	To lose one's head
Quedarse con la boca abierta	To be thunderstruck
Romper el corazón	To break someone's heart
Tener buen/mal corazón	Have a good/bad heart
Tener un nudo en la garganta	Have a knot in your throat
Tomarse algo a pecho	To take something too seriously
Venir como anillo al dedo	To fit like a charm/To suit perfectly

Expresiones y refranes con animales / Expressions and sayings with animals

A caballo regalado no le mires el diente.	Don't look a gift horse in the mouth.
Comer como un cerdo	To eat like a pig
Cuando menos se piensa, salta la liebre.	Things happen when you least expect it.
Llevarse como el perro y el gato	To fight like cats and dogs
Perro ladrador, poco mordedor./Perro que ladra no muerde.	His/her bark is worse than his/her bite.
Por la boca muere el pez.	Talking too much can be dangerous.
Poner el cascabel al gato	To stick one's neck out
Ser una tortuga	To be a slowpoke

Expresiones y refranes con alimentos / Expressions and sayings with food

Agua que no has de beber, déjala correr.	If you're not interested, don't ruin it for everybody else.
Con pan y vino se anda el camino.	Things never seem as bad after a good meal.
Contigo pan y cebolla.	You are all I need.
Dame pan y dime tonto.	I don't care what you say, as long as I get what I want.
Descubrir el pastel	To let the cat out of the bag
Dulce como la miel	Sweet as honey
Estar como agua para chocolate	To furious/To be at the boiling point
Estar en el ajo	To be in the know
Estar en la higuera	To have one's head in the clouds
Estar más claro que el agua	To be clear as a bell
Ganarse el pan	To earn a living/To earn one's daily bread
Llamar al pan, pan y al vino, vino.	Not to mince words.
No hay miel sin hiel.	Every rose has its thorn./There's always a catch.
No sólo de pan vive el hombre.	Man doesn't live by bread alone.
Pan con pan, comida de tontos.	Variety is the spice of life.
Ser agua pasada	To be water under the bridge
Ser más bueno que el pan	To be kindness itself
Temblar como un flan	To shake/tremble like a leaf

Expresiones y refranes con colores / Expressions and sayings with colors

Estar verde	To be inexperienced/wet behind the ears
Poner los ojos en blanco	To roll one's eyes
Ponerle a alguien un ojo morado	To give someone a black eye
Ponerse rojo	To turn red/To blush
Ponerse rojo de ira	To turn red with anger
Ponerse verde de envidia	To be green with envy
Quedarse en blanco	To go blank
Verlo todo de color de rosa	To see the world through rose-colored glasses

Refranes	**Sayings**		
A buen entendedor, pocas palabras bastan.	A word to the wise is enough.	Lo que es moda no incomoda.	You have to suffer in the name of fashion.
Ande o no ande, caballo grande.	Bigger is always better.	Más vale maña que fuerza.	Brains are better than brawn.
A quien madruga, Dios le ayuda.	The early bird catches the worm.	Más vale prevenir que curar.	Prevention is better than cure.
Cuídate, que te cuidaré.	Take care of yourself, and then I'll take care of you.	Más vale solo que mal acompañado.	Better alone than with people you don't like.
De tal palo tal astilla.	A chip off the old block.	Más vale tarde que nunca.	Better late than never.
Del dicho al hecho hay mucho trecho.	Easier said than done.	No es oro todo lo que reluce.	All that glitters is not gold.
Dime con quién andas y te diré quién eres.	A man is known by the company he keeps.	Poderoso caballero es don Dinero.	Money talks.
El saber no ocupa lugar.	One never knows too much.		

COMMON FALSE FRIENDS

False friends are Spanish words that look similar to English words but have very different meanings. While recognizing the English relatives of unfamiliar Spanish words you encounter is an important way of constructing meaning, there are some Spanish words whose similarity to English words is deceptive. Here is a list of some of the most common Spanish false friends.

actualmente ≠ actually
actualmente = nowadays, currently
actually = **de hecho, en realidad, en efecto**

argumento ≠ argument
argumento = plot
argument = **discusión, pelea**

armada ≠ army
armada = navy
army = **ejército**

balde ≠ bald
balde = pail, bucket
bald = **calvo/a**

batería ≠ battery
batería = drum set
battery = **pila**

bravo ≠ brave
bravo = wild; fierce
brave = **valiente**

cándido/a ≠ candid
cándido/a = innocent
candid = **sincero/a**

carbón ≠ carbon
carbón = coal
carbon = **carbono**

casual ≠ casual
casual = accidental, chance
casual = **informal, despreocupado/a**

casualidad ≠ casualty
casualidad = chance, coincidence
casualty = **víctima**

colegio ≠ college
colegio = school
college = **universidad**

collar ≠ collar (of a shirt)
collar = necklace
collar = **cuello (de camisa)**

comprensivo/a ≠ comprehensive
comprensivo/a = understanding
comprehensive = **completo, extensivo**

constipado ≠ constipated
estar constipado/a = to have a cold
to be constipated = **estar estreñido/a**

crudo/a ≠ crude
crudo/a = raw, undercooked
crude = **burdo/a, grosero/a**

divertir ≠ to divert
divertirse = to enjoy oneself
to divert = **desviar**

educado/a ≠ educated
educado/a = well-mannered
educated = **culto/a, instruido/a**

embarazada ≠ embarrassed
estar embarazada = to be pregnant
to be embarrassed = **estar avergonzado/a; dar/tener vergüenza**

eventualmente ≠ eventually
eventualmente = possibly
eventually = **finalmente, al final**

éxito ≠ exit
éxito = success
exit = **salida**

físico/a ≠ physician
físico/a = physicist
physician = **médico/a**

fútbol ≠ football
fútbol = soccer
football = **fútbol americano**

lectura ≠ lecture
lectura = reading
lecture = **conferencia**

librería ≠ library
librería = bookstore
library = **biblioteca**

máscara ≠ mascara
máscara = mask
mascara = **rímel**

molestar ≠ to molest
molestar = to bother, to annoy
to molest = **abusar**

oficio ≠ office
oficio = trade, occupation
office = **oficina**

rato ≠ rat
rato = while, time
rat = **rata**

realizar ≠ to realize
realizar = to carry out; to fulfill
to realize = **darse cuenta de**

red ≠ red
red = net
red = **rojo/a**

revolver ≠ revolver
revolver = to stir, to rummage through
revolver = **revólver**

sensible ≠ sensible
sensible = sensitive
sensible = **sensato/a, razonable**

suceso ≠ success
suceso = event
success = **éxito**

sujeto ≠ subject (topic)
sujeto = fellow; individual
subject = **tema, asunto**

LOS ALIMENTOS / FOODS

Frutas / Fruits

la aceituna	olive
el aguacate	avocado
el albaricoque, el damasco	apricot
la banana, el plátano	banana
la cereza	cherry
la ciruela	plum
el dátil	date
la frambuesa	raspberry
la fresa, la frutilla	strawberry
el higo	fig
el limón	lemon; lime
el melocotón, el durazno	peach
la mandarina	tangerine
el mango	mango
la manzana	apple
la naranja	orange
la papaya	papaya
la pera	pear
la piña	pineapple
el pomelo, la toronja	grapefruit
la sandía	watermelon
las uvas	grapes

Vegetales / Vegetables

la alcachofa	artichoke
el apio	celery
la arveja, el guisante	pea
la berenjena	eggplant
el brócoli	broccoli
la calabaza	squash; pumpkin
la cebolla	onion
el champiñón, la seta	mushroom
la col, el repollo	cabbage
la coliflor	cauliflower
los espárragos	asparagus
las espinacas	spinach
los frijoles, las habichuelas	beans
las habas	fava beans
las judías verdes, los ejotes	string beans, green beans
la lechuga	lettuce
el maíz, el choclo, el elote	corn
la papa, la patata	potato
el pepino	cucumber
el pimentón	bell pepper
el rábano	radish
la remolacha	beet
el tomate, el jitomate	tomato
la zanahoria	carrot

El pescado y los mariscos / Fish and shellfish

la almeja	clam
el atún	tuna
el bacalao	cod
el calamar	squid
el cangrejo	crab
el camarón, la gamba	shrimp
la langosta	lobster
el langostino	prawn
el lenguado	sole; flounder
el mejillón	mussel
la ostra	oyster
el pulpo	octopus
el salmón	salmon
la sardina	sardine
la vieira	scallop

La carne / Meat

la albóndiga	meatball
el bistec	steak
la carne de res	beef
el chorizo	hard pork sausage
la chuleta de cerdo	pork chop
el cordero	lamb
los fiambres	cold cuts, food served cold
el filete	fillet
la hamburguesa	hamburger
el hígado	liver
el jamón	ham
el lechón	suckling pig, roasted pig
el pavo	turkey
el pollo	chicken
el cerdo	pork
la salchicha	sausage
la ternera	veal
el tocino	bacon

Otras comidas / Other foods

el ajo	garlic
el arroz	rice
el azúcar	sugar
el batido	milkshake
el budín	pudding
el cacahuete, el maní	peanut
el café	coffee
los fideos	noodles, pasta
la harina	flour
el huevo	egg
el jugo, el zumo	juice
la leche	milk
la mermelada	marmalade, jam
la miel	honey
el pan	bread
el queso	cheese
la sal	salt
la sopa	soup
el té	tea
la tortilla	omelet (Spain), tortilla (Mexico)
el yogur	yogurt

Cómo describir la comida / Ways to describe food

a la plancha, a la parrilla	grilled
ácido/a	sour
al horno	baked
amargo/a	bitter
caliente	hot
dulce	sweet
duro/a	tough
frío/a	cold
frito/a	fried
fuerte	strong, heavy
ligero/a	light
picante	spicy
sabroso/a	tasty
salado/a	salty

DÍAS FESTIVOS / HOLIDAYS

enero / January
- Año Nuevo (1) — New Year's Day
- Día de los Reyes Magos (6) — Three Kings Day (Epiphany)
- Día de Martin Luther King, Jr. — Martin Luther King, Jr. Day

febrero / February
- Día de San Blas (Paraguay) (3) — St. Blas Day (Paraguay)
- Día de San Valentín, Día de los Enamorados (14) — Valentine's Day
- Día de los Presidentes — Presidents' Day
- Carnaval — Carnival (Mardi Gras)

marzo / March
- Día de San Patricio (17) — St. Patrick's Day
- Nacimiento de Benito Juárez (México) (21) — Benito Juárez's Birthday (Mexico)

abril / April
- Semana Santa — Holy Week
- Pésaj — Passover
- Pascua — Easter
- Declaración de la Independencia de Venezuela (19) — Declaration of Independence of Venezuela
- Día de la Tierra (22) — Earth Day

mayo / May
- Día del Trabajo (1) — Labor Day
- Cinco de Mayo (5) (México) — Cinco de Mayo (May 5th) (Mexico)
- Día de las Madres — Mother's Day
- Independencia Patria (Paraguay) (15) — Independence Day (Paraguay)
- Día Conmemorativo — Memorial Day

junio / June
- Día de los Padres — Father's Day
- Día de la Bandera (14) — Flag Day
- Día del Indio (Perú) (24) — Native People's Day (Peru)

julio / July
- Día de la Independencia de los Estados Unidos (4) — Independence Day (United States)
- Día de la Independencia de Venezuela (5) — Independence Day (Venezuela)
- Día de la Independencia de la Argentina (9) — Independence Day (Argentina)
- Día de la Independencia de Colombia (20) — Independence Day (Colombia)
- Nacimiento de Simón Bolívar (24) — Simón Bolívar's Birthday
- Día de la Revolución (Cuba) (26) — Revolution Day (Cuba)
- Día de la Independencia del Perú (28) — Independence Day (Peru)

agosto / August
- Día de la Independencia de Bolivia (6) — Independence Day (Bolivia)
- Día de la Independencia del Ecuador (10) — Independence Day (Ecuador)
- Día de San Martín (Argentina) (17) — San Martín Day (anniversary of his death) (Argentina)
- Día de la Independencia del Uruguay (25) — Independence Day (Uruguay)

septiembre / September
- Día del Trabajo (EE. UU.) — Labor Day (U.S.)
- Día de la Independencia de Costa Rica, El Salvador, Guatemala, Honduras y Nicaragua (15) — Independence Day (Costa Rica, El Salvador, Guatemala, Honduras, Nicaragua)
- Día de la Independencia de México (16) — Independence Day (Mexico)
- Día de la Independencia de Chile (18) — Independence Day (Chile)
- Año Nuevo Judío — Jewish New Year
- Día de la Virgen de las Mercedes (Perú) (24) — Day of the Virgin of Mercedes (Peru)

octubre / October
- Día de la Raza (12) — Columbus Day
- Noche de Brujas (31) — Halloween

noviembre / November
- Día de los Muertos (2) — All Souls Day
- Día de los Veteranos (11) — Veterans' Day
- Día de la Revolución Mexicana (20) — Mexican Revolution Day
- Día de Acción de Gracias — Thanksgiving
- Día de la Independencia de Panamá (28) — Independence Day (Panama)

diciembre / December
- Día de la Virgen (8) — Day of the Virgin
- Día de la Virgen de Guadalupe (México) (12) — Day of the Virgin of Guadalupe (Mexico)
- Januká — Chanukah
- Nochebuena (24) — Christmas Eve
- Navidad (25) — Christmas
- Año Viejo (31) — New Year's Eve

NOTE: In Spanish, dates are written with the day first, then the month. Christmas Day is **el 25 de diciembre**. In Latin America and in Europe, abbreviated dates also follow this pattern. Halloween, for example, falls on 31/10. You may also see the numbers in dates separated by periods: 27.4.16. When referring to centuries, roman numerals are always used. The 16th century, therefore, is **el siglo XVI**.

PESOS Y MEDIDAS / WEIGHTS AND MEASURES

Longitud / Length

El sistema métrico / Metric system — **El equivalente estadounidense** / U.S. equivalent

- **milímetro = 0,001 metro** / millimeter = 0.001 meter = 0.039 inch
- **centímetro = 0,01 metro** / centimeter = 0.01 meter = 0.39 inch
- **decímetro = 0,1 metro** / decimeter = 0.1 meter = 3.94 inches
- **metro** / meter = 39.4 inches
- **decámetro = 10 metros** / dekameter = 10 meters = 32.8 feet
- **hectómetro = 100 metros** / hectometer = 100 meters = 328 feet
- **kilómetro = 1.000 metros** / kilometer = 1,000 meters = .62 mile

U.S. system / El sistema estadounidense — Metric equivalent / **El equivalente métrico**

- inch / **pulgada** = 2.54 centimeters / **= 2,54 centímetros**
- foot = 12 inches / **pie = 12 pulgadas** = 30.48 centimeters / **= 30,48 centímetros**
- yard = 3 feet / **yarda = 3 pies** = 0.914 meter / **= 0,914 metro**
- mile = 5,280 feet / **milla = 5.280 pies** = 1.609 kilometers / **= 1,609 kilómetros**

Superficie / Surface Area

El sistema métrico / Metric system — **El equivalente estadounidense** / U.S. equivalent

- **metro cuadrado** / square meter = 10.764 square feet
- **área = 100 metros cuadrados** / area = 100 square meters = 0.025 acre
- **hectárea = 100 áreas** / hectare = 100 ares = 2.471 acres

U.S. system / El sistema estadounidense — Metric equivalent / **El equivalente métrico**

- **yarda cuadrada = 9 pies cuadrados = 0,836 metros cuadrados**
  square yard = 9 square feet = 0.836 square meters
- **acre = 4.840 yardas cuadradas = 0,405 hectáreas**
  acre = 4,840 square yards = 0.405 hectares

Capacidad / Capacity

El sistema métrico / Metric system — **El equivalente estadounidense** / U.S. equivalent

- **mililitro = 0,001 litro** / milliliter = 0.001 liter = 0.034 ounces
- **centilitro = 0,01 litro** / centiliter = 0.01 liter = 0.34 ounces
- **decilitro = 0,1 litro** / deciliter = 0.1 liter = 3.4 ounces
- **litro** / liter = 1.06 quarts
- **decalitro = 10 litros** / dekaliter = 10 liters = 2.64 gallons
- **hectolitro = 100 litros** / hectoliter = 100 liters = 26.4 gallons
- **kilolitro = 1.000 litros** / kiloliter = 1,000 liters = 264 gallons

U.S. system / El sistema estadounidense — Metric equivalent / **El equivalente métrico**

- ounce / **onza** = 29.6 milliliters / **= 29,6 mililitros**
- cup = 8 ounces / **taza = 8 onzas** = 236 milliliters / **= 236 mililitros**
- pint = 2 cups / **pinta = 2 tazas** = 0.47 liters / **= 0,47 litros**
- quart = 2 pints / **cuarto = 2 pintas** = 0.95 liters / **= 0,95 litros**
- gallon = 4 quarts / **galón = 4 cuartos** = 3.79 liters / **= 3,79 litros**

Peso / Weight

El sistema métrico / Metric system — **El equivalente estadounidense** / U.S. equivalent

- **miligramo = 0,001 gramo** / milligram = 0.001 gram
- **gramo** / gram = 0.035 ounce
- **decagramo = 10 gramos** / dekagram = 10 grams = 0.35 ounces
- **hectogramo = 100 gramos** / hectogram = 100 grams = 3.5 ounces
- **kilogramo = 1.000 gramos** / kilogram = 1,000 grams = 2.2 pounds
- **tonelada (métrica) = 1.000 kilogramos** / metric ton = 1,000 kilograms = 1.1 tons

U.S. system / El sistema estadounidense — Metric equivalent / **El equivalente métrico**

- ounce / **onza** = 28.35 grams / **= 28,35 gramos**
- pound = 16 ounces / **libra = 16 onzas** = 0.45 kilograms / **= 0,45 kilogramos**
- ton = 2,000 pounds / **tonelada = 2.000 libras** = 0.9 metric tons / **= 0,9 toneladas métricas**

Temperatura / Temperature

Grados centígrados / Degrees Celsius
To convert from Celsius to Fahrenheit, multiply by $\frac{9}{5}$ and add 32.

Grados Fahrenheit / Degrees Fahrenheit
To convert from Fahrenheit to Celsius, subtract 32 and multiply by $\frac{5}{9}$.

NÚMEROS

Números ordinales

primer, primero/a	1º/1ª	
segundo/a	2º/2ª	
tercer, tercero/a	3º/3ª	
cuarto/a	4º/4ª	
quinto/a	5º/5ª	
sexto/a	6º/6ª	
séptimo/a	7º/7ª	
octavo/a	8º/8ª	
noveno/a	9º/9ª	
décimo/a	10º/10ª	

NUMBERS

Ordinal numbers

first	1st
second	2nd
third	3rd
fourth	4th
fifth	5th
sixth	6th
seventh	7th
eighth	8th
ninth	9th
tenth	10th

Fracciones

$\frac{1}{2}$	un medio, la mitad
$\frac{1}{3}$	un tercio
$\frac{1}{4}$	un cuarto
$\frac{1}{5}$	un quinto
$\frac{1}{6}$	un sexto
$\frac{1}{7}$	un séptimo
$\frac{1}{8}$	un octavo
$\frac{1}{9}$	un noveno
$\frac{1}{10}$	un décimo
$\frac{2}{3}$	dos tercios
$\frac{3}{4}$	tres cuartos
$\frac{5}{8}$	cinco octavos

Fractions

- one half
- one third
- one fourth (quarter)
- one fifth
- one sixth
- one seventh
- one eighth
- one ninth
- one tenth
- two thirds
- three fourths (quarters)
- five eighths

Decimales

un décimo	0,1
un centésimo	0,01
un milésimo	0,001

Decimals

one tenth	0.1
one hundredth	0.01
one thousandth	0.001

OCUPACIONES / OCCUPATIONS

el/la abogado/a	lawyer
el actor, la actriz	actor
el/la administrador(a) de empresas	business administrator
el/la agente de bienes raíces	real estate agent
el/la agente de seguros	insurance agent
el/la agricultor(a)	farmer
el/la arqueólogo/a	archaeologist
el/la arquitecto/a	architect
el/la artesano/a	artisan
el/la auxiliar de vuelo	flight attendant
el/la basurero/a	garbage collector
el/la bibliotecario/a	librarian
el/la bombero/a	firefighter
el/la cajero/a	bank teller, cashier
el/la camionero/a	truck driver
el/la carnicero/a	butcher
el/la carpintero/a	carpenter
el/la científico/a	scientist
el/la cirujano/a	surgeon
el/la cobrador(a)	bill collector
el/la cocinero/a	cook, chef
el/la consejero/a	counselor, advisor
el/la contador(a)	accountant
el/la corredor(a) de bolsa	stockbroker
el/la diplomático/a	diplomat
el/la diseñador(a) (gráfico/a)	(graphic) designer
el/la electricista	electrician
el/la fisioterapeuta	physical therapist
el/la fotógrafo/a	photographer
el hombre/la mujer de negocios	businessperson
el/la ingeniero/a en computación	computer engineer
el/la intérprete	interpreter
el/la juez(a)	judge
el/la maestro/a	elementary school teacher
el/la marinero/a	sailor
el/la obrero/a	manual laborer
el/la optometrista	optometrist
el/la panadero/a	baker
el/la paramédico/a	paramedic
el/la peluquero/a	hairdresser
el/la piloto	pilot
el/la pintor(a)	painter
el/la plomero/a	plumber
el/la político/a	politician
el/la programador(a)	computer programmer
el/la psicólogo/a	psychologist
el/la reportero/a	reporter
el/la sastre	tailor
el/la secretario/a	secretary
el/la técnico/a (en computación)	(computer) technician
el/la vendedor(a)	sales representative
el/la veterinario/a	veterinarian

About the Author

José A. Blanco founded Vista Higher Learning in 1998. A native of Barranquilla, Colombia, Mr. Blanco holds degrees in Literature and Hispanic Studies from Brown University and the University of California, Santa Cruz. He has worked as a writer, editor, and translator for Houghton Mifflin and D.C. Heath and Company, and has taught Spanish at the secondary and university levels. Mr. Blanco is also the co-author of several other Vista Higher Learning programs: Vistas, Panorama, Aventuras, and ¡Viva! at the introductory level; Ventanas, Facetas, Enfoques, Imagina, and Sueña at the intermediate level; and Revista at the advanced conversation level.

About the Illustrators

Yayo, an internationally acclaimed illustrator, was born in Colombia. He has illustrated children's books, newspapers, and magazines, and has been exhibited around the world. He currently lives in Montreal, Canada.

Pere Virgili lives and works in Barcelona, Spain. His illustrations have appeared in textbooks, newspapers, and magazines throughout Spain and Europe.

Born in Caracas, Venezuela, **Hermann Mejía** studied illustration at the Instituto de Diseño de Caracas. Hermann currently lives and works in the United States.

TV Clip Credits

page 56 Courtesy of ContentLine.
page 94 Courtesy of Santander Chile.
page 130 Courtesy of Juguettos.

Photography Credits

Cover: Grandriver/iStockphoto.

Front matter (SE): xii: (l) Bettmann/Getty Images; (r) Florian Biamm/123RF; **xiii:** (l) Lawrence Manning/Corbis; (r) Design Pics Inc/Alamy; **xiv:** Jose Blanco; **xv:** (l) Digital Vision/Getty Images; (r) Andres/Big Stock Photo; **xvi:** Fotolia IV/Fotolia; **xvii:** (l) Goodshoot/Corbis; (r) Tyler Olson/Shutterstock; **xviii:** Shelly Wall/Shutterstock; **xix:** (t) Colorblind/Corbis; (b) Moodboard/Fotolia; **xx:** (t) Digital Vision/Getty Images; (b) Purestock/Getty Images.

Front matter (TE): T4: Teodor Cucu/500PX; **T14:** Asiseeit/iStockphoto; **T37:** Corbis Photography/Veer; (inset) Fancy Photography/Veer; **T48:** Braun S/iStockphoto.

Preliminary Lesson
1: Teodor Cucu/500PX; **2:** (t) Asiseeit/iStockphoto; (bl) Mediaphotos/iStockphoto; (br) DGLimages/iStockphoto; **2-3:** Gts/Shutterstock; **4:** Pressmaster/iStockphoto; **8:** (t) John Feingersh/Media Bakery; (b) Michael Simons/123RF; Zeeker2526/Shutterstock; **8-9:** Pla2na/Shutterstock; Jurisam/Deposit Photos; **10:** Cathy Yeulet/123RF; **12:** (all) Carolina Zapata; **13:** Carolina Zapata; **14:** Gallo Gallina/Bridgeman Art Library/Getty Images; **15:** Craig Lowell/Eagle Visions Photography/Alamy; **16:** (tl) Sorbis/Shutterstock; (tr) Vanessa Bertozzi; (ml) Ververidis Vasilis/Shutterstock; (mm) Olivier Tabary/Shutterstock; (mr) ValeStock/Shutterstock; (bl) AGE Fotostock RF; (bm) Gudrun Hommel; (br) Marc Printer/Alamy; Park Jinman/Shutterstock; **16-17:** Robbi/Shutterstock; Madredus/Shutterstock; **17:** (l) Sergey Nivens/Shutterstock; (r) Lmgorthand/iStockphoto; **19:** (t) Andresr/iStockphoto; (ml) Andres Rodriguez/Fotolia; (mr) Skynesher/iStockphoto; (bl) VHL; (br) Nicole Winchell; **20:** Davidf/iStockphoto; **24:** (all)Carolina Zapata.

Lesson 4
25: Franz Faltermaier/AGE Fotostock; **27:** George Shelley/Getty Images; **34:** (l) Javier Soriano/AFP/Getty Images; (r) Fernando Bustamante/AP Images; **35:** (t) Photo Works/Shutterstock; (r) Zuma Press/Alamy; **38:** Jacek Chabraszewski/Fotolia; **49:** Mat Hayward/Fotolia; **52:** Martín Bernetti; **53:** Fernando Llano/AP Images; **54:** JGI/Jamie Grill/Media Bakery; **55:** Rick Gomez/Getty Images; **58:** (tl) Sorincolac/Fotolia; (tr) Albright Knox Art Gallery/Art Resource; (ml) Ruben Varela; (mr) Carolina Zapata; (b) Brian Overcast/Alamy; **59:** (t) Radius Images/Alamy; (mt) Bettmann/Getty Images; (mb) Corel/Corbis; (b) David R. Frazier Photolibrary/Alamy.

Lesson 5
61: Gavin Hellier/Getty Images; **67:** Jeff Greenberg/Alamy; **72:** Gary Cook/Alamy; **73:** (t) AFP/Getty Images; (b) Pierre-Yves Babelon/123RF; **77:** Ronnie Kaufman/Getty Images; **87:** Blend Images/Fotolia; **90:** Carlos Gaudier; **91:** (tl) Corel/Corbis; (tr) Carlos Gaudier; (m) Carlos Gaudier; (b) Carlos Gaudier; **92:** Carolina Zapata; **96:** (tl) Bryan Mullennix/Alamy; (tr) José Blanco; (ml) Carlos Gaudier; (mr) Capricornis Photographic/Shutterstock; (b) Dave G. Houser/Getty Images; **97:** (t) Carlos Gaudier; (mt) Lawrence Manning/Getty Images; (mb) Stocktrek/Getty Images; (b) Carlos Gaudier.

Lesson 6
99: Asiapix RF/Inmagine; **108:** (l) Jose Caballero Digital Press Photos/Newscom; (r) Janet Dracksdorf; **109:** (t) Carlos Alvarez/Getty Images; (bl) Guiseppe Carace/Getty Images; (br) Mark Mainz/Getty Images; **114:** (all) Pascal Pernix; **119:** (all) Martín Bernetti; **120:** (all) Paula Díez; **121:** Paula Díez; **126-127:** Paula Díez and Shutterstock; **128:** Chris Schmidt/iStockphoto; **129:** John Henley/Media Bakery; **132:** (tl) Pascal Pernix; (tr) Pascal Pernix; (mt) Pascal Pernix; (mb) Pascal Pernix; (b) PhotoLink/Getty Images; **133:** (tl) Don Emmert/AFP/Getty Images; (tr) Pascal Pernix; (bl) Pascal Pernix; (br) Movie Prods/REX/Shutterstock.

Índice

A

acabar de + *infinitive* (6) **1B 177**
academic courses (2) **1A 64, 65, 100**
accents (4), **1B 33**
adjectives
    demonstrative (6) **1B 120**
    descriptive (3) **1A 107, 138** (6) **1B 102, 134**
    nationality (3) **1A 108, 138**
    position (3) **1A 114**
    possessive (3) **1A 117**
    ser with adjectives (3) **1A 112**
age questions (3) **1A 107, 125**
al (contraction) (4) **1B 36**
alphabet, Spanish (1) **1A 33**
articles, definite and indefinite (1) **1A 25**

B

b (5), **1B 71**
buildings
    campus (2) **1A 64, 100**
    general (4) **1B 28, 60**

C

campus buildings (2) **1A 64, 100**
classroom objects and people (2) **1A 64, 100**
clothing (6) **1B 100, 134**
colors (6) **1B 102, 134**
conducir (6) **1B 110**
conocer and **saber** (6) **1B 110**
courses (academic) (2) **1A 64, 100**
courtesy expressions (1) **1A 26, 31, 62**
Cultura
    Carolina Herrera (6) **1B 109**
    Las cataratas del Iguazú (5) **1B 72**
    ¿Cómo te llamas? (3) **1A 110**
    La elección de una carrera universitaria **1A 72**
    La familia real española (3) **1A 111**
    Los mercados al aire libre (6) **1B 108**
    Miguel Cabrera y Paola Espinosa (4) **1B 35**
    La plaza principal (1) **1A 35**
    Punta del Este (5) **1B 73**
    Real Madrid y Barça: rivalidad total (4) **1B 34**
    Saludos y besos en los países hispanos (1) **1A 34**
    La Universidad de Salamanca (2) **1A 73**

D

d (6) **1B 107**
dar (6) **1B 113**
dates (months) (5) **1B 64**
days of the week (2) **1A 71, 100**
decir (4) **1B 43, 46**
definite articles (1) **1A 38**
del (contraction) (1) **1A 44**
demonstrative adjectives and pronouns (6) **1B 120**
describing clothes (6) **1B 100, 105, 134**
descriptive adjectives (3) **1A 107, 138** (6) **1B 102, 134**
diphthongs and linking (3) **1A 109**
direct objects: nouns and pronouns (5) **1A 84**

E

estar
    comparing **ser** and **estar** (5) **1B 80**
    present tense (2) **1A 83**
    with conditions (5) **1B 74**
    with emotions (5) **1B 74**
    with health conditions (2) **1A 83**
    with location (2) **1A 83**

F

family members and relatives (3) **1A 102, 138**
farewells (1) **1A 26, 62**
forming questions (2) **1A 79**

G

greetings and introductions (1) **1A 26, 62**
gusta(n), me/te (2) **1A 69, 76**
gustar (2) **1A 76**

H

hacer (4) **1B 46**
hay (1) **1A 40**
health
    conditions with **estar** (5) **1B 74**
    questions (1) **1A 26, 62**
hotels (5) **1B 62, 98**

I

indefinite articles (1) **1A 38**
indirect object pronouns (6) **1B 112**
information questions (2) **1A 79**
interrogative words (2) **1A 80**
intonation, question (2) **1A 79**
introductions (1) **1A 26, 62**
ir (4) **1B 36**

L

linking (3) **1A 109**
location with **estar** (2) **1A 83**

M

months of the year (5) **1B 64**

N

negation with **no** (2) **1A 75**
nouns (1) **1A 36**
numbers
    0–30 (1) **1A 40**
    31 and higher (2) **1A 87**
    ordinal (5) **1B 65, 98**

Índice

O

object pronouns
    direct (5) 1B 84
    indirect (6) 1B 112
occupations (3), 1A 102, 138
ofrecer, present tense (6) 1B 110
oír, present tense (4) 1B 47
ordinal numbers (5) 1B 65, 98

P

Panorama
    Canadá (1) 1A 60
    Cuba (6) 1B 132
    Ecuador (3) 1A 102
    España (2) 1A 98
    Estados Unidos, los (1) 1A 60
    México (4) 1B 58
    Puerto Rico (5) 1B 96
parecer, present tense (6) 1B 110
participles (5) 1B 76
pastimes (4) 1B 26, 60
personal **a** (5) 1B 84
pluralization of nouns (1) 1A 37
poder (4) 1B 40
poner (4) 1B 46
position of adjectives (3) 1A 114
possessive adjectives (3) 1A 117
prepositions often used with **estar** (2) 1A 84
preterite tense (6) 1B 116
professions (3) 1A 102, 138
progressive tense (5) 1B 76
pronouns
    demonstrative (6) 1B 120
    direct object (5) 1B 84
    indirect object (6) 1B 112
    subject (1) 1A 43
    use and omission of subject (2) 1A 76

Q

questions, forming (2) 1A 79
    age (3) 1A 107
    information questions (2) 1A 79
    intonation for questions (2) 1A 79, 80
    question words (2) 1A 80
    tag questions (2) 1A 79

R

regular verbs
    present tense
        -ar verbs (2) 1A 74
        -er and **-ir** verbs (3) 1A 120
    preterite (6) 1B 116

S

saber and **conocer** (6) 1B 110
salir, present tense (4) 1B 46
seasons of the year (5) 1B 64
ser
    comparing **ser** and **estar** (5) 1B 80
    present tense (1) 1A 44
    to show identification (1) 1A 44
    to show origin (1) 1A 45
    to show possession (1) 1A 44
    with adjectives (3) 1A 112
    with nationalities (3) 1A 113
    with professions (1) 1A 45
shopping (6) 1B 110, 134
Spanish alphabet (1) 1A 33
sports and leisure activities (4) 1B 26, 60
stem-changing verbs (4) 1B 39, 43
stress and accent marks (4) 1B 33
subject pronouns (1) 1A 43
    use and omission (2) 1A 76
suponer, present tense (4) 1B 46

T

t (6) 1B 107
tag questions (2) 1A 79
telling time (1) 1A 48
tener
    expressions with (3) 1A 125
    present tense (3) 1A 124
town places (4) 1B 28, 60
traducir (6) 1B 110
traer (4) 1B 46
travel terms (5) 1B 62, 91

V

v (5), 1B 71
vacation vocabulary (5) 1B 62, 98
venir (3) 1A 124
ver
    present tense (4) 1B 47
    preterite tense (6) 1B 117
verbs with irregular **yo** forms (**hacer, oír, poner, salir, traer,**
    and **ver**) (4) 1B 46, 47
vowels (2) 1A 71

W

weather expressions (5) 1B 64
work-related terms (3) 1A 102, 138

Y

years (e.g. 2007) (2) 1A 88